WARLORDS AND MERCHANTS

*To my wife Suzanne Karaki
and to our daughters Catherine-Rima and Maya*

WARLORDS AND MERCHANTS

The Lebanese Business and Political Establishment

Kamal Dib

ITHACA
PRESS

WARLORDS AND MERCHANTS
The Lebanese Business and Political Establishment

Ithaca Press is an imprint of Garnet Publishing Limited

Published by
Garnet Publishing Limited
8 Southern Court
South Street
Reading
RG1 4QS
UK

Copyright © Kamal Dib, 2004

All rights reserved.
No part of this book may be reproduced in any form or by any electronic or mechanical means, including information storage and retrieval systems, without permission in writing from the publisher, except by a reviewer who may quote brief passages in a review.

First Edition

ISBN 0 86372 297 0

British Library Cataloguing-in-Publication Data
A catalogue record for this book is available from the British Library

Jacket design by Garnet Publishing
Typeset by Samantha Barden

Printed in Lebanon

Contents

Foreword		vii
Acknowledgements		ix
Introduction: A Labyrinth of Blood and Money		1
1	Shia Warlords and Druze Emirs	11
2	Maronite Warlords and Sunni *Zaim*s	33
3	The Merchants of Beirut	61
4	Bechara al-Khouri and Michel Chiha	75
5	Camille Chamoun and Emile al-Boustani	83
6	How the Warlord/Merchant Group Shaped the Economy	91
7	Youssef Beidas and Intrabank	103
8	The Golden Years	127
9	The Destruction of Beirut	141
10	Collapse of the National Currency	167
11	Government Decay	181
12	Amine Gemayel and Government Collapse	201
13	Roger Tamraz and Financial Collapse	219
14	Supremacy of the Warlords	243
15	Bachir Gemayel: Last of the Warlords	265
16	Triumph of the Warlords and Merchants	279
17	Rafic Hariri: Last of the Merchants	291
Statistical Appendix		301
Select Bibliography		319
Index		325

Foreword

In a nutshell, I think that ninety-five per cent of the Lebanese people would opt for a secular system of government if they have confidence in their State, if they trust the honesty and good behaviour of the political elite and if the laws of the country provide for equal rights to all.

I think also that in the absence of a secular state system, the Lebanese would accept a consociational democracy based on the distribution of power among religious communities, if the system was well-managed to the benefit of the whole society. This was the type of democracy being practiced during the presidential mandate of General Fouad Chehab (1958–64). In that period one can say that although the "Christian Maronite" political elite was at the apogee of its power in Lebanon, the "Muslim" political elite and Muslim citizens never complained. Social peace prevailed because President Chehab followed a just program of social reform and a wise foreign policy with Lebanon's neighbours.

It is when the State fell back to ugly sectarian attitudes and to unwise foreign policies that the Lebanese people withdrew into their religious cocoons, and subsequently into a situation of strong sectarian feelings that led to violent confrontations. Breakdown and withdrawal from a common national life has occurred three times in the past two centuries: in the period 1840–62, in 1958, and in 1975–90. In the three episodes, the *zaims* – traditional leaders – claimed to represent the sentiments of the religious groups in the country, and installed de facto dictatorships inside their religious communities.

Therefore, since all laws and public institutions in Lebanon are based on religious adherence, it should be no surprise that the people of Lebanon live in fear and hesitate to express their desire for a secular system. Currents at work in the Middle East contributed to this psyche in Lebanon. We should not ignore the predominant atmosphere of clash of civilization and of ethnic and sectarian feelings in the Middle East in the past 35 years. Secular Arab nationalism faltered, while various types of religious fundamentalisms surfaced as a reaction to the political, economic, and military failures of Arab regimes.

However, I remain an optimist.

I believe that the prevailing sectarian mood in Lebanon could rapidly change if the laws and public institutions take a direction that does not condition the legal existence of the Lebanese individual on her or his membership of one of the many religious communities. Religious establishments in Lebanon exercise judicial authority on the civil status of every citizen, and this authority is recognized by the State and remains at the foundation of public order in Lebanon. The Lebanese legal system and constitutional order should be reformed if we want the people of our country to become secularised, i.e., living in a State of institutions and practicing civic principles.

The question of secularism in Lebanon cannot be addressed exclusively by creating an additional "secular" community (i.e., granting a choice to those who want to be outside the religious communities to follow civil laws while maintaining the status quo), as suggested by the famous regulation of the French High Commissioner during the mandate period, which instituted so-called "historical communities" as the basis of public order in Lebanon. Instead, a legal revolution is needed to separate the political management of the country from the religious order. The role of religious authorities as intermediary bodies between the citizen and the State should be stopped; simultaneously, the State should establish a civic legal basis for the existence of every individual away from the theological control of the lives of individuals from birth to death. Such a State should be a body of civilian institutions in direct contact with the citizen.

Of course, in a new legal order, the Lebanese who want to keep their personal status linked to their religious affiliation should be allowed to do so at their age of majority. Constitutional guarantees should also exist to make sure that one religious community does not dominate the others through an electoral system that could be tailored to secure the supremacy of the largest religious group. Through a good electoral system, there are many ways to secure a fair representation of all communities and secular political affiliations.

Georges Corm
Former Minister of Finance
Beirut, 3 February 2003

Acknowledgements

I owe this work to Canada, the land of free thinking and great opportunities.

My approach in writing the manuscript was influenced by two individuals: my economics professor Dr Charles Jeanneret, and my friend Dr Georges Corm, a great writer on Lebanese affairs. Both have humility, authority, and credibility in their life and work, and I wanted to follow in their path. I have also greatly benefited from numerous discussions with Jonathan Higdon, my Irish-Canadian friend who loved Lebanon without ever having set foot there; his observations and insight helped me to clarify my ideas before I put them on paper.

The book would not have seen the light of day without the diligent work of people at Ithaca Press, in particular Emma Hawker, Anna Hines, and Samantha Barden.

Four moral and academic principles guided my writing: (1) "and you will know the truth, and the truth will make you free"; (2) "Let what you say be simply 'Yes' or 'No'; anything more than this comes from evil"; (3) a solid cross-check of the manuscript for consistency and continuity; and (4) a vigilant effort to substantiate and research facts and conclusions.

In writing this book I had the best of intentions, as no reform is possible without a critical approach. However, I may have inadvertently erred and for that I bear sole responsibility.

Kamal Dib

Introduction:
A Labyrinth of Blood and Money

As a child in Beirut, some ten years before emigrating to Canada, I spent many happy hours in the harbour admiring the larger ships as they set sail and then eventually disappeared on the horizon of the Mediterranean. The Beirut of my childhood was different from the city the world has known since 1975. The year 1975 was Year One in a lengthy civil war, followed by ten years of economic hardship. I remember Beirut as wealthy, cosmopolitan, cultured, diverse and an open place. I was five when *The Sound of Music* played in *Cinema Capitol* in downtown Beirut, and I was 14 when I witnessed first hand the end of history in the city. With a sense of existentialism, my generation of young Lebanese was characterized by sadness and futility, left on our own to search for another future in a distant land.

My frequent visits to the country of my birth brought many questions of discovery and self-searching and were, in part, responsible for me writing this book for a Western audience. When the aeroplane approaches the Eastern Mediterranean, you will see not only Lebanon, but also a long stretch of land that has formed an historical crucible for several millennia – that bears the curse of history and holds many bloody memories.

After reading this book, readers may ask whether the warlords of Lebanon see themselves when they watch Francis Ford Coppola's film *The Godfather*. They are certainly not like the mafia that roamed the cities of the United States in the 1920s and 1930s, spreading crime and terror. However, they have certain similarities to the original Sicilian and Calabrian dons whose natural environment was a band of loyal armed men and a mansion overlooking impressive Mediterranean coastal canyons.

While the Calabrian setting might have suited the Lebanese warlords, they would never have adapted to the underworld ways of the New World. In a 1980 interview with an American magazine, Walid Joumblatt, leader of the Lebanese Druze militia, expressed fear of travelling in New York's subway. However, in his mountain fief south of Beirut he was a formidable lord, as he was in control of thousands of militiamen, and resided in a historical palace in the town of Mokhtara. During the 1975–90 civil war, the warlord status of Walid Joumblatt also applied to other Lebanese dons, among whom were the Frangiés, the Gemayels and the Chamouns.

This book emphasizes characters rather than events, and domestic players rather than regional and international personalities. The reason for this dual emphasis is the lack of literature on the Lebanese warlords and their role in the creation and, later, the physical destruction and financial collapse of Lebanon. Written works on Lebanon overlooked or took for granted the "little episodes" of warlord conflicts. Instead, they concentrated on linear interpretations of the conflict as a struggle of ideologies, religions and regional powers. The reality is that the game worked both ways in that both local warlords and the regional powers manipulated each other.

The ruling stratum of Lebanon was and still is tribal, where families or coalitions of individuals are in fact virtual independent district governors. Among the warlords, one finds groups of Lebanese business people who prefer wheeling and dealing in lucrative activities beneath the shiny façades of buildings that line the boulevards of Beirut. The business of commerce was inspired by a long mercantile tradition that started with the Phoenicians in 1000 BC and continued with the merchants of Damascus and Venice and the Levantines of nineteenth-century Beirut. However, modern Lebanon did not undergo a period of entrepreneurial capitalism similar to the one that built Disneyland and invented the cellular telephone. The Levantine culture is a ritual in Lebanon, and the political–business connections go beyond the exchange of goods and services. They colour the social and political life of the country, and become an art unto themselves.

I have written this book with a desire to reach a wider audience and provide a straightforward narrative of a seemingly complex situation. In short, the thesis of this book is that the families that make up the warlord–merchant establishment have a paramount role in the modern Lebanese experience, no matter what amount of influence regional and international foreign powers are assumed to have.

Lebanon is an ancient country that is often mentioned in the Bible. Its historical origins date back to pre-classical times, and its modern rise

Introduction: A Labyrinth of Blood and Money

concurs with the European economic and cultural penetration of the eastern Mediterranean region that began in the seventeenth century. In time, this penetration allowed Beirut to become an international trading centre, boasting several universities, numerous banks and a multitude of business establishments. However, as a society, Lebanon did not have a proper social services network to allow a more equitable economic and cultural development. Even in 1975, Beirut and its vicinity monopolized wealth and knowledge while the peripheral regions were abandoned to feudalism and backwardness.

Before the twentieth century, Lebanon was a land-locked autonomous region within the Ottoman Empire. In 1920, France enlarged the entity and made Beirut its capital. The status of Beirut as a political centre allowed it to extend its economic hegemony over the whole country and, in the next fifty years, it accounted for half of Lebanon's population and most of its economic and cultural activity. The ascendancy of Beirut was a double-edged sword. While it was the hub of Lebanon's strength, its collapse in 1975 meant the demise of Lebanon.

Although Beirut provided the stage for the rise and fall of Lebanon, the roots of the collapse could be traced to neighbouring Mount Lebanon. Social conflicts always started in the mountain region, which was plagued with civil wars among the various communities that inhabited the area. For the past millennium, civil wars in the mountain region had occurred in almost every century, including a bloody civil strife that went on intermittently between 1825 and 1860 and left permanent wounds in the modern Lebanese psyche.

For centuries, the mountain region was home to many religious communities, mainly the Druze, the Maronite Christians and the Shia Muslims. Feudal warlords who competed for hegemony led these communities. Beirut was outside this world. Mediterranean in orientation and in historical development, the city was kept off limits to the mountain people by the successive empires that ruled the Middle East. Towards the end of the seventeenth century, the Ottoman authorities recognized the importance of Beirut and considered it to be one of the major cities of the empire. In the late nineteenth century, they made it the capital of a large *vilayet* (province), which was governed and protected by the Sunni Muslim *zaim*s (bosses) of the coastal cities. However, the empires that ruled the region also recognized the uniqueness of the mountain communities and granted Mount Lebanon a semi-autonomous status.

The development of Beirut and the mountain region as two separate entities, with the Sunnis in political control in Beirut and the Maronites largely in control of Mount Lebanon, lasted until 1920. In 1920, the mountain region and the coast were joined in a state of Greater Lebanon when a coalition of Maronite warlords and Sunni Muslim notables from the coastal cities formed a government and created a pact with participation from lesser important communities. The creation of "Grand Liban" in 1920 shifted the civil conflict to Beirut. In the twentieth century, the warlords maintained a status quo in the mountain region, keeping the well-defined but informal cantons under control in the tradition of their ancestors. However, when appointed to a political role with an office in Beirut, the warlords had an entirely different role and behaved as national political leaders. For example, Sulieman Frangié, the warlord of the Zghorta county in northern Lebanon, became President of Lebanon in 1970 and Bachir Gemayel, leader of the Lebanese Forces (Christian militia) became President of Lebanon in 1982.

Between 1950 and 1975, Beirut became the centre of an essentially feudal and confessional society. Its central location made it accessible to all the cantons, yet it perpetuated their separateness by being so wealthy and dynamic in comparison. The warlords made the most of what Beirut had to offer and ignored the warning signs of a changing society. They considered each spark of violence as "a summer cloud"[1] that would surely pass.

One day, in the spring of 1975, an amalgam of factors including warlord antagonism, social inequities and endless Middle East intrigue exploded, throwing the city and the whole country into violent turmoil.

Viewed from the vantage point of the early twenty-first century, it seems that the massive social upheavals in Lebanon between 1958 and 1990 had little or no impact on the centuries-old clannish arrangements. Even when the warlords achieved peace in 1990,[2] the basis of the new state followed a traditional approach: power was redistributed along lines that were more convenient to the warlords. Since the warlord system had produced a legitimate leadership for almost a thousand years, it could be reformed to *sound* modern. This modern version was encapsulated in 1989 in a new national document called the Taif Accord. The document guaranteed that the warlords would maintain a constant role in the future of Lebanon.

In writing this manuscript, I have relied on personal experiences and observations, as well as published books, news media publications and reports. Many of the books I consulted have a regional focus, and use the local framework to explain the implications of the Lebanese conflict for the Middle Eastern situation. Most books written in English on Lebanon (particularly those published in the period 1982–90) provide more details about the Palestine Liberation Organization (PLO) and its wars with Israel on Lebanese territory than about the Lebanese people themselves. Books published in French have a better focus on the local scene with in-depth analysis of the individual warlord families. This is probably due to the Lebanese habit of publishing memoirs and written material in Paris rather than in London or New York. French writers are also more likely to have a more intimate knowledge of Lebanon and personal connections to the Lebanese establishment.[3]

In contrast, books written in Arabic for the Beirut market dwell mainly on the period preceding the war (1958–75). Arabic books covering the period after 1975 are selective and subservient. For example, a coffee table book entitled *Lebanon 1975–76: Days of Tragedy* by Joseph Chami on the first two years of the war was balanced and professional. However, the second volume, published in 1983, had obvious biases.[4] For example, it focused on President-elect Bachir Gemayel, and portrayed the Palestinians the way the Lebanese right would usually view them, which was not the case in the first volume. Some books published in the United States (for example, *The Lebanese War* by A. Volke, *Operation Snowball* by Zeev Schiff and *From Israel to Damascus* by Robert Hatem, alias Cobra) were also partisan works.[5] These and many others were translated into Arabic, and played well into the propaganda machine of the Lebanese warlords.

With some exceptions, the Lebanese public had more respect for English and French books or for translated tracts in Arabic originating outside Lebanon than for books published locally. Several books that came out in Beirut suggested that the "good people of Lebanon had nothing to do with the wars of the 'others' on Lebanese soil".[6] The "others" meant that the Americans, the Israelis, the Palestinians, the Syrians, the Iraqis or the Iranians had "fought their dirty wars in Lebanon while the peace-loving Lebanese" simply watched.[7] Even leaders and intellectuals voiced this sentiment at times. Though this view is not completely without foundation, the evidence does not warrant acceptance of attempts to collapse the conflict into being about "the endless suffering of the people of Lebanon at the hands of the evil foreigners".[8]

The conflict was inherently a Lebanese one. There were genuine domestic social grievances that surfaced and led to the war in Lebanon in 1975.[9] The warlords on all sides were the ones who invited foreign intervention and benefited from it. If the issue was foreign intervention, then there is no explanation as to why, in the latter part of the 1980s, long after foreign armies had left Beirut, the war continued with the Lebanese killing each other at higher rates. This happened even within the same groups, pitting Christians against Christians and Muslims against Muslims.

The themes of most works on Lebanon can be briefly summarized as follows.

- The war in Lebanon was between Muslims and Christians.
- It was a PLO–Israeli conflict fought in Lebanese territory.
- It was a struggle for Lebanese sovereignty against Syrian hegemony.
- It was a war between modernism and traditionalism ("left" and "right", fundamentalism and secularism, etc.).

These explanations found their way to Western culture and became the accepted wisdom in Europe and North America. In the 1970s and 1980s, the story of Lebanon was repackaged and presented to audiences who became conditioned in a set of standard explanations. In time, a rich discourse developed around the coverage of Lebanon, marred by idioms such as "Muslim West Beirut", "Christian suburbs", "Muslim–Christian fighting" and "Shia villages". These idioms even reached the United Nations peacekeeping force in Lebanon, where the word "Sikh peacekeepers" was used to refer to the Indian battalion in the United Nations (UN) force, making them targets for attacks.

The repackaging helped newsroom editors to choose and present a story that made sense of incoming dispatches in an atmosphere reminiscent of a mechanical assembly line for news reports. The truth was lost in the process of attempting to create a "scientific" and "objective" story of what was going on in Lebanon. The standardization of the story has created a sense of illusory familiarity and déjà vu in the minds of outsiders. People who knew very little about Lebanon would calmly comment on other events in the world saying, "It looks like Beirut", or "Things are moving to Lebanonization of the conflict", meaning into a situation of permanent war and chaos.

Introduction: A Labyrinth of Blood and Money

The simplifying approach to the Lebanese conflict has contributed to the abandonment of Lebanon as a bastion of Western enlightenment and Levantine creativeness. In the 1980s, Lebanon made it to the headlines only when a booby-trapped car exploded or a Westerner was kidnapped. Television networks had their men on the spot showing graphic scenes of burning bodies, and back in the studios in the United States, Arab Americans such as Fouad Ajami or James Zoghby lined up to make comments that sounded more and more like clichés. Dan Rather and Ted Koppel quizzed area specialists to explain the obvious.

Suddenly, images of chic Beirut, "the jewel of the Mediterranean" and the "Switzerland of the East" gave way to a "war-torn" and "death-stricken" city engulfed in violence and the horrors of war. Those who did not know Lebanon or the Levant wrote about the country as "a Third World basket case where wild-eyed fanatics slaughtered each other". Those Westerners who knew Beirut or had lived there for lengthy periods just shook their heads in sympathy and disbelief.

The business of reducing Lebanon to digestible titbits led to a popular consensus in the decision-making countries, and, in turn, this popular consensus in the liberal democracies influenced the attitudes of governments. As democratically elected governments listened to opinion polls and voters' concerns, popular concepts of foreign events usually found their way to policy making. Although largely influenced from outside, the unfolding events in Lebanon convinced public opinion in the West that what they believed was true all along.

Lebanon paid dearly for the media's obsession with standardization. This was illustrated by the fact that as soon as the war ended in 1990, the little country vanished from the scene. Only twice in the 1990s did Lebanon briefly become newsworthy. The first event was in July 1993, when Israel deported a group of Palestinians from the West Bank to southern Lebanon. The second, in April 1996, was when the Israelis attacked Lebanon and committed the massacre at Qana. These events made news headlines and colour photos in weekly magazines.

There was no Marshall Plan for reconstruction and development after the war. The Lebanese government sank into debt in the 1990s trying to finance mega projects to regain part of the past glory of the country.

In the following pages, I have tried to construct an account of the warlord–businessman's role in Lebanon. History books on Lebanon are mainly preoccupied with the different powers that dominated the country:

Arabs, Crusaders, Ottomans, French etc. A possible explanation for this is that writers usually look at the big picture when they try to explain the rise of empires and great events. Details about the mountain people of Lebanon and the merchants of the Levant became less significant.

Therefore, this work is an attempt to make sense of the events that took place in Lebanon between 1975 and 2003 from an economic angle in a context where warlords and business people were the major players. In a small country with a tiny population, individuals make more of a difference and everybody knows everybody else. If I were to give any personal conclusion, I might say that there are no lessons to be learnt from the Lebanese war, because the Lebanese, and for that matter, humanity, never learn from mistakes. The ills of Lebanon are obvious and the medicine is known. The Lebanese simply drift. Analysts could draw general outlines on the future direction of events in the country, but they may not be very different from what has happened before. A modern secular state has to wait for another generation.

NOTES

1. "Sahabat Sayf".
2. It was said that the peace was imposed on Lebanon by regional and super powers.
3. This is true of Eric Roleau, the Middle East editor of *Le Monde*.
4. Joseph Chami, *Lebanon 1975–76: Days of Tragedy*, Beirut, Arab Printing Press, 1977 and *Lebanon 1977–82: Days of Wrath*, Beirut, Arab Printing Press, 1984.
5. Harald Volke, *The Lebanese War: Its Origins and Political Dimensions*, New York, Palgrave Macmillan, 1978. Also, Zeev Schiff, *Operation Snowball*, New York, Simon & Schuster, 1985; Robert Cobra Hatem, *From Israel to Damascus: The Painful Road of Blood, Betrayal, and Deception*, La Mesa, CA, Pride International Publications, 1999; Jean-Pierre Peroncel-Hugoz, *Une croix sur le Liban*, Paris, Lieu commun, 1984.
6. Ghassan Tueni, *Let My People Live* (in Arabic, *Daou Chaabi Yaich*), Beirut, Dar Annahar, 1987. Mr Tueni was Lebanon's ambassador to the United Nations in 1982. At the time he made several presentations to the Security Council in which he formulated his thesis about "the war of the others on Lebanese soil".
7. Pierre Gemayel, leader of the Christian Phalanges Party, August 13, 1976, *al-Amal* newspaper, in which he elaborated on his position that the war was between all Lebanese and international leftist forces allied with the Palestinians in Lebanon.
8. President-elect Bachir Gemayel, in his acceptance speech on 14 August, proclaiming his goal of reuniting the Lebanese Republic's 10,452 km^2 under central

Introduction: A Labyrinth of Blood and Money

authority and extending an olive branch to the Muslim leadership. Quoted extensively in Beirut's daily newspapers *Annahar* and *Assafir*. Also another speech by Bachir Gemayel in the annex to *Assafir*'s supplement "Maronite Leadership from Habib al-Saad to Samir Geagea". Beirut, Arab Information Centre, 1985.

9 A folk story about two families who started a war over a pomegranate tree lying between them became a Lebanese proverb, "The issue is not about a pomegranate; it is hearts full of hatred", meaning that the pomegranate was a pretext for civil strife, but not the real issue.

1

Shia Warlords and Druze Emirs

> Le Levant, c'est le nom qu'on donnait autrefois à ce chapelet de cités marchandes par lesquelles les voyageurs d'Europe accédaient à l'Orient. De Constantinople à Alexandrie, en passant par Smyrne, Adana, ou Beyrouth, ces villes ont longtemps été des lieux de brassage où se côtoyaient langues, coutumes et croyances. Des univers précaires que l'histoire avait lentement façonnés, avant de les démolir.[1]
>
> **Amin Maalouf**

The Levant

Throughout history, different people called the eastern Mediterranean coast and the hinterland area different things. The region was called the Levante by the Venetians and the Machrek or Bilad al-Cham by ancient Arabians.[2] It was also called "Geographic Syria" by historians,[3] *Outre-mer* by the Franks and *Proche-Orient* or simply *le Levant* by the contemporary French. In this work, "the Levant" is the preferred appellation. Not only is it synonymous with the eastern Mediterranean, but it also carries a cultural connotation for its enterprising population and cultural mosaic. It also maintains the term used by the French and the Italians, the first two modern European nations who traded with the region.

The Levant extends some 600 kilometres from Eskenderun in modern Turkey to Gaza, spreading 100 kilometres inland, from the coast to the edge of the desert and is inhabited by some 25 million people. The coastal area is lined with the historical cities of Eskenderun, Latakia, Tartosa, Tripoli, Beirut, Saida, Tyre, Acre, Jaffa and Gaza. These cities served and continue to serve as convenient seaports to the legendary ancient cities of the interior, such as Antioch, Aleppo, Hama, Emsa (Homs), Baalbeck, Damascus, Jerusalem and Amman.[4] In fact, the Levant is a hybrid of the many influences of East and West throughout history, and at times throughout its history too, its peoples have moved freely around the regions to the north, east and west of it.

Stories of the Old Testament consider the whole area comprising the Levant, Arabia, Mesopotamia, northern Syria and Lower Egypt as one continuous region where people in ancient times wandered and knew each other. This explains the cultural affinity that existed between Arabia, the Levant and Egypt and to a lesser degree between Greece and the Levant. (However, the fact should not be ignored that Greece was culturally the closest European country to the Levant.)

Thus three sources of influence shaped the Levant: the north (Greece, and later Western Europe), the east (Persia and Turkey) and the south (Egypt and Arabia). Between 2000 BC and AD 632, Persia, Greece and Egypt competed for dominance. The area was a battleground among these powers and was occupied by one or the other for lengthy periods.

In AD 630, a new force emerged from Arabia under the banner of Islam to rule the entire Middle East until AD 950. Although the Arabians[5] removed the threat of Persia by annexing the Iranian plateau to the Muslim Empire, this only brought the empire into closer contact with different peoples from Asia – for example, the Turks and the Persians. A century after the triumph of the Arabians, the Persian and Turkic peoples, who came within the fold of Islam, gradually succeeded in replacing the Arabians in running the affairs of the Muslim empire. The centre of the Empire moved from Mecca, then to Damascus, to Baghdad (under Persian influence) and eventually to Constantinople (under Turkish influence).

From the north, the European influence persisted through the ages. After Greece (later Byzantium) ceased to be a major power in the region, the crusading Franks stormed the Levant in 1099, and from then on no century passed without an encounter between East and West over the Levant.

At all times, Egypt remained a major contender for hegemony over the Levant. The whole Levantine coast was an Egyptian province in ancient times. Egypt re-established its rule over the Levant between 950 and 1516 (the dynasties of the Fatimids, Memlukes and Ayubids). When the Ottoman Turks took over, Egypt tried several times to retake the Levant, in 1673 (under Ali al-Kebir) and from 1831–9 (under the Khedives). The last attempt was as recent as 1957–61 under President Gamal Abdel Nasser's regime.

South of the Levant lies the huge Arabian Peninsula. Before AD 632, Arabia was a dormant tribal society under Egyptian, Roman or

Ethiopian spheres of influence. However, in the seventh century, led by the Prophet Muhammad and armed with Islam, Arabia mobilized its population and conquered all the adjacent territories. Not only did the Levant fall to the Arabian armies, but also a region extending from the south of France to Central Asia, up to the frontiers of China. This landmass included in between most of coastal Africa down to the Equator and the Middle East. Within ten years of the death of Muhammad, the Arabians defeated the world superpowers of the time: the Greeks at Yarmouk south of Damascus and the Persians at Kadisiya in southern Iraq. Arabian rule was simple and doctrinal in the spirit of desert society, and followed the path of the "Pious Four Arabian Caliphs": Abou Bakr, Omar, Osman and Ali.

The assimilation of the Levant within the Muslim Empire was made easy by a variety of factors, as listed below.

- The fraternal attitude extended to the Arabians by the largely Christian population of the Levant.
- The fact that the population of the Levant had several Semitic tongues (Arabic, Syriac, Aramaic and Hebrew).
- The rejection of the Greek attempts at Hellenization of the populace.

Arabian control over the Muslim Empire ended quickly. Its demise was caused partly by internal feuds and partly by the strength of local cultures outside Arabia. Civil war and internal struggles among the various Arabian tribes began immediately after the death of Muhammad in 632. In addition, the furthest reaches of the empire prevented direct central control from Mecca or Damascus and allowed local autonomy and gradual predominance of non-Arabians. The Arabians never agreed unanimously on any caliphate, and this single issue splits Muslims into Sunni and Shia factions to this day. In fact, solid Arabian rule was ended as early as 660, 28 years after the death of Muhammad. Several Islamic empires emerged in Damascus (*c.* 660), Baghdad (*c.* 750), Spain (*c.* 750), Cairo (*c.* 950), Constantinople (in 1458) and smaller ones in North Africa, Spain, Persia, India and Central Asia.

Despite the decline of Arabia, Arab culture and Islam were well-entrenched in the Levant: the Arabians had succeeded where the Greeks had failed. Since Alexander of Macedonia, the Greeks had tried without success to Hellenize the largely Christian but Semitic Levant. Under the

Arabians, many Levantines embraced Islam, although many mountainous regions in Syria and Lebanon remained Christian. The Christian population of the Levant spoke both Arabic and Syriac. In fact, there was no linguistic demarcation or cultural exclusivity between the Levant and Arabia. Many Levantine Christians were Arabic-speaking tribes (for example, the Ghassans and the Mundhirs) who, like the Christian tribes of Arabia, used Arabic in their prayers and liturgy. Syriac too was used by many Christians in Arabia.

Except for the Crusader period (1099–1291) and brief Crusader incursions between 1298 and the seventeenth century, the Levant was no more than a region within an Islamic state until as recently as 1919. In 1516, the Ottoman Turks descended from Asia Minor, defeated the Egyptian army near Damascus and claimed a huge empire. The Ottoman Empire incorporated parts of central and southern Europe, the whole of North Africa and the Middle East. It was during the Ottoman period that the Levant experienced modern European influences. European commercial and cultural penetration of the Levant grew hand in hand with the dawn of Ottoman rule. While it is true today that the Levant is a hybrid of European and Arabic cultures, it is not easy to pass a judgement on which influence was stronger: it depends on the geographic region and community.

Modern European influence started in the seventeenth century with the arrival of the well-equipped and advanced European states (France, the Italian states, England, Russia and Austria) on the Levantine scene.

It should be noted that in the Levant, history did not evolve alongside the Western tradition – that is, it did not start with Greece and Rome, nor did it pass through the Dark Ages or the Renaissance. Rather, it had its own development as an ancient crossroads, followed by the advent of Judaism and Christianity, which to the population of the Levant are essentially native religions. This was followed by Islam, Crusader, Ottoman and modern European influences. Some historians try to impose a Western schedule on Levantine history by talking about a "feudal period" and a "bourgeois revolution" and so on, or they treat the time of the Phoenician City States as equivalent to the Greek classic period.

Amid these major historical currents, there was a small and beautiful mountain lying magnificently in the Levant, extending 100 kilometres in length and rising 11,000 feet at its highest peak.[6] This place was called *Gabla*, "mountain", in the Phoenician language (better known as Canaanite), "Land of the Sidonians" by the Hebrews of King David and Solomon, *Libanus* by the Romans and *Jabal Lubnan* by the Arabs. The various tribes who inhabited Mount Libanus from ancient times are the forefathers of the modern Lebanese. The roots of the leading mountain tribes could also be traced to other places in the Levant and Arabia. These tribes were headed by powerful warlords who often waged turf wars against each other or engaged in bloody struggles in support of one foreign power against another. Taken in isolation, the place never developed a collective destiny or a national character, a factor that was exploited by successive invaders who played tribes off against each other. On the eve of the third millennium, Lebanon was still struggling to achieve lasting national unity among its diverse communities.

The warlords
It was the Jesuit Professor Henri Lammens who proposed the theory that "Lebanon as a country owes its creation to its function as a shelter for the oppressed minorities in the Levant".[7] In fact, this was a French thesis par excellence, which gave the ideological pretext for the creation of Lebanon. Following the civil war in 1860, the wishes of the Maronite Christians were the single most important factor in the creation of modern Lebanon as a separate entity in the Levant in 1920.

The massacres of 1860–1 had hit the Christians harder than any other group. Those in Damascus were especially targeted for slaughter. A country where the Christians felt safe and had a degree of power was therefore warranted in that part of the world at that time.

Starting in the ninth century, the Maronites settled the northern ranges of Mount Lebanon, and over the centuries they developed good relations with France and, eventually, along with the Druze, pushed for a distinct independent Lebanon. However, the shelter theory could not have been a decisive factor. If it hadn't been for the assertive Maronites, Mount Lebanon could have been just a geographic location, undistinguished from other mountains in the Levant which, incidentally, also served as shelters for minorities, but never became the bases of separate states. In fact, after the First World War, the French pondered the idea of creating an Alawite state (around the Alawi Mountain north of Mount Lebanon) and a Druze state (around the Druze Mountain or

Jabal al-Arab, south-east of Damascus). However, nationalism and hatred for the French won the day over confessionalism, and these "shelters" were dissolved into modern Syria.

The mountains of the Levant are not the Himalayas and were not defensible against ancient military expeditions. In many instances, when Greeks, Arabs or Crusaders wished to reach the mountain communities they were able to do so. The different groups inhabiting the mountain region were able to attack each other in times of conflict. Although religious belief was an important factor that pushed many groups to settle in Mount Lebanon, strong feudal lordships were also common in the region. From the beginning, the Maronites, the Shia and the Druze established warrior societies not much different from the Japanese Samurai-style fiefs. The warrior communities glorified images of chivalry and male strength, and developed into warlord feudal domains.

Although co-existence was a common denominator in the mountain region, civil wars and external attacks marred the valleys and slopes. Tribal fighting was a feature, as it was in the rest of the Levant and Arabia. After the eighteenth century, when modern guns and weapons were introduced to Mount Lebanon, civil wars became more frequent and bloodier.

Although minorities settled Mount Lebanon between the seventh and the twelfth centuries, before that, the mountain region had not been a virgin territory. Since early times, a striking feature of Mount Lebanon that caught the attention of visitors was that it was heavily populated. Even in Phoenician times, there were at least fifty towns and villages in the region separated at times by only a few hundred metres. Recent research has shown that a good portion of the population of the mountain was native and not migrant from other places. As for their religious beliefs, it is possible that the native tribes could have easily converted to the Druze, the Shia or the Maronite faiths. Archaeological works have discovered ancient terracing of the rocky but fertile slopes dating back 5,000 years. Chroniclers of the Macedonian siege of Tyre in 333 BC mentioned native warriors descending from the mountain behind Tyre and attacking the Macedonians to relieve the pressure on the besieged city.

Between the fourteenth and the sixteenth centuries, several tribal homelands or cantons crystallized and prospered in Mount Lebanon. These cantons were ruled by warlords who ran communal armies, maintained peace and order and collected taxes on behalf of the regional power of the day. In the case of the Levant, Mount Lebanon was not a particularly great source of wealth. The relative autonomy of the mountain region cannot be exaggerated. Ruling powers were not generally interested in maintaining a permanent armed presence in the conquered territories; for them, the payment of tribute was a sufficient expression of loyalty. This was true of Egyptians, Persians, Greeks, Arabians, Crusaders, Memlukes and Ottomans. Under the Ottomans, Mount Lebanon, like many other regions, including Romania and Hungary, had local autonomy within the empire. Ancient and medieval empires were plagued by weak communications and logistics as they controlled vast territories and ruled over several peoples. Central governments were unable to extend immediate authority and delegated power through local notables. Central authorities sent armed expeditions only when taxes were not paid or to crush a rebellion.

The undeveloped and rugged terrain of Mount Lebanon allowed a free hand to the proud warlords who enjoyed a degree of autonomy denied to the major towns and territories crossed by the highways of the empires. However, this isolation was a double-edged sword as autonomy was obtained at the expense of foregoing economic and cultural development. The coastal region of the Levant had always been sophisticated and prosperous since the Phoenicians sailed their first boat, but the mountain region failed to produce enough wealth to sustain a meaningful civilization. The autonomy of Mount Lebanon began to erode in the seventeenth century as strong Druze and Maronite warlords attempted to unify the area and enlarge it under the nose of the Ottoman government. Eventually, the feudal autonomy ended in 1842, when British warships transported the last Lebanese emir, Bachir Chehab II to exile in Malta. This was followed by a bloody civil war that continued intermittently until August 1861.

In 1861, the French Army came to the defence of the Christians and the peace that followed allowed the establishment of the "State of Mount Lebanon", administered directly from Constantinople. To allow the new entity to survive, the Ottomans realized that important offices should be held by the leading warlords who represented the various religious communities. This tradition continues to this day.

The supremacy of the warlords in Mount Lebanon existed over a period of 1,200 years – from 640 to 1840. In that period, three communities inhabited Mount Lebanon: the Druze, the Maronites and the Shia. The 1,200 years can be divided into three stages where the warlords of each of these communities dominated in turn. Thus, starting in 640, the Shia[8] dominated the area until 1306, followed by the Druze until 1770 and then by the Maronites until 1843. The Sunnis who belonged to the religion of the empire of the day inhabited mostly the coastal region that was outside Mount Lebanon.

Shia warlords
Shortly after the Levant fell under Muslim rule in 632, the Muslim Empire was rocked by a succession of conflicts and internal feuds. The government system favoured by Muhammad and practised by the "pious caliphs" lasted for less than forty years; it ended in 660 and was replaced by that of the Umayads who ruled the Levant from their base in Damascus until 750. Then the Abbasids took over the empire and established their rule in Baghdad. In 950, Fatimid Egypt broke away from Baghdad and extended its control into the Levant.

Between 632 and 660, the Muslim faith was going through a gestation period out of which would emerge the Sunni–Shia schism that has lasted to the present day. The quarrel among the Muslim leadership over political positions started immediately after the death of Muhammad in 632. The central conflict was over the office of the caliphate (literally, the successor to Muhammad, the supreme commander and leader of the faithful), and involved followers of the Umayad and Hashem clans in Mecca. Over the years, several caliphs were assassinated. Although the rift was largely political and reconcilable, over time the sides were pushed into harder positions. By 660 it became difficult to bring the parties together as the Umayad clan led by Mouaya were entrenched in their domains in Syria and the Hashem clan led by Imam Ali were in Mecca (Arabia) and Kufa (Iraq). After the death of Ali, a cousin of the Prophet Muhammad, the families split into camps and mobilized Muslims against each other. This split created a poisoned atmosphere that led to the first division in Islam between the Camp of Ali (the House of Muhammad, *Ahlul bayt*) and the Camp of the Umayads. These two camps later became religious sects rather than adherents of the different political parties: the Sunnis and the Shia. In 750, the Abbasids formalized Sunni Islam into a state religion while their opponents who embraced the Shia doctrine established their own dynasties in many places: Egypt, Tunisia, the Levant, the Iranian Plateau and Central Asia.

SHIA WARLORDS AND DRUZE EMIRS

The rift between Sunni and Shia swelled over the centuries and covered many aspects of religious beliefs and practices. While the more numerous Sunnis split in turn into only a few schools, it was the less numerous Shia who split into dozens of factions. Today many groups who consider themselves Shia are viewed as heretics by other Shia. The ruling Sunnis considered as Shia all dissident groups who turned against the state including the Kharijis, Jaafari Twelvers, Ismailis, Caramates, Nusairis (Alawis), Batinis, Zaidis, Fatimids, Druze and many others. In the Sunni tradition, these schools were grouped together as heretics.

As early as the 630s, Abu Dharr al-Ghefari, a close associate of the Prophet Muhammad, sought refuge in Lebanon when he became at odds with the rulers in Medina and Damascus. He enjoyed considerable reverence by the Shia. Starting in 750, Shia Islam in its Ismaili and Jaafari forms was establishing itself in Mount Lebanon, and by 950, several areas in northern Mount Lebanon, the Bekaa, the Orontes Valley, Jebel Amil in south Lebanon, and the Alawi mountains, were inhabited by adherents of Shia Islam. Until 1307, Shia inhabited several coastal regions of Lebanon, including the districts of Kesrouane, Jbeil, Batroun, Tripoli, Saida and Tyre. However, these areas never expressed themselves as Shia political centres like Egypt, Tunisia, Northern Syria or Persia, because they lacked the economic base and the population mass. Although dominant in Lebanon at the time, the Shia were tribal communities like the other inhabitants of the mountain region. However there was a Shia kingdom in Aleppo under the Banu Hamdane and another one in Tripoli under the Banu Ammar. The Druze, who are of the Ismaili branch of Shia Islam, created several tiny emirates in Mount Lebanon and Northern Syria, starting in the eleventh century.

When Lebanon fell to the Crusaders between the twelfth and the thirteenth centuries, it was inhabited by Shia, Maronite and Druze tribes. The Crusaders preserved these domains and the Shia and the Maronites traded with, and preferred, Crusader rule to the Sunni rulers of Damascus. However, in the thirteenth century the Sunni Ayubid and Memluke dynasties defeated the Crusaders in the Levant and ended Fatimid Shia rule in Cairo. The Memlukes followed their victory by descending heavily against the Shia and the Maronites of Mount Lebanon. Some historians explain that the relations between the Shia of Mount Lebanon and the Sunni religious authorities in Damascus were not friendly at the time. Consequently, the Memluke assault against the Shia in Lebanon was encouraged by a fatwa (religious edict) from Ibn Taymia, the scholarly mufti of Damascus.

Successive Memluke expeditions attacked the Shia and Maronite cantons between 1283 and 1306, and killed thousands of people in the process. In a 1305–06 campaign, the Memlukes under Sultan an-Nasser Kalawoon waged several campaigns against Kesrouane, killing 15,000 Shia and pushing survivors away from the coast so that contacts with the Crusaders were made difficult. Considering that the whole population of Lebanon at the time was less than 100,000, the killing amounted to genocide, which was followed by a massive settlement of Sunni Kurdish and Turkoman tribes along the coast. Similar raids against the Maronites took place further north, where several thousands were killed, but many others managed to flee to the Island of Cyprus where many Maronite villages survive to this day.

Following these events, the Shia of Lebanon suffered near extinction, as most were either killed or converted to Sunni Islam or Christianity. In the thirteenth and fourteenth centuries, Shia clerics decided to allow their followers to disguise their religion in order to survive, and a fatwa permitted *takiyya* (hiding one's faith). Thus by the end of 1306, the Shia's[9] demise as the dominant community in Mount Lebanon was complete. Following these campaigns, the remaining Shia stayed clear from the coast and from the major cities. Following the defeat of the Crusaders in the Levant and the Fatimids in Egypt, events in Mount Lebanon resembled the fate of Muslims and Jews in reconquered Spain or of the Jews in twentieth century Europe. Evidence of this can be traced in the writings of the Arab chronicler Osama ibn Munqidh, who accused "the greedy and cheating merchants of Beirut as being Shia in disguise practising taqqiya"[10] (insinuating that a greedy and cheating merchant could only be a Shia).

Over the next two centuries, the Shia re-established themselves in fringe areas such as the Bekaa, Jebel Amil (modern south Lebanon) and the Orontes Valley. By the sixteenth century, the Shia had begun to return to Kesrouane and extend their influence in the Bekaa to connect with their co-religionists in south Lebanon. This was possible as passions against the Shia had cooled, and there was encouragement from the Safavid Shia dynasty in Iran, which harboured hopes of controlling the Levant. The Shia were led by the Hamadi and Saghir warlords and their allies. However, the local Turkomen tribes and the Memlukes, and later the Ottoman government, kept the Shia in check as they feared the ambitious Safavid Persia. Eventually, the Turkomen, who were partially Christianized, pushed the Shia back to the Jurd (the heights), and encouraged the Maronites of northern Lebanon to move south to further deter the Shia.

After the sixteenth century, the Shia in Lebanon finally settled in a defined territory that has not changed to this day. The Shia warlords were the Hamadis in the Upper Bekaa (Baalbeck and Hermel), and the Saghirs, Nassars and Chukrs in Bilad Bechara and Jebel Amil (the two cantons of south Lebanon). Although tamed, the Shia continued to cause difficulties to the local Ottoman authorities that contracted local tribes to pacify them. As Jebel Amil was more accessible and slightly more prosperous than the remote and less developed Hamadi warlord domain in the regions of Baalbeck, Hermel and the Jurd in northern Lebanon, the Ottoman governors of Saida and Acre continuously assaulted it to keep the Shia in check.

In the eighteenth century, and as an oppressed minority, the Shia identified with the "Arab" cause against Ottoman rule. While nationalism as a Western concept only came to be known to Arab and Turkish intellectuals at the end of the nineteenth century, ethnic and religious minorities of the large Ottoman Empire struck alliances based on common causes such as language and minority status. There were historical reasons for this development as the Maronites, the Druze and the Shia had always been at odds with Ottoman rule since it began in 1516. An important Shia stand occurred in 1760 when the warlord Nassif Nassar of Jebel Amel and his forces joined the Maronites and the Druze led by Emir Youssef Chehab and the Emir Daher al-Omar of northern Palestine in a fight against the Ottoman authority. This alliance of minorities was encouraged by the governor of Egypt, and both sides had Arabic as a common ground for grievance against the Turks. However, the uprising was crushed and the Shia were wiped out by Ahmad Pasha al-Jazzar, the Ottoman governor of Acre. Al-Jazzar killed many people, burnt down Shia religious schools in the region of Jezzine and the town of Jbaa and confiscated valuable books to use as fire-starters in the bakeries of Acre. The vengeance of al-Jazzar was aimed at punishing the Shia for siding with an Arab alliance against Ottoman rule. A simultaneous revolt combined Daher al-Omar of Jerusalem and the Chehab Emir in Mount Lebanon with an attack on Damascus by Ali Bey al-Kebir of Egypt. The

Shia rose again to support the Druze rebellion against Egyptian occupation in 1838–9.[11]

Druze warlords

The second stage in the development of Mount Lebanon as a political entity was dominated by the Druze and lasted from 1306 to 1770. As early as the eleventh century, the Druze settled in a small canton in Mount Lebanon known as the Chouf. This organized warrior community fared better than the Shia: from the Chouf, they expanded their hegemony over the mountain region and eventually controlled large chunks of the Levant. The Druze trace their religious origin to Ismaili Shi'ism and to other mystic roots of Islam. In the tenth century, an Ismaili group of Fatimids triumphed in North Africa and established an empire in Tunisia and Cairo. The Fatimids extended their rule into Mount Lebanon, where several native tribes were of the Ismaili Shia faith.

In 996, al-Hakem, aged just eleven, became the new Fatimid caliph in Cairo. He preached a version of Shi'ism called "al-Mowaheds" (those who seek unity), and several Ismaili tribes in the Levant embraced the new faith and became Mowaheds. The Mowaheds of Lebanon were harassed and attacked by the Crusaders and the Sunni rulers in Damascus. In response, the Fatimids sent a military expedition from Cairo under the leadership of Anajtekin al-Darazi[12], who arrived in Wadi al-Taim in south Lebanon. This force was eventually engaged with armed groups from Damascus in 1029 in the Battle of Aqhowana at Lake Tiberias on the River Jordan. The victory at Aqhowana was an event of profound importance to Druze psyche. It inspired pride in the hearts of the Mowaheds who later viewed al-Darazi with reverence, and henceforward their faith became known as "the al-Darazi Path" (Mazhab al-Durzi) and its followers as "Druze".

In 1021, al-Hakem disappeared while on a trip to Mount Muqqatam, east of Cairo. His son, who immediately put many Druze in the Levant to the sword, succeeded him. To protect themselves, the Druze practised *takiyya* and hid their faith. Druzism became *din mekhfi* (hidden religion), and still is to this day. However, it is safe to assume that even if details of the Druze faith were made public, these details would not hold any surprises. Druzism is largely based on Islam and the various philosophies and schools that thrived in the Middle East. While sharing many aspects of Shia Islam – including a respect for the last of the "pious caliphs", Ali

– the Druze faith developed a separate path that considered al-Hakem as a Messiah. At first, the Druze were confined to the hinterland areas extending from Wadi al-Taim valley in south Lebanon to the southern slopes of the Taurus Mountains in modern Turkey. Today, large Druze communities inhabit the Chouf, Wadi al-Taim and Hasbaya in Lebanon, Mount Arab (Jabal Druze) and Swaida south of Damascus in Syria and Galilee in Israel. There is also a small community in Jordan.

The first concept of a separate Lebanese entity was developed under the Druze. In the seventeenth century, under Emir Fakhreddine II, Mount Lebanon gained prominence in regional and international affairs and distinguished itself from other regions in the Levant. Druze fortunes further improved in 1516 when the Ottoman Turks arrived in the Middle East as the new rulers. This year signified the start of the modern period in Mount Lebanon known as "the epoch of the emirs", when Druze and Maronite emirs ruled the region between 1516 and 1842.

Between 1306 and 1516, the Chouf range was ruled by various warlord families who were at peace with the Memlukes. They included several Druze warlord tribes – notably the Buhturs, the Maans, the Tanukhs, the Imads, the Abi Nakad, the Abdelmaleks and the Talhouks. As explained earlier, the Kesrouane Range, north of the Chouf, was inhabited by Sunni Turkoman tribes ruled by Assaf warlords, who were partially Christianized. Several Maronite tribes also made their home in Kesrouane. The Maronites of upper Lebanon were led by the Hobeichi warlords who enjoyed good relations with the Assafs.

In the sixteenth century, all the tribes of the mountain region spoke Arabic, and mountain warlords claimed ancestry and/or blood relations to places in northern Syria, Iraq and Arabia. Many of them traced their origins to the Arab tribes who moved to Mount Lebanon between the eighth and the twelfth centuries. On the eastern slopes of Mount Lebanon, Arab tribes, notably the Sunni Chehabs, settled in the Taim Valley in around 1056, while the Druze Maans settled in the Chouf in the village of Baakline in 1120. Soon the Chehabs and the Maans struck up an alliance that ruled Lebanon until 1842.

Shortly after their arrival in 1516, the Ottomans divided the Levant into three *vilayets* (states): Aleppo, Damascus and Acre. These vilayets were governed by Ottoman administrators chosen from the Sunni Turkoman and Kurdish notables. Each vilayet incorporated a portion of Lebanon: the Bekaa belonged to Damascus; the territory north of Beirut belonged to Aleppo; and Saida and Jebel Amil belonged to the vilayet of Acre.

The Ottoman governors appointed local warlords as tax collectors and upholders of law and order. Thus, the Banu Saifa warlords (Turkomen Sunni) took Tripoli and Akkar in northern Lebanon, and the Banu Assaf (also Turkomen Sunni) looked after Kesrouane and its coast down to Beirut. In the areas of Mount Lebanon away from the coast, tax collectors were native Arab warlords. Only the Chouf region was destined to play a major role in Mount Lebanon up until the twentieth century. The role of tax collecting gave the warlords the additional title of *Ayan*.[13]

While most warlords cooperated with the authorities in Acre and Saida, several Druze and Shia warlords rebelled. For most of the sixteenth century, the Ottomans had to send military expeditions to crush rebellions in the Chouf and Jebel Amel. While the Shia canton faced armed expeditions from Saida, the Druze Chouf had enemies on all sides: regular Ottoman Janissaries from Saida, the Banu Assaf from Ghazir (overlooking the Bay of Jounié) and Beirut, the Banu Saifa of Akkar and Janissaries from Damascus. These enemies harassed and attacked the Druze and Shia areas for much of the sixteenth and seventeenth centuries. The Assafs were fortified in Beirut, which had been in ruins since the Crusader era. They renovated parts of it though and reconstructed many of its buildings.[14]

In 1585, the Druze rebellion against the Ottomans reached a climax. In that year, the Saifas accused the Druze of attacking and confiscating state funds coming from Egypt to the Ottoman treasury. In response, the government ordered the Viceroy of Egypt to send a disciplinary expedition to retrieve the funds. An Egyptian contingent ruthlessly attacked the Chouf and killed many Druze, including the Maan Emir Kurkumaz. The death of Kurkumaz and the assault on the Druze and their Shia allies strengthened the legitimacy and popularity of the Maans in the Chouf. This popularity cleared the way for Kurkumaz's son, Fakhreddine II, to claim leadership in 1592.

Fakhreddine was the greatest of the mountain emirs, and remains the greatest national Lebanese hero of all time. As the Ottoman governors became tired of the endless quarrels and rebellions of Mount Lebanon, Fakhreddine was the local warlord they needed to establish law and order in the region. However, Fakhreddine had a hidden agenda as well. When he became emir he vowed to end the threat from the Saifas up north and to rebuild Druze houses, demolished in the Egyptian raid in

1585, from the stones of the houses of the Saifas. Between 1595 and 1608, he succeeded in expanding his domains into a powerful emirate.

Fakhreddine's efforts eventually attracted international attention. With a strong popular base, good organization and a healthy economic position, he started an ambitious independence campaign. To win international recognition, he signed several commercial and defence pacts with the Italian House of the Medicis of Tuscany in 1606–7. He waged a war against the Assafs, chasing them out of Beirut and defeating them at Dog River. He then continued the campaign against the Saifas in Akkar, whom he also defeated, demolishing their houses and removing the stones to rebuild Druze houses as he had planned in Baakline and Deir al-Kamar in the Chouf. Following these campaigns, Fakhreddine annexed Beirut, Kesrouane and the northern ranges, and unified Mount Lebanon under his authority. Then he turned south to Saida where he defeated the governor and annexed the city.

These events were watched by the authorities in Constantinople who ordered the governor of Damascus to restrain the Maans. Damascus sent a military expedition to challenge Fakhreddine. However, the latter confronted and defeated the expedition at Ain Dara in the upper Chouf in 1609. Unwilling to commit more forces to a local affair, the Ottoman government acknowledged Fakhreddine's victories and confirmed him through understandings in 1610 as Emir of the Mountain and all the hinterland areas from the edge of Aleppo down to Ajloun and Hawran near the River Jordan.[15]

While the Ottoman government was pleased with Fakhreddine's stable regime and timely payments, his foreign contacts proved too much to digest. The Italian states were angry at the Ottomans for destroying their commercial links with the Levant. These links, established under the Crusaders, were maintained under the Memlukes until 1516. The Venetians, the Genoese and the Medicis were particularly angry because the Turks disrupted the long-established trade in spices and silk they had enjoyed with the Levant since 1110, a few years after the Crusader conquest.[16] Worse still, between 1605 and 1615, the Ottomans also removed and closed the Italian trading posts in Cyprus. Thus, the Italians paid special attention to Fakhreddine's policies that ran contrary to the wishes of the Ottomans, but were favourable to them.

In 1607, Fakhreddine resumed trade between Beirut and Saida and the Italian states. The Italians, notably the Venetians, were anxious to support rebellions against the Ottomans who had deprived them of their rights to do business in the area. They also supported Fakhreddine's military campaigns. During this period, the Druze and the Maronites received arms supplies from the Venetians in Cyprus. Thousands of musket guns found their way to the warlords who used them against Ottoman Janissaries.[17] Tuscany also assured the Druze of prompt help in time of trouble.

The Ottomans were not sure of the extent of Fakhreddine's ambitions – whether he just wanted to get rid of neighbouring warlords or to seek independence. His verbal allegiance to the Sultan, the payment of taxes and a respectable treatment of Ottoman officials were all signs of loyalty. However, his European connections were feared by the Ottomans. Eventually, their suspicions were transformed into action, and they sent a major disciplinary force against him in 1615. As the Ottoman attack was in full swing, the Italian help failed to arrive as promised and Fakhreddine feared total collapse under the Janissary assault. He eventually gave up and decided to flee to Italy, where he stayed for five years in Naples and Florence, as the guest of Prince Cosimo di Medici. During his stay, Fakhreddine visited Spain and enjoyed wide sympathy in Europe. These sympathizers thought of him as a Crusader knight. One fable, which was convincing to many European rulers, suggested that the Druze were descendants of a fictitious Christian Frank, and that the emir was the Comte de Dreux whose dynasty had flourished in the Chouf since the Crusader period.[18]

Things changed dramatically in the Mediterranean region in 1620 with the accession of an enlightened sultan in Constantinople. With some persuasion from the European representatives in Constantinople, the Ottoman government made the gesture of allowing Fakhreddine to return to Mount Lebanon and restored him as emir. Upon his return, Fakhreddine wasted no time and immediately resumed his emirate-building campaign. On the military side, he organized a warlord alliance that gathered – according to some estimates – 25,000[19] men, comprising mainly Druze, Maronite and Shia warriors. On the economic side, he benefited from the advice of Italian architects and consultants, and rebuilt Beirut and Saida in the Italian style. Historically significant was his decision to move his headquarters from the mountain region to the renovated cities of Saida and Beirut on the coast.

Now at an advanced age, the Emir was more experienced and wary of the extent to which the Italians would help him. Nevertheless, he waged new military campaigns, defeated another *wali* (governor) from Damascus at Anjar and annexed the fertile Bekaa Valley. Initially, the Ottomans, under a new and strong leadership, considered Fakhreddine's manoeuvre as a local concern within their huge empire. They did not object to his rule in Lebanon as long as he paid taxes regularly, recognized central authority and refrained from conspiring with the Europeans. They even confirmed his power over all the areas that came under his control.[20] However, they were alerted by local *wali*s in Syria to the suspicious moves of Fakhreddine and his allies in Syria. As early as 1624, Fakhreddine was organizing an important Druze alliance throughout the Levant. Although this was not instigated from the outside, authorities determined that it was an internal threat to the security of the empire.

The source of this anxiety was the fear of Ottoman governors in Aleppo and Damascus of Druze emirs. At the time, another Druze emirate was emerging in northern Syria, led by the Joumblatts who controlled the cities of Kilis, Aintab and Nisibin[21] north of Aleppo. Like the Maans, the Joumblatt warlords, Ali and Hussain, were troublemakers. They signed treaties with Tuscany in 1606–7, and were involved in battles with Ottoman governors as far away from their home base as Musil in northern Iraq and even in Cyprus.

When the Joumblatts took Aleppo in 1624, the Ottomans decided it was time to check the Druze power in northern Syria. In 1625, they sent a large expedition against the Joumblatts, who were defeated in battle resulting in the demise of their emirate. Facing total collapse, the Joumblatt leaders and their families sought refuge with their ally Fakhreddine and settled in Mazraat Chouf and Mokhtara in Mount Lebanon. After the events of 1625, Fakhreddine was no longer felt to be immune to Ottoman wrath. He understood that the sultan was a learned and liberal ruler, who was opening up to the West. But at the same time, the sultan wanted a secure and stable empire under his control so that he could negotiate with Europe from a strong position with a united home front.

In the 1630s, times were changing for the Ottomans who were on the verge of signing major accords with the European states. As a prelude, and two years before major agreements with France, the Ottomans sent a force to Mount Lebanon in 1633 and engaged Fakhreddine's army. Outnumbered four to one, this attack was the final blow for Fakhreddine who was arrested as a rebel and taken prisoner to Constantinople.

Back in Lebanon, the Ottomans were searching for a warlord to establish law and order and collect taxes. The ambitious Druze Ali Alamuddine offered to replace Fakhreddine and to prove his loyalty he helped the Ottoman expedition crush the Maans and the allied clans. His tribe, the Alamuddines, killed many Maans and Buhturs who were Fakhreddine's immediate uncles on his mother's side. Alamuddine did well, and the Ottomans confirmed him as the tax collector in the area. The situation in the Chouf remained explosive between 1633 and 1635, as the Maans and their allies boycotted the Alamuddines.

Fakhreddine had important friends in the Ottoman capital. The European ambassadors vouched for him, and the government treated him well and even pondered releasing him and restoring his power. The Ottoman governors realized that only a Maan emir could maintain peace and order in the Chouf. To achieve this, efforts were made to release the elderly Fakhreddine and allow him to return to his emirate. However, before this was made public, a Maan rebellion, led by Fakhreddine's eldest son, Hussein, was already under way. The rebels attacked Beirut, now an important Ottoman city, and other places, which angered the central government that summarily executed Fakhreddine in 1635.[22]

Probably the execution of the emir was ill-advised, as his death did not change the government's plan to restore the Maans and remove the Alamuddines. Thus, Druze unity returned under the Maan dynasty minus the power and charisma of Fakhreddine. When the last Maan emir died in 1697, leadership was transferred to their allies, the Sunni Chehabs of Wadi al-Taim. Although power and influence remained with the Druze warlords, they lost internal unity as the wounds created by the Alamuddines continued to run deep. The conflict rose to the surface in 1697 when the warlords split between the Joumblatts and their allies on one side and the Alamuddines and their allies on the other. While nobody objected to the leadership of the Chehabs, each side supported a different Chehab camp to become emir. To arbitrate the issue, the Ottomans intervened and nominated the 12-year old Emir Haidar Chehab, a nephew of Emir Ahmed Maan, the last Maan emir. However, because Haidar was so young, another notable Chehab was appointed as a regent until 1706.

Between 1697 and 1706, Druze infighting continued as the Joumblatts waited for the appointment of Haidar. Haidar was seen to represent the Maans, his uncles, in the dispute among the Druze, and when he became emir, he took it upon himself to revenge the Maans and fight the Alamuddines. In 1711, Haidar, supported by the Joumblatts, defeated the Alamuddines and their allies at the village of Ain Dara in the upper Chouf. Following this battle, Haidar rewarded his allies and extended the title of emir to the Abillama and Erslan clans.

Although Haidar ended twenty years of internal Druze civil strife, the battle at Ain Dara was a dark milestone for the Druze community because it led to the exodus of the Alamuddines and their supporters from the mountain region to the Bekaa and further out to areas south of Damascus. This migration caused the Druze population of Mount Lebanon to drop in comparison with the ever-growing Maronite population. When Fakhreddine II had defeated the Assafs in 1610, he had removed the Maronite Hobeichi warlords from power and appointed the Maronite al-Khazen warlords as his lieutenants in Kesrouane. From then onwards the Maronite warlords of Kesrouane had remained loyal allies of the Maans and were treated as such, being allowed to live in Druze territory and on the coast.

The Maronite move southward occurred in four waves. The first occurred when they were granted the right to inhabit Kesrouane by the Memluke Egyptians in 1291. The second came after 1306, when the Shia were wiped out from the area. The third wave occurred under the Druze emirs between 1400 and 1700. During that period, the silk business was prospering in the Chouf, and under Fakhreddine, the Druze labour force could not match the rising demand in Europe and the Middle East for Lebanese silk. Thus, the Druze warlords welcomed Maronite farmers and encouraged them to move south of Kesrouane. The fourth Maronite move southward occurred after 1711, when the Druze civil war caused a considerable loss of population, and Maronite immigrants were needed even more as the Druze areas suffered serious shortages of manual labour.

Gradually, the Maronites became the largest community throughout the mountain area, from the hinterland east of Tripoli down to the Chouf. Even in the Chouf region they became a majority where the Maronite town of Deir al-Kamar outgrew Baakline, hometown of Fakhreddine II. However, their numbers were not the cause of their rise as rulers of the mountain region. Rather, it was their wealth and education that opened the way for their ascent.

Notes

1. "The Levant is the name given to this string of merchant cities through which travellers from Europe reached the Orient. From Constantinople to Alexandria, passing through Smyrna, Adana or Beirut, for a long time these towns have been home to an intermingling of languages, customs and beliefs. A precarious world slowly shaped over history, before being destroyed." Amin Maalouf, *Les Échelles du Levant*, Paris, Livre de Poche, 1998, p. 3.
2. Derived from *cham'al* (or "north"), in contrast with "Yemen" (*yamin*) or "south" from the standpoint of the Hejaz.
3. Philip Hitti, *History of Syria including Lebanon and Palestine*, New York, Macmillan, 1951. The term "Geographic Syria" was first used by the Romans in the early Christian centuries to refer to that portion of their empire bordering on the eastern Mediterranean sea. Prior to that appellation, the region was an amalgam of smaller entities, such as the various city-states of Phoenicia, the tiny kingdoms and principalities of the Holy Land and Damascus, which was the centre of the Land of Aram. The Romans chose this collective name and it was "geographic" because it was for administrative convenience rather than for historical or cultural reasons.
4. For a colourful account of the region's culture and people, refer to *Tribes with Flags: A Dangerous Passage through the Chaos of the Middle East* by Charles Glass, New York, Atlantic Monthly Press, 1990.
5. Arabians are the inhabitants of Arabia. The term "Arabs" is liberally used in this book to refer to Arabic-speaking peoples who may not be Arabian in origin.
6. The Lebanon mountain range belongs to a series of elevations that start in the Taurus range in Turkey and end with the hills of Galilee and Jerusalem.
7. Henri Lammens, *La Syrie*, Volumes I and II, Beirut, Imprimerie Catholique, 1921.
8. The words "Shia" and "Druze" are already in the plural form; thus, the plural "s" is redundant. In contrast, the words "Sunni" and "Maronite" are in the singular form and need an "s" in the plural.
9. Also called *metawela* (that is, those who pay allegiance to the House of Muhammad or the party of Ali) during the emir's epoch. In the twentieth century, Shia consider the word *metawela* as a degrading reference to the days of oppression and deprivation under the Ottomans.
10. Issam Chebaro, *A History of Beirut from Ancient Times to the Twentieth Century* (in Arabic, *Tarikh Bayrout min Aqdam al-Ossour ila al-Qarn al-Ishtin*), Beirut, Dar Misbah al-Fikr, 1987.
11. For more detail on the medieval history of Lebanon, see the Selected Bibliography.
12. Kamal Salibi suggests that there were two men named Anajtekin al-Darazi in the service of the Fatimids in the early years of the eleventh century. The first was Anajtekin al-Darazi (also known as Mohamed bin Ismael al-Mutahheri), a religious

authority on the Mowahed faith who was assassinated in Cairo in 1017, and the second was Anajtekin al-Darbazi (the added letter "b" in the name is Salibi's researched spelling), the military leader who won the Battle of Aqhowana in 1029. See Kamal Salibi, *An Early History of Lebanon* (in Arabic, *Muntalaq tarikh Lubnan*), Beirut, Dar Nawfal, 1992, p. 69.
13 A derivation from the Arabic word for "eyes", *ayn*; those who oversee or watch the population on behalf of the government. This role is in addition to their role as tax collectors.
14 The Assaf Mosque is an example of an Assaf building that has survived to the present day.
15 See Kamal Salibi, *A Modern History of Lebanon* (in Arabic, *Tarikh Lubnan al Hadith*), London, Weidenfeld and Nicolson, 1965. Arabic edition, Beirut, Dar Annahar, 1971 and 1991.
16 Jan Morris, *The Venetian Empire*, London, Penguin, 1989.
17 The State of Venice was called *Bundukiya* in Arabic. The musket guns donated by the Venetians were also called *Bundukiya*.
18 See *Who's Who in Lebanon 1991*, Beirut, Publitec, 1991.
19 This may be exaggerated. A force of 2,500 would be more reasonable considering the period and the demographic base of the region.
20 Formally, Fakhreddine's domains were confined to the hinterland area that ran from the mountains south of Aleppo to the hills of northern Jordan. The Ottomans confirmed him as Sultan al-Barr over the inlands, which means in Arabic Sultan of the "wilderness" or "rugged land".
21 These cities are now called Kilis, Gazi-antep and Nisip, and are located within modern Turkey.
22 In 1966, Fairuz performed a patriotic dramatized version of Fakhreddine's career, called *Ayam Fakhreddine* (The Days of Fakhreddine). This musical play was written by the Rahbani brothers and ran for over a year in Lebanon. The songs from this drama are a source of inspiration to Lebanese patriotism and steadfastness. In fact, Fakhreddine is one of the few figures respected and admired by all Lebanese. In the 1970s, Kamal Joumblatt called his militia the Fakhreddine Army, and the Phalanges used Fakhreddine's experiences to inspire their fighters. In 1990, a Fakhreddine quote was used by Michel Aoun's supporters to express their refusal to accept Aoun's defeat and subsequent exile. The quote was: "badna nkammel billi bikyou" ("we shall carry on the struggle with the tiny number of those who survived [the catastrophe that has befallen us]").

2

Maronite Warlords and Sunni *Zaims*

Although they constituted a majority in the mountain region, the Maronites played a limited role in the affairs of the emirate before the nineteenth century. After 1770, they became rulers for two periods: 1770–1843 and 1941–75. While the Druze placed Mount Lebanon on the map, it was the Maronites who created the Lebanese idea and later pushed for the creation of a separate state. The years 1861 and 1930 were milestones for the Lebanese ideal. The massacres of 1861 gave Maronite intellectuals an urgent need to create a brand of nationalism unique to Lebanon, centred on two pillars: the Maronite Church and the European link. After 1930 and with the French excavations in Jbeil, the Phoenician heritage became a factor in Lebanese nationalism as will be made clear later.

The Church

The Maronite faith started near Aleppo in northern Syria in the early Christian centuries. Between the fifth and seventh centuries, the Christian clergy of the Byzantine Empire were engaged in a serious debate on the principles of Christianity and the nature of Christ. A Christian hermit, Youhanna Maroun, who lived near Aleppo, preached a different concept regarding the nature of Christ, which ran against the mainstream Jacobite interpretation. At the time, the Christians of Syria were involved in hot debates that eventually turned violent. While individual Maronites had already moved to, and established themselves in, northern Lebanon between the fifth and ninth centuries, the significant wave of Maronite migration occurred after 939, when armies supporting the Orthodox interpretation of the Byzantine emperor persecuted the Maronites along the Orontes Valley and burnt their churches, in the process killing around 350 priests.[1] Several tribes fled to Lebanon[2] and many found refuge around the Wadi Kadisha gorge, a holy valley in the region southeast of Tripoli.

Although there are many Maronite families who trace their origins to the Arab tribes and to villages along the Orontes, unlike the Orthodox Christians, the Maronites in general never accepted Muslim rule. Between the eighth and tenth centuries some Maronite clans known as Marada or Jarajima (originating from the town of Jarjouma in the Orontes Valley)[3] supported Greek efforts to reclaim the Levant. Between the eleventh and thirteenth centuries they allied themselves with the Crusaders and fought with them against the Muslim rulers. This alliance caused the Maronites to pay a heavy price later and produced considerable distress for them when the region returned to Muslim rule in the thirteenth century. In 1293, the Memlukes punished the Maronites and attacked their canton east of Tripoli, killing thousands of Christians, arresting the Maronite Patriarch al-Hadchiti and forcing many into exile in Cyprus, which remained a Crusader territory for some time.

Like other communities in Lebanon, the Maronites did not mix through marriage with other religious sects, although starting in the nineteenth century they mixed to a certain degree with the Greek Catholics and other Catholic groups in the Levant. In fact, the Maronites have championed the cause of Catholicism in the Levant and encouraged the creation of Churches that follow Rome in the region.

Far from the image of the modern Lebanese *joie de vivre*, the Maronite rite adhered very closely to the purity of Jesus's teachings and leading examples of humility and piety. Their patriarchs, clergy and hermits took the issue of worship and a Christian way of life very seriously. This brand of Christianity led the Catholic Church to canonize many Lebanese as saints of the Church.

The Phoenician heritage
Western journalists and academics who talk to Lebanese individuals are usually told that Lebanese heritage goes back 5,000 years and that the town of Jbeil (Byblos) on the coast is the oldest city in the world.[4] Not only is this point emphasized to satisfy the Lebanese fondness for superlatives, but also to reflect the Maronites' ideology of detaching Lebanon from an Arab heritage and predating Lebanese origins to a classical era similar to that of ancient Greece. However, this approach skips almost 1,400 years of Arab and Muslim traditions. While the idea

may serve as a basis for Lebanese nationalism, in fact it led to the alienation of large segments of the Lebanese population.

Between 1930 and 1970, several Maronite intellectuals, such as the poet Charles Corm, have produced enough literature to make a cause for Lebanon's Phoenician ancestry. Other Lebanese writers have played down the Phoenician element and talked instead of a larger regional history, reminding us that a heritage of 7,000 years is not unique to the Phoenicians. Thus, the culture of modern Lebanon suffers from a deep dichotomy. Prior to 1975, official culture and school curricula placed little emphasis on Muslim and Arab heritage from the seventh to nineteenth centuries, highlighting instead two historical milestones to assist Lebanese nationalism:[5] ancient Phoenicia (1700 BC to AD 300) and the epoch of the Maan and Chehab emirs (1516–1840). Little or no mention was made of the long periods of foreign domination or of the history of the territories that were annexed to modern Lebanon in 1920. Some private schools even frown on the mention of indigenous history, and in some instances teachers and parents forbade children to speak Arabic, preferring instead to teach them French and the history and culture of France. The Muslim tradition was notably absent from history books, as was the impact of Islam on the modern development of Lebanon. School books treated the subject in the wider Arab context, but expanded on the emirs and the Phoenicians when they illustrated Lebanese history. A mild attempt was made before the war in 1975 to bring back these obscure episodes in Lebanese history, but by then it was too late.[6]

The Maronites are native to the Levant and have no European roots. If an Arab is someone who speaks Arabic as a mother tongue and lives in a general Arabic cultural heritage, then in today's Lebanon all Lebanese, save the Armenians, are Arabs. Although conversant in French culture, the Maronites share the same general cultural heritage of all Lebanese. They are mountain people and have Arab hospitality, honour, social values and family ties. They speak Arabic, write in Arabic and eat Levantine food. Moreover, Maronite intellectuals are known for saving the Arabic language from certain demise under Turkish hegemony.

To explain the Maronite paradox, one should allow for the importance of religion as a dominant factor in human personality. While some Muslims could very well be descendants of European immigrants who converted to Islam, they willingly embraced Arab culture and heritage without reservation. However, the Maronites, of whom many might be descendants of migrants from Arabia and may have Muslim ancestors, are Western-orientated. Failure to recognize the religious dimension of the conflict by modern intellectuals in Lebanon who studied at Western universities led to many failed attempts at reconciliation between 1975 and 1990.

In response to the Muslims' embracing of Arab nationalism, the Maronites felt strongly about the Phoenician heritage as a defining factor of Lebanese nationalism. Strangely, a discussion among the Lebanese about the origins of the Phoenicians, whose era, by the way, goes back thousands of years, could cause tempers to rise. Sources differ on the origins of the Phoenicians. Some say they came from Arabia in 2800 BC,[7] while others say they originated in Sinai. Yet another opinion says they were native to the Levant and developed there. Some Maronites react emotionally to any critical or academic evaluation of the subject that runs against the established Phoenician connection to modern Lebanon. The Lebanese historian Kamal Salibi was bitterly criticized by the Maronite clergy for having written a book mentioning that the Phoenicians came from Arabia.[8] A Maronite Member of Parliament presented a thesis arguing that the Phoenicians never referred to themselves as such. He was blasted by a radio host as a traitor who loved the "camel-jockeys" (meaning the Arabs).

While Phoenician heritage is rightly a source of pride for Lebanon, it was also a source of pride for the entire Levant, which was home to the Phoenicians. However, one hesitates to consider this as a cornerstone of a unique Lebanese nationalism. Phoenicianism is not exclusive and is shared by many other countries with which the Maronite ideologues do not feel affinity. This heritage is shared by coastal Syria and Palestine (in Ugarit, Aradus and Acre), Tunisia (the site of Carthage), Malta, Sicily and Spain. Loyal to the Muslim and Arabic culture, the people of Syria and Tunisia do not go out of their way to claim Phoenician blood in their veins. Tunisian and Syrian school books give prominence to Phoenician heritage and include Phoenician sites in their tourism publicity. However, the Phoenician link plays little role in their popular culture. During a luncheon meeting with the leading Maronite warlords in Damascus in 1977, President Hafez Assad of Syria joked that if the issue was Phoenicia then he was also Phoenician (born in the Latakia region), and if it was Maronitism then the Maronites' ancestral homeland was northern Syria.[9]

Racially, the Lebanese cannot be distinguished from the population in the rest of the Levant. Continuous invasions and colonization by numerous foreign empires made it difficult to accept any claims of either racial purity or that the modern Lebanese man is a descendant of the Phoenicians. Monuments left by successive invaders on the Dog River, north of Beirut, are strong reminders of the long history of foreign domination. Centuries of Persian, Arabian, Crusader, Greek and Ottoman migrations have created a racial mix in modern Lebanon where in a single family a full spectrum of colours could be found: blond, brunette and dark.

The European link
For much of the twentieth century, Lebanese schoolchildren were taught that the continent of Europe was named after Europa, a Phoenician princess who was kidnapped by Zeus. Zeus had fallen in love with Europa and, in order to kidnap her, he metamorphosed into a bull and approached her peacefully on the shore at Tyre. She rode on his back, but suddenly he jumped into the sea and swam to the island of Crete, where he metamorphosed again into a handsome Greek youth and married the beautiful princess.

Before 1975 and leading up to the 1990s, Lebanese textbooks dealing with ancient history usually followed a Western historical tradition: Phoenicia is placed alongside Greece and Rome as a founding culture of the Western "classical era". This is often followed by a discussion of a "feudal period" under the rule of the mountain emirs, with a "popular uprising" against feudalism and the rise of the "nation state" at the turn of the twentieth century. However, this convenient historical narrative completely ignores the particularities of Lebanon and its surrounding region. It seems that those in a position to decide what goes into history books may well have consulted French school books and borrowed their order of events.

An alternative presentation of Lebanese history would explain that the Phoenicians used a Semitic tongue and shared the major cultural developments of the Middle East and that Lebanon, though ancient, was not part of the Western historical tradition. North American and European history books start with Greece and Rome but give only a passing reference to the civilizations of the Near East, as outsiders to

Western tradition. Western textbooks with chapters on the Near East do not really build a case for a common heritage with the Arabs, although they do seek to establish the Judeo-Christian heritage of the Holy Land.

The European link is further emphasized in the Lebanese school curriculum, which teaches children that for almost a millennium, Lebanon was a province in the Roman and Byzantine empires (333 BC to AD 735). The reality is that the distant historical link with Rome dwarfs in comparison to the Arab link, which left a lasting imprint on modern Lebanon.

Although the Maronites are non-European in origin, their claims to a European connection are valid in terms of the good relations they cultivated with the European states. While the Maronites were at odds with the Greeks in the first few centuries of the creation of the Maronite sect, Maronite links to Europe were strengthened during the Crusader period (1099–1291). Several conferences between the Maronite leadership and papal emissaries took place between 1100 and 1139, paving the way for a strong alliance. In 1180, the Maronites were recognized by the Vatican as co-religionists and the Maronite Church entered in communion with the Roman Catholic Church. In 1203, the Pope appointed an ambassador in Tripoli, and Maronite leaders became frequent visitors to Rome, for example the visit by Patriarch Irmia in 1215.[10] In 1231, the clergy differed on the appointment of the Maronite Patriarch and referred the matter to the Pope in Rome. The selection of the Patriarch by the Pope established a covenant between the Maronites and Rome. Twenty years later in 1251 King Louis of France, a Catholic, recognized the Maronites as "part of the French nation" and extended his protection to them.[11]

Following the Maronite's integration into the Catholic church, their relations with Europe improved tremendously over the next 400 years. A Maronite school was established in Rome in 1584 and the Maronites became fully integrated with the Roman Catholic Church following a religious summit in 1736 at Lowayzé in Mount Lebanon. Italian and French merchants were frequent visitors to the Levant, and a treaty was signed in 1535 between King François I of France and the Ottoman Sultan Sulieman the Magnificent. This was followed by another treaty in May 1560, by which the French acquired many commercial and cultural privileges in the Levant – the first of their kind offered by the Ottoman government.

From the eighteenth century, Maronite children attended French missionary schools and developed a scholarly tradition – an unprecedented achievement that no other mountain community accomplished. The French wanted to instruct societies under their control in French ways and to make Frenchmen of their subjects. The curriculum at schools in Lebanon under the French was distant from the Levantine heritage. Students knew more about the kings and poets of France than about their own culture. In the twentieth century, the Western-educated Maronites and a good segment of the more cultured Lebanese Muslims and other Christians felt alien to the Middle East and its native culture. They exuded a sense of disdain and superiority over the native population.

Towards the end of the nineteenth century, Italy's Foreign Minister, Count Sforza, was shocked while touring the Levant to see young children with dark features singing in unison the French anthem "*Nos ancêtres les Gaullois étaient blonds*!".[12] The cultural alienation of the Maronites continues to this day. While speaking to a receptive audience in 1982, the Maronite warlord Bachir Gemayel welcomed a renewal of Western missionary activities, and then by the same token condemned the "Bedouins of the desert" (meaning Arabs and Muslims), who account for more than 50 per cent of Lebanon's population.[13]

In December 1995, a Synod meeting was held in Rome for the Christian clergy. One of its resolutions was that Lebanon had two cultures – a Christian culture and a Muslim culture. A sermon by the Pope in Beirut in 1999 urged the Christians of Lebanon to open up to the Arab states and understand Islam. Even a French president, Valéry Giscard D'Estaing, forgot that the Maronites were a native, non-transient population of the Levant when he innocently asked in 1980 whether they spoke any Arabic.[14] In fact, if it hadn't been for the Maronites, the Arabic language would not have been as healthy and powerful as it is today. While Turkification of the Levant and assimilation by France of North Africa were under way, the Maronites of Lebanon produced volumes of quality Arabic literature and scholarly work. Maronites such as Butros al-Boustani, Fares Chediac, Ra'if Abillama, Antoun Gemayel and many others contributed greatly to the Arabic cultural renaissance and to the literary movement in Egypt in the nineteenth century. In the period 1900–40, Maronite writers and poets such as Khalil Gibran and Amin Rihani were giants of Arabic literature and remain household names across the Arab world. In the period 1940–70, many Maronites embraced Arab national causes and joined the Palestine movement. Even Camille Chamoun, a representative of the "Evil Maronites" in the eyes of his opponents during the civil war in 1975, fought as a Foreign Minister in 1948 for the creation of a Palestinian state, an effort that earned him the title of the *fata al-Uruba al-agghar* (model Arab youth) in the Arab media.

Maronite dominance
Until the late eighteenth century, the mountain was dominated by the Druze. At first, the Druze did not feel particularly threatened by the Maronites and peacefully co-existed with them. However, the turning point in Druze fortunes came in 1754, during the reign of Emir Melhem Chehab. The extraordinary event was that Melhem's children converted to Christianity and became Maronites. At the same time, the Abillamas (Druze allies of the Chehabs) followed the example and also became Maronites. In 1770, Youssef Chehab, one of Melhem's sons, was declared Emir of Mount Lebanon. Thus, the leadership of the mountain region quietly started to transfer over to the Maronites who were already the most numerous, best-educated and wealthiest community.

Maronite wealth was due to the prospering silk industry and to the migration of wealthy Christians from the Syrian interior to the Lebanese Coast. The establishment of many schools in Maronite areas and the benefits generated from contacts with France and the Vatican increased the education and skills of the Maronites and prepared them for the governorship of Mount Lebanon. However, Maronite dominance was not automatically established under Youssef Chehab for various reasons. For one thing, the Druze warlords did not mind a Chehab emir who was a Maronite as they saw him as merely a figurehead, while they continued to have considerable power at least until 1822. Also, the Chouf remained the Druze seat of power.

Between the seventeenth and nineteenth centuries, Russia represented the main threat to the Ottoman Empire as it was trying to win access to warm waters and expand its territory. Russia's campaign against the Ottomans had a crusading element to it, having as its objectives an empire that would incorporate all Orthodox Christians, including those who were Ottoman subjects, and the acquisition of the ancient Greek city of Constantinople, the Ottoman capital, which Russian propaganda called "Tsarigrad". In the Russian–Turkish war of 1768–74, Russian warships attacked Ottoman coastal cities and supported the local emirs in their bid to free themselves from the Ottomans. This marked the first time in the Ottoman period that a European power would take a direct military interest in the local affairs of the Levant, leading the way for later interventions.

In October 1773, Russian warships attacked the Lebanese coast and bombed Beirut and Saida. This caused major damage to several parts of Beirut, including its walls, and killed many inhabitants. The Russian local allies were Daher al-Omar of Jerusalem, Youssef Chehab of Mount Lebanon and Nassif Nassar of south Lebanon. The Egyptians were also involved in the campaign against the Ottomans. When the Egyptian army entered Palestine in the south, Chehab attacked Beirut, Nassar attacked Saida and al-Omar attacked Acre. The Egyptian–Levantine cooperation was initially successful, with the Egyptians capturing Damascus and the coastal towns falling into the hands of the emirs. However, the success was short-lived as the Russians quickly reaped the fruits of the war and signed a peace treaty with the Ottoman government in 1774. In this treaty, known as Kuçuk Kainardji,[15] the Ottomans made important territorial and political concessions to Russia, including giving Russia the right to protect the Orthodox Christians of the Ottoman Empire. With this outcome, the Russians left Beirut in February 1774 and their admiral, Count Evgeny, surrendered the city to Youssef Chehab in return for 300,000 Ottoman gold coins, although he knew Youssef would not be able withstand a Turkish attack.[16]

Building on the experience of his predecessors, Chehab worked on the assumption that the Ottomans would allow him to control Beirut as long as he paid the taxes. To satisfy the Ottomans and to retrieve the sums he had already paid to the Russians, he imposed heavy taxes on the inhabitants who thought of him as another tyrant and not a Lebanese liberator; in 1774, the Ottomans would not have allowed an important city of the empire, like Beirut, to be outside central authority as they had done with Fakhreddine in 1615.

Over the next two years, the Egyptians withdrew from Damascus, and in 1775, the Ottoman *wali* Ahmad Pasha al-Jazzar re-established Ottoman control in Saida. He attacked the Shia strongholds in Jebel Amil and defeated the Nassars. Then he moved on Palestine, and defeated the emir, Daher al-Omar and killed him. In 1776, he attacked Beirut and swiftly defeated Youssef Chehab as well. Al-Jazzar matched the Mongols in his invasion of Beirut: he ruthlessly punished the inhabitants and demolished much of the European and Christian quarters, turning many churches into mosques.

Following the defeat of Youssef Chehab, al-Jazzar supported another Maronite Chehab, Bachir II, as emir. Bachir II ruled Lebanon for 51 years until 1841 and under his reign Druze power all but disappeared. Bachir was the most important emir since Fakhreddine. Initially, his Maronitism was not a source of concern for the Druze. He compensated for the lack of Fakhreddine's wisdom and vision with diplomacy and firmness. Al-Jazzar was also a different brand of *wali* compared to previous Ottoman governors. He was not satisfied with administering Mount Lebanon from a distance and preferred direct control. Over the next few years, he used his authority to extend his influence to the mountain region. He pressured Bachir into obedience by threatening to support his Chehab opponents, the sons of Youssef Chehab, legitimate contenders for the emirate. This explains why Bachir continued to rely on the Druze warlords and the sons of Daher al-Omar in that period to counter the weight of the greedy al-Jazzar and the other Chehab emirs.

The year 1798 witnessed the arrival of Napoleon Bonaparte in the Levant. Having invaded Egypt, Bonaparte swiftly moved up the coast. While the Maronite community sympathized with French aims, Bachir was apparently lukewarm. He was not certain that the French would be victorious against a British–Ottoman alliance. He feared Ottoman revenge if he took sides and he remembered the destiny of those Levantine emirs who had sided with Russia in 1774, especially his cousin Youssef. However, he maintained communication with the French army in Palestine and sent Bonaparte discreet letters of support.

On the battlefield, the easy conquest of the coastal town of Jaffa led the French to underestimate the strength of Acre, the seat of al-Jazzar, and they immediately moved to attack it. After four months of siege, food and supplies ran short in the French camp and a plague hit Napoleon's men; the French had to withdraw to Egypt.[17] The weak Ottoman response to Napoleon and the death of al-Jazzar in 1804 encouraged the wily Bachir to dramatically change his policies and play down the importance of his Druze and Palestinian allies. He started looking for regional support.

The Egyptian occupation

In some ways, Bachir Chehab followed in Fakhreddine's footsteps. While his abandonment of his Druze and other local allies proved later to be a deadly mistake for the mountain region, his foreign alliances were in line with the Maans' foreign policy. During this period, Bachir forged ties with the French-backed Egypt[18] whose rulers, although nominally recognizing the authority of the Ottomans, had their own designs on the Levant. Bachir also built a legendary Arabian Night palace in the village of Beiteddine near Baakline (capital of the Maans), and another palace in Deir al-Kamar, the largest Maronite town in the Chouf. His several visits to Egypt as guest of its ruler Mohamed Ali al-Kebir brought him closer to Egyptian policy-making.

After 1822, Bachir Chehab began consolidating his authority and undermining the power of the Druze. He started by chasing their leader Bachir Joumblatt out of the country. Many prominent Druze warlords felt threatened and their fears materialized in January 1825, when the Emir's men killed Bachir Joumblatt and several other Druze leaders. It is likely that Bachir Chehab wished to follow Mohamed Ali's example in uniting the country under a central government and ending the rule of the warlords. However, the situation was different as Mount Lebanon did not have the social uniformity of Egypt. Worse, the murder of Bachir Joumblatt backfired and led the Druze for the first time to look at the situation on a sectarian level. They viewed Bachir Chehab as a Maronite despot out to destroy their authority. This was the first recorded incident of a religious backlash that started the long animosity between Maronites and Druze and later split Lebanese society up to the present day.

The Druze's distrust of Bachir Chehab and the Maronites worsened after 1831, when Egypt occupied the Levant and the Emir fought on the Egyptian side against the Ottomans. For his loyalty and friendship, the Egyptians appointed the Emir as viceroy over the mountain region. Egyptian rule of the Levant was not a novelty. The Egyptians had ruled the Levant from 1800 BC to 900 BC, and again in the Fatimid period from AD 800 to AD 1110, then in the Memluke period from 1291 to 1516. The Egyptians viewed the Levant as part of their sphere of influence. They never forgave the Ottomans for wrestling it from them in 1516 and had contemplated taking over the Ottoman Empire and reclaiming the leadership of the Muslim world. To that end, the Egyptian emir Ali al-Kebir briefly took Damascus in 1773, and an Egyptian army invaded the Hejaz in 1816. Egypt was always and still is a major influence in the Levant.[19]

The Egyptian invasion of the Levant in 1831 was preceded by a series of important developments. Inside the Ottoman Empire, a Turkish–Greek quarrel led to a Greek uprising against Ottoman rule in the period 1821–31. The Greeks amassed a strong army and a fleet, and in 1825, their warships attacked Beirut and Alexandria. In response, the Ottomans asked Mohamed Ali al-Kebir to help them crush the Greeks, promising him that he could keep the Morea (an Ottoman province that included modern Greece) for himself. The Egyptians kept their part of the bargain. They attacked the Greek force and took the Morea in 1827. This move provoked the wrath of liberal Europe which saw in the Greeks a classical Athens struggling against Asian despotism.[20] A European contingent rushed to the area, confronted, then defeated the Egyptian fleet at Navarino in the same year.

Mohamed Ali al-Kebir was angered by the loss of the Morea and demanded the Levant instead. The Ottomans did not approve of his demand and in response, the Egyptian army invaded the Levant, defeated the Ottomans and chased the Turkish forces into Asia Minor (modern Turkey). A last-minute intervention from Russia on behalf of the Ottomans saved the empire from falling to Egypt. It is likely that, had it not been for the intervention of Russia, the Egyptians could have brought the Ottoman Empire to an end and occupied Constantinople in 1831. While the French were on the Egyptians' side, the British, who were in the Mediterranean at that time, were worried by the possibility of an Egyptian victory. However, when Egyptian forces were merely days away from Constantinople, only Russia was militarily close enough to prevent an imminent Egyptian takeover of the capital of the Sublime Porte that would have ended the Ottoman Caliphate.[21]

The Egyptians ruled the Levant for ten years. Their rule was enlightened, and they introduced several administrative changes and reforms. The government of Egypt was much influenced by the principles of the French Revolution brought to Cairo by Napoleon when his armies invaded Egypt (1798–1805). The impact was lasting as Egypt allied itself closely with France and sought advice and sent military and civilian delegations to Paris to receive training and learn French ways. During its occupation of the Levant, Egypt made a concerted effort to demolish the Ottoman system of millets that kept religious and ethnic minorities separate but unequal under Ottoman law. The Egyptian reforms introduced in the Levant brought relative salvation to oppressed minorities and modernized the civil administration from the archaic rule of the warlords. Unfortunately, the reforms were short-lived as they were largely repealed following the departure of the Egyptian armies in 1840. Unlike the Ottomans, the Egyptians ruled the area directly and replaced Ottoman gold with their own currency.[22] On the social front, the Egyptians introduced a civil code that treated the Christians of the Levant as equal to the Muslims and not as *dhimmis*.[23] While these reforms made the Christians happy, they offended the Druze who lost their special status and power base, and the Shia who were the underdogs of the empire. Both communities saw in Egyptian laws a further expansion of Maronite privileges. The Sunni Egyptians were not particularly fond of the Druze or the Shia, which were both heretical movements in the eyes of orthodox Islam. In fact, the Egyptians harassed these two communities and consequently, hatred for the Egyptians grew. This was coupled with revived memories of the 1585 Egyptian massacre of the Druze and their emir, Kurkumaz Maan, father of Fakhreddine, and the Memluke massacre of the Shia in 1305.

The Druze were further abused in 1835 when the Egyptians imposed conscription and forced labour on the Druze and the Shia, something the Ottomans had never done;[24] they even requested Emir Bachir to enforce the draft. Some 1,200 youths were arrested and prepared to be sent to the Sudanese deserts to fight in Egypt's local wars in Kordofan. Finding their situation unbearable, the Druze and the Shia rose up against the Egyptians in 1838–9. In response, the Egyptians ordered the Egyptian-armed and Egyptian-trained army of 7,000[25] Maronites to crush the rebellion. The Maronite warriors heeded the call and crushed the rebellion, but they feared that the Egyptians would view them as regular troops and send them to the Sudan as well; thus, the Maronites fled to their villages and kept their weapons without launching further attacks on the other communities. The Maronite gesture was welcomed by the Druze and the Shia, and allowed for a rapprochement among the Maronites, Druze and Shia against Bachir and his Egyptian masters, creating a rare national unity.

Meanwhile, the Ottomans felt confident enough to take the initiative against the Egyptians, and in 1839 they attacked the Egyptian army in the Levant. However, the hastily prepared and ill-conceived Ottoman attack resulted in their defeat at Nezip in July, and allowed the Egyptians to march into Asia Minor and take Konia and Kutahia. After that, Constantinople lay open to them. These setbacks caused the Ottomans to consider surrendering to the Egyptians. However, British diplomacy saved the day in the form of an ultimatum to the Egyptians asking them to withdraw from Syria but allowing them into Palestine. Cairo was in no mood to respond, and in July 1840, the British sent an army led by Commander Charles Napier to help the Turks.[26] A joint Austro–British–Ottoman expedition comprising 31 ships (23 British, three Austrian and five Ottoman) carrying some 18,000 men arrived off Beirut on 1 August 1840. The city was defended by 10,000 Egyptian troops who were well-equipped with heavy artillery.

The joint force landed 8,000 troops at Jounié (12 kilometres north of Beirut) and encouraged the people of Mount Lebanon, including the Druze, the Maronites and the Shia, to rise up against Egyptian rule. On 10 September, the warships opened fire on Beirut, hitting the harbour and the Egyptian military hospital in the Karantina quarter, destroying much of the city and its walls and causing heavy civilian casualties. Fighting raged everywhere and the defeat of the Egyptian fleet in the Mediterranean weakened the coastal defences, opening the way for the allies to take Haifa, Acre, Tyre and Saida. By October, the allies had taken Beirut and secured it in Ottoman hands.

The 1841–61 civil strife

The short Egyptian rule of Mount Lebanon and the Maronite–Druze rapprochement against Bachir Chehab signalled the collapse of the old regime. The situation that followed the epoch of the emirs had needed twenty years of civil warfare to materialize. During the joint British–Ottoman attack that had dislodged the Egyptians from the Levant, the British distributed 30,000 guns to the mountain people.[27] In response to popular demand, the British also shipped Bachir to exile in Malta in 1841 and another Chehab (Bachir III) became emir. Now the Druze wanted to restore their old influence and regain their lands lost to the Maronites under the Egyptians. Although the new emir agreed to restore the Druze's estates, he refused to restore their influence, eroded by his predecessor Bachir II, and he attempted to retain the reforms established by the Egyptian administration, which the Druze found unfavourable to them. His policies endeared him to the Maronite warlords and to Patriarch Hobeich, who was the highest spiritual and political leader of the Maronites. The Maronites saw in Bachir III a means to ensure that power remained in their hands and to avoid a return to the old regime when the Druze controlled the mountain. These differences made the Maronite–Druze peace short-lived and the old wounds quickly reappeared. Civil war was not far off.

In this war, the Maronites outnumbered the Druze but lacked the latter's organization; while the Druze were able to mobilize 15,000 warriors and the Maronites twice as many, their large numbers were without coordination or proper communications. With over 40,000 men on both sides, the stage was set for civil war. From the outside, the British backed Druze grievances and the French adopted a vague policy between mediation and outright support for the Maronites.

In the first phase of the war (1841–3), the Druze were able to reclaim their traditional canton with support from the Druze of Wadi al-Taim and the Jabel Druze south of Damascus. The Ottoman government did not want the situation to get out of hand and restored order in 1843. Benefiting from good relations with Europe, the Ottoman government moved to end local autonomy and the Chehab dynasty, and extended direct rule to the mountain region. This was accomplished by removing Bachir III, appointing an Ottoman civil servant as governor[28] and dividing the mountain region into Maronite and Druze areas – a southern region ruled by a Druze lieutenant (*qa'im makam*) and a northern region under a Maronite lieutenant.

The new arrangement was intended as a *modus vivendi* for the mountain region; however, the population was mixed everywhere and the territorial division did not prevent violence and civil strife from continuing for many years. Between 1850 and 1858, an additional 120,000 guns and 20,000 pistols entered Mount Lebanon, preparing the stage for a wider conflict. While the second phase of the civil war was also between the Maronites and the Druze, it started in the Maronite domains where a social revolution against feudal lords was taking shape. At the time, the predominantly Maronite northern region was controlled by the al-Khazen warlords (brought to power by Fakhreddine in 1611), who were ruling with medieval methods and with no regard to the wishes of the population.

In 1858, a movement called *Harakat al-Amiya* (the Popular Uprising) was led by a blacksmith called Tanyous Chahine. The revolt was supported by the Maronite Patriarch Boulos Mubarak who had been maltreated by the al-Khazens, a major Maronite clan in the mountain region.[29] The uprising turned ugly as crowds attacked the al-Khazens and massacred their leaders, and many of their supporters were forced to flee for their lives. The leader of the uprising, Chahine, followed up the easy win with a declaration ending feudalism and introducing a republican regime.

Encouraged by this success, leaders of the uprising decided to extend their movement to the southern region, home of the Druze warlords. However, although a Maronite uprising against the feudal warlord system would have had potential benefits for most Lebanese, attempts to spread it to Druze areas touched a sectarian nerve and the situation turned into a miserable open war that engulfed the whole region. A foreign observer witnessing the massacres and counter-massacres remarked that "this is a war between two equally vicious communities".[30]

Between 1858 and 1861, the less numerous but more organized Druze were able to rout the Maronites in the Chouf and the Bekaa. By the summer of 1861, the Druze were in total control of the areas south of the Beirut–Damascus road. Their success encouraged them to venture further north and attack Baabda, the hometown of several Chehab notables, and massacre many of them. The Druze attack on Baabda convinced the French that it was time to act and not stand idly by waiting for the Ottoman government to help. Reports circulated in the European capitals signalling that the Christians were losing ground to the Druze in Mount Lebanon and that a terrible massacre of Christians was taking place in Damascus. In August 1861, Napoleon III sent in his gendarmes, who landed at the pine forest south of Beirut and invaded the Chouf. Maronite warriors joined the French attack and pillaged Druze villages, while Maronite exiled leaders returned immediately to Deir al-Kamar and other places in the Chouf.

The civil strife of 1841–61 was catastrophic. In a total population of 500,000, almost 7 per cent or 33,000 people were killed (including 17,000 Maronites, 9,000 Druze, 5,000 other Christians and 2,000 other Muslims), 20 per cent or 100,000 were made homeless, and 10 per cent or 50,000 left Lebanon permanently and settled in the Americas.

Maronite failures were not only a result of disorganization but also of disunity. While the Druze were attacking Baabda, the leader of the Popular Uprising, Chahine, was in Kesrouane planning to help the

Maronites of Baabda and the Chouf. However, the Maronites of Zghorta and Becharri further north, led by Youssef Karam, were angry with Chahine. Youssef Karam, the warlord of Ehden, resented him for what he had done to the al-Khazens in Kesrouane. At that time in the Bekaa Valley, the Druze and their allies were besieging the Greek Catholic town of Zahlé. The population was counting on Karam's promise to relieve the siege and save the city from the Druze. However, Karam chose to attack Chahine and put an end to his popular uprising. Karam's move played well with the Maronite warlords who saw this as a consolidation of the feudal hold and an end to the peasants' revolt. With Kesrouane back under the warlords and the Chouf under French occupation, the Maronite warlords decided that it was reasonable to restore authority in the mountain region to the Maronite emirs as had been the case before 1843. Karam became the champion of Maronite demands, and he started campaigning to become the new emir of Mount Lebanon.

The State of Mount Lebanon
Following the French intervention in August 1861, the Ottomans arrested and executed many warlords and Ottoman army officers who had had a hand in the massacres. The Ottoman government followed this by hosting an international conference in Beirut in September with the "express aim of bringing a lasting peace to the mountain".[31] The conference adopted a modified version of the Ottoman formula of 1844, whereby an Ottoman civil servant of the Christian faith would rule the mountain region, assisted by a council of warlords. To improve the chances of success of this formula, which was called the Mutassarefiya (a system of local government already applied in many places in the Ottoman Empire), the Ottoman government modified it in 1864 and granted Mount Lebanon a greater autonomy.

The Mutassarefiya was welcomed by the Druze but opposed by half of the Maronites. The moderate Maronites of the Chouf and Baabda saw no harm in cooperating with the new system. However, those of Kesrouane and the north, led by the Maronite Church and Youssef Karam and his allies, were dissatisfied. They saw France's acceptance of the Mutassaref regime as a betrayal. Also, the situation was not conducive to accommodating the wishes of the hard-line Maronites; realizing that a Maronite-controlled mountain region was an invitation to more civil wars, the French agreed to the new system and sacrificed the wishes of Karam and his allies. From then on, the Maronites of north Lebanon certainly did not enjoy the prestige and influence of the Maronites of the central region (the Chouf, Baabda and the Metn).

In the Chehab tradition, the Mutassaref government retained Beiteddine and Baabda as dual seats of government.[32] The palace of Beiteddine was made the summer seat of government and Baabda the winter capital. The first Mutassaref was the Armenian Daoud Pasha who appeased the Maronite and Druze warlords by appointing all sixteen of them as cabinet ministers and top administrators. Daoud introduced democratic reforms and parliamentary elections and established many schools.

The northern Maronite opposition to the new regime continued for many years. Although the Maronites of the Chouf, including many Chehabs and their allies, had the lion's share of government jobs, Karam was adamant in his opposition and frequently quarrelled with government troops. Daoud Pasha tried to win over Karam by appointing him as a lieutenant in the county of Jezzine south of the Chouf, but there was no solution acceptable to Karam short of becoming governor himself. Eventually, Karam was exiled to Egypt and later to Europe where he died as an old man.

Between 1861 and 1914, the State of Mount Lebanon enjoyed a long period of peace and prosperity. A warlord council, while retaining the traditional territorial lines, replaced the warring cantons. The Maronites of the Chouf – notably the Chehabs, al-Khouris and al-Boustanis – were dominant in the government. These families participated in every government and have continuously won top positions up to the present day.

By the turn of the century, the northern Maronites still did not have much representation in government affairs. The local warlords of Kesrouane, Zghorta and Becharri held minor positions such as county lieutenants (*Caimacam*). The al-Khazens were again dominant in Kesrouane, while Zghorta and Becharri went to Assad Karam, Youssef Karam's nephew. However, following Assad's death the north was divided into two domains: Zghorta and Ehden under Kabalan Frangié, challenged by Mikhail Mouawad who was supported by the Karams, the Douehis and the Boulos; and Becharri under Najib Daher, who was challenged by the Aridas, the Kairouzes and the Geageas. The Maronites of Becharri, the birthplace of the writer Kahlil Gibran and home of the giant cedars of Lebanon, had the least influence in the Maronite community across Mount Lebanon. The Becharri region was also nicknamed the *Jord* (heights), which is also often used in reference to the countryside people with notorious tempers. Although the most picturesque part of Lebanon, it has remained a less-developed place to this day.

The more cosmopolitan and educated Maronites of the central region easily eclipsed the northern Maronites. Governors of Mount Lebanon preferred to appoint lesser-known Maronites, such as Nemr Chamoun from Deir al-Kamar as finance minister, and ignored the more feudal and rural leadership of the north. The dominance of the central region gradually came to an end after 1970. Between 1970 and 2000, northern Maronites were able to become presidents (for example René Mouawad and Sulieman Frangié) and cabinet ministers. Even a young man from Becharri (Samir Geagea) was able to become the unchallenged leader of the Maronite militia in December 1985.

Under the Mutassaref regime, the Druze became less influential. While this may seem paradoxical, considering their important historical role in the creation of Lebanon, their ever-dwindling numbers and their migration to Syria contributed to the loss of influence. Between 1861 and 1948, Druze representation went to the Erslans (who, like the Abillamas, won the title of emir after the Battle of Ain Dara in 1711). The Joumblatts laid low in this period but came back in force after 1948 under the charismatic leftist leader Kamal Joumblatt.

The Shia remained a fringe group led by outdated and uninspiring warlord families who were interested in winning government jobs but not in improving the lot of the community. Between 1861 and 1970 the north–south split of the Shia continued with the northern part under the Hamadis and the southern part under the Assads. At the turn of the century, the Bekaa Shia were led by Said Hamadi and his son Saad and opposed by the house of Husseini in the Jord. In the south, the Shia came under the control of Kamel Assad, and later that of his son Ahmed and grandson Kamel. The Assads were opposed by the al-Khalils of Tyre.

By 1910, the State of Mount Lebanon was maturing, with a new generation growing up knowing little about pre-Mutassaref society. With French pressure and continued negotiations with the Ottoman government, more powers were granted to the mountain region. In 1912, the Maronites were allowed to have a seaport at Jounié on the coast of Kesrouane and the Druze were allowed their own seaport on the coast of the Chouf at the village of Nabi Younis.

The advent of the First World War brought to an end the stable and brief mountain-state that never rose again. Between 1914 and 1918, Mount Lebanon suffered miserably as tens of thousands of citizens died from famine. A locust invasion, an Allied Forces blockade of the Mediterranean and efforts by the Turkish military administrator Ahmed Jamal Pasha to impose Ottoman banknotes added to the misery and suffering of the Lebanese people. The rugged and unfriendly mountain terrain that grew little food and had no access to the sea made this worse. While farming was the main occupation of the population, even in peaceful times food production satisfied only one-third of the requirement amid extreme poverty, as the warlords (Maronites, Druze and Shia) shared the produce and lived lavishly in beautiful mansions and seraglios.

"Grand Liban"
Following the defeat of the Turks in 1918 and their withdrawal from the Levant, Mount Lebanon was placed under French mandate in 1920. The Maronites welcomed the French as saviours and descended to Beirut's harbour to greet them. The Druze, the Muslims and a majority of Greek Orthodox Christians expressed loyalty to Emir Faisal's Arab government in Damascus. Some Maronite officials of the defunct Mutassaref regime, such as Habib Pasha al-Saad, also showed loyalty to Faisal and worked with his government.

With French support, several Maronite and Orthodox notables of Beirut were able to enlarge the State of Mount Lebanon. Long before 1920, the Maronites had wished to enlarge the "Petit Liban" and create a viable entity. Maronite merchants and professionals, along with Patriarch Elias Hoyek, disliked Faisal's Arab government in Damascus, and pushed for access to the sea and a larger entity. The aristocratic Christian families of Beirut – notably the Bustros, Sursock, Tueni, Chiha and Faraoun – also pushed for a larger Lebanon that incorporated Beirut. Some of the big families who had considerable economic power and who were mostly Maronites were the Bassoul, Faraoun, Hélou, Trad, Naccache, Tabet, Sabbagh, Beyhum, Fayyad and Lahoud.[33] These families signed petitions addressed to the French government to help achieve the goal of a larger Lebanon. The French, with historic links to the Catholic population of the Levant and in response to the wishes of the Christians of Lebanon, expanded Mount Lebanon to include parts of the vilayets of Beirut and Damascus.

The resulting "Grand Liban" had many advantages including a larger population (which doubled from roughly 300,000 to 600,000 inhabitants), important cities (Beirut, Tripoli, Saida and Tyre) and fertile plains (the Bekaa and Akkar – see Table 32 in the Statistical Appendix for the 1921 census information). A new currency, pegged to the French franc, replaced the Ottoman currency and Lebanon was thus linked to the economy of France.

The Druze did not accept the French mandate. Although they welcomed liberation from the Ottomans, the Druze feared the wrath of a French-backed Maronite government and launched a military campaign of resistance. In 1919, a contingent of Syrian soldiers led by a Druze officer, Youssef al-Azmé, stopped the French advance at Maissaloun near Damascus. As the only stand against the French at the time, it was symbolic despite being pushed aside. In another incident in 1920 in Jebel Amil east of Tyre, some Shia were furious at their Christian neighbours who had welcomed the French. A Shia band led by the warlord Abou Khanjar attacked Ain Ebel and killed several Christians. Fearing reprisals from the French, the Shia attackers fled to Jabal Druze south of Damascus. The French authorities learnt of the hideout of the Shia fugitives, attacked the area and killed many Druze. In response, the Druze killed several French officers at Swaida south of Damascus.

The cycle of violence grew year on year with the French waging larger campaigns against the Druze. Druze resistance grew and culminated with the Great Syrian Revolution in 1925, which was ruthlessly crushed by the French.

The Orthodox Christians
The Orthodox Christians, also members of the state religion (originating of course from being part of the Byzantine Empire prior to Muslim rule), prospered and inhabited the big cities along with the Sunnis. While they were less numerous than any of the other communities in Mount Lebanon, they easily outnumbered them as a whole when counted in the Levant. They mixed well with the Sunnis in business and never had ghettos or mountain refuges. They did not suffer from the minority

complex that pushed the Maronites, the Shia and the Druze to the rugged heights of the Levant. Sizeable Orthodox communities lived in every major city of the Levant, engaging in commerce and many aspects of business, and in the civil service of the state, fulfilling the proverb *Si tu ne peux pas devenir roi, fais medicin* ("If you cannot be king, be a doctor"). The Greek Orthodox amassed large fortunes and were well-educated. By the nineteenth and early twentieth centuries they were the aristocrats of Beirut (the Orthodox region of Koura, south of Tripoli, and the Sunni Iqlim al-Kharroub, north of Saida had become *caza*s (counties) in the autonomous State of Mount Lebanon in 1864).[34]

The Sunni Muslims

In contrast to Maronite demographic domination of Mount Lebanon, the new republic of Greater Lebanon had the challenge of winning over the inhabitants of the annexed territories who were largely Sunni Muslims and Orthodox Christians, and who were both imperial sects.[35] Although the mountain region was graced with scenic beauty and an abundance of water, life in Mount Lebanon was cruel and hard at this time, and few lived there. By virtue of their belonging to the state religion, the Sunni Muslims lived in the established towns in the Syrian interior and on the coast. This explains why there were virtually no Sunnis in Mount Lebanon. After the creation of Greater Lebanon in 1920, many predominantly Sunni areas from the vilayets of Damascus and Beirut became parts of the new entity.

The Sunnis of the coastal cities did not accept the artificial separation from their brethren in Syria. For them Beirut and the other coastal towns belonged to the vilayet of Beirut and were governed by Ottoman officials who were chosen from the local Sunni notables, called *zaim*s, or *beg*s. Under the Ottomans, they were first-class citizens with access to government jobs and the right to run for Parliament (*Majlis Mabouthan*). At first, the Sunnis' acceptable minimum was an independent government uniting both Syria and Lebanon. To that end they found solace in the Faisali government in Damascus, which paid extreme importance to the notables of Beirut and the coast. The cities of Saida, Beirut and Tripoli had powerful local Sunni *zaim*s, such as the al-Solhs of Saida, the Salams, Daouks and Beyhums of Beirut, and the Karamis, al-Ahdabs and al-Jisrs of Tripoli.

The Sunni *zaims* therefore opposed the French mandate, rejected a separate Lebanese country and called for a congress in 1920 to consolidate anti-French efforts. The Beirut *zaim* Salim Salam was the chairperson of this gathering, which was called the All-Syrian Congress. Riad al-Solh, *zaim* of Saida, and several other notables were in attendance. The *confrères* demanded unity with Syria and an end to the French mandate. This posed a major challenge to the new entity. Unlike the mountain communities who were based on warrior societies and clan loyalties, the Sunnis were urbane and had enjoyed a long tradition in commerce and administration. Their lack of the warrior sentiment was compensated by the presence of the local police and the Ottoman army, and now they lacked both security and status.

The French and the Maronites were aware of Sunni opposition even before it started to manifest itself. It was clear that the Sunnis had the most to lose. Therefore, from the start, the mandate authorities and the Maronites appeased the Sunni *zaims* in order for the new republic to win the blessing of the largely Sunni Arab world and the local Sunni population. The *zaims* of Saida and Tripoli were the first to be tempted to participate in the government. Between 1928 and 1939, the al-Solhs of Saida (Rida al-Solh was appointed governor of Jebel Amil under the Ottomans) and the Karamis, al-Ahdabs and al-Jisrs of Tripoli moved to Beirut where they were appointed in high places. For example, Abdel Hamid Karami and Kheireddine al-Ahdab were appointed prime minister, while Mohamed al-Jisr was appointed Speaker of Parliament. Thus, the Maronites found partners in the Sunni *zaims* who eventually accepted Lebanon as a separate country.[36] In the late 1930s, the Arab nationalist al-Ahdab participated in an unpopular cabinet. He defended his position publicly: "If the Arabs want to unite, they can do it without me" (i.e., his participation in the Lebanese government would not stop Arab unity).[37]

By 1943, a pact between the Maronite President Bechara al-Khouri and the Sunni Prime Minister Riad al-Solh was reached whereby the Sunnis would not seek unity with Syria and the Maronites would not ask for French protection. The pact was designed as a social contract between the fathers of independence. However, this pact did not stand the test of time. A few years into independence, the Sunnis reinforced their ties with mainstream Arab nationalism following the rise of Nasser in Egypt and the Baath Party in Syria. The Maronite elites, who did not consider themselves Arabs, resumed their warm relations with the West by establishing special economic and monetary ties with France in 1948 and seeking to join pro-American regional alliances.

The psychological dichotomy between Sunnis and Maronites had roots in French and Turkish policies. While the Sunnis went to Muslim schools of the Islamic Benevolent Society, the Maronites attended French missionary schools. In modern Lebanon, the Maronites did not consider Beirut as their capital, and maintained Baabda, capital of the deceased Mutassaref State, as the seat of the Presidential Palace and the Army Command. Sunni prime ministers maintained their offices at the Ottoman seraglio in old Beirut.

Endless stories could be told about the co-existence of the two solitudes. The cultural dichotomy became worse after independence, with the Maronites delving deeper into a Lebanese nationalism, and the Sunnis adopting Arab nationalism based on Islamic and Arab heritage and the past glory of Baghdad, Damascus and Cairo. Even naming streets inspired conflict. Between 1950 and 1970, every main thoroughfare in Beirut named after a Maronite warlord was met by the Sunnis naming another after a Sunni *zaim* or an Arab hero. Boulevard Camille Chamoun was matched with Boulevard Saeb Salam, and Boulevard Pierre Gemayel was matched with Abdalla Al-Yafi Avenue, while Riad al-Solh Square was matched with Bechara al-Khouri Square. In 1991, Rue Verdun, a main Beirut boulevard, became Rue Rachid Karami after the former Sunni prime minister who was assassinated in 1987. Omar Karami, brother of Rachid, explained that the name Karami had more to do with Lebanon than a battle in France.

As for economic activity, the elite of both communities despised farming and dirty work, and preferred clean careers in commerce and government. The Levantine culture was not conducive to manufacturing and farming. Dirt and toil were associated with lowliness, and this belief applied to all communities. Although the majority of the population was engaged in farming, the urbane Sunnis were city folk and the Maronite warlords never ploughed the land. This attitude also went for manufacturing, where an inhibition of getting one's hands dirty became an impediment to the growth of domestic manufacturing.

NOTES

1 Youssef Mahfouz, *A Short History of the Maronites* (in Arabic, *Mukhtassar fi Tarikh al Mawarina*), Kasslik, Kasslik Presses, 1984, p. 37.
2 Butros Daou, *A History of the Maronites* (in Arabic, *Tarikh al-Mawarina*), Beirut, Dar Annahar, 1970.
3 Most sources trace the origins of the Jarajima to the lower Taurus Mountains in south Turkey (Mount Leikam). But Mahfouz, op. cit., mentions that they had Persian origins as well.
4 In the 1930s, a French archaeologist established that Byblos was one of the oldest cities in the world, but Lebanese tourism propaganda made it *the* oldest city.
5 This is typical of all the Arab countries, no matter how small. The emphasis of a national history is thought of as essential to the state's survival. Ideas such as "the Kuwait Nation" proposed by Kuwaiti intellectuals did not save the little emirate from attempts to gobble it up by its neighbours.
6 A high school book was introduced in the curriculum to teach its pupils about the civilizations in Lebanon.
7 Herodotus, *Histories*, London, Penguin Books, 1996.
8 In *Annahar*, June 15 1993, Father Emile Éddé's critique of Kamal Salibi, *House of Many Mansions: The History of Lebanon Reconsidered*, Berkley, CA, University of California Press, 1990.
9 Karim Pakradouni, *Curse of a Nation* (in Arabic, *Laanat Watan*), Beirut, Trans Orient Press, 1991.
10 Salibi, *An Early History of Lebanon*, p. 180–5.
11 Mahfouz, op. cit.
12 Abdul Latif Tibawi, *Islamic Education: Its Traditions and Modernization into the Arab National Systems*, New York, Luzac Publishers, 1969.
13 Speech by Bachir Gemayel to the Order of Nuns of Deir as-Salib in *Assafir*, *Maronite Leadership* (in Arabic, *Al-Zaama al-Marouniya*), Beirut, Arab Information Centre, p. 137. Also Walid Noueihed, *Critique of the Lebanese Idea* (in Arabic, *Nakd al-Fikra al-Lubnaniya*), Beirut, Dar al-Wehda, 1986.
14 Pakradouni, op. cit.
15 A town in Eastern Europe under Ottoman control at the time.
16 The historical context oustide Mount Lebanon is derived from a textbook by Labib Abdel Sater, *History of the Modern World* (in Arabic), Beirut, Dar al-Mashreq, 1983.
17 Napoleon returned to Europe later and a joint British–Ottoman expedition took Egypt from the French in 1805.
18 Many Lebanese politicians sought Egypt's support to counter the weight of another regional power, usually Syria. In 1976, Kamal Joumblatt was anxious to get the Egyptian army to intervene on his behalf against Syria.
19 Even in the twentieth century, Egyptian influence continued in the Levant. In the mid-1950s, Syria became a province in a republic centred in Cairo under the charismatic Gamal Abdel Nasser, until 1963. The efforts of Egypt to extend the united republic to Lebanon triggered a civil war in Lebanon in 1958.
20 Even the famous English poet Lord Byron was fighting with the rebels.

21 The Egyptian withdrawal from Anatolia was significant in restoring the Ottoman government's dignity, because Anatolia was the central plateau of Asia Minor and had been the cradle of the Ottoman Empire since its beginnings in the twelfth century. After the First World War, the Ottoman Empire collapsed and the Turks retreated to their home base of Asia Minor which became modern Turkey.

22 This is the origin of the modern Lebanese word for money, *masari*, from *Masri*, which means "Egyptian" in Arabic. This word is only used in Lebanon.

23 *Dhimmi*s are the non-Muslim inhabitants of Muslim lands who are "protected" by the Muslim government (literally in Arabic "Ala dhimma tul-Islam" or "are protected by Islam"). In the early centuries following the rise of the Muslim empires, *dhimmi*s was a positive word denoting the People of the Book (mainly Christians and Jews) who shared with Islam many of its tenets and lived among Muslims in peace. The only difference at the time was that the *dhimmi*s paid a tax for protection in lieu of serving in the Muslim armies. Over the centuries, the concept developed into a negative trait, especially after the Crusader wars and the European penetration of the Middle East that led to the establishment of strong connections between native Christians and the European powers. These developments made the Muslim majority suspicious of *dhimmi*s and subsequently led to mistrust among the religious communities.

24 At least until 1914, when the Ottomans imposed *sokhra* (forced labour) on the Lebanese.

25 Other sources put the number at 4,000 (for example, Salibi, *A Modern History of Lebanon*, p. 166). Period writings by local Lebanese individuals tend to exaggerate figures. One source quoted in Mahfouz (op. cit., p. 28), suggests that the Maronites could amass 50,000 soldiers to help the Crusaders' invasion of the Levant in 1099. Most probably, this was the total number of the Maronite population in Lebanon at that time.

26 In the nineteenth century, the Ottoman Empire came increasingly under the control of its Turkish elements, especially after the loss of Greece in 1829, and in Western eyes, Turk and Ottoman became almost synonymous. In the latter part of the century, Turkish intellectuals created a brand of Turkish nationalism based on the Turkish language and heritage to the dismay of the participating nationalities of the empire. This was followed by attempts at enforcing the Turkish language at the expense of the ancient and well-established languages of the Middle East, such as Arabic and Armenian.

27 These guns were saved to be used in the civil war in the mountain region in 1841–60.

28 The Croatian Mikhail Latas, who was nicknamed Omar Pasha the Austrian by the natives.

29 Maronite Patriarch Boulos Mubarak Massad al-Amchiti (1805–90) was head of the Maronite Church between 1854 and 1890. His last name denotes his origin in Amchit, a village in northern Lebanon. (Mahfouz, op. cit., pp. 50–1).

30 Chebaro, *A History of Beirut*.

31 Salibi, *A Modern History of Lebanon*, pp. 147–8.

32 Not only was Baabda the residence of many Chehab emirs but also it was located in neutral ground between the predominantly Maronite north and the predominantly Druze south.

33 Kamal Hamdane, *The Lebanese Crisis* (in Arabic, *Al-Azma al-Lubnaniya*), Beirut, Dar al-Farabi with UNRISF, 1998, pp. 80–4.
34 The important Orthodox Christian community has not been discussed in full detail due to the focus of this book. The Orthodox Christians were the dominant group in the Levant on the eve of Muslim conquest in the seventh century. They were settled in the large cities as traders, teachers and professionals, and acquired massive wealth. They were accepted by the Muslims and were never viewed as strangers. The Orthodox Christians of modern Syria are larger in number than those in Lebanon.
35 Sunni Islam was the state religion of the Ottoman Empire, while Christian Orthodoxy was the state religion of the Byzantine Empire.
36 The 1932 census (see Table 33 in the Statistical Appendix) showed that Maronites and Sunnis were the two largest communities in the enlarged republic. The Shias had no power base or a foreign sponsor in the first place, and the important Druze had lost their power under the Chehabs and were ruthlessly oppressed by the Egyptians in the 1830s and the French in 1861 and 1925. The non-Maronite Christians played a minor role in the enlarged Lebanon, but were a very important merchant class. The 1943 social contract was between Sunnis and Maronites. Similar to arrangements in the previous century, these balances alienated other Lebanese and proved to be a time bomb in a country that remained inherently feudal at the end of the twentieth century.
37 Salibi, *A Modern History of Lebanon*, p. 230.

3

The Merchants of Beirut

In December 1986, I was on my way to Lebanon. At that time, there was an international boycott of Beirut airport; only the Lebanese national carrier, Middle East Airlines (MEA), would go there. After a short stop in Paris, I switched planes and soon we were over the Mediterranean. Three hours after take-off, I was able to see the far end of the sea where the Lebanon mountain chain appeared in the distance. With only a few kilometres to go to Beirut airport, I was worried that unless the jet changed direction or ascended rapidly, it would crash into the huge steep mountain. However, as the plane descended and the clouds receded, a tight landmass appeared below, straddling the mountain and the sea. Sure enough, I could now see the huge suburban Beirut lying gracefully on a nine-kilometre long peninsular plateau darting out to the Mediterranean.

Beirut is a place of illusions. Although I was familiar with the political situation, viewed from a plane, I was deceived by the apparent placidity of the city. It looked peaceful and quiet with a greenish-brown mountain background. The illusory tranquillity would welcome the visitor until the plane reached the ground and the travellers disembarked and left the terminal building. On the short strip of highway from the airport to downtown Beirut, the illusion would definitely be shattered, to be replaced by a harsh reality. Indeed, in 1987, Beirut was in its eleventh year of civil war, as foreign armies and private militias roamed the streets and operated the checkpoints.

I visited the downtown area, which was the hub of Lebanese finance and enterprising spirit and my playground during frequent trips with my father before 1975. Walking through the ruins, one would imagine that the place had been blasted by a nuclear bomb. Irreparably damaged and pock-marked buildings dominated the wide boulevards. Wild vegetation grew everywhere as if it had always been there; dogs that looked like hyenas roamed the area looking for human corpses; and other stray animals and rodents could be seen in the small alleyways. It was hard to believe that this was the same place that had competed with the world's financial capitals. Now it was a reminder of the 100,000 people who had died on its streets since 1975.

As we drove past Bab Idriss Street towards the Zeitouni quarter, I remembered a German film I had seen in an Ottawa theatre about the Lebanese civil war in 1975.[1] In those same streets we were driving through now, the film had shown a frightened and dizzy German journalist, his eyeballs bursting, running away from the fighting and gunfire in Beirut's hotel district. He eventually reached an open avenue where fire and smoke covered the buildings in the background. In the middle of the street, a well-dressed Frenchman with a small moustache stood with a bottle of champagne in one hand and a thin glass in the other. Calmly sipping from the glass, the Frenchman offered the German a drink and said by way of a toast: "l'Orient, c'est fini!" ("The East is finished!").

With all its contradictions, for 100 years before 1975 Beirut had been a hybrid of Chateaubriand, Burton's exotic Orient and twentieth-century pragmatic New York. To Westerners, memories of Casablanca, Saigon and Shanghai could very well be invoked when looking at Beirut. To many observers, the city represented one more place where Westerners had lived and functioned until 1975, but which had then fallen prey to incomprehensible forces. As I walked through the hotel district, the pouring rain and the mud made the skeletal hotels look like old Gothic chateaux. What had happened to Beirut was unbelievable. I thought to myself that such a civilized and cosmopolitan city did not deserve such a destiny. The Beirut that had inherited the spirit of ancient Phoenicia down to the Levantine mosaic was now plagued by wars and destruction.

The Phoenician cities of Tyre, Saida, Byblos and Ugarit[2] were centres of culture, manufacturing, shipbuilding, seafaring and commerce. It was at Ugarit in the thirteenth century BC that modern alphabets were invented and in the ninth century BC musical notes were first inscribed. *Orjouane* (murex purple) clothes and other luxury items were made at Byblos, Beirut and Tyre, and traded for precious metals with the kings of the ancient world.[3]

Phoenician commercial expeditions traded not only with the Mediterranean world but also with the British Isles. A Phoenician fleet was commissioned by the Egyptian pharaoh, Nekhaw, to circumnavigate Africa starting from Suez and ending on the Mediterranean coast. Captain Hanno from Carthage also toured the West African coast and landed at the mouth of the Senegal River. Documented sources also mention Phoenician expeditions to the coasts of the Caribbean and Brazil.[4] Along their trading routes, the Phoenicians built important colonies such as those at Marseilles in France, Cadiz and Carthage Nova in Iberia, settlements in Sicily and Malta and the famous Carthaginian Empire in North Africa. The Phoenicians were also state-builders. Their city-states were united under the government of Tyre, which established important relations with the kingdoms of the day. Phoenician Carthage in modern Tunisia was built by the Tyrians after the Levant fell to the Persians and Macedonians. Carthage was the centre of a powerful empire, controlling much of the western Mediterranean under Hamilcar Barca and his son Hannibal who conquered Rome.

A few days after my first tour of downtown Beirut, I made another trip to the historic sites in the city centre. As cars were not allowed to go through Rue Emir Bachir, I parked in the Zkak Blatt neighbourhood and walked on foot towards Government House (the old Ottoman seraglio). Across from the burnt-out edifice, I could see an open area full of Roman ruins that were unearthed by excavators in 1969. I knew from my childhood expeditions in the downtown area that there were more important Roman ruins and columns near Parliament House at Place Étoile and across from the Lazaria (Al-Azaria) Office Towers on Rue Emir Bachir, but the militias in control had barricaded the streets, and the amount of debris prevented me from proceeding. The whole downtown area was a mish-mash of ancient and modern ruins.

In better times, when archaeological work had meant something to a tourism-conscious government, excavation sites revealed massive Roman ruins beneath the city core. Archaeologists have concluded that no matter where you dig in old Beirut, you will find ancient ruins. In 1916, workers discovered several monuments and structures that dated back at least 1,800 years.[5] In 64 BC, Beirut became a resort for the veterans of the Roman army, expanding later into a major cultural and educational centre between AD 200 and AD 633 when a law school was built there. The inhabitants of Beirut acquired Roman citizenship, and in Roman annals, the city was known as Julia Felix Beyrit, after Emperor Justinian's daughter Julia who lived in Beirut.

A tree-lined street in the Clemenceau neighbourhood of Beirut carries the name of Rue Justinian. Also, Rue Général Weygand (named after a French general) is the new name for Via Dicimanus Maximus, a major thoroughfare in old Beirut where Roman troops used to march and which is still used today. The Romans planted a large umbrella-pine forest south of the city and this forest survived as the only significant park area of modern Beirut. It was severely reduced in size following massive Israeli air bombardment in 1982.

The glory that Beirut enjoyed as a Roman city in the fifth and sixth centuries was ended by a succession of earthquakes between 503 and 560. Early in the century, there were various minor earthquakes and tremors, but there was a major catastrophe on 9 July 551. On that day the coast shook violently as the sea ebbed and then flooded and destroyed ships and the port. The city was completely destroyed and the casualties numbered in the thousands, including Roman officers and hundreds of students from Europe attending the schools of Beirut. The city burned for two months and entire structures were either demolished or sank into the mud. Only a few hundred inhabitants managed to flee to the nearby mountain region. Many years later, native residents returned and started a farming community outside the destroyed core. Despite the efforts of Emperor Justinian to rebuild Beirut, it never returned to its former glory under the Romans. Worse still was a big fire in 560 that engulfed the still modest city structures. The fate of Beirut was reflected in several Roman writings of the period.[6]

Signs of these earthquakes are found everywhere in Beirut. Recent renovations of the Grand Mosque on Allenby Street revealed structures and arches of an old Roman temple that extended deep beneath the mosque, confirming that most of old Beirut was buried at a level below the modern city. These excavations were started in 1982 when a company, Oger Liban, owned by the Lebanese-Saudi businessman Rafic Hariri (who became prime minister ten years later), began clearing the debris in the commercial district. The works of this company unearthed the tip of the iceberg of the wonders hidden in the abdomen of the city. From 1988, teams of workers and scientists discovered huge amounts of Persian, Phoenician, Roman and other ancient ruins that will take decades to fully study and document. It was established that the existence of Beirut can be dated as far back as 5,000 years ago.

Several sources mention that by AD 628, Beirut was a great city with almost 35,000 inhabitants,[7] a sizeable urban centre by the standards of the seventh century. However, the Roman presence in Beirut ended in a succession of crises. The Byzantine Romans were engaged in a series of wars with Persia that started in AD 549 and led to a Persian takeover of the Levant. The Byzantines were able to defeat the Persians in another battle in 629 and re-establish their control. However, the Levant fell to the Muslims of Arabia in 635.

The ancient period is not what made modern Beirut, for the earthquakes in the sixth century completely destroyed it. It took six centuries for Beirut to emerge again as a city under the Crusaders. It is this milestone that mattered to the concurrent supremacy of the warlords and merchants in Lebanon. In the twelfth century, Beirut was ruled by the De Ibelin barons who built several castles and churches, including the huge St Jean's Church that has survived to this day as the Grand Mosque of Omar. Between 1099 and 1516, the Levant was engulfed in wars and stagnation, and Beirut changed hands several times among the Fatimids, Crusaders, Zinkis, Ayubids, Memlukes and Turks. During this time, the situation was so confused that Crusaders were allied with Muslims against other Muslims, and Muslims came to the rescue of Crusaders threatened by other groups of Crusaders.

One should not underestimate the impact of the Crusader kingdoms on the Levant. It wasn't only that the native population grew accustomed to the presence of Europeans, but also that the Crusaders became indigenized and proficient in the ways of the Levant. When the last of the Crusader kingdoms fell to the Muslims in 1291, thousands of European families stayed behind and became Muslims or Eastern Christians and were gradually Arabized. Modern visitors to some Shia villages of south Lebanon or to Orthodox Christian villages of the Koura district could see Arabic-speaking families with light features, blue or green eyes and blonde hair.

When the Crusaders departed, the Levant was ruled from Cairo by the Ayubids. Fearful of Crusader attacks, the coastal population moved inland, and the Egyptian Memlukes forbade any native settlements on the coast, filling the harbours with sand and debris to prevent enemy ships from docking. The coast remained in ruins for the next 200 years, until the arrival of the Ottoman Turks in 1516, who built the last of the great empires in the region.

From the departure of the last of the Crusaders left in the city in 1298 to the middle of the sixteenth century, Beirut suffered the toll of warfare and declined in status again to a small village next to its ancient and abandoned harbour. A few hundred yards outside the walled and empty city, jackals and bandits roamed freely in the rugged terrain. For a long time, it was dangerous to travel in that area, especially after the wholesale massacres committed against the native population by both Crusaders and Memlukes. All over the coast, travellers saw destruction and ruins where Saida, Tyre, Acre and Beirut had once stood.

To the north of Beirut, Tripoli had the worst fate. Having existed since Phoenician times, under the Crusaders it became a magnificent commercial and military bastion. After their departure, it was totally destroyed and disappeared from the map. Later, another Tripoli was built inland behind the ancient site, which became the city we know today.

Even after they left, the Crusaders continued to launch raids against the Levant and briefly occupied Beirut and other coastal cities. Eventually, they lost their dynamism in the region as Europe had other concerns. Only descendants of the Crusaders who had inhabited the Levant, and who had an immediate interest in regaining the old Crusader kingdoms of the Holy Land, continued to harass the area from Cyprus until 1570 and from Malta until at least 1798.

The modern Beirut that lasted until 1975 was shaped by the European penetration of the eastern Mediterranean. This took place in 1535, accelerated in the nineteenth century, and climaxed after the European military takeover of the Levant in 1918. The early penetration took the form of commercial links between the Levant and Europe, and was facilitated by the Ottoman government's policies. Sulieman the Magnificent, who became Ottoman sultan in 1520, had agreements with many European powers. He established good relations with France and, in 1535, he granted the French many commercial and cultural privileges. Similar privileges were granted to the Italian states, and to Russia and England. During the Crusader period (1099–1291), the Italian states (Genoa, Venice and Pisa) established important commercial and political ties with the Levant, and in the sixteenth century they were still at the forefront of European trade and commerce with the region.

The old Levant, which had been a centre of conflict among Byzantine, Crusader, Persian and Muslim powers, had long vanished from the scene. By the sixteenth century, it became a place of commerce and mutual interest between the Near East and Europe. Its new role as a commercial and mercantile region began to take shape in the fifteenth century. Perhaps the first orderly use of the word "Levant" in a strictly business sense started in 1413, when Venetian merchants created a company for the sole purpose of trading with the Levant and called it *il Comagnia dell Levante*. Initially, the term "Levantine" was associated with members of this company and with Venetian traders; however, all European traders in the region were eventually called Levantines. By the seventeenth century, it was no longer sufficient to trade with the Levant in order to be called Levantine; traders actually had to be residing in a Levantine city. Along with the native Christian population, the resident European trading communities formed the nucleus of a Levantine culture as it was known to the outside world.

Native Arab Christians of Syria, Palestine, Lebanon and Alexandria, as well as Armenians, Greeks, Italians, Jews and other minorities monopolized business activity with Europe and became wealthy. Over time, visiting and transient European traders no longer qualified for the term "Levantine" as the appellation was restricted to non-Muslim natives and resident Europeans of the eastern Mediterranean. By the late nineteenth century, the term "Levantine" was associated with shrewdness, business skills and knowledge of languages. The large non-Muslim communities were useful in establishing commercial and cultural ties with Europe. Even Alexandria in Egypt was considered Levantine for its mixed population of Arabs, Greeks, Italians and Jews. This was observed by the Arab-American scholar Edward Said, when he resided in Egypt in the 1940s.[8]

In the sixteenth century, the Ottomans encouraged Kurdish and Turkoman Sunni families to settle on the coast and defend the area against Crusader attacks, and at the same time deter the mountain people from giving a hand to the Europeans.[9] These immigrant warlords ruled the coast from Beirut to Tripoli. At that time, Beirut was largely abandoned while most of the core maintained a skeletal existence. Aside from the ruined seaport, the area around the Roman thoroughfare had many damaged structures, including a huge Crusader church and several small hostels and commercial establishments south and north of the church (prior to 1975, these were Souk Sursock and Allenby Street). The Assaf clan, which ruled the small region immediately north of Beirut and was centred in the town of Ghazir, was attracted to Beirut and some Assaf warlords moved there from Ghazir. Emir Mansour Assaf built a mosque on the main Roman road and this mosque has survived to this day as the Assaf Mosque. The Assafs were loyal Sunni Muslims of Turkoman and Kurdish origin who were encouraged to settle the Lebanese coast by the Memluke and Ottoman governments in order to protect it against attacks from Europe and to keep in check the warrior minority communities, chiefly the Druze and Maronites, in Mount Lebanon.

The rise of modern Beirut began in 1618, when Emir Fakhreddine II defeated the Assafs and annexed the small city. Although Fakhreddine made Saida his capital, he gave Beirut special attention. During his five-year residence in Italy, the emir visited Florence and Naples where he witnessed the Italian Renaissance and saw lovely houses and mansions and beautiful roads, all with the natural background that resembled his homeland. When he returned to Lebanon, he invited a team of Italian architects and engineers to create an image of Italy in Beirut. He built forts and palaces, revived and enlarged the Roman umbrella-pine forest and extended it further south as a barrier to sandstorms and a panoramic promenade for people travelling between the Chouf and Beirut.[10] Fakhreddine also built many roads and bridges that helped trade and mobility.

In the same period, Christians and other mountain minorities moved to Beirut, pushing the city's population up into the thousands. Many Muslims started to get involved in the Levantine wheeling and dealing, and eventually the term "Levantine" covered Muslim business people who inhabited the coastal cities, and who traded and made contacts with Europe. Manufacturing and trade flourished, and silk and other products were manufactured and traded with the Italian principalities plus other countries of Europe. By 1635, Beirut had become a sizeable trading centre of 5,000 inhabitants.[11] In 1660, it was made the centre of the *sanjak* (county) of Beirut when the Ottomans created the vilayet of Saida that comprised three *sanjak*s – Beirut, Saida and Safad.

Between 1535 and 1740, the Ottomans granted eight "capitulations" to France, including several commercial and political privileges and a right to protect the Roman Catholic citizens of the Empire. Similar capitulations were granted to Russia in 1774. These included the right to protect the Orthodox Christians of the Ottoman Empire. The French noticed the prosperity of Beirut and named it *Petite Paris*. They even granted French citizenship to a Maronite, Naufal al-Kahzen, and in 1655 appointed him as their consul in Beirut. The al-Khazens, the Maronite allies of the Maans, represented French interests in Beirut for 100 years, when other Maronite families took over the job in 1757.

By 1700, commerce flourished as Beirut's harbour expanded, and more Maronites and Druze descended from the mountain region to work with the Sunni Muslim and Orthodox Christian residents of the city. One could see Greeks, Italians, Armenians, French, Turks, Maronites and Druze working and trading with the common goal of making profit. By then, European merchants and travellers were a common sight in Beirut, which became a permanent abode for many Europeans. From Beirut, the Europeans pushed into the Lebanese and Syrian interiors – to Aleppo, for example – to expand their investments and create new markets for their products.

While it is tempting to draw a rosy picture of Beirut in the seventeenth and eighteenth centuries, its dealings with the Europeans were not always peaceful and friendly. As an Ottoman city, it paid the price of the Ottoman government's foreign policy and its wars with Russia and Austria. The city became a frequent target of the gunboat diplomacy of the European powers. Between 1773 and 1912, warships anchored off Beirut and lobbed their shells into the city and on many occasions, sea blockades were imposed.[12] However, these incidents were mere interruptions in Beirut's path towards growth and prosperity. By 1839, Beirut was a major city with a population of 15,000, the fourth largest town in the Levant, and with the largest harbour in the eastern Mediterranean. In the nineteenth century, its urban growth also expanded into areas east of the seaport, where the Egyptians built a military hospital and a quarantine facility, and west of the port where large hotels were built with both native and European capital.

After 1840, Beirut began its modern period of prosperity, which lasted until 1975.[13] Between 1840 and 1860, several banks, hotels and commercial enterprises were opened. Finance companies had already been established early in the century, and French enterprises invested large sums, for example with the establishment of the Ottoman Bank in 1856 and a branch of Crédit Lyonnais in 1875. In 1863, a beautiful building was built on the waterfront to house the Ottoman Bank, three kilometres from old Beirut. In 1867, a city hall was built as Beirut was already eclipsing in importance not only the coast and Mount Lebanon but also the whole of the Levant and the Syrian interior. Recognizing the importance of Beirut, the reformed Ottoman government made the city the centre of a new vilayet and formalized it as "the vilayet of Beirut" in 1888. This vilayet covered the whole Levantine coast from

Latakia to Acre, and comprised the important cities of Tripoli, Saida and Tyre with almost 900,000 inhabitants in an area of 30,500 square kilometres.

Between 1850 and 1870, the city expanded from the old core of the harbour front into new neighbourhoods as far west as the Ras Beirut district and as far east as the Achrafié quarter. Both neighbourhoods were inhabited by wealthy Orthodox Christians along with a large number of Sunnis who were either Ottoman civil servants or merchants and farmers. Institutions of higher learning, such as universities and technical colleges, were being established in previously undeveloped areas and wild terrain. In 1866, American Presbyterians built the Syrian Protestant College, later named the American University of Beirut.[14] This university occupied several acres of prime land in Ras Beirut. Many Lebanese Christians who converted to Protestantism enrolled in this university.

Not to be outdone by the Americans, French missionaries built a Jesuit university in 1875, close to the Achrafié quarter, east of old Beirut. This institution was officially known as Université St Joseph, although the general public knew it as the Jesuit University (*Al-Yassouiyé*). Other schools and universities were also opened by Western missionaries. Broadly, all the Western institutions taught subjects such as law, medicine, the arts and engineering. However, they differed in their missions. The Americans emphasized the Protestant ethic that had inspired the early pioneering Americans, while the French emphasized Jesuit discipline and the superiority of the Christian spirit that had inspired the French colonial heritage.

Transportation gained a central prominence with the advent of the modern economy. France completed the Beirut–Damascus Road in 1857,[15] and in 1892, a Christian from Beirut set up a partnership with a French interest to build a modern harbour in Beirut to replace the old antique seaport. This was completed quite rapidly in 1892 by the standards of the time. In 1895, a railway was built to connect Beirut with Damascus and the interior. Between 1900 and 1940, things could not have been better for Beirut: its status and wealth rose astronomically.

Levantine financiers

In the minds of both natives and Westerners, Beirut became associated with the perfumed, elegant and wealthy merchant who was in eternal pursuit of money and business deals. His eyes shone with intelligence and his tongue moved through several languages: Arabic, French, English, Spanish, Italian, Armenian, Turkish, Russian and Greek. Indeed, one could not be a Levantine merchant without knowledge of at least three important languages. It intrigued observers how people in such a tiny place could command so many languages and skills. This was no mystery, however. While Arabic was the mother tongue in the Levant, there were large pockets of Armenian and Greek resident communities who maintained their own languages. French, British and Russian missionary schools had been spread throughout the area since the seventeenth century. As for Italian, two factors contributed to its popularity in the Levant. The first was the old and continuous Italian trade with the Levant and the presence of Italian residents in Beirut; the second factor was attributed to special connections between the Maronites and the Vatican. From 1584, the Vatican had granted scholarships to young Maronite clergymen who went to Rome to learn Italian and study theological subjects.

The Levantine philosophy of the eighteenth and nineteenth centuries had no sense of belonging or nationalism. It represented a *capitalisme sauvage* that recognized no borders, save the extent to which it might go to search for fortunes. A Greek or an Italian is perfectly at home in Beirut, but so is an Arab Christian who paid little attention to the ancient glory of Byzantium, or a Muslim Arab who both considered the ancient glory of Byzantium, the *Golden Odes*[16] and the golden glory of Abbasid Baghdad as private matters that should not stand in the way of doing business. The wealthy families of Beirut were mainly Christian Orthodox along with some Maronites and Greek Catholics. Prominent among them were the houses of Sursock, Bustros, Takla, Faraoun, Tueni and Chiha. These families maintained excellent contacts with the French and very good relations with the Sunni notables of the city.

Before 1920, Mount Lebanon had a special status as an autonomous land-locked region. However, it maintained special relations with Beirut and the coast since much of Mount Lebanon's and the Syrian interior's trade with Europe went through Beirut. Conversely, the wealthy families of Beirut owned summer homes in the mountain region, and had many relatives and business contacts there. Several important Orthodox and Catholic Christian families of Beirut originally came from Mount Lebanon, as well as from Damascus, Latakia and Aleppo in Syria. These Christians were not mere menial workers; they were lawyers, doctors and merchants, and their contribution to Beirut was enormous. Soon the Christians of Beirut began subscribing to the idea of creating a Lebanese state with Beirut as its capital. Many Christians preferred the concept of a federated Levant of Lebanon and Syria where Beirut could play a central role, but the Lebanese state idea won the day. Petitions, signed by prominent Christians and Muslims, were submitted to the French consulate in Beirut, while a delegation headed by the Syrian business man Georges Samné lobbied in France for an independent Syria with a special status for Mount Lebanon.

On the eve of the First World War, Europeans controlled virtually all economic interests in the Ottoman Empire. When the Levant finally fell to the Allied Forces in 1918, the French General Henri Honoré Gauraud marked the significance of the moment by standing at the tomb of the great Muslim hero Saladin in Damascus, and boasting, "We came back, Saladin!" in reference to the defeat of King Richard the Lionheart by Saladin in 1190. In 1920, Beirut became the capital of Greater Lebanon, a welcome event for many Christians but a sad moment for the Muslims who saw it as a separation from their co-religionists in Syria and as a lowering of their status in a new entity where Christians were in the majority. The marriage of economic convenience between Beirut and the mountain region had adverse effects. Along with the objection of the Muslims, the explosive social climate of the mountain warlords was brought to Beirut when city and mountain region were joined in this way. The fabric of the city was transformed into a mix of enterprising Levantines and feudal warlords.

While the Levantines were not particularly nationalistic, at least not as the intellectuals of Damascus were, they eventually realized that their interests lay in independence and the termination of the French mandate. To their dismay, France did not turn out to be a benevolent power. French imports dominated the domestic market, and much of the tax collection was siphoned off as either payments to French interest on Ottoman debt owed to France or to finance the unpopular mandate administration. Thus began a struggle between the Levantines (including native Muslims) and the French. On the other extreme there were the native Francophiles, who were backed by the French and the Maronite Church, and who wanted not only to maintain the mandate but also to strengthen the ties to France. The independence-minded group was led by the houses of al-Khouri and Chiha and the major Christian families of Beirut. The second group was led by the Francophile Maronite lawyer Emile Éddé, who returned from France with the Allied Forces aboard a French warship in 1919. During the French mandate, there was a struggle between these two predominantly Christian groups. More families with strong economic and social presence were added to the Beirut elite circles of the rich and famous, and were, like their predecessors on the scene, mostly Maronites. These included the Sahnaoui, Essaili, Arida, Aramane, Ghandour, Jabre, Nawfal, Kettané, Nakad and Taraboulsi.[17]

In the 1930s, new utilities were formed with joint capital, namely Électricité du Liban, the Water Company, the Harbour Free Zone and the Régie du Tabac. The latter was a French company that largely replaced the defunct cotton industry, especially in south Lebanon. Also in that period, the service sector, the favourite profession of the Levantines, became the dominant sector as farming and manufacturing stagnated. In 1936, to advance the commercial role of Beirut, an airport was built at the hamlet of Khaldé, south of the capital, and in 1938, the single-basin harbour was expanded and a second basin added to receive more ships. After independence in 1944, Lebanon profited from the disasters that hit the world and the Middle East. During the Second World War, the presence of large British and French armies on Lebanese territory benefited the country. Between 1940 and 1945, these armies spent massive amounts in Lebanon (a United Nations report put the amounts at 607 million pounds sterling.)[18] When Jewish settlers proclaimed the state of Israel in 1948, skilled and wealthy Palestinians fled to Beirut, and Beirut thus replaced the ports of Palestine as the dominant port on the eastern Mediterranean.

Later events in the Middle East also benefited Lebanon. The Egyptian coup that removed the Khedive dynasty and brought Gamal Abdel Nasser to power eliminated the competition of Alexandria, and pushed many wealthy merchants to move to Lebanon. Between 1950 and 1970, the whole Middle East became involved in wars and coups. Since socialism was the norm of these coups, many wealthy Arabs migrated to Beirut. With the demise of the non-Arab Levantine class of the Middle East (Italians, Greeks and Jews), only the Lebanese continued to carry on the spirit of the Levant. Lebanon became a country with a culture peculiarly its own in terms of commerce, social life, food, architecture, history, Western philosophy and oriental mysticism, which were all present in a unique blend. By the 1950s, Beirut was the Levantine city par excellence.

Notes

1. *Die Fälschung* (The Circle of Deceit), 1981, directed by Volker Schlöndorff, starring Hanna Schygula and Bruno Ganz. The film addresses the moral and psychological experience of a German journalist during the first two years of the civil war in Lebanon (1975–6).
2. The town of Ras Shamra in the modern state of Syria.
3. Julian Huxley, *From An Antique Land*, London, Max Parrish, 1954, pp. 67–92.
4. *As-Sayyad*, December 1995. Article on the Lebanese researcher Youssef Mroué.
5. Of course, much older ruins going back to the Pharaohs and the Assyrians are found elsewhere on the coast.
6. Chebaro, *A History of Beirut*. See also Philip Hitti, *A History of Lebanon* (in Arabic, *Tarikh Lubnan*), Beirut, Dar al-Kitab al-Lubani, 1980, pp. 286–8.
7. Mohamed Ali Maki, *History of Lebanon between 732 and 1516* (in Arabic), Beirut, Dar Annahar, 1977.
8. Edward Said, *Out of Place*, New York, Vintage Books, 2000.
9. See Chapters 1 and 2.
10. The fort was a famous monument and in the twentieth century, long after it was demolished, its location in downtown Beirut was still known as Sahat al-Bourj, or Fort Square. The official name was Place des Martyres after the Turks executed several Lebanese nationalists in May 1916.
11. However, Beirut was still tiny compared to other Levantine cities such as Damascus, Saida, Tripoli, Acre and Tyre.
12. This did not change in the twentieth century – in 1983 Western ships were still arriving and firing their shells.
13. However, the attacks on Beirut didn't stop until well into the twentieth century. Even rising Italy wanted a piece of the action, and in 1911 it attacked Ottoman territory and took over Albania and Libya. In response to Ottoman resistance of these occupations, Italian warships shelled Beirut, causing massive damage to its seafront and to several ships in its waters.
14. The name was changed to the American University of Beirut in 1924.
15. Kamal Hamdane, *The Lebanese Crisis* (in Arabic, *Al-Azma al-Lubnaniya*), Beirut, Dar al-Farabi with UNRISF, 1998, p. 80.
16. The Golden Odes are the ten standard poems of great Arabian poets that preceded Islam. They are posted in golden embroidery on the holy shrine of Mecca, and are now called "the ten hanging poems" (*al-Mouallakat al Ashra*).
17. Hamdane, *The Lebanese Crisis*, p. 88.
18. The Allies also built a 100 km railway from Beirut to Nakoura in the south. This project helped the economy and employed tens of thousands of Lebanese workers. Abou Abbas, a very old man from Markaba in south Lebanon who worked on the railroad, tells a story about an English supervisor who had rough manners. The Englishman was irritated that the workers did not readily understand English so he kept pushing them while yelling every now and then: "Fuck these people, Fuck 'em, Fuck 'em . . .". The illiterate peasants took this as a compliment since the word *Fakm* in Arabic meant "great, wonderful". However, Abou Abbas understood the meaning and complained to the Englishman who laughed and became friendlier.

4

Bechara al-Khouri and Michel Chiha

The creation of "Grand Liban" did not secure the leadership of the Maronites; they had to wait until 1941 to establish it throughout the country. Meanwhile, the stage continued to be dominated by Maronite infighting, which started in 1861. Under the Mutassaref regime, Maronite leaders, such as Patriarch Hobeich and Youssef Karam, stood against the new international arrangement for Mount Lebanon and pushed for a Maronite-led government. The Maronites of the central region, who were groomed under successive Maan and Chehab emirs, supported the State of Mount Lebanon and participated in its government. The French were better connected with the more traditional Maronites of Kesrouane and the north, while the British befriended the more liberal and mercantile Maronites of the centre.

When the French arrived in Beirut in 1920, they quickly caused animosity amongst the Muslims and the Druze when the French Commander, Robert Colandre, made a speech to the effect that "France came to Lebanon to save its Maronite friends".[1] The largely receptive Maronites in the audience applauded the speech and, in celebration, fired their guns into the air. It seemed that despite their historic connections with the Levant, the French still needed a few more years before they became familiar with Lebanon. In the beginning, their style was dull: the French maintained the Ottoman tradition of appointing a council of seventeen Lebanese notables and the only change they introduced was to replace the Ottoman civil servant with a French civil servant as the council administrator.

Under the French mandate the Maronite infighting was led by two people: the Francophile Emile Éddé (of the Jbeil county north of Beirut) and the more open Bechara al-Khouri of the Chouf. Emile Éddé was popular among the Maronites of Kesrouane and the north, while the Maronites of Beirut and the central region supported Bechara al-Khouri, who was one of the al-Khouri Saleh warlords of the Chouf Jord (heights) region and was a relative of Habib Pasha al-Saad. Bechara al-Khouri was a law graduate who had practised in Emile Éddé's office in Beirut in 1912. In the transition from 1918 until the proclamation of the mandate in September 1920, he was an assistant to Habib Pasha al-Saad, who was made governor of Mount Lebanon by Prince Faisal's Arab government in Damascus.

While the British had promised the Arabs independence following the defeat of Turkey, they also had agreements with France to split the Levant into zones of interest. In 1920, the French had their own agenda for Lebanon. Accordingly, they declared that "Grand Liban" should be ruled by a French High Commissioner and assisted by a sectarian council. Emile Éddé was chosen as Assistant Commissioner, while Habib Pasha al-Saad, the Faisal-appointed governor of Mount Lebanon, was removed from the seat of government at Baabda. This made Bechara al-Khouri the senior figure in the liberal Maronite party. He was also appointed as cabinet minister in the mandate administration, and in 1922, he married the sister of the financier Michel Chiha. Both moves strengthened his political and financial influence in Beirut.

The appointed council continued until 1926, when, in accordance with the League of Nations mandate, a constitution was written under the chairmanship of Chiha to graduate Lebanon into statehood. Chiha was an open-minded business man committed to the Latin rite of the Roman Catholic Church, a rarity in Lebanon, and who descended from an Iraqi Christian family. He was a far-sighted intellectual who knew that the future of Lebanon lay not with France but with the surrounding Arab and Muslim worlds. His touches are clear in the constitution that made Arabic the official language along with French, emphasized the absence of a state religion, and established merit and qualifications, not religious affiliation, as the passport to government jobs. Chiha's philosophy was that the major task for the new country was to bring in the Muslims as partners in the new republic.[2]

With a new constitution and a parliament, the search was on for a president. The financier class that included many notable Muslims and Christians took up the task of containing the massive Muslim and Greek Orthodox opposition to French presence and to Maronite hegemony. To that end, the Greek Orthodox Charles Debbas was chosen as the first President of Greater Lebanon. Although Debbas was a Francophile who studied in Paris, the traditional Maronites and the French were not happy with the choice. To provide balance with the Maronite leadership, between 1926 and 1930, Debbas allowed Bechara al-Khouri and his nemesis Emile Éddé to take turns to act as prime ministers.

Eventually, al-Khouri emerged as the stronger leader as he was backed by the Chihas and their millionaire cousins the Faraoun family. Éddé represented the hard-line Maronites who emphasized the idea of a Christian homeland linked to France. The French were aware that the Maronites of the Central Region (the Chouf, Baabda and Metn) were more liberal-minded and at ease with the Muslim communities in Lebanon and the neighbouring countries than Éddé and his entourage of northern Maronites. On the other hand, while Éddé, France's main ally in Beirut, was talking about the "Arab dangers to the Christian Lebanon",[3] Bechara al-Khouri toed Chiha's line in extending the hand of friendship to the Muslims of Lebanon and to the Arab countries. The liberal Maronites realized that the financiers and merchants of Lebanon needed the Arabs as business partners and that the Arab countries were an area vital to the growth and prosperity of Lebanon.

While credit can be given to the liberal camp, it should be noted that the al-Khouri camp was equally sensitive about the preservation of a Christian-dominated Lebanon, and strongly opposed unity with Syria. However, its style was more conciliatory and diplomatic than the aristocratic and dogmatic style of Éddé and his followers, who looked down on the Muslims with an air of contempt for the natives reminiscent of the French colonials in North Africa. While al-Khouri wished to appease the Muslims of Lebanon, Éddé cared less for this idea and preferred to conquer them with France's help. When al-Khouri became prime minister under Debbas, he sought rapprochement with the Muslims and befriended them, but Éddé's intentions were apparent when he became prime minister under Debbas in 1936.

Despite the clear philosophies of the warring camps, an episode in the early 1930s demonstrated that political pragmatism could produce the most illogical events in Lebanon; it was Éddé, and not al-Khouri, who supported a Muslim deputy to be president of the country. In 1930, thanks to encouragement from Debbas, Mohamed al-Jisr, a Sunni deputy from Tripoli, joined the government in Beirut as a Speaker of Parliament. When Debbas's term ended in 1932, Éddé was alarmed that al-Khouri had an excellent chance of becoming president as he enjoyed the support of many like-minded Maronites, plus a majority of the Muslims and the Greek Orthodox. To break the enemy's alliance and defeat al-Khouri, Éddé made the historic decision to back the Muslim Mohamed al-Jisr as president. When al-Jisr accepted Éddé's backing, the Muslim and Greek Orthodox figures that at first had supported al-Khouri switched sides and supported al-Jisr instead. Even the Maronite Patriarch Arida supported al-Jisr because he wanted to see al-Khouri defeated.

The French, who had intended to create a predominantly Christian Lebanon, were shocked by such Maronite behaviour that pushed the country into electing a Muslim president, and were certainly against such a step. The French High Commissioner intervened and extended Debbas's mandate by one year, followed by the appointment of the now elderly Habib Pasha al-Saad as president for two years. In this period, the pro-Éddé newspaper *L'Orient* attacked al-Khouri and his supporters as a "group of financiers out to control Lebanon and run it as their own". The pro-al-Khouri paper, *Le Jour*, which was owned by Michel Chiha, was equally vociferous, branding the Éddé supporters as "lackeys of the French and believers in outdated ideas".[4] Charles Hélou, a Maronite who was a Jesuit graduate and a nephew of Chiha, wrote many articles in *Le Jour* and became President of Lebanon in 1964, but at heart he was purely Francophile.[5]

In 1935, the French allowed a resumption of constitutional life and permitted the elections of a new president. Fearing the ambitions of the al-Khouri camp, who wanted an end to French economic domination and sought British help to lead the country into independence, the French backed Éddé. Éddé became president in September 1935, but now he was more dependent on the French, and particularly on their omnipresent commissioner in Beirut. The al-Khouri camp was furious at the choice of Éddé, and between 1935 and 1941, they waged a campaign for full sovereignty. The British government supported the al-Khouri camp; their representative in Beirut, General Sir Edward Spears, promoted the idea of Lebanon's independence, for which actions a major street in Beirut was named after him.

In his capacity as president in 1936, Éddé encouraged Western missionaries and embraced the idea of an exclusive "Phoenician nationalism", which he made part of school curricula. Éddé's mentor was Charles Corm, another Francophile who pushed for a Lebanese nationalism based on the Phoenician heritage. This issue was particularly important, because it was at this time that French archaeologists were visiting Lebanon and unearthing important Phoenician ruins throughout the country. In the early 1930s, French experts unearthed important ancient Phoenician ruins in Beirut and Byblos. This discovery spurred an upbeat study of Phoenician heritage in Lebanon and Europe, especially in academic circles in France, Germany and Italy. Many Lebanese intellectuals jumped at the opportunity to prove that there was a unique Lebanese heritage.

Meanwhile, the Muslims of Lebanon were impatient with French manoeuvering and held pan-Syrian congresses in 1933 and 1936. The Christians' divided response to these congresses was as expected: the Greek Orthodox sent delegations, while the Maronites boycotted the discussions. The 1936 congress was especially patriotic. Its declarations, as well as the statement from the Beirut Sunni notable Salim Salam, called for an end to the mandate and for unity with Syria. Such declarations stirred public opinion and encouraged the Muslim population to rise in rebellion against the mandate, which alarmed the pro-French camp in Lebanon.

On 15 October, the country was on the brink of a Mount Lebanon-style civil war, with Beirut as the main stage. Muslim and Maronite militants had fist fights in the Jemmayzé quarter in downtown Beirut; however, Greek Orthodox militants of the Syrian Nationalist Party (Parti Populaire Syrien) supported the Muslims. Many people were killed in the incident. Responding to popular demands and bowing to British pressures, the French gave in and agreed to grant Lebanon full independence in three years (in 1939).

The events were a revelation for Éddé, who was humbled by the experience and was by now gaining political shrewdness and moderating his position. Grasping the idea the al-Khouri camp had taken for granted all along, he understood that it was important to win the Muslims over to the idea of a Lebanon separate from Syria. In 1937, he appointed the first Sunni prime minister, a Tripoli notable, Kheireddine al-Ahdab. This grand gesture became a tradition in Lebanon, and from then on, the prime minister's office always went to the Sunnis. To satisfy the supporters of the warring Maronite camps, al-Ahdab had to reshuffle his cabinet five times in two years.

The French were not too keen on abandoning their empire in *le Proche Orient*, and when the Second World War broke out in 1939, they imposed direct military rule in Lebanon. This move angered the now patriotic Éddé, who expressed dismay by withdrawing further from public life, noting that he was not treated with much dignity by the French as president of Lebanon. To maintain respect for his position as president, he stayed at home and ignored invitations to see the French Commissioner. Eventually, he resigned in 1941 and reopened his law firm.

Busy with the war effort, the French wasted little time and appointed the Maronite Alfred Naccache as president and the Sunni Ahmed Daouk as prime minister. Daouk resigned after one year and was replaced by a judge from Saida, the Sunni Sami al-Solh.

The British did not stay idle. They protested that the French had not kept their word regarding Lebanon, and in 1942, London recognized a de facto independent Lebanon and immediately appointed General Spears as their ambassador in Beirut. In April 1943, Spears encouraged general elections that were held in September under the watchful eyes of a British team. Predictably, the al-Khouri camp won by a vast majority and the new parliament of 55 deputies elected Bechara al-Khouri as president on 21 September 1943, with a vote margin of 44 to 11. Al-Khouri appointed his Sunni ally, Riad al-Solh, as prime minister, and the government swiftly amended the 1926 constitution and declared independence. This move angered the French and their Lebanese supporters, and the French commissioner ordered the arrest of the Lebanese leaders, including al-Khouri, al-Solh and four cabinet ministers. This was followed by a reconciliation with Éddé, whom he re-appointed as president on 11 November.

With two cabinet ministers, Emir Majid Erslane and Habib Abichahla still at large, the French found the situation to be out of hand. The two ministers escaped to the Chouf and in the absence of the full cabinet acted as a caretaker cabinet in the town of Bchamoun with help from General Spears and the British army, so that the country could continue to have a skeletal legitimate government.[6] Within one week, the French had released the Lebanese officials and al-Khouri returned to Beirut. The French finally had succumbed to the idea of Lebanese independence.

Al-Khouri appointed the Chehab emir, General Fouad Chehab, as commander of the new national army, and the French and the British withdrew in December 1946. It turned out that the al-Khouri camp provided most of the presidents of Lebanon over the next fifty years, who later came to be known as the "Chehabists" or the *Nahj* group, after General Chehab's term as president in 1958–64. Only twice did the presidency fall outside Nahj hands – under Sulieman Frangié in

1970–6, and under Amine Gemayel in 1982–8. Presidents Elias Hrawi (1988–98) and Emile Lahoud (1998–) also followed in the Chehabist tradition. In an independent Lebanon, the Christian financiers of Beirut, the Sunni notables of the coast and the warlords of the central region became the new rulers of the country.

In 1943, Lebanon had a population of 1,064,000, 70 per cent of whom lived in the rural areas. Beirut was a city of 220,000. It would take 25 years before the proportions were reversed and the rural population dropped to 30 per cent. Relatively speaking, Lebanon's independence was not hard-won. Unlike the Algerian War of Independence from France where hundreds of thousands died, or the French resistance against German occupation in the Second World War, the Lebanese won independence by negotiating with the mandate power and conducting a series of political meetings. There was a single demonstration against the French in Beirut that turned rather violent when the Senegalese Foreign Legionnaires opened fire and killed one person and injured several others. With independence secured, those who led the country unfortunately did very little to improve the lot of the annexed territories; instead, they spent the next ten years in improving their own lot, and that of their immediate clans.

Notes

1 Salibi, *A Modern History of Lebanon*, p. 207.
2 Michel Chiha, *Visage et présence du Liban*, Beirut, Presse Orientale, 1964.
3 Salibi, *A Modern History of Lebanon*, p. 218: "Eddé was disliked by the Muslims of Lebanon for his open contempt for Arabs and his warnings of the dangers of Arab unity."
4 *L'Orient* and *Le Jour*, 1935, quoted by Salibi, op. cit., p. 225.
5 His biography, published in 1995, could easily be the memoirs of a retired French statesman. Charles Hélou, *Memoirs* (in Arabic, *Muthakaraat*), Beirut, Dar Annahar, 1995.
6 The British had a community school and a military base in the town.

5

Camille Chamoun and Emile al-Boustani

The economy of independent Lebanon followed Levantine business ethics with a natural bias towards services. This was a successful formula for the private sector. However, in the public sector, the Ottoman-style nepotism and patronage that had dominated the government of Mount Lebanon remained a trait of the new republic.

Supporters of al-Khouri won the best jobs and the lucrative contracts, with members of the president's immediate family and entourage benefiting from their connections in the government. Al-Khouri's brother Salim built a fortune and the president's wife amassed a vast wealth. This behaviour angered not only the opposition, but also many al-Khouri supporters – chief among them Michel Chiha and cabinet minister Camille Chamoun.

Chamoun was born on 13 April 1900 to a Maronite family of Deir al-Kamar, the largest town in the Chouf region. His father, Nemr Chamoun, was the Finance Minister of the Mutassaref government of Mount Lebanon, and his mother, Antoinette, hailed from a large Kamarite family, Dib-Nehme. In 1916, during the First World War, the family was exiled to the Turkish hinterland for anti-Ottoman sentiments, but returned in 1918. Camille studied law at the Université St Joseph in Beirut and graduated in 1923 to start practising law the following year. From 1926, he contributed articles to the Beirut French daily, *Le Reveil*, and in 1929 he was elected to parliament. In 1930, he married Zalfa Nicolas Tabet, daughter of an aristocratic Beirut family, and subsequently had two sons – Danny and Dori. In the 1930s and 1940s, Chamoun was a Member of Parliament for the Chouf region, and held several important positions as ambassador and cabinet minister.

In the late 1940s and early 1950s, Camille Chamoun monopolized Maronite public opinion and struck up an alliance with the young firebrand Druze leader Kamal Joumblatt. Their opposition waged large protests against the regime, calling Salim al-Khouri, the president's brother, "Sultan Salim" (a reminder of the Ottoman sultans), and parliament questioned al-Khouri's wife about her wealth. In 1952, President al-Khouri asked Fouad Chehab, the commander of the army, to crush the opposition, but he refused. This situation, plus the murder of Prime Minister Riad al-Solh in the previous year on a visit to Jordan, convinced al-Khouri to resign. The parliament duly elected the popular Camille Chamoun as president on 1 September 1952.[1]

Chamoun's mandate witnessed a period of unprecedented growth and prosperity in Lebanon. In the 1950s, the Lebanese economy grew rapidly as foreign investment poured in. The war in Palestine, general social and political changes in the Middle East and Arabian oil made Beirut an international financial centre. In the 1950s, Lebanon became an important outpost of Western economic interests. Everything that happened in Beirut had an international ring to it. Oil companies and consulting firms made Lebanon their headquarters in the Middle East, and rich Kuwaitis and Saudis spent large sums in Lebanon resulting in prosperity and drawing increasingly more investors and sales representatives to the area.

The United States' business interests were significant and the construction of the Trans-Arabian Pipeline (Tapline) from Arabia to the coast south of Saida made the place more important. In this period, the large Western business community in Beirut had more banks than New York and more newspapers than London at their disposal. More confidential business newsletters were published in Beirut than in New York, Paris and London put together, and half of the world's gold trade was transacted through the city.[2]

These gains came at a cost. After the Second World War and especially in the 1950s, the Middle East felt the impact of the Cold War between the United States and the Soviet Union. The Soviets resumed their centuries-old southward thrust into the Near East, and the Americans inherited Britain's position in Arabia while confirming their cultural ties to the Levant. Their cultural and educational contributions and the absence of a colonial heritage made the Americans more successful than the Soviets in the Levant.

The Americans were not newcomers to the Middle East. Shortly after independence in 1776, the US leadership was seeking trading outlets to replace the reliance on British-controlled markets and eventually was able to sell cotton and other products to the Middle East. However, trade with the region was not a safe venture and occasionally America fought battles with the Barbary kingdoms of North Africa in the period 1801–5 over shipping rights in the Mediterranean. However, piracy resumed until France took over Algeria in 1831. Before the United States took military action, President Thomas Jefferson was content with paying ransom to release US ships and their crews who were brought to the harbours of Algeria, Tunis and Tripoli.[3] Between 1850 and 1865, cotton farming in the Levant and Egypt prospered as the USA experienced a bloody civil war. However, following their war, the USA resumed its activities in the region, and American missionaries and educational delegations made important inroads in the Levant in direct competition with France. Several American schools were established, as well as the Syrian Protestant College (built on Beirut's waterfront in 1866).

In 1919, the League of Nations was deciding the fate of the former Ottoman territories in the Middle East. While the French and the British pushed for placing these territories under their mandate, the Americans insisted on establishing an international commission of enquiry to investigate the wishes of the local population. President Woodrow Wilson, upon the recommendation of Dr Howard Bliss, the dean of the American University in Beirut, wanted to make sure that the former citizens of the Ottoman Empire accepted the mandate and did not want total independence. Facing a lack of interest from France and Great Britain, President Wilson sent his own delegation headed by two commissioners, Henry King and Charles Crane to investigate the situation. On 28 August 1919, the commission produced the *Report of the King-Crane Commission of Enquiry* which strongly recommended independence for Syria, autonomy for Lebanon within Syria, and a warning against the establishment of a Jewish state in Palestine. Although Great Britain and France ignored the report, it was still instrumental in shaping the American attitude towards the presence of the two European powers in the Near East.[4]

The last outburst of the old colonial powers came in 1956 when France and Britain decided, along with the new state of Israel, to attack Egypt. At the time, Egypt was ruled by the charismatic leader Gamal Abdel Nasser, who had removed the Khedive dynasty in 1952 and nationalized the Suez Canal in 1956. The Americans disapproved of the tripartite attack, and led an international chorus of condemnation that led to UN resolutions requesting a return to the status quo. The attackers withdrew in autumn 1956 and Nasser declared victory.[5] From then on,

US supremacy in the region was established with important allies in several Arab states as well as in Israel, Turkey and Iran.

The Soviets, whose internal struggles lasted from the Bolshevik Revolution well into Stalin's rule and after, started making headway in the area in the 1950s in cooperation with Egypt. This made the Middle East the stage for a major power competition. To counter the Soviet threat, the Americans forged a pro-Western alliance of several countries under the Baghdad Pact. Lebanon, which was pro-Western, could not remain immune to superpower rivalries, nor to the winds of change sweeping the Middle East. Simultaneously, a renascent Egypt was now vying to restore its old image in the Middle East.

This mixture of superpower rivalry and a rising Egypt was manifested in Beirut in the form of competition between Egypt and the United States. President Chamoun, pro-Western by nature, was nourished by the memories of the 1860 civil war and by Western culture by his father Nemr; he was against any serious Arab unity under Egypt. Instead he wanted to join the Baghdad Pact. On the other hand, his Lebanese opponents pushed for unity with the United Arab Republic (UAR, the Arab unity forum led by Egypt). Syria (the big neighbour of Lebanon) had already joined the UAR as a province, and Nasser, the arch-enemy of the Baghdad Pact, was looking for more countries to join.

The situation was complicated by the Lebanese parliamentary elections in June 1957, when the American, Soviet, French, British and Egyptian embassies contributed funds to the various candidates. It was reported that foreign intelligence agents were roaming Beirut like nowhere else and Beirut was an important station for the likes of Kim Philby.[6] In the elections, Kamal Joumblatt, Hamid Frangié, Rachid Karami and several other opposition personalities lost their seats, prompting accusations of fraud and treachery against Chamoun. The election's outcome quickly developed into an open crisis that polarized the country as the opposition charged Chamoun with working towards a docile parliament to allow himself a second term as president.

The internal situation was exploited by the UAR and the superpowers that were supporting and arming the protagonists. While Chamoun and his allies were already armed, weapons were smuggled to the opposition from Syria and Beirut was shut down as trenches were erected in many neighbourhoods. Two such neighbourhoods were the predominantly Muslim Basta, led by the notable Saeb Salam, and the predominantly Christian Achrafié, led by the Phalange leader Pierre Gemayel. Both neighbourhoods remained symbols of unity and disunity, even in the 1975 civil war. Any cracks in national unity showed up immediately as a rivalry between Basta and Achrafié. Ultimately, the Mount Lebanon conflict had moved to Beirut.

Initially, Chamoun was steadfast in his palace at Baabda, feeling confident and turning down mediators. Faced with the rejection of General Fouad Chehab, commander of the army, in using force against the opposition, Chamoun supplied his supporters with guns and used the police force of the Ministry of the Interior for this purpose. Commercial activity in the country was brought to a halt, and the confrontation rolled into action after a pro-opposition figure, Nassib Matni, editor of the newspaper *Al-Telegraph*, was assassinated in Beirut on 7 May 1958.

Fighting covered several regions and the opposition was effectively in control in many places. A coalition of warlords was fighting another coalition of warlords: while most Sunnis were in the opposition camp, several Maronites were against Chamoun, following a traditional split in the Maronite camp that bid the Maronite warlords against each other. The opposition camp included many powerful figures such as the Maronite Frangié and Mouawad warlords of Zghorta (in the north), the Sunni *zaim* Rachid Karami (also in the north), the Sunnis Saeb Salam and Abdalla al-Yafi (in Beirut), the Druze Kamal Joumblatt (in the Chouf), the Shia Ahmed Assad (in the south), the Shia Sabri Hamadi (in the Bekaa) and the Druze Chebli Aryan (also in the Bekaa).

Chamoun had allies everywhere and was a match for his opponents. Along with the Sunni prime minister, Sami al-Solh, who spoke Arabic with a Turkish accent, Chamoun was supported by the Douehi clan, the enemies of the Frangié in Zghorta, Emir Majid Erslan, the Druze foe of Joumblatt in the Chouf, and Kazem al-Khalil, who was the Shia foe of the Assads in south Lebanon. The Maronite Pierre Gemayel also supported Chamoun for Beirut and the Metn region. Fighting lasted for six months and the future of Chamoun was in the balance. When Joumblatt made advances on the ground and controlled the mountain region south of Beirut, Chamoun feared defeat and invoked Point IV of the Baghdad Pact. He claimed that Lebanon was a victim of "a communist conspiracy" led by Nasser and called upon the USA to intervene.

In July, the Lebanese representatives Emile al-Boustani and Fawzi al-Hoss, plus several Western representatives, decided to mediate in the conflict. Al-Boustani was an MP who had held several government positions. He hailed from Debbieh, a town in the Chouf region, and moved on to become a wealthy businessman, the owner of CATS, a company specializing in agrarian equipment and development-related projects. He encouraged policies that allowed foreign aid, especially American and Western, to pour into Lebanon. The mediation of al-Boustani and the others brought Nasser and the USA to agree to the election of General Fouad Chehab as president, and the appointment of the Sunni Rachid Karami as prime minister. However, on 14 July, a nationalist coup in Iraq succeeded in removing the King of Iraq and his pro-Western prime minister, Nouri Said, from power in Baghdad. This encouraged the Nasserite camp to boast that after the fall of Baghdad to nationalist forces, Chamoun and King Hussein of Jordan were next on the list.

The American administration became worried and, fed by a dark picture of the situation in the Middle East, ordered the Marines, who had already been posted off Beirut's shore for some time, to land. When the Marines landed at Khaldé south of Beirut, they found a different picture: there were no Nasserite armed hordes on the beach but Lebanese sunbathers and women in smart bikinis. Before they knew it, they were accosted by hordes of boys selling American soft drinks and chocolate bars. The Marines' mere presence cooled the fighting in Lebanon and over the next two months the combatants established a formal end to the conflict. In September, General Fouad Chehab was elected president and he appointed Karami as prime minister. The Marines left without firing a single shot.

This war showed that a mere dozen years after the French had left, the Lebanese were already acting contrary to the minutes of the national pact of independence. Western companies tried to broker an agreement but, as a US embassy official put it to Sandy Campbell, president of Tapline: "What else can we expect? To hope that the Lebanese won't resort to violence again is like hoping dogs don't chase cats."[7] But the American businessmen who had seen their Lebanese friends in sensible pursuit of business profits were not aware of the dichotomy between Beirut and the rest of the country, or the nature of conflict in the mountain region; they did not accept the US diplomat's assessment.

Almost 4,000 people were killed in 1958, combined with a flight of capital, a drop in foreign investment and other economic difficulties.

Even after the guns were silenced, at least 120 US companies were worried about the future stability of Lebanon and a smaller number of other Western companies re-evaluated their presence there. However, considering the explosive situation in the Middle East, Lebanon remained a relative oasis of tranquillity with its liberal economy and banking secrecy amidst a sea of Arab socialism and revolution – this meant that Beirut could not be replaced as a commercial and financial centre.

The warlords made peace and "kissed each others' beards", as the popular Lebanese saying goes, and Saeb Salam announced the happy ending of the 1958 civil war with the famous words: "No victors, no losers" and "One Lebanon – not two". Everybody won, or it felt like it: the Maronites were reassured by the swift Western support, while the Sunnis were satisfied that Syria and Egypt had not abandoned them. Both sides felt safe enough to resume business as usual.

However, after 1958, things were no longer the same in Lebanon. The republic of 1960 was not the same as the feudal society of 1860. New economic and financial forces had emerged in Lebanon since 1943; demands for a wider democracy were voiced by non-Maronite and non-Sunni elements in the country, and Shia and Druze aspirations were taking shape. Blind to these new realities, the warlords and their merchant allies chose to focus on the confrontation with the reformist and anti-warlord President Fouad Chehab. The next twelve years were dominated by the emergence of the annexed territories and the dominance of Levantine mercantilism over a modern economy.

Notes

1 Riad al-Solh was assassinated in 1951 during a visit to Amman, Jordan, by members of the outlawed Syrian Nationalist Party (called the *Parti Populaire Syrien* under French mandate). The assassins were avenging the execution of their leader Antun Saadeh by a firing squad in Beirut on 8 July 1949. This execution had been approved by al-Solh 24 hours after the arrest of Saadeh on charges of rebelling against the state. Saadeh was a Greek Orthodox Lebanese émigré who returned to Lebanon in 1947 to lead a secular movement that aimed at uniting Syria, Lebanon, Jordan, Palestine, Iraq, Kuwait, Cyprus, Sinai, Eskenderun and Cilicia (in modern Turkey). His ambitions went against the Lebanese establishment who saw in his bid a challenge to their sectarian-based political system and to the independence of the young republic. Saadeh's supporters point out the speed

at which the sentence was made as a sign of the brutality of the sectarian regime against a non-conforming intellectual, and that al-Solh did not give him a chance for a decent hearing in a proper court.
2 Confidential business newsletters were pamphlets not sold in libraries or news-stands, being obtainable only through subscription. Usually they contained reports exclusive to the publication and privy to subscribers. These publications still exist today but they charge above-market rates compared to mainstream business magazines.
3 A. B. C. Whipple, *To the Shores of Tripoli: The Birth of the U.S. Navy and Marines*, New York, William Morrow and Co., 1991.
4 Abdel Sater, *Modern History of Lebanon and the Arab Countries* (in Arabic, *Labib, Al-Tarikh al-Mouasser: Lubnan wa al-Dowal al-Arabiya*), Beirut, Dar al-Machreq, 1983, p. 186. For the text of the commission's report see *The Israel-Arab Reader: A Documentary History of the Middle East Conflict*, edited by Walter Laqueur and Barry Rubin, London, Penguin Books, 1985, pp. 23–33.
5 The French and the British were in retreat everywhere in Africa and Asia. The British eventually left India in 1949 and France suffered defeat at Dien Bien Phu in Vietnam in 1954.
6 Miles Copeland, *The Games of Nations*, London, Weidenfeld and Nicholson, 1969, pp. 192–200, and Said Abu-Rish, *Beirut Spy: The Story of the St Georges Hotel*, London, Bloomsbury, 1990. The Lebanese became familiar with the identity of so many spies in the 1950s that they thought of intelligence work as a profession like any other. A joke circulated about a Western spy who arrived in Beirut and was instructed to call on his local contact Youssef Haddad. When he arrived at the address and rang the bell, an old man answered the door. When the spy asked for Youssef Haddad the man said, "Yes, I am Youssef Haddad, but don't you want Youssef Haddad, the spy, who lives on the second floor?"
7 Miles Copeland, op. cit., p. 199.

6

How the Warlord/Merchant Group Shaped the Economy

Between 1943 and 1975, warlords, *zaim*s and Levantine business leaders acted as mediators between the Middle East and Europe – a role that fitted the self-proclaimed official mission of Lebanon. The distinction between warlords and business people became blurred, as many individuals were both. The financial and economic landscape was increasingly shaped by the divergent interests of the warlords and the business people, but not by the requirements of national development. Even the private sector was plagued by favours and patronage appointments.

The population of the annexed territories (Tripoli, Akkar, the Bekaa and the south) believed that the creation of a larger Lebanon made no difference to their well-being and had brought no material gain. The annexed areas remained underdeveloped while the mountain region and Beirut prospered. Before 1920, apologists for a greater Lebanon argued that Mount Lebanon needed fertile lands to feed its population, and that was the reason why the Bekaa was annexed. However, under the enlarged entity, agriculture deteriorated and became the least important priority for the government. In 1944, although 70 per cent of the population lived outside the cities, Lebanese agricultural products only contributed around 20 per cent of the GNP (this ratio fell to 12 per cent in 1964 and to 9 per cent in 1974). Even in the 1970s, the fertile Bekaa Valley and the arable areas of the Akkar Plain and southern Lebanon remained forgotten. Their situation was no better than it had been 200 or 300 years before. In some villages, families did not have running water at home and continued to rely on ground water from wells that had been dug by charitable organizations and wealthy individuals as long ago as 1760 and 1812. Sometimes, such wells, despite being museum pieces, were still in use as recently as 1975 in the absence of government water projects. It was the case that political and business leaders were more interested in services and commerce, and had no intention of devoting effort to farmland and the countryside. They had inherited Lebanon's role as the service centre for the Levant; it had proved profitable and they did not intend to change a natural comparative advantage.

This neglect was unwarranted as the annexed territories held huge economic potential. The fertile Bekaa had once been a granary of the Roman Empire and there was a site of magnificent Roman ruins located in the city of Baalbeck. These ruins include the Temple of Bacchus, which boasts the highest-standing Roman columns in the world. While most of the Bekaa was ignored by the central government, the opening of a modern road in the 1950s connecting Beirut to Damascus created a corridor of prosperity centred around the towns of Zahlé and Chtaura. In addition to its scenic beauty, its arable land and historical sites, the Bekaa has most of the country's water resources. The largest rivers in Lebanon, the Litani and the Orontes,[1] flow from the Bekaa in opposite directions: the Orontes flows across the border into Syria and the Litani flows south-west to the Mediterranean. In the 1950s and 1960s, grandiose projects to exploit the Litani for irrigation were introduced but later abandoned, although the creation of a dam and a small lake were achieved.

Starting in the 1930s, farmers in the northern Bekaa who were aiming to outbid the Levantine money-banking skills of the warlords and *zaim*s in Beirut and the mountain region planted hashish on a large scale. The drugs industry prospered as export markets, especially to neighbouring countries, were developed to the extent that the Egyptian government sent memoranda in 1940 to the Lebanese government to curtail the drug business. Hashish farmers were undeterred and in fact expanded their business after 1970, introducing modern methods to produce other drugs and processing them on a scale that matched the laboratories of Columbia. By 1980, in the middle of the civil war and in the absence of state authority, the Lebanese drug industry was a multi-billion dollar business.

The discrepancies in the levels of economic and social development in the country were apparent at many other levels. In 1970, the peripheral regions remained rural and underdeveloped; the annexed towns of Tripoli, Sidon and Tyre, normally glorified by Lebanese nationalists as "the Pride of Phoenicia" and oft-mentioned in school textbooks, remained abandoned and forgotten as "too provincial". In the early 1970s, visitors wouldn't have been able to see a single modern café, modern hotel or sizeable theatre in Saida, Tripoli, Tyre or Nabatié. In 1974, the harbour of Saida and the surrounding area looked as if the Crusaders of 600 years ago had only just left. Visiting Sidon at night, the shabby looking ruins and the few ghostly pedestrians in the alleys made one wonder whether a Crusader knight would suddenly jump out of one of the tiny alleyways. In Sidon's harbour, a few fishing boats, probably more appropriate in a scene for a documentary on Phoenicia, were still in use and still lined the little docks.

Lebanese manufacturing fared a little better than agriculture but did not expand very far either. The few manufacturing firms that did exist were concentrated in and around Beirut at the expense of the peripheral provinces. Far from helping Lebanon to graduate as an independent nation, the French swamped the market with their own products, which retarded domestic manufacturing. After independence, authorities provided no adequate protection or tariff walls for domestic manufacturers to grow and establish themselves against French competition. The service industries by nature were against manufacturing as they concentrated on shipping, re-export and transit, requiring almost unfettered entry and exit of foreign products. Businesses and those with a political interest in the service industries argued that Lebanon would suffer if protection against imports were introduced.[2]

Between 1948 and 1974 manufacturing stagnated, growing by only 2 per cent annually. Like other economic activity, most manufacturing firms were located in Beirut and its suburbs. This concentration loosened in relative terms in the 1950s as the proportion of manufacturing plants in Greater Beirut fell from 78 per cent in 1954 (against 22 per cent in the annexed territories: 5 per cent in the Bekaa, 5 per cent in the south, and 12 per cent in the north), to 61 per cent in 1957 (or 407 out of 665 establishments). However, the concentration increased in the 1960s as the proportion for Beirut rose again to 83 per cent in 1964 against just 17 per cent in the annexed territories (3 per cent in the south, 4 per cent in the Bekaa and 10 per cent in the north), and was even more concentrated in Greater Beirut in the 1970s. The major manufacturing centres around Beirut were located mostly in the suburbs: the Industrial City (*al-Madina al-Sinahia*) in the eastern suburbs of Sinn al-Fil, Jisr al-Basha, Tell Zaatar and Mkalless, and the southern industrial area at Nahmé and Kfarchima.

Lebanese manufacturing was overwhelmingly concerned with the production of consumer goods. Between 1918 and 1964, foodstuffs, footwear and clothing accounted for almost 75 per cent of manufactured products. A considerable shift in output from consumer goods to raw materials occurred in later years.[3] Semi-processed and final products accounted for a small portion of manufacturing output. This suggested a structural weakness in production relations as little organic links existed among the various manufacturing sub-sectors. Raw and semi-processed materials used in manufacturing had to be imported, as did equipment. For example, in the construction industry paint factories imported everything they used in order to operate, from colours and powders to machinery. Developers bought paints and cement locally, but imported lifts and aluminum for the windows.

Between 1950 and 1970, employment in manufacturing stagnated. In 1950, the average firm had ten employees and a capital base of LL100,000, and in 1970 it still had ten employees but a capital base of LL175,000. In the same period, the number of firms increased twice as fast as the number of manufacturing workers. In 1960, the average firm had fewer workers than in 1950, but after 1960, the trend was towards larger firms. Another development was the increased capital intensity in manufacturing and the heavier use of machinery. The capital/labour ratio was sixteen to one in 1970 against seven to one in 1950. The reason for the small size of firms and the low number of employees was the prevalence of family-orientated businesses in Lebanon. This created a problem of scale and became an obstacle to Lebanon's regional and international competitiveness. The small size of the domestic market also hindered the growth of efficient and economically sound manufacturing plants.

The Lebanese economist Nadim Khalaf warned that the reliance on services would lead to an imbalance in Lebanon's trade position and to a chronic merchandise trade deficit, because Lebanon was importing most of its basic goods and exporting only some of domestic products. He predicted that this would lead to a loss of sovereignty.[4] When the crisis struck in 1975, the service industry, making up two-thirds of the economy, was the first to go down.

Following the 1975 civil war, rather than exploiting the resources of the peripheral regions and developing a strong and diversified economic base and a balanced economic structure, the Lebanese government and business sector concentrated its activities in Beirut and the mountain region in the service industries. Banking became a major industry in Lebanon and Lebanese bankers boasted that a "Phoenician business ethic" drove their efforts, mimicking the "Protestant business ethic" of America. As one banker put it: "Lebanese capitalism is now out to conquer the world as Phoenicia once did ... economically."[5]

The banking sector
After 1943, the al-Khouri camp and its entourage were effectively running the government and largely controlling the economy. This did not go unchallenged by other traditional camps who were finally able to depose al-Khouri and elect Camille Chamoun in 1952. However, in 1958 the presidency was again in the hands of another Nahjist, General Fouad Chehab, and the struggle continued on all political and economic fronts. Events showed that the opponents of Chehab believed that it was acceptable to hurt the economic interests of his supporters even if this was not in the best interest of Lebanon. Although the golden period of Lebanon resumed with Chehab, the prosperity was haphazard and aimless. The future was a dark mystery for those responsible for administering the country and those running the economy. The 1960s were the best years for economic prosperity, but they were marred by economic and political crises.

In October 1966, a financial crisis rocked Lebanon and left its internationally renowned financial market in ruins. This crisis was known as the Intrabank Crisis, after Intrabank (International Traders), the largest financial institution in the Middle East at the time. The financial crisis and the public inquiry that followed exposed the practices and inherent mismanagement in Lebanese banking. The sheer size of Intrabank made it the leading rogue, and a commission of enquiry treated Intrabank and a number of other banks harshly. Observers differed on the interpretation of the Intrabank crisis. Some pointed out that Intrabank was a victim of the Lebanese warlords and financiers who wanted the Palestinian-owned and Chehabist-backed Intrabank to collapse. Indeed, Intrabank's collapse would have been avoidable had the government intervened in time.[6]

Banking in Lebanon owes its origins to the small finance houses of the early nineteenth century. Under Egyptian rule (1831–40), discount houses and finance shops offered banking services to finance economic transactions of the affluent merchants of Syria and Lebanon who were engaged in the growing import–export business. The first European bank to open in Beirut was the French-owned Ottoman Bank in 1856, followed by the French bank Crédit Lyonnais, which opened a branch in Beirut in 1875. In the period 1875–1920, several other European and Lebanese banks also started up. After 1920, many prominent families such as the Chiha, Faraoun and Sursock were involved in banking.

During the French mandate, the French Banque de la Syrie replaced the Ottoman Bank as a central bank for Syria and Lebanon with exclusive rights of note issue and custody of government funds. Almost 85 per cent of its shares were held by French and British interests, and only 15 per cent were held by nationals. The name of the bank was changed in 1924 to La Banque de la Syrie et du Liban (BSL), but remained headquartered in the old Ottoman Bank building on Beirut's waterfront and maintained six branches in Lebanon and six in Syria. Since the president of the bank and most of the board of directors resided in Europe, executive powers were delegated to a managing director in Beirut. Following important political developments in Syria and Lebanon in 1936, a 1937 convention established the BSL as the fiscal agent for Syria and Lebanon. Thereafter, each government dealt separately with the bank. By 1938, Syria and Lebanon had two separate currencies issued by BSL.

Independence and the end of the Second World War brought stability, prosperity and foreign investment to Lebanon. Deposits at financial institutions grew ten-fold from LL27.5 million in 1939 to LL227.1 million in 1945.[7] This increase was due to the capital inflow that the Allies used to finance their war efforts in the region. Nevertheless, the inflow created huge inflationary pressures. After the war, deposits grew moderately reaching LL259 million in 1951, while the number of banks increased from seven in 1945 to 11 in 1951.[8] Up to 1966, new banks were established almost every year, reaching 21 in 1954, and 99 in 1966; deposits increased from LL392 million in 1954 to LL1,585 million in 1963, while commercial credit rose from LL318 million to LL1,333 million in the same period. Banking activity was also growing rapidly as the number of cheques cleared in Beirut increased from 5 million (worth LL94 million) in 1943, to 803 million (worth LL3.6 billion) in 1963. The Credit Risk Office of the BSL also operated a clearing house for the commercial banks.

While credit was available, the financial market did not offer funds for business projects in the real sectors, since many of these deposits were invested in Europe and in gold and foreign exchange assets.[9] In the 1950s, half of the world's gold transactions passed through, or were handled by, the Beirut market. Arbitrage in foreign exchange assets was a profitable venture. Financial institutions used foreign currency to extend credit in the domestic market since they considered these assets as part of their liquid holdings and readily convertible into lira. They also met depositors' claims by converting dollar assets into lira, should their liquid reserves have been inadequate. A sizeable portion of the banks' holdings was kept in offshore investments. This tradition continued into the 1990s.

The break-up of the monetary union between Lebanon and Syria, and the dissolution of the customs union and the joint exchange office, took place in 1950. By 17 May 1952, Lebanon had removed all remaining foreign exchange restrictions and allowed a free movement of funds at current market rates. From then on, the official exchange rate, published by the BSL, was used solely for internal government finance to set customs duties and foreign currency revenues and expenditures. The Foreign Exchange Department of the BSL continued to handle government transactions in foreign currencies such as royalties from oil transit in Lebanese territory and the accounts of diplomatic missions (diplo trade).

For the remainder of the 1950s, Syria and Lebanon concentrated their efforts on putting their houses in order, by building national institutions and asserting sovereignty by wrestling as much power as possible from the BSL. The absence of a regulatory framework for money and credit led to abuses by the BSL. Between 1925 and 1956, due to its profit-motivated activities the BSL sometimes functioned contrary to the needs of Syria and Lebanon. It pursued discount and credit policies that were inappropriate to the objectives of overall monetary stability. For example, the Bank increased liquidity by moving securities to its issue department against the issue of additional banknotes, which was harmful and inflationary to Lebanon at the time.

While both Syria and Lebanon faced similar problems, they developed separate monetary policies and different economic systems. Between 1952 and 1956, Syria adopted nationalistic policies by introducing Law 151, which imposed controls on the currency and on foreign investment, and created a central Bank of Syria to end its dependence on the BSL. Lebanon moved in the opposite direction and towards more liberalization, with little control over financial markets. The creation of a fully functioning central bank in Lebanon had to wait until the mid-1960s. Camille Chamoun's presidency (1952–8) was associated with opening up the economy to foreign investment. Many elderly Lebanese remember Chamoun as the president who introduced banking secrecy in 1956, imported luxury goods (such as televisions and fridges) into Lebanon, and initiated major public works and modern roads. Perhaps Chamoun is especially remembered for the elegant municipal stadium to which he invited important foreign dignitaries to watch sports events.[10] Slowly, Lebanon was consolidating the gains of independence and strengthening its liberal economy.

Lebanon moved further ahead by liberalizing capital markets to attract foreign capital. The banking secrecy law was introduced on 3 September 1956, so that bank accounts could not be disclosed without the consent of the client. This law set Lebanon as an entrepôt for those who wanted a safeguard for their wealth. The law was timely, coming amid massive political and social upheavals in the Middle East. Socialism was in vogue in the Arab world and the Arab militaries wanted to follow the Egyptian example of Nasser by overthrowing the decaying regimes. Wealth found a safe haven in Beirut, encouraged by Lebanon's stability, growth potential and liberal economy. Foreign firms used Lebanon as a springboard for business contacts with the rest of the Middle East.

Despite the growth of the financial market in Lebanon, the situation was chaotic in the 1950s with no banking law or guidelines. Few laws were introduced to establish order in the banking sector. The minimal legislation comprised a 1962 law requiring Chart A banks to be members of the Credit Risk Office of the BSL,[11] and a new Code of Commerce which included several articles dealing with deposits at financial institutions and with commercial credit. The minimum capital base for establishing a Chart A bank was one million lira, half of which was payable up front.[12]

In the 1950s, liquidity and safety were the major problems facing the financial market in Lebanon since banks maintained a tiny reserve ratio and invested in speculative activities outside the traditional fields. Small sporadic events foretold the type of difficulties the Lebanese financial sector would encounter: many institutions experienced a run-down in their reserves when faced with major withdrawals; the BSL came to their rescue and hedged these banks by rediscounting bills. To meet the liquidity needs, branches of foreign banks in Beirut dealt directly with their head offices abroad.

In the 1960s, banking was the major industry in the Lebanese economy. Much wheeling and dealing went on behind the façades of the apparently normal buildings that housed the banks of Beirut. Operating in a risky but profitable environment, Lebanese banks concentrated their activities in short-term commercial credit and loans, and gave little attention to mortgages and long-term credit to manufacturing and agriculture.[13] The government handled problems in the financial sector on a case-by-case basis. Between 1948 and 1964, it aimed at freeing the financial system from dependence on the French franc and creating an open financial market. The Banking Secrecy Law was very helpful in attracting Arab capital and a variety of hard currencies. Now the task was to regulate the industry and encourage direct foreign investment in the country.

The year 1963 was a milestone in Lebanese finance. It witnessed the introduction of a law to regulate financial activities in the country: the Law of Money and Credit. The Law stipulated the appointment of a Money and Credit Board whose first *ordre du jour* was to create a central bank for Lebanon. Such a bank was created in the same year and progressively accumulated the functions of a central bank: it became responsible for maintaining a stable currency and efficient financial markets; and it introduced a credit policy compatible with stable prices and full employment (although the debate goes on around the world as to what a central bank can do about the seemingly incompatible goals of stable prices and full employment). The creation of the Bank of Lebanon faced stiff opposition from the Bankers Association, which was apprehensive about regulation. Antagonism developed between the Central Bank and the Association, and this became a dominant theme of Lebanese finance.

The relationship between financiers and warlords in Lebanon was developing further. Aside from fellowship of money – where wealthy families and individuals befriended each other to the exclusion of all others – ties extended into blood relations, family alliances and sectarian solidarity. Bankers were involved in many more activities besides banking. Several banking institutions were fronts for larger operations that mixed aspects of banking and business enterprises. Beirut's nightlife provided the backdrop for deals struck among the warlords and financiers – usually during endless cocktail parties, which filled the social pages of the morning papers. In some instances, rational considerations of loss and profit were not a major factor for an investor to start a bank. The prestige that came with the ownership of a bank was equally valuable in a country where status and position were very important. Status and position were then used to build connections, and these connections opened the door to lucrative deals. Bank ownership guaranteed membership of the Lebanese Bankers' Association and led to contacts with influential people in the warlord business community. The bankers would use these connections and, with patience, careful manoeuvering, the necessary signatures and backing, big money would be their reward. Although the price tag of starting a bank was prohibitive, many people managed to find enough capital to start up shop.

Among the new bank owners were Lebanese émigrés who had made their fortunes abroad and returned to Lebanon to open their own business. These returnees were quickly picked up by the local media as potential new members of the Beirut upper class. Although wealthy, many of the émigrés were illiterate farmers who had left Lebanon 20 years earlier to toil in the Amazon or the jungles of West Africa. Back in Lebanon, they figured prominently in the social pages. In the early 1970s, radio stations broadcast live programmes from the airport, interviewing the returning Lebanese and playing favourite Lebanese songs.

The banking sector also worked as an important bridge for financiers who want to get involved in politics. As early as the 1960s, at least 25 per cent of Lebanon's politicians had had a head start in banking. The architect of the constitution and the philosopher of Lebanese nationalism, Michel Chiha, was a banker;[14] his sister was the wife of President Bechara al-Khouri and her son, Michel al-Khouri, also a banker, became the Governor of the Central Bank (1977–84 and 1991–4). Elias Sarkis, another banker, became the Chief of Staff of President Fouad Chehab (1958–64), and then the Governor of the Central Bank (1966–76). He became President of Lebanon in 1976. The Sunni Salim al-Hoss, another banker, was chairman of the government's Banking Control Commission between 1967 and 1976, four times prime minister of Lebanon (between 1976 and 2000) and always a prime minister in-waiting like all the Sunni *zaim*s of the coastal cities. Farid Roufael, the founder of the Banque Libano-Française, was Minister of

Finance with Sarkis in 1976. Several warlords and *zaims* who had either retired, left the government or lost their seats in parliament found a place in banking and were hired to sit on boards of directors, as bank owners figured that they would benefit from the connections and family background of such individuals. Najib Salha and Rafic Naja[15] were two examples.

Since independence, and through extending loans and grants and financing election campaigns, banks have built a network of connections with the warlord and *zaim* families. The latter returned the favour in kind. In the 1957 elections, the press reported that large sums of money were spent by candidates to buy votes. In Zahlé (in the Bekaa), candidates spent two million liras (US$600,000) to buy votes.[16] In the 1968 and 1972 parliamentary elections, the proportion of spending on campaigns per candidate was one of the highest in the world – almost twice the amount spent in the American Congressional elections.[17]

Such was the atmosphere in the financier-warlord-*zaim* world when the Intrabank crisis hit in 1966.

Notes

1 Called *al-Assi* (the Rebel) in Arabic, because it flows upstream towards northern Syria.
2 This changed in the 1990s as protective measures were introduced.
3 In the Statistical Appendix, Table 7 shows the sectoral structure in manufacturing between 1918 and 1964, while Table 8 shows factor intensity and value added in each sector.
4 Nadim Khalaf, *Economic Implications of the Size of Nations with Special Reference to Lebanon*, London, E. J. Brill, 1971, pp. 1–25.
5 Youssef Salamé, *Memoirs* (in Arabic, *Hadathani Ya Sine Qal*), Lind, Dar Neilsen, 1988, p. 76.
6 See Youssef Salamé, op. cit.; Morris West, *The Tower of Babel*, New York, William Morrow and Co., 1968; Abdul Amir Badruddin, *The Bank of Lebanon: Central Banking in a Financial Centre and a Financial Entrepôt*, London, Pinter, 1984.
7 They dropped to LL180.6 million in 1949.
8 Of the six national banks, two were French while the rest represented Italy, Britain, Iraq and Jordan.
9 The type of credit available took the form of discounts, advances on securities and overdrafts for less than a year, usually against property or endorsements.
10 The stadium was destroyed by Israeli planes in 1982 and rebuilt in 1995.
11 Decree No. 9860 of June 1962 and Decree No. 10412 of August 1962.

12 Decree No. 8004.
13 Not all banks were commercial. Four non-commercial banks were established before 1964 with the aim of extending credit for meaningful economic activity. The Société de Crédit Agricole et Industriel du Liban (SCAIL) and the Banque de Crédit Agricole, Industriel et Foncier (BCAIF) were backed by government guarantees of LL55 million, as loans from the BSL at an annual rate of 2 per cent. These two banks extended long-term credit to agriculture, manufacturing, construction and mortgages, charging interest rates of 5 per cent to 9 per cent. There were two more non-profit institutions – namely, the Société Mediterranéenne de Placement et de Gestion and the Mont de Piété Egyptien. Those were French companies involved in advances and small loans. By 1974, only BCAIF was still functioning, and its role was limited to extending credit to farmers and manufacturers who did not qualify for commercial credit. New banks for long-term credit were established in 1973, namely the Banque pour le Développement du Tourisme et de l'Industrie, which was a public–private initiative. A second bank was established in the same year as a joint venture with foreign capital.
14 See Chapter 3.
15 See Chapter 7 for more on Salha and Naja.
16 Leila Meo, *Lebanon: The Improbable Republic*, Connecticut, Greenwood Press, 1972; Meo quotes from an article by Georges Naccache in the Beirut daily, *Al-Jarida*. Naccache, a very well-known journalist of the period has coined the oft-quoted phrase: "Deux négations ne font pas une nation", a sceptical reference to the two renouncements by Christians and the Muslims of their foreign allegiances, which were not enough to forge a nation.
17 Michael Hudson, *The Precarious Republic: Political Modernisation in Lebanon*, New York, Random House, 1972.

7

Youssef Beidas and Intrabank

> I am convinced that the Intrabank affair was the beginning of the disintegration of Lebanon. The old style of Lebanese government plunged the nation into a civil war that threatened its very survival as an independent state.[1]
>
> **Najib Alamuddine**

Youssef Beidas, president and co-founder of Intrabank, was a Palestinian Christian from Jerusalem. His origins go back to the Russian immigrants who settled in Palestine in the nineteenth century.[2] His father, Khalil was a man of letters who wrote in Arabic, but was also fluent in Russian. Youssef was born in Acre in mandate Palestine in December 1912. He acquired little education and when he became successful later in life, he scorned degrees and academia. In the 1930s, he started his banking career as a clerk at Barclays Bank in Jerusalem, and then moved to work as a director of the Arab Bank Ltd in the Jerusalem branch. His outstanding performance there was recognized by his superiors and this recognition earned him several promotions. As a senior executive, he expanded the activities of the Arab Bank Ltd, and built working relationships with many important institutions and individuals. In the 1940s, his reputation as a banker spread throughout Palestine. He married the Lebanese Widad Salamé, a niece of the Lebanese parliamentarian Mounir Aboufadel.

When the Palestine war struck in 1948, 104,000 Palestinians, including Beidas, fled to Lebanon. In Beirut, he opened a small exchange office near the harbour and with other Palestinian financiers, and shortly afterwards started an import–export business that was eventually transformed into a banking project. Intrabank was established in 1951, by which time Beidas had become well-known as a banker in Lebanon and the Middle East. Over the next eighteen years, he proved to be unique. He was a workaholic who used social events to strike deals and discuss business. In his long banking career, he maintained offices and apartments in several major cities around the world. He hated intermediaries and commissions, and preferred to slice the cake himself. His foresight was astonishing and he felt the coming importance of Arab oil. At a dinner in 1963, he told David Rockefeller, chairman of the Chase Manhattan Bank: "In the near future the finance ministers and businessmen of the industrialized countries will visit Riyadh, Kuwait, Qatar and Abu Dhabi, looking for opportunities and loans."[3] Which they did.

Beidas's style was one of simplifying the most complicated issues, and his creativity in banking practices, good or bad, was unheard of in Lebanon, Europe or the USA. He invested huge sums outside the sectors traditional for banks, and his philosophy on money was a favourite topic of conversation. Like the wealthy J. Paul Getty, he said that the true value of money was in investing not in spending.

In 1960, Beidas was ready to expand to the USA, and in 1961 he went to New York and hired several individuals – one of whom was a Lebanese business graduate, Youssef Salamé, to whom he was related through his partner, the Lebanese parliamentarian Mounir Aboufadel. Beidas told Salamé that Intrabank was on its way to becoming an international player in finance, and that he was considering entering the American market through its financial gateway, New York. He said that Intrabank had good working relationships with many American banks, especially the Bank of America and Chase Manhattan. At the time, Salamé, a graduate of a US business school, was an employee of a New York-based investment house which specialized in stock and bond trading. He explained to Beidas that banking in the USA was different from in Europe and the Middle East, and that running a bank in New York required specialist technical expertise and local knowledge that was not available amongst the staff of Intrabank.

Beidas did not take any notice. He answered in his usual style: "Don't worry about those things now!" He told Salamé: "Your mission is short and simple. First, start work immediately to acquire a banking licence; this requires an application and a brief report on both the Lebanese economy and Intrabank to the Auditor of Banks of the State of New York. For that, we have the support of Chase Manhattan Bank and the Governor of the State of New York, Nelson Rockefeller, who is the brother of my friend, David, the president of Chase. Second step, buy a building on an important street in New York. When you equip the offices and hire the necessary technical and support staff of your choice, you announce to the public the date the branch will be open for business. After you have finished both tasks, delegate one of the active managers as president, then fly to Beirut to join me at headquarters."[4]

Salamé left his job with the New York firm, joined Chase Manhattan as a trainee, appointed the American lawyer William Eaton as a legal consultant and applied for a licence. In fourteen months the preparations were almost complete and Intrabank decided on a location in the heart of Manhattan. On 1 March 1963, Beidas was in Paris visiting the Intrabank branch on 12 Avenue Montaigne and Salamé was negotiating with a real estate agency headed by the New York developer William Zeckendorf over the purchase of a skyscraper at 680 Fifth Avenue for US$4 million. The building, known as Canada House, was owned by a group of Canadian financiers who built it in 1957 and wanted to sell it. They appointed Zeckendorf to negotiate the deal on their behalf.

After six hours of negotiations, interrupted by telephone calls from Beidas who was anxious to finalize the deal, the documents were ready for signature. However, Zeckendorf's representative announced that Columbia University, which had agreed to lend Zeckendorf US$3 million (75 per cent of the value of the deal), had backed off and that the deal with Intrabank could not go through. When everybody started to pack up and leave, Salamé panicked because Beidas was waiting for good news to announce to the Beirut media. Salamé discussed with his associates the possibility of Intrabank taking over the financing. He had US$1 million dollars in cash; the rest of the money could be paid through a US$3 million bond, issued and guaranteed by Intrabank and payable at year-end with interest. William Eaton, the consultant, disagreed, reasoning that as a foreign bank with no presence in the USA, Intrabank could not guarantee the bond.

Salamé disagreed with Eaton. Instead, he went ahead and made an offer that the Canadians liked. Then he called Beidas in Paris and explained Zeckendorf's inability to finance the acquisition, adding that Intrabank could replace Zeckendorf by paying 25 per cent in cash and the rest in a one-year bond. Beidas was pleased: "Issue the bond." Salamé was unsure about a number of difficulties: first, whether Beidas had the authority to make the decision without going back to the board of directors in Beirut; second, whether a new bank in New York could make such an issue; and third, that he himself did not have the legal authority to sign such a bond. Beidas's mind was sharp: "Issue the bond to the Canadians now and tell them that in half an hour they can confirm with Chase Manhattan that you are delegated to sign it on behalf of Intrabank of Beirut." With a single sentence, Beidas had solved all three problems. The documents were signed and the acquisition went through.

Soon afterwards, Beidas arrived in New York for the opening ceremony and held a cocktail party at the Waldorf Astoria. The party was attended by American and foreign executives and bankers, as well as by politicians and diplomats from Washington. The ceremony was covered extensively in the Beirut dailies, which called it "The Lebanese financial invasion of the heart of capitalism". Intrabank opened for business in New York, and its first deal was to finance exports of American wheat to Lebanon and the Middle East – a very lucrative market. Over the next few months, the property doubled in value and on a subsequent visit Beidas stood on Fifth Avenue across from the skyscraper looking at the Lebanese flag flowing above it. He addressed his aides: "It is now worth US$10.5 million dollars! How cheaply we bought it! Tomorrow our grandchildren will come here and recognize the Lebanese flag and say Beidas bought this property so cheap!"[5]

Meanwhile, Intrabank quadrupled its paid-up capital to LL20 million liras (US$7 million) from LL6.4 million, and established branches in Lebanon, Syria, Jordan, Iraq, Qatar, Sierra Leone, France, West Germany, Italy, Britain and the USA. Subsidiary banks and investment companies with different names were established in Lebanon, Switzerland, Liberia, Nigeria and Brazil. A New York-based subsidiary was engaged in exporting American cars to Lebanon and the Middle East, and was expanded to incorporate Intrabank's varied activities. By 1966, the bank was at the peak of its glory; deposits came in from people of all walks of life – the average members of the public, businessmen, foreign investors, Lebanese expatriates – and from all sectors of the economy such as tourism, real estate and manufacturing.

Due to its stability and size, Intrabank became the de facto bank of banks in Lebanon for the smaller institutions and their deposits. In 1966, there were 99 banks in Beirut totalling 133 branches. Out of these banks, fourteen were French, three American, two British, and ten of other nationalities. Intrabank was the largest bank accounting for 40 per cent of deposits (Tables 24 and 30). Intrabank's assets and reserves accounted for 56 per cent of the Lebanese banking system's total, outrunning the next competitor by a ratio of eleven to one. The eight banks after Intrabank in size jointly controlled only 15 per cent of total assets in the sector.

Fifteen years after its establishment, Intrabank became the fulcrum of Lebanese finance, influencing interest and exchange rates in Beirut and shaping Lebanese banking and the country's economic landscape. To realize a favourable spread over the interest paid on its deposits, the bank engaged in long-term investments. It owned controlling interests in the national carrier, Middle East Airlines (MEA), the Beirut Harbour Corporation, Radio Orient in Beirut (previously French-owned), the Marseilles Harbour in France, a French shipbuilding company, and had other investments in real estate, manufacturing and tourism such as Hotel Phoenicia in Beirut's chic Zeitouni district, the Lazaria Office Towers in downtown Beirut, Casino du Liban, the Storage Company and a large hotel in Logano in Switzerland plus a stretch of properties on the Champs-Elysées in Paris and a hotel on Park Lane in New York, as well as a myriad of other properties in Lebanon, France and the USA.

Despite all this growth, Intrabank had two problems. First, most of Intrabank's fixed- and long-term assets were obtained by using short-term liabilities, such as demand deposits. This was at the root of the Intrabank crisis that dealt a deadly blow to the Lebanese financial system in 1966. The second problem, paradoxical as it may sound, was Beidas himself. Despite the success of Intrabank and the dynamism of its founder, Beidas underestimated the clan politics and family ties that underlined Lebanese culture which had shaped public life for centuries. His ignorance of the local setting proved fatal when the crisis was at hand. The warlords' racist dislike of the success of a Palestinian project was showing its face. Intrabank's success was like a genie out of the lamp, and the Lebanese clans who had initially welcomed Palestinian capital could not stomach the Palestinian individual behind the capital or his skills at banking and finance. Although Beidas obtained Lebanese citizenship, perfected his Lebanese accent and built cordial relations with people in the government, he failed to understand that in Lebanon the wheeling and dealing of the ruling Lebanese families meant more than the conduct of innocent money and banking affairs in a cosmopolitan city, especially at very high levels where it started to get personal.

In the Lebanon of the 1960s, both government and business continued to have their roots in warlord traditions. The titles of emir, *beg* or *zaim* were as significant in 1966 as they had been in 1750. Public figures were still being addressed as Emir Adel Chehab, Emir Maurice Chehab (the curator of the National Museum), Emir Farouk Abillama,

Sheikh Amine Gemayel (the former president), Saeb *beg* Salam (the former prime minister) or Walid *beg* Joumblatt. This much Beidas understood. However, he felt that by befriending the Chehabists, a group of influential people who were loyal to President Fouad Chehab (1958–64), he would be immune. As we saw earlier, in the early 1960s these Chehabists (or the *Nahj* group) seemed to be ruling the country and operating in every important government office.

Although President Chehab was himself a warlord emir, he was also a true statesman who attempted to curtail the power of the warlords and create a modern state with unified social goals and aspirations. For this, Chehab was not befriended by the warlords, who saw in him a determination to curtail their authority. Chehab initiated important social reforms, including a labour code, a regional development plan, and a social security fund, and introduced legislation to establish a progressive personal income tax. His policies were frowned upon by the warlords and their business associates as "socialism in disguise", inspired by President Gamal Abdel Nasser of Egypt who had a hand in the election of Chehab. As mentioned previously, before the election of Chehab in 1958, the Maronites were always divided: between the Éddés and the al-Khouris in the 1940s, and among the Chamouns, the Gemayels, the Éddés and the Frangiés in the 1950s. However, Chehab's policies caused many warring families to join forces.

Chehab made life difficult for the traditionally powerful families in the country. A professional soldier, he relied excessively on the Deuxième Bureau (military intelligence), to rule the country. Under his regime, the Bureau had a finger everywhere, sometimes compromising democratic principles and the rule of law, a situation that the warlords cleverly pointed out in the media which damaged Chehab's reputation as an honest broker. For example, it made sure that loyal candidates would win parliamentary elections and that traditional leaders would lose. Chehab was also becoming cynical. In 1961, following a failed coup led by an army colonel who had the blessing of Chamoun, a group of prominent Beirut notables called on Chehab to congratulate him on his safety. On that morning, Chehab was having his beard shaved and did not wish to interrupt this morning ritual, so he nodded to the barber to continue the job saying: "Shave, my son; those people would have come anyway to congratulate the new ruler if the coup had succeeded!"[6]

Chehab paid little lip-service to the prominent families, instead grooming a group of Maronite and Muslim civil servants and public figures who lacked the power base enjoyed by the families. His chief of staff was the colourless Elias Sarkis (who was President of Lebanon between 1976 and 1982) and his assistant was the dull Francophile Charles Hélou (President in 1964–70). Both were outside the recognized clans: Sarkis hailed from the small mountain village of Chebanyé and had started as an employee of a railway company; Hélou was a well-connected lawyer and journalist who worked with his uncle, Michel Chiha, on the French daily *Le Jour*. The traditional leadership was biding its time in putting an end to the Chehabists' growing power.

The Palestinian Youssef Beidas felt safe with the Chehabists. He believed that money was power and applied the cool principles of finance to the incomprehensible Lebanese labyrinth. He felt that the Lebanese people would appreciate his services, and that the warlords and the financiers would forget about him in a cosmopolitan Beirut. However, the Lebanese families looked at him and his compatriots at Intrabank as Palestinian intruders, despite the efforts of Beidas and his friends to assimilate in Lebanon and despite the fact that Intrabank was not entirely Palestinian, although it had this reputation. The bank was established on 7 November 1951 by Beidas and two Lebanese businessmen, Mounir al-Khouri and Mounir Aboufadel. Aboufadel, who later became the deputy speaker of parliament, was related to Beidas through the latter's marriage to Aboufadel's niece. The government licence[7] to Intrabank to have a formal written permit to start operations was backed by ministers Abdalla al-Yafi and Philip Boulos and by President Bechara al-Khouri one year before he stepped down. The bank also enjoyed support from top *Nahj* politicians and individuals in the government and the private sector.

Beidas's main Palestinian partners at Intrabank included Badre Fahoum (Muslim), Badih Boulos, Emile Mussalem, Mounir Haddad, Fritz Marwam and Georges Eshtakalf (all Christians). Despite their Arabic language and their Levantine accents, these Palestinians were strangers in Lebanon. Their native accent was apparent in a country where "two-bit Palestinian" (*shakfet falastini*) was used as an insult following the arrival of the Palestine refugees in 1948. Even in 1975, people had fun quizzing someone suspected of being of Palestinian background by asking him to repeat the Arabic word for tomatoes (*banadoura*), as Palestinians pronounced it *"bandora"* (as in Pandora's Box). Aboufadel, a frequent visitor to Jerusalem, was sympathetic to his Palestinian partners. He spent time training and helping them assimilate in Lebanon. They eventually obtained Lebanese citizenship and some of them claimed as their birthplace one or the other of the towns in the Chouf or the Metn regions.

Beidas showed some skills in adapting to Lebanese ways. He befriended President Chehab and his entourage and was soon able to count among his personal friends Elias Sarkis (Presidential Chief of Staff), Abdalla al-Yafi (Prime Minister and Minister of Finance) and Philip Takla (Governor of the Central Bank and Foreign Minister), as well as many leaders of political parties and members of military intelligence and military personnel.

In the early 1960s, Beidas felt very confident. Encouraged by the success of Intrabank, he thought that the future was bright for the bank and ultimately for Lebanon, and that Beirut was destined to be a Singapore or a Hong Kong on the Mediterranean. He said that the suggestion by Camille Chamoun that Beirut would soon be an "international whorehouse" (*kara-khané*) that was open for business was already becoming a reality. Beidas believed that the stability of the country under Chehab meant that Chehabism would run the country forever, or at least for the next twenty years. His contacts with top government officials gave him the privilege of being informed ahead of time on economic and financial policies. In turn, the government took his opinions and suggestions into consideration.

In 1964, Chehab's mandate ended and Beidas welcomed the election of the Chehabist Charles Hélou as president. However, Beidas did not realize that Hélou was not an enthusiastic follower of Chehab and his entourage, but was closer to the Emile Éddé camp than to Bechara al-Khouri in the language of the 1930s. Under Hélou, Beidas's ties to the government suffered.

The plot against Intrabank
Initially, Hélou's presidency did not make a difference to Beidas: the Chehabists were still in power and it was business as usual. But two years into Hélou's mandate, the Chehabists began planning for the 1968 parliamentary elections and the 1970 presidential elections, and they

involved Intrabank in their calculations. To that end, in August 1966, Elias Sarkis and a group of politicians, financiers and beneficiaries of the regime asserted the necessity of the survival of Chehabism at the helm of the country after the end of Hélou's mandate in 1970. They figured that the current economic, financial and social conditions were suitable for this continuity, while the popularity of former President Chehab and his policies were additional assets in this plan. The group endorsed Elias Sarkis as the candidate for the presidential elections of 1970, while another Chehabist would be groomed for the 1976 elections (there was a long list of prominent Chehabists who were effectively "presidents in waiting").

Beidas's cooperation was essential in financing the election campaigns. The Chehabists' contact with Beidas was his closest aide, Edouard Baroudi, who brokered a meeting with President Hélou to draw up a plan. Since the new Law of Money and Credit allowed the Central Bank to extend credit to banks against certain guarantees, and since Intrabank held a large amount of stocks of important companies, Beidas was to request the Central Bank for a loan of LL100 million (US$35 million).

Beidas argued that he could not prove that Intrabank needed the money and wondered how a request for a loan by Intrabank could help the Chehabists to become re-elected. The Chehabists explained that the current Beirut inter-bank rate was 6 per cent, and the official terms of the loan to Intrabank would be fixed in the prospectus so that Intrabank would pay a fixed rate of only 3 per cent. The remaining 3 per cent and the subsequent spreads of 3 per cent would fund the election campaign. Annual interest payments of LL3 million or more would accumulate in a fund to finance the estimated LL10 million, the total cost of the campaign, and the fund would continue to grow to finance the 1976 campaign as well.

Beidas liked the idea and thought that if he went along with the plan, Intrabank would dominate Lebanese finance and politics. With successive administrations of like-minded Chehabists, what was deemed good for Intrabank would be equally good for Lebanon. Hélou, a reluctant Chehabist but a disciplined Jesuit graduate with important ties to the traditional clans, was not fully informed of the details of the plan, as the core Chehabists knew about his half-hearted leanings. The core Chehabists were everywhere in the government and were confident of their ability to run the show, but Hélou's support was crucial in obtaining the loan from the Central Bank.

The Chehabists assured Beidas that the meeting with Hélou would go well. In the meeting, Beidas would talk about the success of Intrabank and its excellent performance, then the president would casually ask why, under the circumstances, Intrabank was not investing enough money in Lebanon (a question frequently asked not only by the Lebanese opponents of Beidas but also by the Syrians who wanted Beidas to invest in their country). According to the planned script, Beidas would answer that opportunities in Lebanon were limited as almost all investments required cash payments, while Intrabank's profits were invested in long-term ventures abroad where the bank could get the necessary credit and liquidity. Then Hélou would ask what could be done to facilitate investments to bring Lebanese standards to parity with practices in Europe, and to this Beidas would answer that the Central Bank could extend credit to the banks and this was permitted by the Law of Money and Credit. When Hélou declared his readiness to help, Beidas would explain that he needed LL100 million to initiate new investments in Lebanon. The meeting would end with a promise from Hélou to look into it.

The Chehabists could not guarantee that Hélou would be positive about the request for the big loan as he was likely to say only that he would look into it. They said that if Hélou did not like the loan idea, he would not actively oppose it. It was enough for them to have Beidas discuss the loan with Hélou and for Hélou to say that he would look into it, as they could claim that it had the President's blessing and in Lebanon that would carry the weight of a recommendation from the President. For example, Hélou could mention to his brother-in-law, the deputy governor of the Central Bank, Joseph Oghourlian, the idea of a loan facility to Intrabank against proper guarantees and within existing laws.

Beidas agreed to the plan and waited for a suitable amount of time, but things moved faster than his calculations. When the meeting with Hélou was approaching, a financial crisis was already underway in Beirut, and Beidas was out of town inspecting his business interests in Paris and New York. By the time he returned and met Hélou, events were leading to a catastrophe for Intrabank.[8]

The crisis
Early in 1966, the US dollar began to appreciate noticeably in the foreign exchange markets in Europe, rising by 8 per cent in a single

day. Lebanese bankers bid against the odds and invested their available liquidity in speculative activities against the dollar. At that time, US and European bankers and financiers – notably David Rockefeller of Chase – were touring the Middle East offering attractive rates to countries already doing their banking in Beirut. Attracted to the rising dollar, foreign capital was leaving Beirut in droves for Europe and the US, further exposing Lebanese banks who began to experience a serious liquidity problem. While Beidas and his board of directors were confident that the rumours would disappear, they overestimated Intrabank's ability to overcome the crisis even when collapse was just weeks away.

Initially, Intrabank had no liquidity problem and the shortage hit other financial institutions; but the depth of the crisis was influencing the whole sector, warranting a major government response. Beidas feared that a government investigation into the crisis would expose existing banking practices and negative revelations would throw into doubt the survival of many financial institutions. He knew that he had to set his house in order; he therefore moved to tidy up Intrabank's practices and restructure its board. Beidas figured that Intrabank needed to be free of the external influence of politicians, exerted through its founders whose connections with public figures were too obvious. He discussed with Najib Alamuddine, chairman of Middle East Airlines (MEA) and a member of Intrabank's board of directors, the need for reform to strengthen Intrabank against the current financial crisis. They agreed that a consulting firm should be hired to recommend reforms, and for this, they appointed the American Paul Parker, a vice-president at the Bank of America.

Parker came to Beirut and reviewed the records. He found that Intrabank had a strong asset position but a very shabby liquidity position. In mid-September, Beidas was worried when Parker explained to him that Intrabank was in trouble as foreign and domestic banks were withdrawing their deposits almost on a daily basis. Parker feared that if the news spread to small depositors and to the public at large, it would place Intrabank in serious trouble. Beidas hurried through the reforms, and in consultation with Alamuddine, reshuffled the board of directors, appointing clean and competent people at the top. He himself resigned from the post of chairman. The parliamentarian Najib Salha was elected chairman of the new board, which confirmed the strength of Intrabank and played down the current difficulties as a temporary shortage of liquidity.

The new board quickly adopted the decision to request a loan from the Central Bank to offset the shortage in liquidity against its fixed and less-liquid assets. Beidas knew that such a plan was not workable at that time not only because of the situation but also because of Intrabank's bad relations with the Central Bank and the animosity he had developed with several leading warlords and *zaim*s. Another concern Beidas had was that public disclosure of such a request by Intrabank would have an adverse psychological impact on the market. However, he went along with the pre-arranged meeting with Hélou and talked to him about the loan. As expected, Hélou dumped the request on Joseph Oghourlian, the deputy governor of the Central Bank.

Beidas knew that Oghourlian, an Armenian Lebanese, hated him – as did many of the traditional warlords. When Beidas talked to Oghourlian in New York and told him about Intrabank's investments in Lebanon and the plans to do more, the governor's prejudices came to the fore. He said to Beidas: "Why did you invest in Lebanon? You are not Lebanese and Lebanon does not want you to control its economy."[9] In the opinion of Oghourlian (both of whose parents were Armenian), it made no difference that Beidas had Lebanese nationality and a Lebanese mother, wife and children. While there were grounds for the Central Bank to help Intrabank, and while Oghourlian knew about the strength and size of Intrabank and the impact of its collapse on Lebanon, he refused to handle the loan and threw the ball into the Sunni Muslim leadership's lap. He argued that such matters were the province of the Sunni Prime Minister and Minister of Finance, Abdalla al-Yafi. Oghourlian called al-Yafi and related to him Hélou's suggestion. Al-Yafi promised to look into it, but promptly called his important ally and mentor, the Sunni *zaim* Saeb Salam.

Salam, it seemed, had also a bad experience with Beidas. In his memoirs, Youssef Salamé asserts that Saeb Salam, an important Beirut *zaim* and several times prime minister, had applied for a loan from Intrabank in 1965 to build a mansion at Doha, south of Beirut, and that Beidas had rejected the request.[10] Other commentators support Salamé's suggestion that Beidas had not given the Lebanese families enough to "munch on". Fouad Chehab himself called these families the *fromagistes*.[11] When Beidas needed all the help he could muster, even from the Sunni leadership that had stood against the government in 1958, including Abdalla al-Yafi and Saeb Salam, he was refused any such help. With their refusal, other potential sources of support to Intrabank also disappeared. After that, the issue became a taboo and many people stayed away, afraid of the possible consequences if they helped Intrabank.

This chain of informal consultations, starting with Hélou, spread the news that Intrabank was requesting a loan. There were rumours in the financial markets that Intrabank was in trouble and was looking for a bail-out. Other rumours asserted that Intrabank was on the verge of putting up its assets for sale or collateral. In a culture that readily subscribed to conspiracy theories, the public began to believe that Intrabank was collapsing.

Beidas knew that many leading families were foes of the bank: they disliked the bank's Palestinian identity, its relations with the core Chehabists and its monstrous size and hegemony over Lebanese banking. In fact, no one could attest whether Beidas cared much about being Palestinian or Lebanese, or for that matter, whether he cared about belonging to any nationality. He cared about business and money; loyalties were good as long as they expanded business opportunities. He was a typical Levantine like any other Syrian, Lebanese or Palestinian. In his quest for profits, he collided not only with the Lebanese elite who did not view him amicably but also with mainstream Palestinians who proved to be equally hostile. Soon, Palestinian capital abandoned him; the newly established Palestine Liberation Organization (PLO) withdrew its deposits with Intrabank and opened an account with the Arab Bank Ltd;[12] and the Syrian monetary authorities made it a criminal offence for Syrians to maintain secret accounts in Beirut. Petty politics in the Levant seemed now to have replaced rational business behaviour.

To ease the crisis, Beidas ordered his associates to transfer deposits from branches abroad to Beirut and considered selling part of the assets. "Rescuers" and bargain hunters, including several American business interests, jumped at the chance of the potential bargains that would materialize if Intrabank fell.

Towards the end of September, Herbert Brunel, a former US Secretary of Justice under President Eisenhower and a well-known lawyer, contacted the New York Intrabank branch to make a presentation on behalf of Daniel Ludwig, a successful American businessman. At that time, Ludwig owned several firms including the large National Bulk Carrier (NBC). Brunel requested a meeting for Ludwig to see Beidas "concerning important matters related to the financial crisis in Lebanon", and presented a schedule of topics. Ludwig was a practical man with no time for Levantine jargon. In the meeting, he expressed his wish to buy Middle East Airlines (MEA) from Intrabank and, in return, he would help Beidas to solve the liquidity problem. As a bonus, Ludwig would work with Beidas to get an oil-drilling licence from the government of Iraq. Beidas answered that he would cooperate on all matters except on the topic of MEA; the airline was not for sale.

Two days later, Beidas was visited by the Lebanese businessman Carlos Arida. Arida started in the Levantine manner by asking about family and health, and then got to the point. He said that he had confidential reports that Intrabank's situation was not promising and, driven by altruistic motives, he was offering to purchase MEA. Beidas was curious about the offer, since he knew that Arida was the former owner of the small airline Air Liban, which had been bought by Intrabank a few years earlier and integrated into MEA. Beidas calculated that Arida's assets were tiny compared to the value of MEA. When he asked Arida how he planned to finance the offer, Arida answered that he had influential and wealthy friends who were ready to help, and that he wanted to get back into the aviation business. Beidas explained that he had already rejected an offer from Ludwig and Arida replied that he had heard about Ludwig's offer but he thought that Beidas would not reject his offer for the sake of friendship. After all, Arida added, MEA would remain in national hands. However, Beidas did reject Arida's offer and later learnt that Arida was working on behalf of the American billionaire Howard Hughes.

Other offers were made to buy the property on New York's Fifth Avenue, but Beidas was negative about selling that, too. Meanwhile, he did not sit idle. He sought help from friends and acquaintances in banks and financial institutions in Europe and the USA, but his efforts were not sufficient.

In September 1966, Intrabank had a liquidity ratio of 3.5 per cent, a criminal offence anywhere else in the world. Then came the threat of withdrawals by the big clients – the Saudis, the Kuwaitis and the Soviets. For a variety of reasons, these clients were pondering the idea of withdrawing their deposits. King Faisal of Saudi Arabia was upset with the Beirut media. Lebanese editorials attacked him daily and praised President Nasser of Egypt. At the same time, the Saudis were visited by

Swiss bankers who offered them lucrative deals. The Saudis saw Intrabank as a Lebanese bank and decided that they had no reason to maintain their cash in Beirut where their king was insulted in the Lebanese media every day. The Kuwaitis had different reasons. They were under pressure from the British to channel their deposits from Beirut to London to help the struggling British pound against the US dollar. While the Soviets were communist and had little to do with capitalist banking, as part of their regional policy and the Cold War, they maintained an active account with Intrabank that had a balance of US$6 million. The Soviets wanted to pull out of the bank for reasons related to the changing situation between their allies and foes in the Middle East.

In October, the Saudis and the Kuwaitis opened accounts with British and Swiss banks and deposited cheques against their balances with Intrabank, requesting clearance within ten days. The Soviets also withdrew their deposits. Such requests accumulated and reached LL100 million in a single day. The Central Bank was alarmed and ordered a three-day shut down of the financial market to cool off the fears of depositors. A stampede at the banks began as the public and smaller clients requested their deposits from banks that were short on cash despite their wealth. Meanwhile, Intrabank's new board of directors was assuring the public that the bank was in good health.

On 9 October 1966, panic was the dominant sentiment in Beirut as the crisis deepened and its biggest institution, Intrabank, was at the forefront. Huge crowds lined up outside the banks to withdraw deposits. Beidas, now in Paris, received several telex messages from Iskandar Ayoub, director of Intrabank's largest branch in the Bab Idriss area, with details on the volume of withdrawals. The Ras Beirut (Rue Jeanne D'Arc) branch was equally badly hit. Things were only getting worse for Intrabank. President Hélou and Prime Minister al-Yafi, along with Oghourlian of the Central Bank and many other government officials were procrastinating as Intrabank was nearing collapse by the hour.

In one telling episode, Oghourlian even tricked Intrabank into a trap that only quickened the pace of its collapse. He promised to loan the bank LL15 million (a fraction of the amount requested) on condition it agreed to use its holdings of bonds and stocks as collateral and have these securities delivered to the Central Bank in utmost secrecy. The light-hearted Najib Salha, a Beidas associate, agreed to this and shipped the securities. However, Oghourlian seized the opportunity and made a public display of Intrabank's collateral in the Central Bank's lobby. Observers started calling everywhere, sending shock waves that Intrabank had given up its assets to the Central Bank at salvage value.[13]

On Friday 14 October, with Intrabank facing total collapse, the government decided to act. Hélou called an emergency meeting at the presidential palace at Baabda to address the situation. The governor of the Central Bank, Philip Takla, was not even present: he was attending the regular meeting of the International Monetary Fund (IMF) in New York. The emergency session was attended by Prime Minister Abdallah al-Yafi (who also held the finance portfolio), several Cabinet ministers, the chairman of the Lebanese Bankers Association Pierre Éddé, Joseph Oghourlian, Elias Sarkis, Najib Alamuddine, the head of MEA, plus other influential bankers and politicians. Najib Salha, now chairman of the board of Intrabank, accompanied by Rafic Naja, joined the meetings while Paul Parker, Youssef Salamé and other senior officials from Intrabank were on hand with documents to help Salha.

During the meeting, news spread that Intrabank had become bankrupt. Many people were joining and leaving the meeting, including individuals that knew nothing about banking. The prime minister hated Beidas, referring to him as a "crook" and a "thief", but he had no quarrel with letting the bank go under. Nobody, not even the ministers present, thought for a minute to look at the documents that Parker had brought along, and which confirmed that the bank was still very strong with massive assets in Lebanon and abroad. They thought of Parker as an employee of Beidas and therefore that he carried no weight. Parker naively behaved as if this was an American-style meeting, and stuck to his book-keeping and legal framework to prove his point. Later that night, Daniel Ludwig arrived with Alphonse Arida, brother of Carlos, to discuss with the government his offer to buy MEA, even before Intrabank was declared bankrupt, which revealed much about the negative intentions of the meeting.

When the meeting was over, it was made known that the government had made no commitment to save the bank, pending an official inquiry. The preferred action was to let things take their course. Butros al-Khouri, a prominent member of the al-Khouri clan and a close friend of Beidas, was present at the meeting. When he left, he told the media that "Beidas should not come back to Lebanon since the meeting was a slaughterhouse of Intrabank, and that Intrabank was the bull that fell and the butchers were numerous".[14] Instead of discussing ways to save the banking system, many prominent individuals pointed an accusing finger at Intrabank and the atmosphere became an inquisition blaming Intrabank for the financial crisis.

On the same evening, Intrabank's board of directors realised that the government would not act to save Intrabank. They held a meeting at the bank's headquarters in Beirut and decided it was time to call it quits. Intrabank declared default on payment and bankruptcy on the evening of 14 October, and stopped payment and closed its doors on 15 October. The bank was declared bankrupt on the 16th. Due to its sheer size as holder of almost half the Lebanese banking activity and assets, its demise meant the death sentence for what should have been an important international financial market. Fearing the worst, the government closed down the financial market for three days, and the Central Bank hurried through financial support to all the banks except Intrabank.

In the autumn of 1966, instead of handling just Intrabank's problems, government experts now had a whole financial sector to revive. This sector was chaotic long before the crisis hit, as financiers used the Secrecy Law of 1956 to abuse the system. The 1966 crisis exposed the Central Bank's lack of experience and leadership in implementing the Law of Money and Credit. The commercial banks belittled the Central Bank. Indeed, they viewed it as an obstacle to their lucrative operations and created barriers to prevent it from fulfilling its supervisory role.

The government recognized the weakness of the Central Bank and was determined to give it teeth. In 1967, Philip Takla, governor of the Central Bank, resigned and Elias Sarkis replaced him. The appointment of Sarkis helped to cool the market as his reputation carried weight in banking circles. A commission of inquiry called the Banking Control Commission was established in the same year under the chairmanship of Salim al-Hoss to investigate the practices that had led to the crisis, and to audit the books and activities of several banking institutions. The Commission's review of the books made disturbing revelations. Some banks' boards of directors existed only on paper, while some annual financial statements were entirely fabricated by the directors.

In hearings before the commission, government lawyers repeated the same accusation, that many of the assets of several banks existed only on paper. One lawyer, Elias Salamé, denied the existence of any of Intrabank's assets abroad. He said that the skyscraper in New York, like all the assets abroad, "was a fabrication of the thief Beidas". When William Eaton, the lawyer of Intrabank New York, confronted him with documents showing Intrabank's ownership of the property, Salamé murmured that he knew this but that the Superintendent of Banks of the State of New York had taken over the property and the Lebanese government could not claim it. Even the hotel in Logano, Switzerland, was thought of as another of Beidas's lies. However, when Parker showed him the documents, the prosecutor agreed that the hotel existed but that its book value of US$14 million was inflated.

In some cases, the government claims were true. Records revealed that some banks had requested credit from the Central Bank to pay off loans that never existed or had asked permission to reduce their reserve requirements claiming that the size of deposits had fallen, which was not true. Bank employees drew cheques against the deposits of the banks. One such bank was al-Ahli, which extended loans amounting to tens of millions of dollars to its own managers and to members of the board.[15] Some legally established and respected institutions were, in fact, havens for looting, fraud and illegal practices. Huge sums were involved in these illegal practices. Investigations revealed that some banks were involved in pay-offs to politicians, friends and intermediaries.

At least twenty MPs were involved in these illegal activities. They were found to be using false financial records of non-existent corporations with no capital base to engage in banking and to commit various crimes under the Law of Money and Credit. Most of the big loans that the banks extended were invested in long-term projects which had almost no short-term returns, thus placing depositors' money at higher risk. Even when records and receipts of these loans were found, the government could not recall these loans on short notice.

Under the commission's recommendations, ten out of the eighty-five banks were ordered to shut and another four were ordered to end most of their activities. The Secrecy Law was lifted on four other banks, which were thoroughly investigated. When the process ended, 73 banks remained and these were assisted or bailed out. New guidelines were introduced to impose limitations on the areas of investments carried out by the banks, and the practice of mixing banking with investments in real assets was forbidden. All banks were required to register as associate financial institutions,[16] with a capital base of no less than LL3 million (increased to LL5 million in 1972).

Intrabank was taken over by the government in order to liquidate its assets and pay off depositors and other claims. A committee was established to run Intrabank and manage its assets, headed by four individuals: Bechara Francis, Chawkat al-Mounla (a retired judge), Elias Sarkis and Pierre Dagher. Their task was to appoint a new board of directors, estimate and sell the assets and hire a consulting firm to assist in these tasks. Kidder, Peabody and Co., an American financial consulting firm, was hired to recommend a course of action, and its agent in Beirut, the Lebanese Roger Tamraz, became the government's consultant on Intrabank.[17]

The board of directors of Intrabank were brought to court and accused of fraud, theft and purposeful bankruptcy. Even the honest and naive Salha was arrested and jailed under the same charges. The plan, presented by Tamraz on behalf of Kidder, Peabody and Co., recommended the creation of a new entity. Parker's plan to save Intrabank was dismissed on the grounds of conflict of interest. Parker's simple plan called for a temporary support from the government until Intrabank could recover and resume its business affairs. However, the plan proposed by Tamraz won the day. He did not go as far as selling the assets to pay off creditors. Instead, he reasoned that since Intrabank had defaulted on payments and lacked liquidity, and since it owned massive illiquid assets, the solution was to transform the assets into shares and make shareholders out of the depositors. The government asked how it would be possible to get depositors to agree to the plan. Tamraz answered that this was not necessary as the government could impose the plan by force of law. Through a decree, deposits could be transformed into shares. Kidder, Peabody and Co. received millions of dollars in consulting fees for recommendations that would not have been acceptable in a US or Canadian context, since an important institution like Intrabank would not have been left to collapse and would have been able to be rescued.

Thus, by law, many legal shareholders lost everything and a new board was appointed to represent the new shareholders. In time, small depositors had their money returned while the new administration enjoyed the surplus that remained after meeting the claims. The building that housed the branch in New York was put into receivership under the New York State Auditor of Banks and was later auctioned for US$15 million to pay depositors. After settling all the claims in the USA, the New York branch still had a surplus of US$8 million.[18] Intrabank's remaining assets were divided between a strictly banking institution, Banque al-Machrek (which was a joint enterprise between a consortium of Lebanese financiers and the Morgan Guaranty Trust of New York) and an investment firm called the Intrabank Investments Company. The Lebanese government owned 45 per cent of the new entity, while 25 per cent was owned by Kuwait and 10 per cent by Qatar.

After 1966, the Central Bank grew successively stronger, aided by the Control Commission that exerted immediate supervision over financial institutions. The Central Bank was named as the body responsible for the Commission's functions, setting up its budget and periodically reviewing its work. The Commission helped to regulate the financial market and consolidate the Central Bank's control over credit expansion and note issue. Following a recommendation from the Commission, the government imposed a freeze on the right of establishment of new banks by nationals for the next ten years. A report by the Sunni banker (and later, prime minister) Salim al-Hoss showed that the number of banks where the majority of shares were owned by nationals had dropped from 60 per cent in October 1966 to only 45 per cent in 1968. Between 1968 and 1974, the number of foreign, especially American, banks increased and exerted greater influence over the banking sector.

The big banks in Beirut were now American: the Bank of America, Chase Manhattan and Citibank. The influence of foreign banks was strong, and media rumours suggested that some American and European banks were behind the Intrabank crisis. A notable Lebanese economist, Hisham Bsatt, bitter over the financial crisis, wrote a paper in which he accused the USA of staging the crisis in order to control Beirut's financial market and service the entire Middle East. Foreign banks were even the target of attacks by extremist groups in Beirut.

With Beidas and his friends out of the way, the control of Intrabank fell into Lebanese hands and was also subject to important Kuwaiti and Qatari interests. As for Beidas himself, the crisis shortened his life. In the days leading to Intrabank's collapse, he was monitoring the situation from New York. He was advised by Parker and Salamé to return to Beirut to face his accusers, but emissaries of a leading Lebanese warlord threatened to kill him and his family if he ever set foot in Lebanon again.[19] In his memoirs, Beidas revealed the name of this warlord and the names of many other Lebanese politicians who had been involved in dirty business against Intrabank and against the Lebanese economy. However, these memoirs never saw the light and remained confidential.[20] As for his personal wealth, his aides in New York suggested that he withdraw US$2 million from the New York branch, a small amount out of massive total. They warned he would become a poor man if his empire collapsed. However, he rejected the offer and was satisfied with whatever amount he had in his name. He did not become a poor man when Intrabank collapsed and, sufficiently wealthy, he moved from one country to another and eventually settled in Lucerne, Switzerland, where he died on 28 November 1968 at fifty-six years of age.

Iskandar Ayoub, one of Beidas's aides, was hired by other financial institutions, then became a journalist for *al-Hawadeth* weekly until he died in June 1991. Daniel Ludwig pursued new adventures elsewhere. In 1982, at eighty-five years old, Ludwig bought a large chunk of territory in northern Brazil to develop a pulp industry. He shipped huge pulp mills from Japan for that purpose. When he gave up on the project, the *New York Times* called it "the largest and most costly entrepreneurial effort ever made by one man".[21] However, he remained one of the world's richest men. In October 1991, *Forbes* magazine estimated his fortune at US$1.2 billion. He died in Manhattan on 27 August 1992.

Despite the disappearance from the scene of many of the main figures of the Intrabank saga, the Intrabank empire survived and lived to the day when it was rocked by a bigger crisis. After transferring ownership to the big depositors, Intrabank remained the largest finance company in Lebanon for the next twenty-five years. In the 1980s, the champion of the second crisis that rocked Intrabank was Roger Tamraz, the Kidder Peabody consultant who helped restructure the bank in 1966. In the years after the crisis, Roger Tamraz became a financial superstar in the Middle East, and in 1983 he became the chairperson of the Board of Intrabank.

The 1966 financial crisis in Lebanon led to greater government intervention in the financial system. The Central Bank's newly won ability to enforce laws was curtailed over the years by the usual web of personal connections. Some Lebanese bankers who had the support of the warlords and the *zaims* were able to ward off any legislation or policies they deemed too interventionist. No matter how much effort was made to beautify the garden of Lebanon by modernizing the economy and building a state of law and order, it seemed that the ancient weeds always returned to choke the budding roses; the immediate interests of the warlords and merchants took precedence over the prosperity of future generations.

Notes

1. Nagib Alamuddine, *The Flying Sheik: Story of Middle East Airlines*, London, Quartet Books, 1987, p. 140.
2. Many Russians settled in the Levant following the 1917 Revolution. A restaurant situated on Hamra Street in Beirut had a Russian barman who had been an Admiral in the Russian Navy and there was a furniture firm, "Meubles François et Nicolas", behind the Cappuccin Church on the same street, run by the sons of Russian immigrants. However, by the 1960s most Russian immigrants were integrated in the society and were able to speak Arabic.
3. Salamé, *Memoirs*, p. 67.
4. Salamé, *Memoirs*, p. 72.
5. Quoted in Salamé. Beidas would have never guessed that those Lebanese children would not be able to do that in the end. When the banking crisis struck in Beirut, the New York Auditor of Banks took over the New York branch, including the building and the liquid assets.
6. Fouad Awad, *The Road to Power* (in Arabic, *Al-Tariq ila al-Sulta*), Beirut, np, 1976, p. 213.
7. Decree No. 6647, 1951, to license Intrabank.
8. Najib Alamuddine, head of Middle East Airlines and a close associate of Beidas, provides a different version to the story told by Salamé about Beidas's encounter with President Hélou. In his memoirs *The Flying Sheik*, Alamuddine, who met both Hélou and Beidas in early October 1966, reveals that each side contradicted the other's account of what had gone on between them. When Alamuddine met Hélou, the President told him "I have been requested by Beidas to ask the Central Bank to help Intrabank because it is in real trouble" (*The Flying Sheik*, p. 135). The same night, Alamuddine called Beidas in New York to confront him with Hélou's disturbing revelation about the request for assistance. "Beidas swore to me on the lives of his children that this was not the case, and that it was Hélou who asked him to increase Intrabank's investment in Lebanon, and that the government would help him. The President had then mentioned a possible figure of LL150 million – [and said] 'go see Joseph Oghourlian'" (pp. 136–7). In the next 35 pages, Alamuddine exonerates Beidas from any wrongdoing and makes clear that he believed his account rather than the President's.
9. Alamuddine, p. 136.
10. Salamé, *Memoirs*.
11. *Les fromagistes* in Lebanese folklore are a group of greedy cheese-eaters who had the task of inspecting and weighing a piece of cheese while they sat around a table. But no one would pass the cheese to the next person before taking a sizeable bite. So the cheese got smaller as it moved around the table till it ended up only a small morsel that the last person on the table finished off. The story is told about

politicians or business people who would not participate in a project unless they got a certain percentage of the budgeted amount. This kind of corruption exists also in the Persian Gulf states where people receive commission on business transactions in return for approvals. They were called, for example, Mr 4 or Mr 5 per cent (in reference to the percentage required to let the deal go ahead).
12　This bank became the largest in Lebanon in 1981.
13　Alamuddine, p. 146.
14　Salamé, *Memoirs*, p. 97.
15　Salamé.
16　Société Agregée Libanaise (SAL).
17　Tamraz worked briefly with Hani Salam, brother of Saeb, and would play a major role in Lebanese finance in the 1980s.
18　The property in New York was worth US$100 million in 1987.
19　Alamuddine, p. 139.
20　Ibid.
21　Jerry and Lerry Shields, *The Invisible Billionaire: Daniel Ludwig*, New York, Houghton Mifflin Co., 1986, p. 234.

8

The Golden Years

Between 1966 and 1974, Lebanon continued on the path of growth and Beirut reached its zenith, achieving unprecedented levels of progress and prosperity. The global oil crisis and the subsequent quadrupling of oil prices were translated into an influx of huge amounts of money into Lebanon. Oil money placed a big demand on Lebanon's service industries and inflated real estate prices. Skyscrapers began to spring up everywhere and a stretch of real estate on Hamra Street became more expensive than similar property on the Champs-Elysées in Paris. The rush of Arab and European tourists to Lebanon's scenic resorts meant greater wealth and prosperity was coming into Lebanon and strengthened its national currency, the lira. In the early 1970s, the US dollar was declining in Beirut, hitting a low of LL2.61 in 1973, LL2.33 in 1974 and LL2.20 at the beginning of 1975.[1] The stability and strength of the lira led to its acceptance as a form of international payment and the inauguration of Beirut as an important international financial centre.

As a child between 1968 and 1974, I accompanied my father to his office on Allenby Street in old Beirut. I used to take the opportunity to go on a private tour of the downtown maze. I wandered in the alleyways filled with shoppers and business people, or in the wide boulevards where banks, retail establishments and plazas rose in magnficence and shone in the Mediterranean sun. Wealth was in the air and the sidewalks seemed paved with gold. Touring the old souks where churches and mosques hugged each other in an atmosphere of prayer and sacredness, and walking into open areas where office towers dominated the skyline, I had mixed feelings about time and space. Such was the mystique and prosperity of Beirut.

However, the prosperity was concentrated in a few hands and this prevented a meaningful economic development of Lebanon. A study by two Lebanese economists on the concentration of economic power revealed a high level in Lebanon in the early 1970s.[2] A review of the family background of Lebanese business showed that 438 families controlled the boards of directors of the 207 largest Lebanese companies. (Family was defined as immediate blood relations.) Thirteen families (3 per cent of the total) controlled 50 per cent of all companies. These families also had 47 per cent of all capital investment in Lebanon, 30 per cent of all capital investment of banks and finance companies, 24 per cent of all service companies, 29 per cent of transport companies and 14 per cent of all real estate companies. At least five families had links to foreign capital.

The thirteen big family names listed in this study were: al-Khouri (i.e. Butros al-Khouri and Sheikh Fouad al-Khouri), Arida and Ghandour in Tripoli, Sehnaoui, Jabre, Kettané, Sinno and Jabbour, Assaf (i.e. Tawfic Assaf), Essaili, Salha, Doumit and Jallad. Of the thirteen families, eight were Christian and five Muslim (two Sunni, two Druze and one mixed).[3] This study exemplified the concentration of political and economic power in Christian hands on the eve of the war in 1975.

In those years, nobody would have believed that something could shake Beirut, let alone lead to its collapse. Even when Lebanon was on its way to civil war in 1975, domestic and foreign observers failed to realize that the isolated sparks of violence were more than a passing cloud like the events in 1969 and 1973. People believed that the violence would not last very long; it was as if the war had caught the country by surprise after an expensive and rowdy party. However, this was not the case. Lebanon had been warned often enough that the accumulation of a host of problems would soon lead to a social explosion that might bring about its end. Despite this, it seemed the best solution in Lebanon to any problem was to let things take their course and not do anything.

Very proud of the economic system of *laissez faire sauvage*, the banking secrecy law and Napoleon's dogma, *l'argent fait tout*, the Lebanese establishment wanted things to run on their own. The way to do that was simply to benefit from Beirut's harbour and the talents of the population, and to serve whoever was prepared to pay. An immediate result of this mentality was the dominance of a single sector – services – at the expense of farming and manufacturing. Indirectly this led to a chronic merchandise trade deficit, which was always balanced by current account items such as transfers and remittances and trade in illegal drugs (or what some ingenious Lebanese economists called the "trade in invisible items"). Income maldistribution was also a serious problem, and several reports and recommendations warned against the consequences of social inequalities.

The wealthy classes paid very little in taxes, and nepotism and corruption were rampant in the public sector as each warlord had people under his control in various departments. Indeed, sharp imbalances were evident when comparing the level of social and economic development of city and country, between Beirut and the rest of Lebanon, and between Mount Lebanon and the periphery.

Although some Lebanese economists wished to see the country transformed into a Singapore or a Hong Kong of the Middle East, lacking raw materials and a manufacturing base Lebanon was destined to have a service-orientated economy. The growth of the service industries and the prosperity they brought convinced the government and the private sector that specializing in services was the right path to take. These services, including banking and tourism, represented almost 68.5 per cent of GDP in 1974, and banking and tourism were the largest industries of the Lebanese economy, representing 30 per cent of GDP in the same year. The non-service sectors played a minor role in the economy. The share of farming in GDP deteriorated rapidly in the late 1960s and early 1970s, accounting for a mere 9 per cent in 1974 against 16 per cent in 1957. Manufacturing fared better and accounted for 23 per cent of GDP in 1974, against 15 per cent in 1957, but its growth was stagnant.

Together, farming and manufacturing contributed around 30 per cent of GDP in 1974, but engaged 40 per cent of the labour force. Manufacturing[4] contributed LL1.85 billion in 1974 and employed 120,000 workers against 96,000 workers in 1970. In contrast, agricultural products (mostly fruit) were valued at LL745 million in 1974, and had employed 130,000 workers. Farming suffered from a lack of investment and from urban expansion. By the early 1970s, ugly concrete buildings had sprung up in the most picturesque and fertile areas of the Lebanese countryside. The government contributed small grants to farming (LL25 million in 1961–5, and LL123 million in 1965–9), but overall, investment in agriculture remained low. Land reclamation projects whose purpose was to expand cultivated land worked against farming. Reclamation increased land value several fold and the land ended up in the hands of speculators who purchased the plots at low prices and then sold them in the booming real estate market. Landowners viewed investment in agriculture as a non-starter; it was more profitable to zone the plots for speculation or build luxury apartment blocks on them than to start farming activities.

Although the annual growth rate of investment in manufacturing was 15 per cent in the 1960s, this dropped to an average of 8 per cent in 1970–4. Few attempts were made to help this sector. A 1971 government decree increased the tariffs on imports of luxury items. However, lobbying by business people protesting the increase, and abuse by those who circumvented the decree through numerous inventive ways, led to very limited success for the government's attempts to help manufacturing. Some business people used illegal means to flout the regulations. For example, some imported luxury items were placed in boxes labelled as products that required no tariff payment. Customs officers found boxes full of Du Pont gold lighters and fancy golden pens marked as canned tuna. Yielding to pressure from traders and lacking the enforcement power, the government dropped the plan.

The stock market
While the service sector was the main occupation of the Lebanese, its growth was chaotic and misguided. In the financial industry, for example, aside from banking, other financial activities such as investing and trading in stocks and bonds were negligible in importance. The Beirut Stock Exchange was tiny, with few participating firms. In 1973, the Bourse listed some thirty-two manufacturing firms, nine real estate firms, seven power plants and two miscellaneous firms. A Beirut Chamber of Commerce report explained that the reason behind the weakness of the stock market was the family-orientated nature of Lebanese business, which prevented the establishment of incorporated firms or the issuing of shares. There was no social capital to permit a national trust among business people to start up big ventures. Maintaining family control was important. Firms preferred financing through bank loans rather than through commercial paper or stock issue. In 1973, out of 675 sizeable establishments in Lebanon, only 44 (or 6.5 per cent of) manufacturing firms were shareholding companies.

An immediate factor in the stagnation of the stock market was the legal requirement that trading information (amounts, parties and prices) be made public. While this is the practice in other countries, it worked less successfully in Lebanon. The Lebanese Bankers Association (LBA), for example, viewed this requirement from the angle of the Banking Secrecy Law, which stipulates that the investor's identity should be protected.

Despite the potential problems of extending investor anonymity to stock trading, the exchange authorities were ready to adjust the rules to accommodate potential firms, hoping that this might attract banks and other establishments into the Bourse.

The Bourse was at odds with foreign dealers who used Beirut as regional headquarters to sell foreign stocks and siphon off the payments to foreign exchanges. Investment in foreign stocks by Lebanese citizens deprived the Beirut market of an important pool of funds for local businesses.

The Beirut Bourse also suffered from a lack of information on the traded shares. Aside from information on stocks in the financial sector, investors knew little about price developments or the strength of participating firms, and investment safeguards were lacking. There were no government decrees setting out administrative guidelines or standards to encourage investment in securities, nor was there a securities commission. The size of the market for private issues was not well known and the public viewed the exchange more or less as a bazaar where everything was permissible. The modern stock exchange that attracts investments and channels savings into meaningful economic activities was simply not there. Quick profits and cut-throat competition were the order of the day. The use of insider information was not a crime, and fierce battles among investors led to speculative trading and meant prices were constantly swinging.

In this casino-like environment, prices meant little, trading was sporadic and the volume was volatile: it dropped 57 per cent in 1969 against 1968, but rose 404 per cent in 1970, 36 per cent in 1971 and 199 per cent in 1972. In 1973, the volume of trading reached 353,000 shares of 27 establishments (worth LL51.6 million). This was in fact a drop from the previous year as the political situation had deteriorated which led to frequent shutdowns of the Exchange and to a 65 per cent drop in trading in the second quarter.[5] In April 1973, the Lebanese army clashed with the Palestinians, and this escalated into an open war in May and June. This conflict led to an economic blockade by Syria and to intermittent curfews in Beirut in the week of 12 May. The Bourse recovered in the fourth quarter of 1973, and compared to the previous year the volume rose 173 per cent and prices by 71 per cent.

In 1974 and early 1975, the Bourse was planning for a larger role as Lebanon had good economic prospects in an environment of rising exports, new investments and a stable currency. Ten new applicants were admitted in 1974, the largest of which were Tourisme et Téléphérique, the Lebanese White Cement Company and the French company OGIMO. Commercial paper issues of Hydro Nahr Ibrahim were also traded on the Exchange, and hydro power companies were moving towards more active share and debt issues.

When the civil war started in 1975, the Bourse closed down for extended periods. In the autumn of 1975, the building housing the Beirut Exchange, on Rue Patriarch Hoyek in the commercial district, received direct hits from the fighting and was burnt down. In 1977, the damage was repaired and business returned on a small scale, continuing in peaceful periods between 1977 and 1990. It was not until 1996 that the Bourse resumed its full operations. Between 1980 and 1995, the challenge to the Bourse was from another institution rather than from the fighting in the country. In 1980, a new entity known as the Lebanese Finance Company (SOFL: Société Foncière du Liban) was established. This company overshadowed and took over many roles of the Bourse. The October 1987 world stock market crash showed that many Lebanese had been investing in foreign stocks all along and as a result incurred massive losses.

Although the Lebanese experience with the stock market was unsuccessful, it was remarkable for the Middle East as despite the massive wealth and the volume of economic activity, there were no other stock markets in that part of the world. Family businesses and personal contacts were essential to economic activity, and it was a common belief that a stock market was simply a casino, a place for speculators and gamblers. Turkey and Kuwait set up their own stock markets but the movement in volume and prices in the Istanbul Stock Exchange and the Almanac Kuwait Exchange resembled the experience of Beirut.[6]

Apples and hashish
In the early 1970s, Lebanon experienced a boom in merchandise trade, enjoying a trade surplus with the Arab countries. However, it suffered a deficit with Europe and North America, the main sources of imports. With a small real base, Lebanon's economic prosperity was threatened. The chronic deficit in merchandise trade became a constant theme of Lebanon's balance of payments. Since the service industries relied on stability and peace, any threat to public order was essentially a threat to

two-thirds of the economy. Food security was the second important economic threat. Farm products, fruits and vegetables, were essentially cash crops destined for export, while essential food staples, such as cereals and meat, were imported. The trade deficit was usually offset by the capital account, which included mainly remittances from Lebanese expatriates.

Lebanon imported manufactured goods and farm products, usually from Europe and North America, and exported fruits and vegetables and some manufactured goods, usually to the neighbouring Arab countries. Farm products were mostly cash crops destined for the export market, while farm imports were mainly cereals, dairy products, cattle and feed. On balance, Lebanon showed a chronic deficit in farm products, mainly because of cereal imports. Farm exports accounted for 33 per cent of total exports in the 1960s, and grew at a rate of 9 per cent in 1970–4. Even in 1990, fruit continued to be the major agricultural export and cereals the major agricultural import. Lebanese citrus fruits, apples, cherries and bananas were popular in the oil-rich Arab countries. These markets dictated the composition of Lebanon's agricultural output, and almost 84 per cent of exported fruits were apples, oranges and lemons.

The Fruit Marketing Board contributed to the development of export markets for Lebanese fruit. Before 1975, the Arab market for Lebanese fruit was becoming even larger, thanks to population growth and the affluence of Saudi Arabia and the Gulf states, so ever larger amounts were being shipped to that region. In 1974, farm exports were valued at LL338 million. Lebanese apples were particularly popular. They were given as gifts by Arabs and treated as a gourmet product in Egypt (and named *tufah lubnani*). Between 1970 and 1974, competitions were held to judge the best drawings of apples as the best promotional idea.

Lebanese bottled water was also exported to the Gulf. Lebanese spring water (for example *Soha* and *Sannine*) became very popular in the Gulf where the only available water came from the desalinization plants. In the Middle East, bottled water is much more expensive than petroleum. During the war years, the business of bottled water spread so thinly that by 1990, there were 170 businesses selling it. In 1999, the Department of Health discovered that the majority of these businesses were not following health standards and that at least 40 businesses were selling tap water that was already available in households.

Manufactured exports fared well. Until 1965, only small quantities of manufactured goods were exported, varying in value between LL10 million and LL30 million annually. However, this changed in the period 1966–74, as manufactured exports accounted for 75 per cent of total exports and progressively became more prominent relative to total exports, growing to LL87 million in 1967 and to LL129 million in 1968. Rapid growth started in the early 1970s, when manufactured goods exports grew by 29 per cent annually in 1970–3, against a growth rate of 13 per cent in agricultural exports in the same period. The value of manufactured exports reached LL1.5 billion in 1974.[7] On the other hand, manufactured imports grew substantially in the same period, accounting for 30 per cent of total imports and doubling in value from LL150 million in 1959 to LL350 million in 1969 (see Tables 9 to 11 in the Statistical Appendix).

Despite a chronic merchandise trade deficit, the Lebanese external balance of payments was almost always in surplus. In 1970, the value of merchandise imports was five times greater than the value of merchandise exports, which was an improvement over 1960 when it had been at a ratio of almost ten to one. The trade deficit was very acute in the 1970s, growing from LL2 billion in 1971 to LL6 billion in 1981 (see Table 14), but Lebanon was able to balance its books from the sale of services to foreigners, remittances from expatriates and the "invisible trade" in drugs.

Remittances were the main item that levelled the balance of payments. They came mainly from Lebanese workers in the Gulf Region and West Africa. They amounted to US$200 million per month in the late 1970s, dropping to US$150 million per month in 1983 and to less than US$100 million in the late 1980s. Trade in services covered 40 per cent of the trade deficit. Long-term and short-term capital inflows both to the private sector and to government also covered a portion of the current account deficit. Foreign investors were attracted by the free movement of capital, a strong national currency and an experienced capital market. In 1971, the net inflow of capital going into the banking sector was LL471 million, six times greater than the average annual inflow in 1960–70. This doubled to LL919 million in 1972.

Another item that supported the expensive foreign shopping list of the Lebanese was the export of hashish. Grown in the Bekaa Valley, annual revenues from drug sales were estimated at billions of dollars. Growers netted US$500 million annually between 1976 and 1990, and the various militias and whoever mattered on the ground from local politicians to foreign armies shared US$2.5 billion in drug sale proceeds. This trade was so elaborate that distributors guaranteed delivery anywhere in the world. Warring militias and armies worked together when it came to the drugs business. The shipments could leave Lebanon to any destination via the illegal seaports on the Lebanese coast; through Syria, Larnaca (in Cyprus), Turkey, Israel or Egypt. There were many instances of Lebanese individuals being arrested around the world with large quantities of heroin and other drugs with a street value of millions of dollars.

The Lebanese government and public opinion strongly opposed the illegal drugs trade. In 1974, government troops raided the fields in the northern Bekaa Valley – traditionally the poorest area in the country. The army burnt hashish fields and engaged armed gunmen belonging to the Hermel and Baalbeck warlords. A programme to develop alternative agricultural products followed the raid. One government programme was to encourage farmers to plant sunflower seeds for vegetable oil production and promising to buy the crop at good prices. This was good, but then hashish was planted side by side with the sunflower seeds and growers cut the money both ways. The northern Bekaa had been neglected and abandoned by the central government since independence and remained poor until the early 1970s. However, visitors in the late 1970s noticed manifestations of wealth in the construction and development and in business expansion. Schools, hospitals and shopping centres were built everywhere.

Even before the war, it had become very difficult to curtail the illegal drugs trade in Lebanon albeit for an international effort. These efforts resumed in 1991 with little success, as the drugs business became active again in the late 1990s, when farmers in the Bekaa became disillusioned with the empty promises of serious financial assistance. In 2001, the production of drugs was again the subject of media reports in Lebanon and elsewhere. The drugs trade was a further sign of the general breakdown of law and order.

Personal income
Despite being without oil, any natural resources or a sound industrial base, the Lebanese economy fared very well before 1975 and national income was constantly growing. But in the years after independence, meaningful information on the Lebanese economy is sporadic. Between 1943 and 1962, there was no government statistics bureau to collect

economic data. The Economic Research Unit at the American University of Beirut produced data on national income for the years 1948–50 with projections to 1958, and the American Embassy in Beirut produced another series for 1954–7. In 1962, a central statistics office was established which used a simplified version of the French system of national accounts.

Starting in 1965, the bureau published frequent bulletins on national income and other economic data (see Tables 1 and 2). These data sources show that national income grew from LL3.2 billion in 1964 to LL3.5 billion in 1965. The cumulative economic growth between 1950 and 1966 was 158 per cent (or 9.8 per cent annually), and between 1966 and 1973 it was 83 per cent (or 10.4 per cent annually). The year 1972 was exceptional as national income rose LL5.9 billion. Lebanon achieved its highest level of income in 1974 at LL8.14 billion, with a rate of growth from the previous year of 11 per cent. Per capita income rose from LL1,754 (US$585) in 1971 to LL2,675 (US$1,300) in 1974. However, income distribution was skewed, and this produced sharp social problems. The rosy picture of Lebanon as an affluent country, where it was possible to swim in the Mediterranean in the morning and ski on snowy slopes in the afternoon, was an alien concept to many Lebanese with limited means. Wealth and power were so concentrated in Beirut and Mount Lebanon that before the civil war broke out in 1975, people of the annexed territories, from southern Lebanon and the Bekaa Valley and Akkar, were economically depressed and forgotten. In 1974, demonstrators from remote villages carried placards in front of Parliament House in Beirut that read: "We are part of Lebanon, Mr President."

While much of Beirut and Mount Lebanon resembled western Europe, slum areas teeming with Palestinian refugees, as well as poor Lebanese and Kurds, were common. The poor slums of Beirut, indistinguishable from the Indian city of Calcutta, existed next to modern chic neighbourhoods. At least thirteen slums ringed Beirut on all sides. These went from north to south in a semi-circle: Dbaye, Haret al-Ghawarné, Maslakh, Karantina, Nabaa, Camp Trad, Tell Zaatar, Jisr al-Basha, Bourj Brajné, Sabra, Chatila and Mar Elias. The inhabitants of these slum areas experienced the horrors of the war that started in 1975, as the militias of all stripes systematically destroyed and razed them, killing thousands of people in the process. Between 1965 and 1975, many Lebanese in fancy clothes sat in beautiful coffee shops discussing their next trip to Paris.

Jean-Paul Sartre and Federico Fellini were household names to the affluent, while thousands of slum dwellers negotiated their lives day by day. Families having as many as twelve members were crammed in one room with no sanitary facilities, electricity or running water.

Under President Chehab (1958–64), the Lebanese government focused on the imbalance in social progress and income distribution, and invited a team from the French Institut International de Recherche et de Formation Éducation du Développement (IRFED) to study the social and economic development of Lebanon. The team studied the situation from 1959 to 1962, and in 1963 IRFED presented its results in a three-volume report that became an oft-quoted classic in Lebanese circles. This report warned of the country–urban imbalance and presented disturbing figures on income distribution. It showed a sharp rift between the upper 4 per cent of the population and the lower 49 per cent. The upper 4 per cent were extremely wealthy with high incomes, and this percentage figure became a cliché in the ammunition of the opposition parties against the ruling elites and was often used in discourses against the government. Fifteen years after IRFED's report, Kamal Joumblatt, leader of the opposition, was still talking about "the gang of 4 per cent that swallows 60 per cent of the GNP."[8]

President Chehab took IRFED's recommendations seriously. He introduced legislation and established several bodies to improve the imbalance. His labour code and the social services were crucial to the survival of many Lebanese in the depression of the 1980s.

In 1966, another study was conducted by the Ministry of Planning, which showed an improvement in income levels but a worse distribution. The lower middle income group increased from 49 per cent to 57 per cent in three years. Starting in the 1960s, the poor neighbourhoods and the refugee camps provided most of the manual labour needed in agriculture and manufacturing. Excluding Palestinian and Syrian workers, Lebanon's labour force grew from 450,000 in the mid-1960s to some 650,000 in 1974. The number of Palestinian and Syrian workers grew from 150,000 to 300,000 in the same period (see Table 4, which shows the distribution of the labour force by sector for the years 1967 and 1970). Some 25 per cent of the labour force was engaged in agriculture, 15 per cent in manufacturing and 60 per cent in services.

The warlords, the financiers and the business community would have liked Lebanon to be a country in Europe or even to be an island, as their anxiety had much to do with geography. The flood of victims of the endless wars in the Middle East and the fragility of Lebanon's service sector in an exploding region were serious challenges.

In 1948, the tiny Lebanese army fought alongside the other Arab states in the Palestine war against the creation of a Jewish state in mandate Palestine. In the process, Lebanon lost seven villages and received 104,000 Palestinian refugees who had been forced to flee from their own homes. At the time, the general belief was that the refugee problem was temporary, and the Palestinians were placed in camps near the major cities – where they remained for the next fifty years. Before the Palestine war, Armenians fleeing atrocities in Turkey arrived in three stages (1915, 1925 and 1939), finding refuge in Lebanon where they became citizens. Between 1965 and 1974, with the rise of the Palestinian Resistance movement launching attacks on Israel from southern Lebanon, another refugee situation was created. This time Lebanese from the villages bordering Israel were caught in the crossfire between the Israelis and the Palestinian fedayeen.[9]

Economically, Lebanon benefited enormously from the tragedy of the Palestinians and Beirut became the only major Arab port in the Levant. Palestinian capital and valuable human resources came to Beirut. Arab consumers in the Gulf relied more than ever on Lebanese citrus fruits and other staples, and on Lebanon as an outlet for tourism, leisure and business deals. Although the 1966 financial crisis resulted in the collapse of Intrabank, in the 1970s the Palestinians came back with a larger institution, the Arab Bank Ltd, where the Palestine Liberation Organization (PLO) deposited its legendary wealth, estimated at billions of dollars.

Between 1967 and 1971, another 100,000 Palestinians fled to Lebanon after the June 1967 Arab–Israeli War and the Jordanian civil war (1969–71). By 1974, there were almost 400,000 Palestinians residing in a dozen camps around Lebanon, amid a native Lebanese population of 2 million people.

Syria, surrounding Lebanon on three-quarters of its borders, was another source of both headaches and benefits for Lebanon. Following each coup and each socialist decree in Syria, wealthy Damascenes and other Syrians were trickling into Beirut with their money and skills. By the 1970s, aside from a large resident community, almost 500,000 Syrians visited Lebanon every year for work and pleasure. Many sectors in the economy relied on Palestinian and Syrian labour, while road access to Arab markets went through Syrian territory. Apart from the Mediterranean in the west and a tiny strip of border with Israel, which had been shut down since 1948, Lebanon is entirely surrounded by Syria. The Lebanese in power knew that they had to keep the Syrians happy to survive.

Access through Syria was the lifeblood of Lebanon since the Arab market absorbed 84 per cent of Lebanese manufactured exports and 75 per cent of agricultural exports, and the harbour of Beirut was the passage for the important transit business. Almost 250,000 Lebanese workers were in the Gulf States and sending their remittances to Lebanon. Saudi Arabia alone accounted for 35–40 per cent of Lebanese exports. In the war years after 1975, the Saudis became even more important for Lebanese exports.

Most of the Arab trading partners of Lebanon – namely Syria, Jordan, Saudi Arabia, Iraq, Kuwait and the other Gulf states – are located to the east. Goods destined to these markets from Beirut were therefore obliged to take the overland routes available to Lebanon – i.e. through Syria, then through the Syrian–Jordanian border at Rumtha or the Syrian–Iraqi border at Alboukamal. The access through Syria was not entirely safe. On 8 May 1973, following clashes between the Lebanese Army and the PLO, the Syrian authorities imposed a land blockade on Lebanon to show their dismay about the Lebanese move against the Palestinian Resistance. This blockade continued for three months until August 1973, at a cost of LL50 million (US$20 million) per month to Lebanese trade with the Arab Middle East. Most of the perishable produce and poultry was either damaged and spoiled or dumped into the domestic market at give-away prices. Ships flowing with imported goods destined for the Arab countries were stranded at the harbour and Syrian guest workers who did much of the construction work in Lebanon stayed at home in Syria bringing the construction industry to a standstill.

Between 3 and 18 May, the violence in Beirut kept potential tourists away. Hotels and other establishments in the service industries experienced heavy losses. Fighting in the refugee camps between the army and the PLO overflowed, and Palestinian artillery shells fell on the airport runways forcing the airport to shut down. The Lebanese army used warplanes to fight the Palestinians, and the country was on the verge of a civil war as many Lebanese groups sympathized with the Palestinians and wanted to fight alongside them. In October 1973, Syria again took control of Lebanese airspace during the 1973 Arab–Israeli War.

This was the atmosphere in Lebanon in 1974: chaotic economic growth, social inequities and injustices, indifference to the Bekaa and the south, a sectarian division of power and endless battles between the Palestinians and the Lebanese army. Newspapers reported daily clashes between the PLO and Israel in southern Lebanon. These events were met with a resigned shrug and a "business-as-usual" attitude. Up until the eve of the civil war, and even several months into the conflict, government and business leaders behaved as if everything was all right. The cruel reality was that the situation in 1969–74 had needed only a spark to set off the powder keg.

NOTES

1. *Bulletin trimestriel de la Banque de Liban*, 1971–4.
2. Kamal Hamdane and Roger Hage, "The Financial Junta in Lebanon", *Al-Tariq*, No. 4, 1979. Cited in Hamdane, *The Lebanese Crisis*, pp. 116–17.
3. Hamdane and Hage, op. cit., p. 117.
4. Mostly construction and construction materials, foodstuffs, textiles and petroleum products.
5. Beirut Chamber of Commerce, *Lebanese and Arab Economies* (in Arabic), 1973.
6. David Lamb (correspondent of the *Los Angeles Times*), *The Arabs*, New York, Random House, 1988.
7. Distributed as follows: 23 per cent metal products, 14 per cent textiles, 9 per cent mining, 7 per cent chemical products, 7 per cent clothing, 16 per cent foodstuffs, 4 per cent paper and print, 4 per cent leather products and 16 per cent miscellaneous products.
8. Kamal Joumblatt, *Pour le Liban*, Paris, Stock, 1978.
9. For a solid account of the Palestine tragedy, see publications by Edward Said listed in the Select Bibliography.

9

The Destruction of Beirut

Although the civil war that started in 1975 was a complex event, its basic ingredients were not that different from those of the civil wars of the previous 100 years. Between 1861 and 1975, the scene had been dominated by the traditional leadership of the warlords and *zaim*s. On the eve of the war, the Maronites were still divided between north and south, and after 1952 the southern Maronites were split further between the Chehabists and Chamouns. The leading Sunnis of Beirut, Tripoli and Saida remained the houses of Salam, Karami, al-Yafi and al-Solh. Druze leadership had returned to the Joumblatts, but other leading Druze families were still influential. The Erslans, who had won the title of emir in 1711, challenged the Joumblatts' leadership and Emir Majid Erslan was a cabinet minister on several occasions. Najib Alamuddine (a descendent of the Alamuddines whose power was eradicated in 1711), had been chairman of Middle East Airlines (MEA) since its creation in 1951. The Shia leadership remained in the hands of the Hamadis in the north and the Assads in the south.

In 1970, the term of President Charles Hélou ended, and the Chehabist Elias Sarkis ran in the presidential election and lost by one vote against the warlord Sulieman Frangié. Frangié, leader of the northern Maronites, was chosen by the warlords. This development signalled a gradual decline of the Chehabist influence at least until Frangié left office in 1976. Frangié's consultants were aware of the social changes in the country and the new president appointed the Beirut *zaim* Saeb Salam as prime minister to head a Cabinet of young ministers (*hokomat al-chabab*). A purge against the Chehabist centres of power in the government and the armed forces followed, and many leading Chehabists were either fired or jailed. The Maronite commander of the Lebanese army, Jean Njaim, a leading Chehabist, mysteriously died in a helicopter crash over the coast.

By 1972, the "Youth Government"[1] had already incurred the rage of the warlords with its new ideas and modernizing policies.[2] Submitting to the pressure, Frangié fired his Cabinet and appointed a new one containing traditional faces. However, Lebanon in 1974 was a powder keg, and the appointment of a traditional cabinet was viewed by the public and the media as only buying time. With the shelving of social reforms, Lebanon was to have only two more years of peace.[3] Failing to deliver the expected reforms, Frangié had to encounter the rising opposition that was making its voice heard. Kamal Joumblatt spearheaded the opposition against the system as he had done since the early 1950s. Throughout the period between 1950 and 1974, Joumblatt had allied himself with a variety of Maronite warlords but failed to achieve the aspirations of his small Druze community. In 1969, he changed his strategy, abandoning the traditional alliances in favour of the marginal Lebanese Left and the rising Palestinian Resistance movement.

The disparate Lebanese Left, a collection of small parties led by sentimental intellectuals determined to remove warlord hegemony, joined Joumblatt and began to engulf the country. Before the 1970s, lacking in warlord and popular support, the leftists had had no say in Lebanese politics. Joumblatt's sponsorship was their greatest opportunity in fifty years and their best bet for achieving political power (and this happened after the parliamentary elections in 1992). As Minister of the Interior in 1969, Joumblatt gradually licensed the communists, the nationalists and other leftists. He even outdid the Sunnis with his close ties to the Palestinian Resistance. Thus, between 1969 and 1975, Joumblatt was single-handedly able to bring together a large and serious opposition. By 1975, the leftist coalition, with Joumblatt as its spiritual godfather and chairman, was on the offensive against the Lebanese system.

The first battle of the war, which actually started in late 1974, took a traditional twist, bidding Maronites against Druze militiamen in the mountainous village of Tarchiche. However, the war was more generally waged between the leftists and Palestinians on one side and the Christian rightists on the other. The traditional Muslim leadership (including Kamel Assad, Saeb Salam, the al-Solh family, Imam Moussa Sadr and so on) was leaning towards supporting the existing system instead of joining Joumblatt's venture.

Who were the leftists?
The Left in Lebanon was an amalgam of liberal democrats, communists, socialists, Arab and Syrian nationalists and notables who espoused social

and political change. It comprised members of the communities left out of the arrangements of 1861, 1920 and 1943. These members mainly came from the Shia, the Druze and the Greek Orthodox communities. There was also a significant number of Sunni leftists who opposed the traditional Sunni *zaim*s. They created several Arab nationalist organizations based on the popularity of Egypt's leader Gamal Abdel Nasser.[4] In the parliamentary elections in 1972, these Sunnis shocked Saeb Salam in Beirut and Rachid Karami in Tripoli. They were instrumental in defeating the traditional candidates and voted in the Christian Najah Wakim, vice-chairman of a Nasserite organization, and the Sunni socialist Abdel Majid Rafei in Tripoli.

In the same period inside the Shia community, the mention of the Shia warlords Kamel Assad, Sabri Hamadi and Kazem al-Khalil brought rage and denunciation from Shia youths.[5] Most leaders of the leftist coalition were Orthodox Christians – for example, Najah Wakim (Nasserite), Georges Hawi (communist), Abdalla Saadé (nationalist), Albert Mansour (independent nationalist) and Inaam Raad (nationalist). The remaining leftist leaders in the coalition were the Shia Mohsen Ibrahim (communist) and Assem Kansou (nationalist), the Druze Kamal Joumblatt (nationalist) and the Sunni Ibrahim Kuleilat (Nasserite).

The destruction of Lebanon
With a coalition that included the disgruntled and deprived groups in Lebanon, Joumblatt pushed for a secular system to break the Maronite-Sunni hegemony.[6] In the spring of 1975, Joumblatt tried to ban the Phalanges Party. This task was not possible as the country descended into a cycle of violence. In the civil war that followed, Lebanon and its jewel Beirut were destroyed. For a while, the leftists had thought their goal was attainable. Between March and June 1976, they controlled 80 per cent of Lebanon's territory, and their forces converged on east Beirut and Jounié, the capital city of the Maronite canton. At that time, Joumblatt was at his house in the neighbourhood of Musaitbé in west Beirut waiting for Bachir Gemayel and the Maronite warlords to visit him and agree to his list of reforms. As described later, subsequent events resulted in the defeat of the leftists and a return to the status quo.

The destruction of the commercial district

In the first eighteen months of the civil war, the destruction of the physical infrastructure of the Lebanese economy started in the business district of Beirut (*al-aswak al-tijariya*). Although the exact date of the beginning of the civil war is disputed, most people agree on 13 April 1975. Phalange gunmen in the southern Beirut suburb of Ein Rummané opened fire on a bus killing its 27 passengers, all of whom belonged to a Palestinian faction. This was the immediate spark, although many commentators place it in a context of a long battle between the Christian parties and the Palestinians dating back to 1969. It took six months following this incident for the battle lines to be drawn which separated Beirut into east and west and for the major violent confrontations to start.

Unfortunately, Beirut's commercial district, the symbol of Lebanon's dynamism, straddled the battle lines. Heavy fighting for control of the commercial district started on 18 September. Fires consumed its massive structures and shopping complexes. The Lazaria business complex, owned by Intrabank, was hard-hit by shells and fire, which required the Damascus Fire Department to control the inferno. Hotel Urabi, frequented by low-income workers, was burnt down and 37 clients roasted inside. Large-scale looting by the militias started in broad daylight. After the first few months, neither the police nor the army were prepared to intervene any longer. This allowed free reign for looting and banditry.[7]

In the commercial district, debris and fallen buildings filled the once picturesque Place des Martyres with its "talking" clock made of flowers and roses. The charred shells of the public buses littered the area and became barricades for the gunmen.

In the months between September 1975 and March 1976, movie theatres, banks, stores, the gold and jewellery marketplace and the entire city centre were burning incessantly. Although most of the modern theatres were located in the western suburb of Hamra far from the battle lines, and therefore were not hurt by the war, the downtown theatres known by people of all ages and walks of life, and a source of intimate memories – namely, the Empire, Rivoli, the Capitol, the Byblos and Le Grand Théatre – were totally destroyed.

The heart of Beirut was burning out of control and estimates of the damage ran at a cost of US$1.5 billion.[8]

The destruction of the hotel district

The hotel district on Beirut's sea front, better known as the Zeitouni neighbourhood, was the second casualty. Before the violence started, driven by profits and optimism, everybody thought that 1975 was going to be better than 1974 for tourism. Early in 1975, super-hotels with hundreds of rooms were preparing to receive guests. The massive structures of the newly built Holiday Inn, the Hilton and the Sheraton hotels figured prominently in the Beirut skyline. In September, the Phalanges Party militia was in control of the areas reaching into the heart of west Beirut, extending from the harbour district to the Zeitouni and Ain Mriessé neighbourhoods. The Phalanges also had a presence in the Kantari and the Sanayeh neighbourhoods, and casual checkpoints on Wardiyé Square and Raouché deep in west Beirut.

For some time there had been talk in the leftist–Palestinian coalition about driving the Phalanges out of Kantari and the hotel area. Starting in October 1975, the fighting spread to this area of Beirut. On the night of the 25th the leftist–Palestinian forces attacked the Kantari neighbourhood. Kantari, a residential area and home to many aristocratic Lebanese families (including the mansion of Henri Faraoun), was pillaged. Expensive chandeliers, carpets, furniture and jewellery were taken away from the houses in daylight. To cover up the looting, the militiamen burnt the place to the ground. A second wave of looting followed: windows, doors, floorings, fixtures, toilets and anything else that could fetch a price was pulled out.

The Kantari battle brought the leftist coalition to the main avenue leading from Murr Tower to the Holiday Inn. On 8 December, with Kantari under control, the coalition attacked the hotel district. The attack was concentrated a few blocks from Kantari, where the reputable and long-established Lebanese Phoenicia and St Georges hotels were located, along with several smaller hotels such as the Vendôme and the Palm Beach. The Phoenicia and the St Georges were internationally known. Books and travelogues were written about them; film directors had chosen them as a location for shooting movies; spies, diplomats and foreign correspondents frequented their bars and lobbies.[9] It took the militias one day to storm the St Georges and burn down the Phoenicia. The fighting in the area lasted for one week and ended with a truce on 15 December as the coalition forces were unable to cross a stretch of road on the seafront that was exposed to Phalange gunners.

After the fighting subsided, many hotels were unrecognizable as a result of fire, explosions and looting. In terms of destruction and looting, the destiny of this area was no better than Kantari's. A few months later, only the ruins of walls remained, the area behind which was filled with human excrement and garbage. News reports showed footage and graphic detail of the actual fight for the area. It was an understatement to call what happened to beautiful Beirut a nightmare.

After the hotel battle, a truce was established lasting three months. However, fighting continued elsewhere in the country. In March 1976, the front line in the hotel area ran from Kantari and ended at St Georges on the seafront. While roads were open between east and west Beirut, preparation for the next round of fighting was underway. Bigger weapons and equipment were brought in. On 11 March 1976, a Lebanese army officer, Brigadier Aziz al-Ahdab, staged a coup broadcast on television, to which nobody paid attention, as the country was in a pretty much lawless situation.[10] On 13 March, the second Battle for the Hotels (*harb al-fanadek*) resumed, this time with bigger weapons. The leftist–Palestinian alliance aimed to remove the Phalanges from west Beirut. The Phalanges were well-entrenched in the giant hotels, bigger than the medium-sized St Georges and Phoenicia. From their positions, the Phalanges were able to repulse the coalition attack and wage their own counter-attack with 29 tanks, which travelled from the Starco Centre to the Holiday Inn. Heavy fighting lasted for the next ten days. Dozens of militiamen on both sides were killed, and more big fires burned out of control. Eventually the attackers took over the Holiday Inn and from there house-to-house and building-to-building fighting took place. The fighting caused massive destruction to property and irreparable damage to the tourism industry. Some 40 per cent of the quality hotels in the country with a total of 2,461 rooms between them were destroyed in this battle.

For several weeks, hordes of armed men from both sides were seen leaving the area with truckloads of merchandise, furniture, clothing, jewellery and other luxury items. The Starco shopping centre, with its exclusive and unique boutiques, was looted and burnt. The grand hotels were stripped of their belongings, and later windows, doors, floors and anything of value was looted. One militia leader was nicknamed "Zuhair Ajami" for the preference of his men for Persian rugs. To the Lebanese, this episode became known as the Battle of the Thieves.

The aftermath of the battle was total destruction. Near the Murr Tower there were burnt and bullet-ridden bodies of militiamen rotting in the rain. Debris and damaged cars filled the street, and buildings were peppered with rocket fire and covered by traces of black following the fires. Down the avenue, one could see giant smoke clouds over the hotels, while tongues of fire leaped out of the windows of the Holiday Inn. Business establishments and hotels were looted and burnt down kilometre after kilometre from the St Georges down to the Place des Martyres in old Beirut.

Beirut harbour
As the war front moved deeper into the commercial district, the battle began for the control of Beirut harbour. In 1974, the harbour, the largest in the Middle East, had received 3,792 commercial ships moving 5.1 million tons of merchandise from all over the world to the Middle East, and 200,000 commuting passengers.

In March 1976, following the fall of the hotel district to the hands of the coalition forces, the Phalanges moved back to fortified positions north of the Place des Martyres. The latest front line marked the old Beirut–Damascus Road, and the fighting turned into trench warfare with fixed positions that were held for the next fifteen years. The demarcation line passed parallel to Allenby Street behind the Fattal Building and up to the Regent Hotel on Rue de l'Argentine that bordered the Place des Martyres. From the Place des Martyres the front extended from the Empire Theatre to the Achmoun Building and then continued in a straight line to the Sodico Crossing. From there, it straddled the Stade de Chayla down to the Beirut race track in the southern suburbs. This demarcation became the "green line" that effectively divided Beirut.

On 8 April, the battle for the harbour started as both sides raced to burn and loot another symbol of Beirut's prestige. The value of the looted goods was estimated at US$1 billion and the fires consumed equally as much.[11] Fires and black smoke from the cellars of the harbour could be seen from fifty kilometres away. A militiaman told a Western journalist: "We are fighting for you!" (meaning "for the West"). The fighting for the port continued for another month. On 4 May, the coalition attempted more assaults to take over the facility from the Phalanges. At that time the war underwent a dangerous development as both sides started to use long-range artillery. Soviet-made GRAD missiles were used for the first time in Lebanon on the night of 29/30 May when the port was systematically shelled with rockets.

The immediate material losses from the fighting over Beirut harbour were trivial compared to the economic cost to the country of losing its harbour. International trade between the Middle East and the rest of the world came to a halt, and private harbours owned and operated by the militias proliferated on the Lebanese coast. While much of the trade was lost forever, the private harbours and the Syrian port of Tartous, which had been modernized and expanded, picked up the slack. The fall of Beirut harbour also robbed the government of much-needed revenues.

In subsequent years, the harbour was shelled frequently by the various militias and armies; its depots were burnt down one by one. Officially, the Harbour Corporation continued to function with a fraction of its normal business under the administration of the financier Henri Faraoun and Ibrahim and Hassan Baltaji. When the harbour was operational, the corporation paid off the various groups to prevent bombing and pillaging of the facility.

The destruction of Beirut's international airport

Beirut's international airport at Khaldé, south of Beirut, also suffered. The number of travellers through the facility had climaxed at 2.3 million in 1974. In 1977, the first year of peace after the eighteen months of fighting, the number of travellers dropped to 1.5 million, but never recovered to the 1974 level, even by 2000. In the war years, the majority of travellers were departing. Before 1975, 146,000 tons of goods were shipped through the airport, but this dropped to less than half in 1977. In 1974, new air routes were being planned to North America with Kuwait Airlines, and were supposed to start in early 1975. After 1975, thousands of shells fell on the airport's terminal and runways, and forced the facility to shut down frequently for periods of up to one year.[12]

On 7 June 1976 several shells landed on the runway, and the airport closed until 19 November (the authorities tried to re-open the facility on 23 June 1976, but more shells fell on the runway and hit an MEA Boeing, killing the pilot). The terminal was abandoned and the runways became empty. Horses from the nearby Beirut race track were released by militiamen and found shelter in the terminal building. In June 1982, during the Israeli invasion, a major battle took place on the runways as the Israeli army searched for alternative routes to advance into Beirut after being stalled by fierce resistance at the strategic Khaldé crossroad south of the city. A joint Lebanese–Palestinian unit offered stiff resistance to the superior Israeli army. In this battle, the runways and the terminal were severely damaged, and tank battles were waged on the second runway.

Despite the losses and the damage to the airport and the national carrier, the years 1977–80 were still relatively better than the chaos that was to come in the following decade. With the cycle of violence growing larger in Lebanon, kidnapping of foreigners and hijacking of civilian planes became a frequent occurrence. After 1983 nobody wanted to visit Beirut; only casual visitors, journalists and Lebanese nationals, who were by then numb to the war, used the airport. Foreign dignitaries had to use the airport while frequent gunfire and shelling from the various militias hit the runways. In May 1983, as a sign of the times, the *International Herald Tribune* showed on its first page a picture depicting United States Secretary of State George Shultz's plane taking off from Beirut airport's runway with a background of gunfire and artillery smoke that could be seen in the nearby hills.

The various local militias had a great deal of influence over the airport and its operation, obtaining easy access to the terminal building and the runways. More than dozen plane hijackings were reported in 1985. The hijacking of a TWA jet in 1985 was reported live on television – evidence of the low that the country had reached. The TWA hijackers landed in Beirut and smuggled the passengers out of the airport to the nearby southern suburbs. Western audiences saw on television turbanned and bearded men, not government officials, in the control tower, negotiating with the hijackers to release the hostages. Another hijacking of a Jordanian Airlines jet to Beirut ended with the plane being blown up on the runway, while another group hijacked an MEA plane to protest at the Jordanian incident. Hijacking of planes was committed for the simplest of grievances. In another hijacking an airport employee commandeered an MEA plane going to Cyprus to protest about low wages. Things happened on the ground as well. Militiamen in Land-Rovers drove onto the runway and picked up friends arriving on incoming planes.

These events added to Lebanon's isolation. Following the TWA incident, the US government requested all foreign airlines to avoid Beirut's airport,[13] and it was not until 1998 that Washington partially lifted the ban on American travel to Lebanon.

Along with the demise of the status of Beirut's international airport, the national carrier MEA suffered a serious decline. Before the war, MEA, along with Trans-Mediterranean Airlines (TMA) accounted for much of the air transport in the Arab world and beyond. These two institutions had started as a private effort by private businessmen. MEA was established by Najib Alamuddine in 1951 and became a world-class airline in the 1970s. In 1975, it became the second-largest employer in Lebanon after the government civil service, hiring some 5,600 engineers, pilots, stewards, skilled workers, administrators and other staff. However, MEA was not amenable to the politically explosive environment. In 1969, in retaliation to a PLO attack on Israeli targets in Athens, Israeli commandos landed at the airport and attacked the MEA fleet. Thirteen MEA civil carriers were totally destroyed in the Israeli attack. During the October 1973 Arab–Israeli War, Syria imposed an air blockade on Lebanon as a precaution against Israeli air attacks via Lebanon, and the airport had to close for the period of the war. After 1975, MEA incurred heavy losses every year. A 1981 annual report calculated annual losses at US$22 million in 1975 and 1976, and US$6 million each year after 1976.

In 1975, TMA was planning to expand capacity and acquire a Boeing 747.[14] However, the orders were cancelled after the start of violence. In the air travel business, Lebanon also had the edge in catering. The Abela brothers, who owned a small catering agency, were able to transform it into an international catering institution that served hot meals to airlines in thirty airports.

Collapse of manufacturing
The cycle of violence and destruction engulfed the commercial district, the harbour and the airport; next it reached the manufacturing establishments.

In the spring of 1976, Syria decided to intervene militarily to stop the leftist–Palestinian march against the Phalanges and to support President Frangié. On 3 June, their tanks moved into position at the Khaldé crossroad south of Beirut and imposed a blockade on west Beirut. Surrounded from the east by the Phalanges, from the west by the Mediterranean Sea and Israeli gunboats and from the south by the Syrian army, west Beirut was cut off from the world.[15] For two weeks, water supplies, food, electricity and communications were all interrupted.

At the same time, the Phalanges were encircling Palestinian and Muslim areas which had become isolated islands deep inside east Beirut. Fighting intensified around the slum areas of Tell Zaatar and Nabaa in east Beirut and in the commercial district.

While long-range bombing engulfed the city, actual street fighting was taking place on several fronts. The industrial city in the eastern suburbs of Beirut was a site of violent battles as it was located next to the Palestinian camps. The Phalanges were determined to oust the Palestinians and their leftist Lebanese allies out of the largely Muslim neighbourhoods and Palestinian camps, whose territory overlapped with that of the industrial city. The battle for the Palestinian camps of Tell Zaatar, Jisr al-Basha and the Lebanese neighbourhoods of Dikuané and Nabaa in east Beirut lasted for two months. Nabaa and Dikuané fell to the Phalanges on 6 August, while the camps fell after a 62-day siege on 12 August.

A few days after the fall of Tell Zaatar, a truce was implemented to allow an Arab peacekeeping force to evacuate survivors of the camp. Beirut looked like a giant slaughterhouse. Almost 3,000 civilians had been killed in Tell Zaatar, and reports on that day talked of the evacuation of the remaining 5,000 from Tell Zaatar and almost 30,000 from other areas in east Beirut that had fallen to the Phalanges. That afternoon at the Museum Crossing, the first evacuees from the inferno of Tell Zaatar arrived. The people that emerged from the peacekeepers' trucks barely looked human: their legs were rotting from wounds and their bodies were covered with unknown skin diseases. Many other poor people followed on foot in black clothes, but with dignity on their faces, resembling the crowds along the *Via Dolorosa* where Christ marched with the cross to his crucifixion. The war would last for another fourteen years after that day.

Destruction of the tourist resorts

While battles raged in and around Beirut, a new front was started in Mount Lebanon. By the early 1970s, the mountain region was very important for the Lebanese tourist industry. In the first year of the civil war, fighting was restricted to Beirut and its environs. On 17 March

1976, skirmishes in the mountain region east and south of Beirut quickly developed into open warfare. The first round of the mountain region war was limited to the county of Upper Metn north of the Beirut–Damascus highway, more specifically in the towns of Aintoura and Tarchiche. In October 1976, the second round was enlarged to cover the tourist area of Aley, Bhamdoun and Sofar, quickening the pace of Syrian military intervention.

In October 1976, the Syrian army, already in control of the Bekaa Valley, advanced to the mountain region. The confrontation between the Syrians on one side and the Palestinians on the other took place amongst the jewels of Lebanese tourism along the strip of Aley, Bhamdoun and Sofar. Several hotels in Bhamdoun were shelled and a major stand-off between the warriors caused extensive damage to Sofar. However, the comprehensive destruction of the region took place several years later beginning with the Israeli invasion of 1982, continuing with the Druze–Maronite war in 1983–5 and the US Marine bombing in 1983. By 1984, almost 79 per cent of tourist establishments in Bhamdoun had been destroyed. This ratio was higher in Aley where almost 94 per cent of buildings were destroyed. Elsewhere in the mountain region, the extent of destroyed buildings was 87 per cent.

In Aley, hotels and restaurants that had hosted wealthy Arabs and Westerners before 1975 were in shambles. Large and brightly coloured posters dating back to the glory of 1974 announcing famous Arab singers such as Warda, Abdel Halim Hafez and Farid al-Atrash were still recognizable amid the destruction. The place looked like a ghost town, with streets full of broken glass and walls decaying and falling down.

The southern part of Aley was particularly hard hit. Between September and December 1983, in response to intimidation from the various Lebanese militias, and fooled into action by the false pretensions of some Lebanese warlords, various US warships anchored off Beirut, including the USS *New Jersey*. They opened their big guns on Aley and the neighbouring villages, and on south Beirut. The action was initiated in support of President Amine Gemayel, and to stop the advance of the Druze militia on the strategic town of Souk al-Gharb, a stronghold of a Lebanese army garrison led by General Michel Aoun. The result of the bombardment was nightmarish. The one-ton shells of the *New Jersey* were so powerful that they caused deep craters in the mountain terrain. The extent of the damage was very severe by Lebanese standards.

On the western side of Aley, Phalange militiamen in the town of Kahalé, less than a mile from Aley, blocked the main highway to Beirut. They hoped the blockade would help defend the mountain reaches to the east of Beirut. With the main highway closed, most travellers took the tortuous mountainous unsurfaced route through the rugged Chouf hills south of Aley. A trip that used to take fifteen minutes by car from Beirut to Aley via Kahalé before 1976 took upwards of ninety minutes during the war in the rugged terrain and steep roads.

The town of Bhamdoun was the second victim in the battle for the mountain region. It had several hotels and restaurants, and boasted dozens of villas and palaces built by Arab emirs – notably the rulers of Kuwait and Qatar. In 1976, the Lebanese leftist coalition and the PLO confronted the advancing Syrian army at Bhamdoun and the fight that ensued destroyed much of the town. Tourist establishments lining the main thoroughfare, such as the Hotel al-Karma, were charred by bombs and bullets, and burned for days on end. The next round of Bhamdoun's destruction came in 1983.

Following the invasion in June 1982, the Israelis wanted to block the supply routes of the Syrian brigade locked in Beirut, so they quickly advanced on the Chouf to reach the Beirut–Damascus highway. Aware of the Israeli aim, Syrian tanks at Jamhour (west of Aley) and at Ain Dara, near the Damascus–Beirut highway, confronted the Israeli advance. However, the Israelis eventually pushed forward and took over the stretch of highway between Aley and Sofar.

At the same time, the Phalanges took advantage of the Israeli presence in the mountain region and sent their militiamen to control the Chouf in order to impose their will on the Druze. This was ill-advised as the Phalanges did not heed the Maronite Patriarch Nessralla Sfeir's warning against the venture on the grounds that it would jeopardize Maronite–Druze co-existence in the Chouf. The Druze, who had stood by during the Israeli invasion, proved to be a surprising match for the Phalanges. During 1983, Maronite and Druze militiamen were engaged in a series of massacres and counter-massacres. The Israeli withdrawal from the mountain region in September 1983 quickened the pace of a large-scale confrontation. A pro-Druze army of 3,000 militiamen invaded the Aley, Bhamdoun and Sofar strip and crushed the Phalanges. This confrontation was exceptionally violent as the Phalanges offered serious resistance and were determined to hold their ground. Flattened buildings covered the area and pessimistic estimates put the number of dead Phalange combatants at 2,000 (more conservative estimates put the number of dead at 700). The important Maronite village of Deir al-Kamar continued to be blockaded by the Druze and their allies until 1985.

While the tourist area in the central mountain region paid a heavy price for straddling the strategic Beirut–Damascus highway, most of the other tourist areas further from the highway were safe. North of the highway, the Hotel Printania in Broummana, the al-Boustan in Beit Mery and other smaller hotels along with those on the coast in Jounié and Tabarja and Bouar north of Beirut were almost untouched by the war, but suffered a major drop in occupancy compared to peaceful periods.

Other more distant establishments were not as lucky. Many hotels deep inside the residential areas of east and west Beirut were exposed to frequent shelling, and many others were occupied by displaced civilians or by militia leaders. In 1976, the chic cottage paradise south of Beirut at Khaldé and Saint Simon and Ouzai became home to Muslim refugees forcefully evacuated by the Phalanges from Nabaa and the slums of Maslakh and Karantina. Most of the Palestinians who were evacuated by the Phalanges from Tell Zaatar took refuge in the equally forcefully evacuated Maronite town of Damour, south of Beirut. Damour had been assaulted by the Palestinian–leftist alliance early in 1976 and its Maronite residents fled to east Beirut where they occupied homes of the displaced Muslims and Palestinians.

The war against the tourism industry spread further north to the city of Tripoli. In 1975, the government had finished the construction and furnishing of a new government rest-house in Tripoli to help tourism in this second largest Lebanese city. However, a few days after the opening ceremony, the rest-house was looted by a local militia and transformed into a military base. A smaller rest-house north of Tripoli (the new Arida rest-house), which was opened on the same day, operated for just one day before succumbing to a similar fate.

Cost of the war

In the 1980s there was not much left to destroy on the front lines as each area in the country became a law unto itself. Regional division was rampant away from the lines of confrontation. Tourism in these areas flourished, and several modern hotels and entertainment complexes were built in the suburbs of Beirut – namely Summerland (south of Beirut), Aqua Marina and Safra (north of Beirut). These establishments relied on Lebanese clientele and foreigners who had the courage to venture into Lebanon. They needed armed guards to operate, and had independent power and water lines that would serve for several weeks if the city supplies were interrupted. Oddly, the number of travel agencies increased from 179 in 1974 to 270 in 1981, but they did mainly rely on Lebanese travellers.

As people were fleeing the country, establishments owned and operated by Lebanese sprang up outside Lebanon, such as hotels and restaurants in Paris (where the Champs-Elysées alone boasted several Lebanese restaurants), London, Montreal and in the Gulf states.

The truce that was established in 1977 quickly faded away. Attempts by President Elias Sarkis to bring national reconciliation among the different factions did not work. From February 1978, the Phalanges and their Syrian supporters were fighting against each other in east Beirut;[16] in March 1978 Israel invaded southern Lebanon and got as far as the Litani River. The Israelis invaded Lebanon again in June 1982, this time getting as far as Beirut. Although November 1976 denoted the formal end of the civil war, it was merely a milestone in the strife that lasted until 1990. However, the significance of the November 1976 milestone was that it marked the defeat of the leftist coalition and the re-emergence of the traditional warlords.

Faced with a deterioration in the situation in 1977, plans for reconstruction and development had to be shelved. Government authority was reduced, and the Lebanese police could only control the government complex in the Sanayeh neighbourhood in Beirut and the presidential palace at Baabda. Government finances also suffered as revenues disappeared: government enterprises showed little or no profit and taxes were collected by the militias. The government matched shortfalls by borrowing from the Central Bank and commercial banks. With Parliament granting the government borrowing authority, deficits were financed by debt issue. Borrowing took place largely through the issue of Treasury bills offered to financial institutions and the general public.

The magnitude of loss in the tourism sector was catastrophic. Tourism revenues dropped from LL1.5 billion in 1974 to LL700 million in 1975 and LL250 million in 1976. This improved slightly as revenues rose to LL400 million annually in the periods of relative peace between 1977 and 1990. Even with repairs and the creation of new establishments, Lebanon never won back its cherished place. The number of hotel rooms in Beirut dropped from 6,400 in 1974 to 4,000 in 1977, and the number of guests dropped from 650,000 in 1974 to an annual average of 100,000 during the war. The occupancy rate in Beirut's hotels dropped from 69.4 per cent in 1974 to 22.3 per cent in 1977. Some 71 per cent of tourism employees lost their jobs and many left the country or changed occupation. Additionally, 60 per cent of furnished apartment blocks were taken over by the militias, while the brave owners paid protection money to them. Other establishments were exploited for illegal activities such as gambling and prostitution with most of the profits going to the militias.

In the period from 1975 to 1982, the once prosperous and rich Lebanon became wretched; its economy was destroyed, its institutions shattered, the industrial and commercial districts in ruins, with the flower of its young and educated people either dead or gone abroad. The winners were the militias. They destroyed the country but also generated massive war-time revenues. Between 1975 and 1990, the value of the physical destruction of the country and the revenues generated by the militias was estimated at US$75 billion to US$100 billion.[17]

A breakdown of the cost of the damage and the revenues generated by the militias is provided in the table on page 157. For a number of years in the period 1975–90, revenues generated by the militias far exceeded the Gross National Product (GNP) of Lebanon. The economic cost of the first two years of war was estimated at US$3.2 billion.[18] These included a US$600 million loss to the public sector, US$650 million to manufacturing establishments, US$430 million to services establishments, with the remainder taken up by the other sectors (for example farming, tourism and private property).

Every conceivable act of piracy, banditry, murder, thuggery, robbery, forgery, drug dealing, kidnapping and smuggling was committed by the militias. There is a public perception in Lebanon that the militias enriched themselves at the expense of ordinary folk or from pillage. However, contrary to this perception, the amount collected from the people, whether voluntarily or by force, only represented about 1 per cent of militia revenues as can be seen in the following table.

Militia revenues and physical damage from their infighting (1975–90) (in billions of US dollars)[19]

Revenues	
Pillage	
Beirut harbour	1.5
Commercial district	2.0
Banks	1.0
Militia tax collection	0.7
Sales	
Hashish and drugs	12.5
Transfers from foreign governments	15.0
Embezzlement of banks	0.5
Other sources[20]	7.0
Total revenues	40.2
Physical damage	
Physical destruction by militia fighting	31.0
The Israeli Invasion[21] (1982)	2.0
Other Israeli invasions and attacks	1.0
Total	74.2

Over two-thirds of revenues ($27.5 billion) came from the sale of illegal drugs and transfers from foreign governments that had a hand in the war. Pillage of public and private property and embezzlement of commercial institutions brought in around 12 per cent and the rest came from miscellaneous sources (see endnote 20).

Financing the war

The machinery of war was an expensive business. Between 1973 and 1990, almost US$16 billion worth of arms and ammunition were reported to have been imported by the various militias. Each of the hundreds of millions of bullets and rockets fired in Lebanon was paid for in hard currency. As the civil war progressed, more expensive and larger guns were introduced. In 1975 all the militias had used small guns ranging from shotguns to automatic weapons (Kalashnikovs (AK47s), FALs and M16s). Later in that year, larger weapons began to be employed including shoulder-held rocket propelled grenades (RPGs in models B2, B7 and B10) and recoilless artillery (81mm, 106mm, 122mm and 130mm). In 1976, the warring militias started using Soviet GRADs, American 155mm Howitzers, 160mm artillery and armoured troop carriers and tanks. In 1978, multi-barrelled launchers were added to the war machine. By 1988, long-range 240mm artillery that could shoot targets up to seventy kilometres away was trained on residential areas. Tank-led attacks were not uncommon as the war progressed.

In 1989, with the country economically crippled, the minimum wage at US$75 a month and poverty hitting low income families hard, a partial list of ammunition prices was as follows: a single 240mm shell cost US$9,500, a 160mm shell US$1,500, the 155mm US$1,300, the 130mm US$700 and the 122mm shell US$300,[22] and a Kalashnikov bullet dropped in price from 50 US cents in 1976 to 30 US cents in 1989. Beirut became a free trade area for all kinds of weapons from East and West. Everyone knew the price of a Kalashnikov gun or a Smith and Wesson pistol. Guns were sold on the sidewalks next to smuggled cigarettes and whisky.

The militias were trigger-happy. In November 1984, a battle between the Shia *Amal* and the Druze militias cost US$27 million in explosives, rockets and equipment. According to knowledgeable observers, on New Year's Eve in 1985, the Lebanese fired US$5 million worth of bullets into the air in celebration. In 1990, the war for the domination of the Christian enclave between the Christian militia and the Lebanese army under General Michel Aoun cost US$1.5 billion in economic and military losses.

A love of weapons runs deep in the Lebanese tradition. In the period 1610–85, the people of Mount Lebanon received musket guns from Venice with which to fight the Turks,[23] and in 1840, many Lebanese acquired Smyrna guns from the British and the Turks to fight the Egyptians. These guns were hidden and later used in the 1860 civil war. Today they can still be seen in Lebanese homes as wall decorations. In the 1958 civil war many Lebanese acquired American M16 rifles, which they kept and used again in subsequent conflicts.

Who was paying for the arms at a time when the civilian economy was in ruins? Most of the money and shipments came from the Middle East as well as from eastern and western Europe. Occasionally, the same countries and arms dealers sold weapons to both sides. While the PLO and its allies received weapons from several Arab and east European states, the Phalanges were more eclectic in their choice of suppliers.[24]

The arming of the Lebanese population occurred in many stages. In the late 1960s, Chamoun's Tiger militia and several other smaller

Christian and Muslim groups had small guns and pistols left over from the 1958 crisis. Even before the war in 1975, men in their forties and fifties were likely to own British Sten guns, Egyptian Port Saids, Belgian FALs and American M16s. Chamoun's militia, which was put together in the 1958 war, continued to function in the 1960s and became an organized paramilitary group. In 1967, following a meeting of the Maronite warlords at Chamoun's palace at Saadiyat, south of Beirut, the Tigers of Chamoun marched in a military display on the main coastal highway.

Between 1969 and 1974, realizing that the Lebanese army could not be used as a tool for the Maronite leadership's purposes, Chamoun and his Tiger militia acted as guardians of Maronite interests, and the Maronite public considered Chamoun as a second patriarch. In the early 1970s, the Tigers replaced the state security in action against misbehaving Muslims and leftists, since government action would have been viewed as biased. In 1974, a strike by leftist students at the American University in Beirut ended in violence when the Tigers attacked the campus.

Even if the Tigers enjoyed prestige as a strong militia between 1958 and 1974, when the war started in 1975 it was the Phalanges Party[25] that led the Maronite camp. Lacking the prestige of Chamoun as a traditional warlord, the Phalanges relied on organization and support at the popular level. By 1969, they were already in possession of M16 rifles, Czech M58s and other small arms.[26] After several skirmishes between the PLO and the Lebanese army in 1968 and 1969, Lebanon was polarized along sectarian lines and the Maronite leadership needed a strong proxy to replace the fragile Lebanese army in the fight against the PLO. The Phalanges wanted to play that role. In order to balance the threat to the system from the PLO and the Lebanese leftist and Muslim groups, the Phalanges started arming themselves on a large scale.

When the war started in 1975, the Phalanges used the hundreds of millions of dollars that had been looted from the harbour, and the US$100 million stolen from the vaults of the British Bank of the Middle East, to purchase heavier weapons.[27] Expatriate Lebanese in the Americas, sympathetic groups and foreign governments contributed generously to the Phalanges' arms procurement. Weapons were bought from communist countries to fight the communist cause in Lebanon. A shipment of weapons arrived in September 1975 at Jounié from dollar-starved Bulgaria, which was valued at US$10 million. The deal was made with the Bulgarian state agency Texim and the weapons were delivered on a Bulgarian ship. Other weapons used by the Phalanges were simply taken from Lebanese army barracks. When the Lebanese army split early in 1976, both the Phalanges and the Lebanese leftist coalition took over the large army arsenals and acquired tanks and heavy artillery.

The PLO and its Lebanese allies received most of their weapons from eastern Europe, and the shipments arrived through sympathetic Arab states. They also bought weapons on the open market. Initially, weapons arrived to the PLO through Syria but after the split with Damascus in 1976, they were shipped through the Lebanese harbours of Sidon and Tyre. The PLO was heavily armed and it owned weapons manufacturing plants in Beirut. As the Lebanese war became a major regional conflict that attracted many players, the PLO used progressively more sophisticated weapons, including T54 and T62 tanks, SAM anti-aircraft missiles and triple launchers. It even trained pilots to fly MIGs in Yemen.

Following the victories of the leftist–Palestinian alliance in the spring of 1976, the Phalanges decided that bigger and more powerful weapons were needed. Consequently, they sent emissaries to London, Paris, Teheran (under the Shah) and Washington, as well as to conservative Arab states, and arranged for rapid purchases of arms. However, all the money raised by the Phalanges and the gifts they received from well-wishers were not enough to finance the war efforts or to match their Palestinian and Lebanese leftist foes. At this stage, Chamoun decided he was "ready to deal with the devil" so that he could stay put and defend the Christian areas. In May 1976, Israel started to make deliveries of Soviet-made weapons captured from Arab armies to the Phalanges. Shipments were received at the Aqua Marina yacht inlet near Jounié. In subsequent deliveries, several boats unloaded Russian mortars and Dushka guns, as well as Super Sherman tanks that were usually being supplied to Israel.[28] With a major stake in the Lebanese war, the Israelis armed the Phalanges with all kinds of weapons so that their common enemy, the PLO, could be stopped.

In 1976, heavier armaments, including 160mm guns, appeared on the battle fronts. Beirut was flooded with weapons from everywhere, not only for the war effort but also for sale on the secondary market. Apples and bananas were replaced with pistols and hand grenades as the commodities on street stands. Dealers came from all over the world.

The West German Günther Leinhäuser sold 300 tons of weapons in Beirut. The Lebanese–Armenian dealer Sarkis Soghanalian, who was based in New York, visited Beirut representing several US firms including Colt, and gave a press conference that was publicized by the US Embassy.[29] One of his sales orders included 3,000 prestige chrome-plated pistols. The arms dealer Hubert Julian also came to Beirut to offer his services. The PLO and the Phalanges bought German equipment and military trucks from the same West German dealer, who later mysteriously disappeared in Beirut.

The Beirut arms market was booming, and soldiers of both the Israeli and Syrian armies were frequent customers. It was reported that 4,000 guns from Israeli arsenals were sold by Israeli soldiers in the secondary Lebanese arms market.[30] The Lebanese warlords were not left out of the action. The arms business would not have existed without their seaports and the cooperation of their militias. Chamoun sent his son Danny on several missions to complete the business in arms transactions.[31]

Estimates for the cost of imported arms by the Lebanese ran into US$1 billion annually. The PLO used its huge cash deposits in Beirut, reportedly between US$8 and US$13 billion, plus the transfers from many governments, to build a strong arsenal. The Phalanges purchased or received weapons to the value of US$250 million annually. British journalist Anthony Simpson estimated the Phalanges' weapons purchases at between US$250 million and US$600 million in 1974–6, and Kamal Joumblatt quoted a figure of US$250 million for weapons bought on the open market by the Phalanges in Europe up to 1975.[32]

The leftist coalition received weapons from Fatah, the largest PLO faction, as well as from Iraq and Libya. Funds to these militias arrived regularly in Beirut banks in amounts ranging between US$15 million and US$50 million. The Iranian Embassy gathered US$100 million annually to support Hizbollah between 1985 and 1991, and upped this amount to between US$200 million and US$300 million in 1992 to finance the resistance efforts against the Israeli occupation of southern Lebanon.

Via Dolorosa – the cost in human lives
The flood of weapons of destruction and killing was not for display only. In sixteen years of war in Lebanon, the human losses were massive.

Out of a population of three million people, more than 143,000 were killed in 1975–90, 60 per cent of whom died in 1975–6 and 1982.[33] About 40,000 people died in 1975–6 alone, and 15,000 to 25,000 during the Israeli invasion in 1982. The internal wars in each canton also caused massive losses. In 1987–9, the Shia war between *Amal* and *Hizbollah* caused 2,000 deaths, while in 1990, the Maronite war between the Lebanese forces militia of Samir Geagea and the Lebanese army faction of Michel Aoun caused 1,900 deaths. A report in *Le Monde* puts the number of children under fifteen killed in the war at 40,000.[34] A UNESCO report shows that 90 per cent of the children died from falling rockets and bombing, while another 50,000 who were hit and survived were left with physical handicaps.[35] It is estimated that only 5–10 per cent of those killed belonged to the militias, while the rest were civilian bystanders.[36] The Lebanese paramilitary organizations numbered 32,000 fighters, while the Palestinian factions accounted for 12,000 fighters (see Table 34 in the Statistical Appendix).

About 500,000 people permanently left the country for safety, resulting in a critical loss of skilled labour.[37] In the first eight years of war, Lebanon lost much of its labour force, including a 30 per cent loss in the construction sector and 50 per cent in manufacturing. Increasingly in the 1980s, it became difficult for employers to find skilled workers. There were severe shortages of carpenters, mechanics, electricians, machine operators and maintenance workers. The shortages in these semi-specialist areas were also attributed to demand in the oil-rich states in the Gulf where legendary salaries and attractive bonuses were offered. As of 1990, the net drop in the population of Lebanon, counting births, was estimated between 500,000 and 800,000.

Another crime against the people of Lebanon was the kidnapping and counter-kidnapping. Between 1975 and 1990, estimates of Lebanese and Palestinian kidnap victims who never returned to their homes or who were believed to have been killed by their captors approached 10,000. This tragedy was a case study of the torture of the civilian population by the warlords.

Newspapers casually reported discoveries of dead bodies everywhere in the country: in abandoned car trunks, in forests, in destroyed buildings and in the debris of the commercial district of Beirut. Most of the time, victims were gruesomely killed with necks and fingers cut or eyes slit. In the Maronite–Druze war in 1983, skulls of civilians were hung at the entrances of villages and Canadian television reports showed militiamen playing a game of football with human skulls near the village of Kfarmatta. The population was terrified by the escalating violence and the killings and kidnapping, and civilians left Lebanon in their tens of thousands.

The barbarity and bestiality of the crimes against civilian life and property did not attract enough world attention to ease the pain of Lebanon. However, the fate of a dozen Western hostages proved more important than that of thousands of Lebanese and Palestinian hostages. Stories on these Western hostages dominated news coverage of Lebanon in the Western media for many years. Books and memoirs about their experiences in Lebanon became abundant, with long expositions about their psychological traumas. Dominant in these memoirs was the simplistic linking of hostage-taking to religion and fanaticism.

Unfortunately, these simplified explanations of the causes of the kidnapping were readily accepted by a sympathetic audience in the USA. In fact, these acts could not be detached from the general kidnapping activity in Lebanon, and from the secret deals and dirty games that had been played out on Lebanese soil since 1975. Among these factors were the Arab–Israeli conflict, the plight of the Palestinians, the social imbalances of Lebanon and the Iranian influence following the fall of the Shah. Every foreign army and local militia engaged in the destruction of Lebanon claimed to be acting in the country's best interests.

NOTES

1. The Saeb Salam cabinet was called the "Youth Government" as it was a departure from the previous practice of inviting only traditional leaders, mainly warlords, to make up the cabinet. Aside from the relatively young age of its members, the new ministers were university educated and were new to the political scene. They were dismissed by the traditional leaders as rookies and "technocrats" (a derogatory term used in Lebanon to belittle educated and promising individuals, claiming that they did not have what it took to be in politics).
2. The Minister of Finance, Elias Saba, a graduate of the American University of Beirut, proposed imposing higher import tariffs on luxury items, but this was defeated by business-warlord pressures. Saba later quit the government.
3. Sarkis had another chance at the presidency in 1976 when he was helped by Syria to get elected. Sarkis remained in power until 1982, when the Israeli army invaded Lebanon. The Israelis tried their luck in playing the Lebanese game and

the pro-Israel Bachir Gemayel, leader of the Phalanges, was elected president. Two weeks after his election, he was assassinated at his militia's headquarters.
4 There were at least half dozen Arab nationalist movements inspired by the Egyptian President Gamal Abdel Nasser. The largest Nasserite organizations were: *al-Mourabitoun* (the Independent Nasserite Movement), led by Ibrahim Kuleilat, *al-Tanzim al-Nasseri* (the Nasserite Organization) of Saida, led by Moustafa Saad, and *Itihad Qiwa al-Chaab al-Amel al-Tanzim al-Nasseri* (the Union of Working People's Forces Nasserite Organization) led by Kamal Chatila and Najah Wakim.
5 For centuries, the Shia were the least developed community and the most illiterate. Despite their long tradition of religious learning, the Shia did not receive the modern education of the twentieth century that the Maronites, for example, had. However, this started to change in the 1960s, when poor uneducated Shia began to send their children to schools and universities. Soon, many young Shia rose in the ranks of the educated and the cultured in Lebanon and joined leftist political parties, dismissing in the process their traditional warlords and seeking more equality in the Lebanese system.
6 Kamal Joumblatt, *I Speak for Lebanon*, London, Zed Books, 1983, Chapters 1–3.
7 Even establishments located in relatively peaceful areas fell victim to hooligans and looters. Crowds of civilians and militiamen attacked Spinney's shopping plaza, a large three-storey shopping centre in Beirut's West End selling food items and other commodities. People walked or drove in to carry away or fill their cars with canned food, sundries and kitchenware. One father of four filled his car with food to discover when he got home that it was all cat and pet food. His complaint to his neighbours was philosophical: he could not believe that with all the poverty going around in the country, stores would have the nerve to sell pet food. Another man's experience was no luckier. After filling his car with boxes of food and bags of cereal, he went back in for more, but somebody else took advantage and stole the car with its load. The owner of the car stood outside yelling that one could not trust leaving one's car unattended in Lebanon (Jean Makdisi, *Beirut Fragments*, New York, Persea Books, 1990).
8 Georges Corm, "Militia hegemony and the reestablishment of the State", in Deirdre Collings, editor, *Peace for Lebanon? From War to Reconstruction*, Boulder, Lynne Rienner, 1994.
9 See Said Abu-Rish, *Beirut Spy: The Story of the St Georges Hotel*, London, Bloomsbury, 1990.
10 Al-Ahdab announced his coup from a government television station. However, the following day, the media commented that he had staged a "television coup" because his control was limited to the TV station and had no military force to take over other government buildings. He went home shortly after he made the announcement, and the public never heard about the coup again.
11 Corm, op. cit., p. 3.
12 Aside from brief shut-downs in sixteen years of war, the airport was closed for lengthy periods between 1975 and 1990: five months in 1976, five months in 1978, 44 days in 1979, a month every year in 1980 and 1981, from June to October in 1982 (following the Israeli invasion), 37 days in September–October 1983, March to May in 1987 and ten months in 1989. It remained open after 1989.

13 An unnecessary punishment to the whole country, since no more hijackings took place after 1985 and security has been tightened since then.
14 TMA was established in 1965 by Munir Abu Haidar with one plane and was transformed into a world-class shipping carrier with a client base from Tokyo to London.
15 This seige was to be repeated in 1982 when the Israelis replaced the Syrians at the same crossroads.
16 Bachir Gemayel epitomized the historical Lebanese nationalist who would not stand even a hint of unity with Syria. The Maronite nationalist ideology called for an independent Lebanon, distinct and separate from Syria (see Chapter 2).
17 Corm, op. cit., and *Cahiers de l'Orient*, "Le Chantier Libanais", numbers 32–3, Paris, Centre d'Études et de Réflexion sur le Proche Orient (CERPO), IV, 1993 and I, 1994.
18 Ghassan Ayache, *Crisis of Public Finance in Lebanon 1982–1992* (in Arabic, *Azmat al-Maliyya al-Amma fi Lubnan 1982–1992*), Beirut, Dar Annahar, 1997, p. 37.
19 Corm, "Liban: hégémonie milicienne et problème du rétablissement de l'Etat" in *Maghreb-Machrek* No. 131, January–March 1997; *Cahiers de l'Orient*, Paris, CERPO, 4ième Trimestre 1990; Georges Corm in *al-Hayat* daily, 17 September 1993.
20 Trade in toxic waste, contraband dealings with foreigners, theft from foreign aid assistance, piracy, sale of government and army property, etc. A huge volume of pieces were removed from the National Museum and other historic sites throughout the country. Most of the pillaged treasures found their way to Switzerland and the USA where they fetched tens of millions of dollars.
21 Boutros Labaki and Khalil Abourjeili estimate the cost of the Israeli invasion at US$1.8 billion for Beirut, south Lebanon and the mountain region in *Bilan des Guerres du Liban 1975–1990*, Paris, L'Harmattan, 1993. This included: destruction of educational institutions, US$77 million; hospitals, US$70 million; manufacturing, US$88 million; farming, US$50 million; hydro utilities, US$72 million; Beirut airport, US$30 million; private property, US$825 million; and commercial establishments, US$465 million.
22 In *Al-Diyar*, a Beirut daily, 9 May 1989, quoted in Makdisi, *Beirut Fragments*, pp. 230–1.
23 The Arabs call Venice *Bundukiya* and a gun in Arabic was called the same thing.
24 The Phalanges purchased their weapons from a variety of countries, including communist countries and Western countries, as well as from individuals, businesses and government agencies.
25 *Al-Kataib* in Arabic.
26 Anthony Simpson, *The Arms Bazaar: From Lebanon to Lockheed*, New York, Bantam Books, 1978, p. 19.
27 *The International Herald Tribune*, 29 November 1976, quoted in Simpson.
28 Joseph Fitchett, *The Observer*, 18 July 1976, quoted in Simpson, p. 24.
29 Simpson, pp. 13–24.
30 Robert Fisk, *Pity the Nation: The Abduction of Lebanon*, Oxford, Oxford University Press, 1991.
31 Anthony Simpson provides a detailed account of the Chamoun's arms business during the Lebanese war in Simpson, op. cit., pp. 22–31. Camille Chamoun died in 1987 (*Time* magazine, 17 August 1987) and his son Danny led his father's

party and family business until he was assassinated in 1991. Danny was followed by his brother Dory Chamoun as leader of their father's *Parti national liberal*. A sympathetic account of the Chamoun family's war experience is recounted by Danny's daughter, Tracy Chamoun, in *Au nom du père*, Paris, Édition Jean-Claude Lattés, 1992.

32 Simpson; Joumblatt, *I Speak for Lebanon*.
33 Reports on 1 May 1991 (in daily newspapers from Reuters and AP) put the figure at 180,000 dead but that is debatable. Ayache estimates that in 1975–6 alone, 15,000 were killed and 13,000 wounded (*Crisis of Public Finance in Lebanon 1982–1992*, p. 37).
34 *Le Monde*, 4 April 1990.
35 UNESCO's report was presented at the International Peace Research Institute conference on Peace and Development in Lebanon, Paris, 11–13 April 1990.
36 Simpson.
37 Ayache estimates emigration at 400,000 in 1975, 300,000 in 1976 and 260,000 in 1977–82 (p. 39). However, there is a consensus in Lebanon that almost half of them returned.

10

Collapse of the National Currency

In 1982, seven years into the war, people thought that the Lebanese economic miracle would survive. Their bet was that Lebanese inventiveness and private initiative, plus a strong national currency, the lira, would keep things going. The lira was a symbol of Lebanese resilience and a reminder of Lebanon's golden years. However, after 1983, even that symbol was destroyed and with it went the dreams of quick economic recovery.

The general economic collapse, the destruction of the physical infrastructure and the flight of capital and human resources were the main reasons for the decline of the lira in the 1980s. However, the rapidity of the decline after 1983 was largely attributed to the undeterred speculation against the national currency and the weakness of the Central Bank.

When the lira started to fall in 1985, everybody rushed to participate in the gamble. Speculation in currencies was a lucrative business in Beirut in the late 1970s, and this accelerated in the 1980s. Hundreds of small shops sprang up everywhere and sidewalk exchange vendors mushroomed on every main street. The exchanges with a fixed outlet were mainly working from small kiosks,[1] not much larger than washrooms. These kiosks would have two or three employees armed with walkie-talkies, transistor radios and small pocket calculators; sometimes a Kalashnikov gun could be seen lying behind the counter just in case.

The exchangers used walkie-talkies to communicate minute-by-minute exchange rates and business transactions. Fearing outlaws who might listen in, the exchangers developed their own code of communication. For instance, during a visit to Lebanon, I asked a vendor to exchange a few hundred Canadian dollars for Lebanese liras; I was told that the exchanger did not have enough liras to pay for the dollars I was offering. The man immediately placed an order for liras by yelling *arnab* ("one rabbit") into his walkie-talkie, which meant a million liras, and ended the conversation by saying: "Send it with Rambo", which meant send it with an agreed-upon person who is known to both sides but

[167]

unknown to gangsters who listen in to trace deliveries. Newspapers casually reported robberies where bank employees making deliveries of banknotes were held up and the money they carried was stolen.

Radio stations played a prominent role in the psychological war against the lira. Keeping listeners on the edge of their seats, radio broadcasts of foreign exchange bulletins were the hottest item on the news; the dozen radio stations in Beirut competed in announcing the latest rates every fifteen minutes. The currency bulletins even preceded news on the political and security situation. Both exchangers and ordinary folk turned on their small transistors to learn the vicissitudes of the dollar. Students skipped or finished their exams early to exchange their few dollar bills in the hope of making a profit. The Beirut US dollar market was almost independent of international influences. Even when the US dollar was falling against the major currencies in Europe and the Far East, it continued to rise in Beirut.

When I visited Beirut in 1987, I found it amusing to see a new generation of exchangers on foot – dozens of men carrying piles of dollar bills going about the exchange business as if they were in a vegetable market. These men had no knowledge or experience in the business, except for small cash and a cheap pocket calculator. They travelled the sidewalks and negotiated the transactions as if they were vendors of ice-cream. I noticed that at times clients were more knowledgeable about the market than some of these walking exchangers.

Like other commodities, the price of foreign currencies was also negotiable. Before quoting a price, the exchanger would want to know if the prospective client was buying or selling, and what the amount was. The exchanger would then quote a price of, say, LL941 per dollar. Unlike in North America where foreign exchange prices are more or less fixed, bargaining is a sacred art in Beirut. People do not walk away if the price is unsatisfactory as both sides know that this is only the opening quote. Laborious negotiations follow, as the client tries to bid the price down. I could watch these transactions take place in the streets of Beirut. One customer would say: "I bought yesterday at 925 liras", or "Your neighbour offered 950 liras", or, if he was not very interested, "Is that your last word?" The client would check with several exchangers before deciding on which one to do business with. Usually, the sidewalk exchangers offered better rates than the kiosk exchangers as they had no overhead costs, commissions, salaries or rent to pay.

Collapse of the National Currency

Some sidewalk changers became owners or managers of kiosks. One such example was Karim. In one of the fancier boutiques on Hamra Street I met Abou Mahmoud who told me his story in the exchange business. Abou Mahmoud owned two shops on this fashionable street, selling clothes and fresh flowers. In his best days, sales to Westerners and affluent Lebanese made him very happy and rich. However, when things turned sour in Beirut he lay low and waited for better times. Until he was approached by Karim.

Matouk, 28 years old, was a showcase of a dynamic, street-smart, sidewalk exchanger. Although he had little in terms of formal education, he understood the basics of foreign exchange. After working the sidewalk for several months he approached Abou Mahmoud with a partnership project and convinced him to convert a store into a take-out sandwich business, "since people bought more sandwiches than flowers in these bad days". In return Karim would pay him a good percentage of the profits. Abou Mahmoud agreed and converted the place, across from the Strand Movie Theatre in the heart of Hamra Street, into a falafel parlour. Anxious for the venture to succeed, the old man tended the cash register while Karim served the hot sandwiches. In a few weeks business picked up.

Karim's ambition was beyond shawarma and falafel sandwiches. He wished to make more money and wanted to run the place by himself. He confided to Abou Mahmoud that he wanted to start an exchange business and would pay him LL75,000 a month (US$200) in rent – a sum several times higher than he was receiving from the fast food business. Abou Mahmoud could not resist the offer and allowed Matouk to go his way. In one week, the new exchange store replaced the sandwich parlour. Karim became a busy man handling large amounts of cash, boasting a telephone, a desk calculator and a walkie-talkie to communicate the latest quotations, do his bidding and give offers.

Casually, Karim would ask Abou Mahmoud whether he wanted to make some "extra money" as the dollar was expected to rise, and Abou Mahmoud would agree. On one occasion, Karim placed an order on the walkie-talkie for LL300,000 worth of dollars on Abou Mahmoud's behalf. Within three days the dollars were sold and the sceptical Abou Mahmoud received a handsome LL25,000 in profits without having committed any funds. Abou Mahmoud warmed to the idea. He wanted to be a partner with Karim in a business "that yields pure gold instead of the torturing hours selling jeans and skirts at the other store to whining customers". The exchange business flourished as more people deposited their savings with Karim on the promise that they would receive up to 50 per cent in profits in one month.

One morning, Abou Mahmoud arrived at the store to find the doors locked and many people lined up outside. Karim had fled with LL30 million liras in his pocket and left Abou Mahmoud alone to face the crowd. Abou Mahmoud, believing he understood the business, decided to continue alone hoping to recover the amount owed to depositors. Unfortunately, at that time the dollar was declining and Abou Mahmoud had no idea of the dynamics. In a matter of days he lost an additional LL5 million and had to stop before sinking deeper in debt. He returned to the flowers and clothing business.

When Abou Mahmoud finished his story with a sigh, I offered to pay for the flowers I bought from him, and I took out of a plastic bag a pile of LL250 bills amounting to LL20,000 and handed it to him. He took LL17,500 and returned the rest to me, which I promptly put back in the big bag of Lebanese currency which I exchanged for a handful of dollars.

The rise and collapse of the lira

While sidewalk and kiosk money changers were amusing to watch and kept themselves busy, it was doubtful if they had any influence on the market. The big transactions and speculations were undertaken by the Central Bank and financial institutions, as well as by wealthy individuals and organizations who dealt in large amounts. The public encounter with the fall of the lira was reflected in inflated consumer prices. The purchasing power of the lira fell a factor of 1,000 in a matter of ten years. In 1980, street vendors quoted the price of one kilo of bananas at one lira. The price shot to LL100 in 1985 and to LL1,000 in 1989. There was a time when one Lebanese lira was worth 54 French francs, but in 1991, 166 liras were required to purchase one French franc.

The Lebanese lira had its glory days between 1949 and 1975, and met a dismal end in the 1980s. After the First World War, Lebanon and Syria came under French mandate and a new currency, the *livre* (lira), based on the French franc, replaced the Ottoman banknotes and became the common currency of Lebanon and Syria. An Anglo-French committee supervised the issue of this currency by a French commercial bank, the

Banque de la Syrie et du Liban (BSL), and between 1920 and 1941 the Libano-Syrian lira was rigidly pegged to the French franc and was backed completely by Franc-denominated assets. The lira was redeemable by cheque in Marseilles and Paris, and the note cover consisted of French Treasury securities, foreign reserves and eligible commercial paper. The lira was divisible into 100 piasters and was set at 20 francs in the exchange market (this explains why in Lebanon a 5-piaster coin was called a franc).

The French franc began to face difficulties in 1936. By 1944, the franc dropped so low against the lira that the latter was valued at 54.35 francs. In that year, the monetary authorities in Syria and Lebanon negotiated an agreement with France to drop the French exchange standard, and the Libano-Syrian lira was linked to British sterling. A new law was introduced on 24 May 1949, setting an independent Lebanese lira under the gold standard at 405.512 milligrammes of pure gold or 45.66 US cents (LL2.19 against one US dollar). In a further step, the Lebanese Treasury took over the issue of coins from the BSL. Under the BSL authority, banknotes were covered 50 per cent in gold and foreign currency reserves and 50 per cent in foreign government securities, particularly T-bills and bonds. However, the Lebanese Ministry of Finance took over the determination of the components of each cover and started issuing Lebanese government T-bills.

By 17 May 1952, Lebanon had removed all remaining foreign exchange restrictions and allowed free movement of funds at current market rates. From then on, the "official exchange rate", published by the BSL, was used by the government to set customs duties and evaluate government foreign currency revenues and expenditures. The Foreign Exchange Department at the BSL continued to handle government transactions in foreign currencies, such as royalties from oil transit in Lebanese territory and accounts of diplomatic missions.

In order to massage the sharp fluctuations in the foreign exchange rate of the lira, the government established an Exchange Stabilization Fund, composed of several officials from the BSL and the Lebanese government, and headed by the Lebanese Minister of Finance. The Fund exercised control over gold and foreign currency reserves that were not earmarked as a buffer to support the national currency. Building on the strength of the lira, the Fund became a major purchaser of US dollars in the period 1949–63. Its first intervention was to stop the decline of the US dollar in Beirut on the eve of the Korean War in 1953, by heavily buying US dollars and preventing the appreciation of the lira. As capital inflows continued, the Fund intervened more frequently with a greater injection of liras into the system.

Although Lebanon pursued a liberal foreign exchange policy, the Fund maintained a LL3.01 to LL3.21 band to the dollar in the period 1953 to 1963. When capital inflows became excessive and the dollar was falling, the Fund intervened by injecting additional liras to absorb the surplus dollars. This policy was abandoned in 1964 as money supply was rising unnecessarily, creating inflationary pressures.

From its introduction in 1949, the Lebanese lira followed an ascending path; declines were the exception. The dollar jumped from LL3.26 in 1949 to LL3.73 in 1951. However, after the start of the Korean War, it fell steadily, moving to LL3.15 in 1959, LL3.01 in 1962 and LL3.07 in 1964.[2]

The 1958 civil war led to a flight of capital from Lebanon and to a drop in foreign investment. The lira was able to maintain its stability in the years that followed the 1958 crisis, aided by the eruption of many regional conflicts in the Middle East. In that period, the dollar remained within the prescribed band. It peaked from LL3.01 in 1962 to LL3.17 in May 1963 but stabilized at LL3.10 by the end of 1963. To achieve this stability, the fund sold large quantities of dollars for the first time, which depleted much of the amounts accumulated since the 1950s. After 1963, the lira was artificially kept strong, since it was weakened by higher global interest rates and the flight of foreign capital out of the Middle East. Between 1963 and 1967, Beirut became less attractive to foreign investors as interest rates in Tokyo reached 6 per cent against only 2 per cent in Beirut. The US dollar ceased to be abundant in Beirut and Lebanon's balance of payments became less favourable. Between 1958 and 1963, Lebanon received US$12.5 million in foreign aid from the US.

Following the difficulties in 1963–4, the official exchange rate of the dollar, which had been set at LL2.19 since 1949, was adjusted in January 1965 to LL3.08. Experts maintained that the right path for the government to stabilize the monetary system was to increase interest rates and to issue Treasury bills, and not to depreciate the currency and generate more liquidity issue as it did. Simultaneously, the Fund decided to end its frequent interventions and the pegging policy. Thus, the market was freed from the frequent interventions and the lira took an independent course.

Collapse of the National Currency

Between 1966 and 1971, the dollar appreciated slightly from LL3.08 to LL3.22, but subsequent events reversed this trend. The lira was again on a rising trend following the crisis in the world monetary system in the early 1970s. In February 1972, gold prices jumped from US$35 to US$37 per ounce in the world market, and the reaction in Beirut was an adjustment in the value of the lira similar to the 1965 adjustment.[3] With the depreciation in the value of the dollar from 886.71 milligrammes of gold to 851.30 milligrammes in February, the lira appreciated against the dollar. This was not the end of it. In May of the same year, gold prices rose again to US$42.22 per ounce and pushed lower the gold value of the dollar to 736.67 milligrammes. The Bank of Lebanon reluctantly depreciated further the value of the dollar in Beirut.

On 15 August 1972, US President Richard Nixon announced that the United States was abandoning the Gold Standard, leading to a re-alignment of the major currencies in the world. With this development, the dollar went into a long-term decline in Beirut. It hit a low of LL2.61 liras in 1973, LL2.33 in 1974, and LL2.20, its lowest level in twenty-five years, at the beginning of 1975. The global oil crisis in 1973–4 and the subsequent quadrupling of oil prices was translated into an influx of huge amounts of money into Lebanon from the Arab states of the Gulf. Oil money placed a big demand on Lebanon's service industry: banking, tourism, hospitals and schools. Real estate prices were inflated as skyscrapers sprang up everywhere. The rush of Arab and European tourists to Lebanon's scenic resorts brought more wealth to the country and additional strength to the lira.

The stability and strength of the lira led to its greater acceptance as a form of international payment and the inauguration of Beirut as an important international financial centre. In 1972, a consortium of fifteen Lebanese banks underwrote a bond issue by the State Bank of India for LL15 million, opening the door for further issues by foreign sovereigns in Lebanese currency. In 1973, thirty-three banks underwrote a bond issue by the World Bank for LL75 million, while ten banks underwrote a bond issue by the Renault Automobile company of France for LL50 million; and in 1974, the Government of Algeria issued a lira bond amounting to LL50 million. Further loans and deals were negotiated with several African and Asian countries. The Central Bank's foreign currency reserves grew from LL1.186 billion in 1970 to LL1.725 billion in 1971 and to LL2.041 billion in 1972. The bank's foreign exchange liabilities were as little as LL5 to LL6 million in the same period.

In the period 1970–4, healthy economic activity and the huge gold reserves gave enough momentum to the lira, which helped it survive the first eight years of civil war (1975–82). In February 1975, the US dollar stood at LL2.20 but in December 1976, after the first eighteen months of war, it rose to LL2.91. As economic stagnation and destruction continued in the country, the dollar rose further to LL3.44 in 1980. After 1980, foreigners lost hope that Beirut would regain its former glory and the economy remained stalled. It took only a few months for the lira to deteriorate further, and the dollar was trading at LL4.31 in 1981 and at LL4.73 on the eve of the Israeli invasion in June 1982. In 1983, with the prospects of peace and the intervention of the Multinational Force (the US, the UK, France and Italy), the dollar fell slightly to LL4.53.

In perspective, the lira lost 50 per cent of its value from 1974 to 1983, fetching 44 US cents in 1974, 34 cents in 1976, 29 cents in 1980 and 22 cents in 1983. The declines between 1975 and 1983 were minor compared to what came after 1983. In the first eight years of war, the economy was resilient and the country retained the confidence of the early 1970s. The real catastrophe arrived in the mid-1980s.

Starting in 1984, the dollar went on a course of unprecedented hikes that caught the country off guard. Before they knew it, the Lebanese were facing hyperinflation. Between 1984 and 1992, the dollar was breaking a record almost every month. Reaching LL6.51 in early 1985, the dollar climbed to LL16.42 later that year. Gone were the days of the 1950s and 1960s when the monetary authorities imposed bands on the dollar or complained that the dollar was falling too low in Beirut. In the 1980s, the ability of the Central Bank to influence foreign exchange markets as a player eroded and was not sufficient to stop the free fall of the lira.

In February 1986, the dollar traded at LL28. At the time, the Central Bank considered that level as harmful. To stop the deterioration in the lira, the Central Bank intervened heavily in the market and in a matter of weeks dumped US$500 million (a large sum in Lebanese standards), which stabilized the foreign exchange market and pulled the dollar down to LL19. The governor of the Central Bank was confident of this intervention and declared the LL19 level as a threshold that would be maintained for the next six months. However, in a matter of three weeks, the lira resumed its downward trend. By April, the dollar was trading again within a range of LL24 to LL30 liras, thus eliminating the impact of the February intervention. By late 1986, the dollar reached LL38.37, and the lira was effectively trading at 2 US cents.

Unable to intervene effectively in the foreign exchange market and realizing the proportion of bank accounts in foreign currency denominations, the Central Bank aimed to curtail the growth of money supply and tighten credit through higher reserve requirements. This policy crippled commercial credit amid a growing government deficit. The failure of the Central Bank to establish itself as a credible defender of the national currency was felt in the market, and an open season against the lira by speculators and gamblers was underway. The governor wished to intervene more forcefully but expert advice was against such policy and the lack of reserves curtailed the Bank's influence.

The public's rush to buy foreign exchange funds pushed the percentage of hard currency-denominated deposits at the financial institutions from 28 per cent of total deposits in 1984 to 86 per cent in July 1987. The Central Bank accentuated the panic by purchasing US dollars for liras beyond its needs for foreign currency intervention and government financial requirements. The flight to foreign currencies could not possibly be checked as the Law of Money and Credit does not specify the size of deposits in foreign currencies and would not allow the Central Bank to intervene in order to put a cap on these deposits. Changing such laws was not possible, as the Cabinet was not meeting. Additionally, Cabinet ministers were simultaneously leaders of the private militias.

In May 1987, officials from the Bank of Lebanon met a team from the International Monetary Fund in Paris to review the 1986–7 financial and economic developments in Lebanon. In this meeting, the International Monetary Fund (IMF) approved the Bank of Lebanon's policy of increasing reserve requirements to control credit expansion and of obliging commercial banks to buy government securities. The IMF suggested additional measures to contain credit expansion and protect the national currency, with emphasis on controlling the growth of money supply and requiring financial institutions to increase their capital base. On the fiscal side, the team suggested spending restraints by the government, especially in the areas of defence and public subsidies.

Controlling the budget deficit and imposing a limit on the amount of cash advances from the Central Bank to the government were strongly recommended.

The IMF recommended lifting government subsidies as almost all subsidies to fuels and wheat were wasted because of the absence of control over prices. Businesses were making large profits by buying goods at subsidized prices and selling them at market prices. In addition, subsidized products were smuggled out of the country and sold to foreigners. Effectively, government funds were wasted in order to subsidize domestic businessmen and consumers in the neighbouring countries.

The team criticized the frequent interventions by the Central Bank in the foreign exchange market to defend the national currency, and recommended limited interventions with small amounts as the Central Bank needed to build its foreign currency reserves. In 1987, the Central Bank took in 73 per cent of the private banks' liquid assets through secondary reserve requirements (government securities), cash requirements and special bills. These actions limited the market's ability to extend credit or to maintain a healthy cash ratio, which led many banks to recall their private loans, exposing promising investments to financial difficulties.

The IMF report also dealt with the financial troubles that rocked Lebanon. Between 1984 and 1986, money supply (currency in circulation and demand deposits) grew exponentially, at a rate of 24 per cent in 1983–4, 56 per cent in 1985 and 172 per cent in 1986. The preference of the public for foreign currency led to sharp increases in the domestic price level. In the same period, foreign currency-denominated deposits accounted for 68 per cent of total deposits, and a good portion of currency in circulation was in foreign currencies.

The large surges in the value of the dollar started in 1987. In June 1987, the exchange market experienced almost daily jumps in the value of the dollar. Hysterical rises in the dollar occurred in October, a dismal month in which the international stock market crashed in the same year. On Thursday 1 October 1987, the value of the dollar started at LL287.25, and remained at that level until 10 October when it jumped to LL300–LL350. A bandwagon effect followed and traders went wild with the dollar. It increased at a rate of LL10 to LL20 every day, until it hit LL400 on 15 October.

After a pause of ten days the wild race resumed on Monday morning, 26 October. On that day, the rate of decline in the value of the lira accelerated and the LL10 to LL20 rise in the dollar was now happening every four hours. The dollar closed at LL475 on Monday, LL530 on Tuesday and LL600 to LL700 on Wednesday. The mad decline suddenly abated on Thursday morning, 29 October, and the dollar closed at LL580, falling further to LL500 on Friday 30 October. The net increase in the value of the dollar in October was LL211.50.[4]

The October crash of the lira was attributed to speculation and to the public loss of confidence in the national currency. The deterioration in economic conditions also eroded the support of the real base of the economy as all economic sectors were deteriorating. A study conducted by the Department of Money and Banking at the American University of Beirut showed that aside from economic factors, speculation in the foreign exchange market against the national currency contributed 40 per cent to the rise in the value of the dollar in Beirut.[5] In the absence of a strong leader like the Central Bank, market participants pushed the lira into a deep abyss. Even moral influence from the Central Bank was lacking. In late 1987, the dispute between the Central Bank and the Bankers' Association reached a critical level and depositors were afraid that their lira deposits may be frozen by decree or lose their value altogether due to the continued collapse of the currency. The banks were furious at the Central Bank's policy of forcing them to swallow the Treasury bill issues. The Central Bank absorbed only a portion of the Treasury bill issues as the banks would take the main amount, and in turn this led to monetization of government debt and to further banknote issue, effectively increasing the money supply.

By 1987, aside from fruit and vegetables, most other commodities such as clothing, appliances, jewellery, durables and automobiles were priced in US dollars to the extent that it became increasingly difficult for the average citizen to effect daily transactions in the national currency. The dollarization of the economy that was once feared finally became a reality. Almost 75 per cent of consumer and producer goods were imported and paid for in foreign currency.

Although it was a criminal offence to reject the lira as a form of payment for transactions, it was not forbidden to quote prices in foreign currencies or to use foreign money in the conduct of economic activity.[6] The Lebanese Criminal Code states that: "Whoever rejects the lira as a proper form of payment for a commodity will be fined LL5 to LL50."[7] However, this law was not enforceable under the circumstances and many businesses chose not to observe it. Even if it had been possible to enforce the law or to bring offenders to justice, a fine of LL5 to LL50, which had probably been meaningful in the 1970s, was insignificant to violators in the 1980s. The powerless and paralyzed judiciary was unable to bring to justice violators of the Criminal Code or speculators using illegal methods.

Government investigators routinely compiled reports on speculation activities and violations. Individuals were interviewed by government inspectors in private but no charges were laid as connections and influences played their role in the conduct of the courts. To curb the spread of speculation, the Minister of Finance announced Saturday to be a day of rest for financial institutions. However, the announcement made little difference as trading continued at Friday's closing rate.[8] Sidewalk and kiosk exchangers benefited from the closure of financial institutions and conducted exchange business.

The year 1988–9 witnessed the worst fighting in the Lebanese war and the lira fell further with the dollar reaching the LL1,000 limit. In 1988, the scene was dominated by the presidential election campaign. An unwritten convention allowed any Lebanese Maronite to run for the post. In previous elections, only a few candidates had come forward but almost everybody withdrew when a particular candidate seemed to enjoy the support of foreign powers and was able to secure a majority of votes in Parliament. By early summer 1988, there were 99 presidential candidates vigorously campaigning for the position. However, no election took place in September as Parliament failed to obtain a quorum. In response, the Maronite warlords, fearing effective authority would fall into the hands of the Muslim prime minister Salim al-Hoss, gathered at the Presidential Palace and appointed the commander of the army, General Michel Aoun, as prime minister, until circumstances could allow presidential elections to take place.

Aoun, a Maronite, was not a bad man, and aspired to unite the country, thinking himself to be another Chehab who could build central authority and curtail the power of the warlords. However, he forgot that in the 1960s Chehab had lost and the warlords had won, and Lebanon was condemned to live through the same story again. As early as February 1989, Aoun waged a limited assault against the Christian militia of Samir Geagea to guarantee the backing of the Christian heartland and to appease the Muslims with the good intention "that he started with their foes". In March 1989, he declared a war to "liberate Lebanon". Aoun's six-month war against Syria and its Lebanese allies and against the Christian militia was the worst episode of violence in Lebanon's fifteen years of war. In these circumstances, the dollar went wild in Beirut rising to LL900 to L950 in one week. Aoun stayed in power until October 1990, and then sought refuge in Paris.

Parliament finally met near Tripoli in autumn 1989 and elected René Mouawad who, a few months into his mandate, was assassinated in Beirut. Parliament met again and elected Elias Hrawi who revived hopes for an end to the war. With these developments the dollar fell to optimistic levels and traded at a range of LL500 to LL600 in early 1990. However, with the advent of the Kuwait crisis and Aoun's resistance to give up authority and allow the elected president to move to Baabda, the lira fell and the dollar rose to LL1,250 and LL1,400. In the Gulf War over Kuwait, Lebanon sided with the coalition against Iraq and an international understanding developed that Syria, a member of the coalition against Iraq, would run over the enclave held by Michel Aoun, which it did, and peace returned to Lebanon by the power of the gun. Before 1990 was over, the dollar fell back to the pre-October 1987 level of LL500 to LL600.

Relative peace was not enough; with the economy destroyed and the government bankrupt, Lebanon needed massive inflows of funds. They did not materialize. Even in April 1991, by which time Lebanon had already taken brave steps towards internal peace, the dollar was still trading at LL945, dropping marginally to LL892 in the summer of 1991, despite signficant injections from Saudi Arabia totalling several hundreds of millions of dollars,[9] and promises of aid from Germany and Italy.

Aside from the lack of funds, the situation in the south of the country continued to be as explosive as it had been since 1968. In February 1992, fighting between the Israelis and the Lebanese resistance dealt another blow to the cause of peace and the dollar broke another threshold, trading at LL1,400 and stabilizing at LL1,150 in March 1992. The continued economic stagnation and inflationary pressures led to another eruption in the dollar in April and May 1992, when the Beirut market quoted the dollar at the giant sum of LL2,600. Eventually, the Hariri cabinet that took over in 1992 was able to stabilize the exchange markets by setting a fixed rate of the dollar at LL1,500, which remained in effect for the next decade.

NOTES

1 The Beirut-corrupted version of kiosk is *kishk*. Curiously, there is a national food staple made of yogurt and wheat which is also called *kishk*.
2 All exchange values of the US dollar in the Beirut foreign exchange market are from the Bank of Lebanon quarterly bulletins.
3 Article 229 of the Law of Money and Credit sets the value of the dollar at 886.71 milligrammes of pure gold and that of the lira at 405.51 milligrammes.
4 *Annahar* weekly economic reports in October–November 1987.
5 Institute of Money and Banking, *1988 Seminar Proceedings – Bank Mergers in Lebanon* (in Arabic, *al-Damj al-Masrifi fi Lubnaan*), Beirut, American University of Beirut, 1990.
6 Lebanese Criminal Code, Paragraph 6, Article 767, "Violations Against Public Trust".
7 Decree No. 83/112.
8 The official exchange rate is published daily by the Central Bank but does not entail a managed or controlled foreign exchange market. The market operates freely, and rates are determined by the forces of supply and demand. However, the closing rate announced by the Central Bank is usually considered the leading closing to direct the market. Markets in Beirut open at 8:30 am and close at 12:30 pm. The official rate is chosen by the bank shortly after 11 am and would prevail until the following open. Market participants are in constant contact with each other, and after the banks close exchange kiosks and sidewalk exchangers operate into the night.
9 "Saudis give Lebanon US$60 million", *Al-Hayat*, 6 April 1991.

11

Government Decay

While the period 1975–80 witnessed the physical destruction of Lebanon and the entrenchment of the cantons in each region, the theme of the 1980s was general collapse. Ferocious and more violent fighting took place between 1981 and 1990, and hyperinflation ruined all aspects of economic life. As in Weimar Germany, people in Lebanon had to carry large bags stuffed with bundles of money just to buy basic food items and clothing.

With the ever-increasing possibility of being killed, the Beirut of the 1980s became a living hell. Street scenes resembled the American Wild West. Where chic ladies and smart-suited businessmen had walked a few years ago, militiamen now roamed complete with cowboy hats and shiny handguns at their belts. Some gunmen wearing dark sunglasses and smart sheriff hats were reportedly riding horses. In the absence of law and order, neighbourhoods had to cooperate with each other in order to survive and somehow residents managed to make functional sense of the chaos.

Law enforcement and quality control over consumer goods disappeared, leaving the public to the mercy of undeterred merchants. Essential staples such as sugar, rice, flour and eggs mysteriously disappeared following deliveries of large shipments, only to resurface later in the black market at inflated prices. Pastries used a cyclamate sweetener that could cause cancer if consumed large quantities. Honey, pastries and baklava were made with cyclamate, and suppliers of this chemical boasted that cyclamate sweetened forty times more than sugar. Some businesses imported beef and fish past its sell-by date and sold it as fresh. Similarly, out-of-date canned foods were imported and new labels with new dates were affixed to them to be offered as new products. Some firms in Italy, France and other places held aside expired and damaged products, normally destined for the garbage dump, for Lebanese merchants. With the absence of coast guards, all kinds of import and export commodities went unchecked through the illegal harbours.

A scam involving several Lebanese businessmen and politicians was revealed in 1988, when a shipment of deadly and extremely hazardous chemical and nuclear waste was found on a beach north of Beirut. It was reported that some Lebanese businessmen had struck deals with firms in Europe to import industrial waste into Lebanon at a fee of several million US dollars. These Lebanese individuals had the necessary import licences and the seal of approval of the Lebanese government, so it did not raise the suspicion of the authorities in Europe. In the absence of a proper government authority, everything, including licences, was available in Beirut for a fee.

The helpless government, or what remained of it, tried to control the situation but to no avail. Consumer Affairs Minister Victor Kassir created a commission to watch over prices and fraudulent products. Publicly, the militias promised cooperation and in one week the commission issued 120 fines against violators. However, public statements were one thing, but the reality on the ground was another. Two months after the commission was established, Kassir, his wife and his daughter narrowly escaped assassination when a bomb planted under their car exploded. The minister got the message and found it appropriate to dissolve the commission after it came head-on against the interests of the militias and their rackets and neighbourhood bosses.

Hyperinflation

Between 1943 and 1972, Lebanon enjoyed steady growth and low inflation. However, between 1973 and 1982, prices rose steadily and Lebanon experienced a foretaste of even higher prices when inflation pressures accelerated. Between 1983 and 1991, consumer prices rose uncontrollably and when the currency collapsed, hyperinflation crept in.

Similar inflationary pressures had been experienced during the Second World War. The only available information on inflation for the period 1940–59 is the consumer price index (CPI), which was released by the Ministry of the Economy. This index used a basket of consumer goods that reflected typical household consumption.[1] The data showed that from 1939 to 1945, domestic prices increased 1,100 per cent (11 times). In that period, the lira was linked to the French franc. With the massive inflow of funds from the Western governments who maintained a huge armed presence in Lebanon and Syria during the Second World

War, and with the collapse of the French franc, prices rose astronomically. However, they moderated after the war and remained stable for the next 25 years.

By 1960, a new CPI had been published by the Bureau of Statistics at the new Ministry of Planning, and the oil companies published other price index series. Companies such as MobilOil and ARAMCO (the Arab-American Oil Company) maintained their Middle East headquarters in Beirut and published their own CPI. In 1962, the Government Bureau did a survey of 2,600 families, following which new weighted averages reflecting prices of a new basket of household consumer items were used to arrive at a new CPI.[2] This basket showed a substantial shift in consumption towards luxury items, and reflected an improvement in the standard of living. The percentage spent on food was only 14 per cent against 38 per cent in 1940, while inessential items (such as cigarettes or house cleaners) represented 16 per cent, compared to less than 5 per cent in 1940.

Hiring house cleaners is a sign of affluence in Lebanese society. For centuries, well-off Lebanese families had kept house cleaners, and this tradition continued into the twentieth century. With the Lebanese distaste for menial work, very few Lebanese women took jobs as house cleaners. Instead, they came from remote and poor Lebanese villages and from Alawite villages in Syria. In most cases, the parents of the young girls garnered their pay. From the 1950s, the expansion of Middle East Airlines (MEA) to West Africa and the wealth accumulated by Lebanese expatriates made it possible to hire house cleaners from French-speaking Africa. In the 1980s, the Lebanese market for house cleaners had a further reach: they were hired from as far away as the Philippines and Sri Lanka. In the late 1980s, house cleaners from the Philippines and Sri Lanka were paid in US dollars at a salary twice as high as the average salary of a Lebanese government employee.

The CPI, established at par in 1964, rose at an annual rate of 3 per cent to 122 in 1971. In 1973 as Lebanon imported 40 per cent of its consumer and capital goods, the inflationary pressures in the global economy spiralled into Lebanon through higher import prices. That year, the food price sub-index rose 24 per cent to 145 and the clothing sub-index rose 17 per cent to 156. The impact of these increases on the general price level was minimal, as many other sub-categories experienced no change in prices.

In the early 1970s, the price system was rampant with rent controls, subsidies and a chaotic tax system that distorted the CPI and gave the impression that inflation was insignificant. In 1973, the housing index rose a mere 1 per cent to 105.7 per cent, and the miscellaneous index rose 4 per cent to 107.8 per cent. Controls on rental accommodations kept spending on housing in check for decades, causing its share of total household expenditures to decline as income levels rose. The laws were geared to favour low-income tenants. However, everybody benefited at the expense of the landlord. A family who paid LL50 in rent and earned LL300 per month in 1960 still paid LL50 in rent in 1970 but earned LL600. Throughout this period, the weighted ratio of housing in the consumption basket was maintained at 19 per cent, which gave this sub-index a greater weight than it really had.

Government policies aimed at improving income distribution through subsidies and progressive taxation also contributed to price distortions. These policies were mainly expansionary and accentuated inflationary pressures, but were not reflected in the CPI. Efforts to isolate the impact of subsidies did not succeed. Subsidized goods such as meat, sugar and flour were imported and paid for in hard currency but were distributed at low prices. Private imports of foodstuffs were exempt from duties and import licences were not required. Instead of introducing anti-inflation policies, the government contributed to inflation by increasing the proportion of disposable personal income, freeing more spending money and increasing aggregate demand. In an attempt to alleviate the burden of the low-income families, the government encouraged the system of cooperatives, which were low-price consumer outlets financed by government interest-free loans.

Given such distortions, by the early 1970s the basket of goods was no longer a proper monitor of inflation. However, it was still possible to monitor actual inflation from other economic signs. Commercial credit, at LL500 million in 1971, rose by merely LL74 million to LL574 million in 1972, but leapt to LL1,389 million in 1973. Capital inflows, mainly from Arab countries, pushed real estate prices through the roof, depressed the affordable rental housing market and created a market for furnished and luxury apartments and houses for sale. Other signs of inflation were also reflected in labour costs. In the 1970s, the highly unionized Lebanese labour force pushed for more frequent wage increases and was able to gain raises in the range of 10 per cent annually.[3] The government gave a lead in implementing these wage adjustments shortly after the agreements and was followed by the private sector.

In 1974 the government set up a National Council on Wages and Prices, known as the "Committee of the Six".[4] The Minister of Finance, Joseph Chader, presented the plan to the Beirut Chamber of Commerce on 19 March 1974. The committee recommended higher taxes to curtail consumption and supplement government revenues, including a 10 per cent increase in personal income tax, progressive taxes on monthly incomes over LL12,000, capital tax on gains from the sale of property, a lump-sum tax on the goodwill payment on commercial properties and user-fees on public services. To control the rise in food prices, the government introduced a ban on the export of food items it deemed lacking in the domestic market. However after six weeks, the government backed off and lifted the ban.

The Central Bank used moral suasion with banks to control inflation and increase the interest rates to stop credit expansion. There were suggestions to sell petroleum products at market prices and lift the subsidy, but this was not done until 1989 after the government looked at the issue again. Early in 1975, progress on these plans was slow as the country experienced the first signs of the civil war.

After 1975 inflation accelerated, and between 1976 and 1982 prices rose at an average of 19 per cent. In the context of the period 1975–90, the inflation of the 1970s was still small compared to the large jumps experienced in the 1980s. While inflation moderated in 1983 at only 6 per cent, the pace quickened in the following years with the CPI rising 18 per cent in 1984, 64 per cent in 1985 and 104 per cent in 1986. Commodity prices rose several times faster than wages, especially after the lira began its slump against the US dollar. Inflation peaked in 1987 at 403 per cent, and moderated to 154 per cent in 1988 and 70 per cent in 1989, thanks to the fiscal and monetary restraints imposed by the government and the Central Bank.[5]

Wage-earners tried to cope with inflation. For example, in 1986 wages rose at a rate of 80 per cent to 100 per cent. The increase in wages in the second half of 1986 gave those with an annual salary ceiling of LL96,000 a raise of 45 per cent, and amounts higher than LL96,000 per annum were increased by 35 per cent. The whole salary spectrum was increased by amounts ranging between LL14,400 liras and LL78,000 per annum. On 1 January 1987, the minimum salary was LL51,600 per annum, but the adjustments were hardly sufficient to offset the loss in purchasing power and real wages kept falling. In US dollar terms the salary dropped from US$2,244 per annum in 1975 (equivalent to LL240,000 in 1987 exchange rates) to US$420 per annum in 1987 (equivalent to LL51,600 in 1987 exchange rates), or an 80 per cent drop in dollar terms. As these levels were abnormally low, subsequent wage adjustments brought the minimum annual salary to US$1,200 in 1990 and to US$1,440 in 1991.

To put the drop in the standard of living in perspective, perhaps I might make an assumption about the potential of the country had the war not taken place. If Lebanon had had no war between 1975 and 1990, it would have achieved an annual rate of growth of 6 per cent (based on the average realized in the period 1964–74) within a 4 per cent inflation rate economy. Based on these figures, computations show that annual per capita income would have been US$6,600 in 1990, compared to the actual US$1,440. Thus in 1990, actual per capita income dropped to less than 22 per cent of potential income, and incomes in 1991 stood at 60 per cent of the level Lebanon had achieved in 1974.

Salaried employees carried the burden of inflation, watching their salaries become worth less and less while paying inflated prices for everything. They were never ahead even with the wage adjustments, as the market quickly absorbed wage rises through higher prices. Businesses adjusted their prices as a matter of routine, following each wage raise. The collapse of the national currency further eroded the purchasing power of salaried employees, and wage increases ironically became a net loss to them since they inflated the currency and increased money supply.

Aware of the climate, workers quickly exchanged their earnings into US dollars and other hard currencies before further collapses in the lira. Fearing the government and the private sector would resist wage adjustments on grounds that they contributed to inflation, the Lebanese Labour Union argued that the rising dollar was behind inflation and not wage adjustments. Between December 1986 and March 1987, the dollar rose LL41 (51 per cent) to LL106, and the CPI jumped by 50 per cent in the same period. Meanwhile, salaries rose by less than the rise in the CPI. Between April 1986 and March 1987, salaries rose 307.5 per cent but the CPI rose 530 per cent in the same period.

Consumers of essential goods also suffered as Lebanese products found their way to those who paid more outside the country. With the decline in the national currency and the relatively high lira prices fetched for Lebanese products abroad, endless queues of trucks filled with agricultural and manufactured products lined up at the Syrian borders on their way to the Arab markets. Many basic fruits and vegetables went missing from the domestic market. Even pitta bread was baked in Lebanon and shipped to Syria and Cyprus while households in Lebanon searched for the rare staple.

During the war, the Lebanese became used to the public provision of many amenities of life such as schools, housing, utilities, bread, fuel and electricity. Although the government's revenues had vanished or were swallowed by the militias, the public and the media cried out against the government each time prices rose or a government department defaulted on delivery of services. The government treasury was depleted from subsidizing consumer goods, the public abuse of electric power, lost utility revenues and from maintaining the wheat and energy funds. Despite the laissez-faire economy and the absence of government intervention, public subsidies were even more generous than those in a socialist country. In 1987, electricity, fuel and grain subsidies were costing the government LL103 billion, of which LL8 billion went to the Wheat Subsidy Fund and LL95 billion for the Fuel Subsidy Fund, of which LL8 was spent on fuels that fed power stations.

The power utility
Power shortages and abuse of government-subsidized electric power were common on a small scale before the war but became widespread after 1975. Between 1940 and 1953, hydro output increased threefold from 57 million kWh to 164 million kWh. But between 1953 and 1973, output increased tenfold reaching 1,790 million kWh in 1973. This represented an average growth of 50 per cent annually. Despite the rise in output, demand was always higher and outages and shortages were part of the culture. In 1973, to meet the extra demand, work was begun to produce power by means other than hydropower, as water was becoming increasingly scarce in Lebanon and the Middle East. Electricity shortages were more acute during the war. In 1983, the absence of revenues and the abuse led to a reduction in output and the country ended up importing 15 per cent of its needs from Syria for the first time in history, after having being a net exporter.

In the 1980s, the power company, Électricité du Liban, was facing a severe deficit. Large factories and wealthy establishments defaulted on payment and risked throwing the whole country into darkness. The Kadisha Power Station filed a suit against the Arida Brothers Company for failure to pay arrears dating back many years and amounting to hundreds of thousands of dollars.[6] A 1986 study found that the utility was better off not collecting the dues. The report explained that the cost of enforcement and collection of dues was larger than the estimated amounts to be collected, and that money could be saved by supplying power at no charge until a meaningful schedule was established and reinforcement was possible. By 1983, the company was incurring annual losses in the area of US$40 million to US$50 million. Costs were real. The two power stations at Jiyé (south of Beirut) and Zouk (north-east of Beirut) used 600,000 tons of imported oil annually to produce electric power at a cost of US$10 a barrel.

Despite the heroic efforts by the utility to provide service and repair damaged lines in areas where fighting was taking place, the public abused the utility to the extreme. The abuses ranged from default on payment of dues to instalment of private wires onto the main arteries by individuals and the militias who stole power for their own purposes. Consequently, the utility had to place entire regions on rationing on a rotation basis. Neighbourhoods sometimes went for months without power. Still, when the company failed to repair a line, the militias and the media were fast at denouncing the "corrupt government" and the "imperialistic conspiracy against the people".

The Fuel Subsidy Fund
The Fuel Subsidy Fund accounted for 80 per cent of all subsidies and represented a big chunk of government expenditures. In 1987, the fuel subsidy amounted to US$382 million, of which US$352 million went on public consumption and US$30 million went to the power utility.

Between 1940 and 1953, annual output of oil products increased five-fold from 100,000 tons to 545,000 tons. Between 1953 and 1973, production rose four-fold reaching 2 million tons in 1973. After 1973, production of oil did not match consumption as output capacity rose 9 per cent, but consumption rose 23 per cent. Contrary to accepted wisdom in the West, being an Arab country did not immunize Lebanon against the 1974 oil crisis. Following the 1973 Middle East War, oil prices also quadrupled in Beirut. Lebanon paid world prices for oil but nonetheless shared the bad publicity directed at Arabs in the Western media. To manage the crisis the authorities imposed restrictions on consumption and introduced rationing where cars with even-numbered licence plates could be used one day and odd-numbered the next. The crisis was eased after Iraq started supplying oil to a small refinery at Tripoli in northern Lebanon at slightly lower prices until July 1975. This experience led the government to give serious thought to greater subsidy of oil products.

Oil consumption doubled between 1975 and 1985. This was largely because of the excessive number of motor vehicles in the country compared to the tiny size of the population. In 1983, government records showed 550,000–600,000 registered vehicles, of which 80–90 per cent were for private use. This easily placed war-torn Lebanon in the rank of countries with the highest number of cars per capita. In 1998, the number of motor vehicles reached 1.5 million.

In October 1984, the country was hit with another rise in oil prices, and the Fuel Subsidy Fund started to incur an annual deficit of LL5 billion to LL7 billion as oil had to be imported at world prices in hard currency and sold for token money to the public. This was made worse by the decline in the value of the national currency. As an illustration of the loss ratio, in 1986 the government paid LL12.5 billion for the imported oil but sold it for LL7.10 billion to the public.

Several groups and rackets abused the oil subsidy and extorted maximum benefit at public expense. Owners of gas stations amassed large quantities of oil at the subsidized price and sold it at a price several times higher than the official rate; others exported oil for profit to neighbouring countries. The public was outraged that the government and the media would announce the arrival of huge shipments of oil while gas stations claimed they had run out. Everybody knew that the stations lied and that those who could afford the black market price got what they wanted.

In light of this situation, the Central Bank called for the subsidy to be abolished, especially at a time when the government was borrowing heavily to pay for it and was allowing the import of oil by private citizens in the hope of creating a competitive environment and of breaking the monopoly of black marketeers who would be forced to lower their prices.

The Central Bank insisted that the government had no business subsidizing oil in these hard times and the world price was a fair one for the market. The subsidized price was not available anywhere, and 20 litres cost LL15,000 in 1990 during the Kuwait crisis against LL1,200 to LL1,600 in 1987 – a far cry from the LL7.35 per 20 litres in 1975.

Lebanon processes oil at two refineries: one at Zahrani (south of Beirut) and a smaller one at Tripoli (in north Lebanon). The Zahrani refinery was the major oil facility in the country. In the 1980s, it employed 250–300 people and processed 15,000–17,000 barrels per day (with 160 litres per barrel), which were paid for by the Ministry of Industry and Oil at a cost of US$16–18 per barrel. Due to its proximity to areas of tension in southern Lebanon, the refinery was not immune to frequent Israeli raids. Israeli attacks in 1976 and 1978 caused extensive damage to the refinery, which was shut down for several months each year. The 1976 raid caused a 50 per cent loss in the refinery's production capacity of 17,500 barrels per day.

No sooner had the refinery resumed production when another raid in 1981 closed it down for three months with additional loss in capacity. The company resumed activity later in 1981 with lower capacity, but another Israeli attack was not far off. In June 1982, the Israeli forces damaged the Trans-Arabian Pipeline (Tapline), as well as several parts of the facility, the administration buildings and the storage tanks. Each Israeli raid cost the refinery at least US$5 to $10 million in repairs. The refinery was repaired after the Israeli withdrawal in 1985, and full capacity was restored.[7]

In the war between Aoun and the Christian militia in east Beirut, several rockets hit the Dora oil storage facilities and set them aflame with damages reaching US$50 million. For weeks, burning oil could be seen from as far away as 50 km.

Social services
Faced with sharp social imbalances, Lebanon had struggled to institute a welfare structure since the early 1960s. Public provision of social services was viewed by the private sector and warlords as socialism, and was frowned upon by legislators and executives. Several privately run social and health insurance firms sprang up in the country, but access to them was limited to the high-income group that could afford treatment in

Paris or Switzerland. The Social Security Fund was created by an Act of Government in 1963, although it took until 1971 to launch the Fund. The Fund had an administrative council of thirteen members: five representing labour, five employers and three the government. The size of the council doubled in 1978 to better satisfy the Lebanese formula of religious representation, as every sect was represented by at least one member on the council.

The Social Security Act stipulated four functions of the Fund: health and maternity, unemployment insurance (including industrial accidents compensation), family allowance and retirement security. The act was considered the single most important piece of legislation to benefit the average citizen. It became the only body to provide universal coverage of health insurance, hospitalization costs, old age, maternity, unemployment and retirement. At least one-third of Lebanon's active labour force was covered by the Social Security Fund by 1975, and this rose very little in following years.

Starting in 1986, the Fund ran into deficits and defaulted or deferred payment of benefits. Many contributors were unable to pay for prescriptions and essential treatments, especially in the health and maternity programmes. The government fully compensated the claimants at prices that were much higher than the Fund's ledgers would permit. The standard of living of the average family dropped so low that the number of eligible claimants rose several times over. Faced with this flood of claims, the Fund paid claims of less than LL3,000 without verification, but scrutinized and asked for authentic receipts for large claims.

The situation worsened after the retirement of a number of doctors, which the Fund could not replace. The chronic absenteeism among civil servants weakened the programme further. Even in peaceful times, some civil servants preferred to stay at home and report to work once every month to collect their pay, since their salaries were hardly enough to justify the cost of commuting and a lunch. With the lawless state of affairs, employers got away without paying the contributions, although they deducted contributions before paying salaries to the workers. In some instances the contributions were paid to the private militias as they were the real authority on the ground. The Fund found a way around delinquency by linking recognition of claims to the payment of contributions.

The Fund applied strict guidelines and rate schedules to hospitals. However, since the rate schedules did not follow a cost of living adjustment clause to reflect inflation, they required a lengthy and complicated process in order to be adjusted. The proposed adjustment had to go through several stages from the General Directorate of the Fund to the Executive Council to the Board of Trustees. At each level disagreements and conflicting interests arose, delaying any decisions indefinitely. Eventually, hospitals and clinics benefited from the incompetence of the Fund's administration and were able to get away with the excessive charges. Claimants suffered from the excessive charges as they paid the difference between the rigid schedule and the actual cost. Even when the Fund delivered a new schedule in May 1987, inflation rendered the new schedule meaningless two months after its introduction. Hospitals paid little attention to the new schedule, but imposed higher charges anyway.

Inflation touched other programmes in the Social Security Fund. The Retirement Security Programme, which was partly implemented when the war started in 1975, faced serious difficulties. Instead of a fully funded pension fund, the retirement plan involved a lump-sum "end-of-service" reward. This approach proved difficult to apply in a fluctuating economic environment and was not immune to the inflation of the 1980s. This loophole in the retirement plan caused considerable damage to the Fund. The lump-sum payment was linked to the last salary paid upon retirement. However, contributions were based on the actual lower salaries received by the employee in all the years prior to retirement.

As wages rose, the reward rose proportionately – hence, the sum of the contributions fell below the end-of-service reward. The employer was required by law to pay the shortfall between the reward and the contributions. In the 1980s this problem became worse as salaries were doubled frequently by decree and the reward had to be paid based on the last salary. The relationship between wages and the retirement reward became disproportional, as benefits far exceeded contributions. Employers quarrelled with the Fund about who should pay the bill, while the employee went without any benefits.

From 1987, the deficit in the Social Security Fund was due to the collapsing economy and the environment of lawlessness that led to abuse by both contributors who failed to pay and claimant abuse. In the early 1970s, the Fund paid LL150 million to LL200 million in benefits to medical care, maternity, retirement and family allowance claims. After sixteen years of serving the public, the Fund was suffering an annual deficit of LL1 billion out of the LL12 billion comprising total expenditure. The books showed that it would have been possible to eliminate the deficit if contributions were indexed to the 1987 wages. Collections fell to 20 per cent of potential contributions despite the existence of a fine for defaulters.

Pondering a possible demise of the Fund, the government considered privatizing social insurance and imposing mandatory private insurance on employers as an alternative to the safety net the public fund provided. Supporters of this scheme argued that the idea of privatization and deregulation was gaining currency worldwide and experts argued that the businesses of health care, unemployment and retirement insurance were better handled by the private sector, which allowed premiums to be determined by market forces. The idea was explored, but a close review showed that the insurance industry in Lebanon was not ready for the idea. The available health insurance firms provided only a small part of the benefits covered by the Fund. Even in that area not everything was covered, since private plans met hospital cost but not prescription drugs or doctors' visits.

Difficulties with the idea of privatization were further compounded due to the lack of a regulatory mechanism of the private insurance firms. Standards and guidelines governing the practice were covered in the National Insurance Review Act, which was introduced in 1968 and which called for the establishment of the Insurance Review Board and a Superintendent of Insurance position. The Minister of Economic Affairs who overlooked consumer and corporate affairs was formally the head of such a board. But these regulatory functions were stillborn as both business and parliament disliked any public regulation or supervision, dismissing the Insurance Review Board as a "Chehabist legacy".

Facing such enormous obstacles in privatizing the Fund and eliminating the subsidies, the government backed off and preferred to study the best way to allow a morally defensible retreat from the provision of social security.

Municipal services
In the 1980s, Lebanon was divided into 635 municipal units of varying sizes, from Beirut with one million people to the smallest village of a few hundred people. Municipal authorities provided many indispensable services, such as the provision of roads, sewers, public health and safety and garbage collection. Municipal revenues were largely raised through

traffic fines, property taxes, sales taxes, import duties, amusement taxes, licensing and utility taxes. Municipalities lost most of their revenues during the war, and had to rely on the central government for needed funds.

Aside from local taxes and licence fees raised by some municipalities, much of municipal revenue came from levies collected by the central government. Revenues were usually allotted by the Ministry of the Interior's Division of Townships and Villages according to a prescribed formula. Municipal workers unions received 25 per cent of the allocations and municipal authorities received the rest.[8] For many municipalities this levy represented their only revenue. The public paid the levy as a component of utility charges on power and water, while a portion came from the profits of Casino du Liban, a gambling and entertainment complex north of Beirut. Municipalities were allotted LL26 million annually in 1983–6 from the profits of Électricité du Liban, and LL24 million annually from the water company. The levy on the casino's profits went entirely to the smaller municipalities (210 towns and villages).

Until 1977, municipal revenues were collected and distributed in an orderly fashion, averaging LL104 million annually in 1973–6, of which 35 per cent went to Beirut. In 1980, these revenues dropped to LL81 million, of which 60 per cent went to Beirut, as it was the most hurt by the civil war.[9] During the war, it became difficult to collect taxes and dues, let alone adjust them to inflation. An existing law stipulated that fees and taxes should be adjusted for inflation,[10] and this law was re-emphasized in 1977.[11] In accounting terms this meant windfall revenues to the municipalities, but the adjusted schedules were never introduced and municipal authorities assumed that nobody would pay the adjusted fees under the chaos prevailing in the country. The other levies and taxes were taken over by the militias or went largely unpaid. By 1985, revenues sharply declined due to evasion and to the pressure of inflation. Government loans to the city of Beirut reached LL1.9 billion in 1981–5.

By 1985, municipal debt amounted to LL3 billion, 50 per cent of which was owed by Beirut at interest rates reaching 21 per cent. In 1986, Beirut's revenues stood at LL278 million and spending at LL349 million, a deficit of LL72 million. The city's records indicate that a total of LL191 million in taxes and fees were unpaid for the period 1978–85, large enough to eliminate the deficit. Revenues dropped to a mere LL86 million in 1987 (US$307,000) against LL270 million in 1975 (US$108 million in 1975 exchange rates). The Ministry of the Interior calculated that with adjustments for inflation and enforced collection, municipal revenues should have been at least LL2 billion in 1987. The amount paid to individual towns became so insignificant in 1987 (LL25,000–50,000 annually), that it was not enough to pay even one monthly salary. To supplement municipal revenues, the government created a special fund of LL14 million, and extended loans and grants to pay for salaries and expenses. Some LL2 billion was handed out annually by the government to the municipalities to keep them running. However, the support was not enough and the municipalities, already running large deficits, were defaulting on payment of salaries and expenses.

The situation was most acute in the city of Beirut where most of the 15 years of fighting took place. With the de facto halving of the city, municipal authorities had to duplicate efforts. The garbage treatment plant at Karantina located in east Beirut was off limits to garbage from west Beirut. City equipment and vehicles were either stolen or destroyed in the fighting, and the city had to resort to contracting private firms to manage its affairs. By the 1980s, most of Beirut's streets were damaged, with no light and with crater-sized holes. The heart of the city became a wasteland with trees and wild plants growing on the streets. What had once been the commercial and cultural centre of the Middle East was reduced to a heap of rubble in the first round of fighting in 1975–6. A World Bank team made a field study of downtown Beirut in the period February to March 1983, and estimated the cost of clearing the debris at US$223 million. Many firms were commissioned, and the company Oger Liban began clearing the rubble and debris and preparing the area for reconstruction. Oger Liban was owned by Rafic Hariri, the Lebanese financier from Saida, who held Saudi citizenship.

Housing
Serious overcrowding conditions prevailed in all of Beirut. In the first two years of civil war, the Phalanges cleared the largely Muslim Lebanese citizens and Palestinian refugees from the eastern suburbs. In the western sector, the Lebanese left and their Palestinian allies forced the residents of the largely Maronite Damour to move to east Beirut. Beirut, east and west, suffered disproportionately relative to the rest of Lebanon as it was the destination of most of victims of dislocation and war. The flood of

internal refugees imposed a massive demand on Beirut's already scarce resources. Proprietors refused to pay property taxes, claiming that almost every building was either damaged by the bombs or occupied by refugees from other places, or that the rent they received was not enough to pay the taxes because of inflation.

Residential buildings were deteriorating and the city infrastructure (including water supplies, sewage and electricity) was outdated. The sewage system, already a scandal before the war, became a threat to public health, polluting drinking water and the beaches. In many a neighbourhood, because of clogged pipes in the winter season, sewers flooded periodically and low-level houses were filled with dirt and disease. A 1983 World Bank study estimated the cost of a new sewage system for Lebanon at US$15 billion.

Lebanon's acute shortage of housing became very serious after 1982. Although the government made a decision to construct 20,000 housing units in 1980,[12] studies conducted in 1983 showed that 135,000 units were needed immediately to house the homeless and cope with the internal refugee situation. Most of Lebanon's population is urban and a typical family lives in an apartment block. Aside from single-home ownership in the small towns and villages, city dwellers reside in high-rise apartment blocks. In the cities, single-family homes are considered a rarity and, where available, are owned only by the very rich.

The housing crisis stemmed partly from the rent control laws that had been in place since independence. These laws required annual rental rates to be set in perpetual lease contracts. Once signed, the rental amount could never be changed unless the tenant agreed or moved out. This arrangement proved to be a gold mine to tenants who became virtual owners. This explains why almost no tenants ever moved, creating one of the most immobile populations in the world. It is normal in Lebanon to maintain the same address for upwards of fifty years but still pay a rent set many years beforehand. By 1987, the monthly rental fee of some apartments amounted to less than one US dollar.

Faced with this dilemma, property owners most often gave generous rewards, usually large amounts of money, to long-term tenants to convince them to move. Once vacant, proprietors either demolished or converted the apartments into luxury condominiums or, if they could not afford to demolish or convert the apartments, leased them at exorbitant rates to new tenants or allowed their children to move in when they got married.

Although private financial institutions provided mortgages at attractive rates, a market for mortgages was almost non-existent in Lebanon and cash payments were always required when buying property. Considering the rent control laws in Lebanon, the shortage of mortgage funds cannot be seen as an impediment to housing.

Although public-funded housing is an idea that never materialized in Lebanon, the Ministry of Housing and its arm the Independent Housing Fund provided some support for affordable housing. The Fund extended credit at easy terms to help those who lost their homes during the civil war or to repair damages incurred during the fighting. The maximum amount of the loan was initially set at LL100,000.[13] However, with the increasing inflationary pressures the law was amended on 1 July 1987 to modify credit conditions and to link mortgage financing to income levels. The maximum amount of a loan was increased to LL200,000, but this remained much lower than the rise in inflation. The real problem facing the Fund was the chronic default on payment and the lack of enforcement by the central government to pressure defaulters to pay. Hence, loans became de facto handouts and the public saw them as such. The same mentality which held that government services should be free allowed borrowers from the Fund to believe that they had a right to the money.

Aside from the middle-class and low-income housing, there were many well-off Lebanese who could easily afford to build or acquire property. This group had access to credit from a private bank, the Housing Bank, which extended credit to safe investments. This group also kept the construction industry afloat even in the direst moments of the war.

It was not unusual to see construction workers doing their jobs with bombs falling around them, as in an environment of economic collapse and depression, investors found a safe refuge in real estate and construction. Construction accounted for 4–5 per cent of the GDP in the years 1965–74 and, during the war, demand for building permits maintained a healthy pace, encouraged by the decline in the value of the lira and the influx of US dollars from expatriates eager to take advantage of the relatively low price of property.

In the first six months of 1987, an amount of US$300 million was invested in construction in Lebanon. Building permits covered 2.3 million square metres, or the equivalent of 12,000 apartments at 180 square metres each.[14] This compared to building permits for an area of

6.2 million square metres, or the equivalent of 32,000 apartments in the entire period from 1980 to 1986. Even in the best boom years in Lebanon before the war, construction never attained that level of growth. Permits covered 2.1 million square metres (12,096 apartments) in 1972 and 1.6 million square metres (9,500 apartments) in 1973.

While metropolitan Beirut is a large urban conglomerate extending as far as the adjacent province of Mount Lebanon, government records on housing in Beirut cover only the area within its municipal boundaries, which received a relatively small number of building permits. Although construction firms advertized housing opportunities in Beirut, the majority of the building permits were for Beirut's suburbs which are formally located in the province of Mount Lebanon.

After 1985, payments for transactions in the construction industry were made in US dollars. As most building materials were imported, developers needed to purchase large amounts of hard currency to finance their construction projects. Payment for the purchase of property was also made in US funds. Property value rose dramatically in the 1980s. In 1987, depending on location, property was priced at US$20–55 per square metre for average quality buildings and US$100–140 per square metre for high rise and luxury apartments. Modern and well-equipped apartments fetched as much as US$300–350 per square metre. The greatest demand came from wealthy residents and expatriate Lebanese. A typical apartment that sold for LL104,000 in 1974 was offered for LL16 million in 1987. However, it was actually cheaper in dollar terms, at US$42,000 in 1974 (US$1 = LL2.48) and US$35,000 in 1987 (US$1 = LL457). Lebanese individuals working in the Gulf region and West Africa topped the list of home-buyers, followed by those in the Americas. Expatriates accounted for at least 85 per cent of homes bought in 1987.

As a major economic sector that used hard currency as a mode of payment, activity in the real estate business weighed on the value of the lira and contributed to inflation. The construction price index that reflects the cost to developers jumped from 287 per cent in 1985 to 1,278 per cent in 1987. Cement, wood and iron were the prominent components of this index. In 1972, the construction index stood at 106 per cent, moving to 164 per cent in 1973 (in 1973, cement prices rose 6 per cent, wood 113 per cent and iron 109 per cent). The index had its largest rises in 1987. The exponential rise in construction costs was not due entirely to the exchange rate. It also reflected rising demand for cement. Records of the Cement Company of Lebanon and the National Cement Company show that demand skyrocketed from 310,000 tons in 1985 to 1.2 million tons in 1986, a rise of more than 300 per cent in a single year. To match the demand, the two firms expanded capacity, which meant greater imports of machinery, equipment and raw materials.

With the continued decline in the lira, import prices rose, leading to higher prices for the final product. Consequently, in 1974 a ton of cement cost LL75 at factor cost, rising to LL9,420 in 1987. When converted to dollars at the exchange rates prevailing in the two periods, the cost was US$30 in 1974 against US$33 in 1987 (US$1 = LL280). In other words, the price of cement in terms of US dollars rose only marginally between 1974 and 1987.

The decline in the value of properties is partly explained by the drop in demand by foreign investors and rich Arab nationals and the stagnant wage levels in the construction industry. Labour, priced in terms of the domestic currency, was not adjusted enough to reflect the rise in inflation. Compared to a construction price index of 1,274 in 1987, the wage index was 226 (1971 = 100). Hence, the tiny rise in labour costs since 1974 meant lower wages. The unit labour cost was US$22 per ton in 1974 against only US$7 in 1987 (a 300 per cent decline), while unit material cost rose from US$8 to US$26 (a 350 per cent increase) in the same period. Developers made huge profits because of relatively cheap labour. The share of labour in the unit cost dropped from 70 per cent in 1974 to 20 per cent in 1987 (against 70 per cent for material inputs and 10 per cent for other costs in 1987).

Notes

1 The weights used were: food, 38 per cent, housing, 23 per cent, clothing, 17 per cent and other items, 22 per cent.
2 Food, 14.07 per cent, housing, 19.21 per cent, clothing, 12.44 per cent, health, 6.06 per cent, education, 5.86 per cent, personal needs, 1.23 per cent, leisure, 7.97 per cent, commuting, 11.23 per cent, telephone, mail, telegrams, 0.79 per cent, cleaning, 1.37 per cent, maids, 2.47 per cent, cigarettes, 2.84 per cent and miscellaneous, 1.52 per cent. Mentioned in the Beirut Chamber of Commerce', *Lebanese and Arab Economies*, 1974.
3 Lebanese workers are organized into four big unions, which in turn form the umbrella General Union of Syndicated Workers.

4 The committee had six members, most of whom had a Ph.D. in Economics from an American university. The experts were Salim al-Hoss (prime minister for the majority of 1977–90), Mohamed Attallah (later president of the important National Council for Reconstruction and Development in 1977), Samir Makdisi, an American University of Beirut professor, Rawakara Oglan, an insurance broker, Issam Achour, a businessman and Khalil Salem (later director at the Finance Ministry).
5 Makdisi, *Beirut Fragments*, p. 8.
6 This was the same Arida family who tried to convince Beidas in 1966 to sell Middle East Airlines to an American financier.
7 From a study by Ghaleb Ahmad, director of the refinery, published in *Annahar Economic Report*, 1987.
8 Decree No. 1917 of 6 June 1979.
9 *Official Gazette* No. 52, 25 December 1980; Decree Nos. 3675 and 3676.
10 Decree No. 68 of 5 August 1967.
11 Decree No. 118 of 6 June 1977.
12 Decree No. 6/80 of 17 May 1980.
13 Decree No. 3686.
14 Annual Report of the Civil Engineering Syndicate of Lebanon, 1990, Beirut.

12

Amine Gemayel and Government Collapse

In a state of nature, man becomes victim to the absence of law and order; everyone looks out for themselves as life becomes "brutish, selfish and short".[1] This Hobbesian scenario does not apply in the Levant. When everything was breaking down in Lebanon, private initiative saved the day. Even in more peaceful periods, chaos was the norm in Lebanon. A story is told in Lebanon about a Belgian economist who visited Lebanon in the 1940s. Shocked with the way business was conducted there, but pleasantly surprised with the prosperity, he became convinced that there was no other way to run the country. His observation went down in the annals of Lebanese wisdom: "We don't know how or why, but if it works, don't touch it".[2]

This non-interventionist principle is at the core of Lebanese capitalism, and often serves as a prescription for a limited role for government. In the late 1950s however, this rudimentary capitalism did not strike a chord with President Chehab who, in 1959, invited a group of experts from the Institut International de Recherche et de Formation Éducation du Développement (IRFED) to study the development prospects of Lebanon. IRFED produced a report after three years, which Chehab took very seriously. Indeed, he began a programme of reform that touched on many aspects of life. One of his legacies was the creation of a civil service Conseil de Discipline (al-Majlis al-Ta'adibi), which was part of his personal war against corruption in the civil service and politics.

Nepotism and patronage go a long way back in Lebanese tradition. The 1864–1916 Mutassaref system would have failed had it not satisfied the demands of the various warlords and *zaim*s. This also applied to twentieth-century Lebanon. In fact, Kamal Joumblatt would not have parted ways with Chamoun in 1952 had it not been for Chamoun's reluctance to reform the civil service and to start an inquiry into alleged abuses by senior bureaucrats and public figures, such as former president Bechara al-Khouri and his entourage.

The Lebanese civil service was a product of the Levantine culture. Government departments suffered from chronic absenteeism and an Ottoman legacy of corruption and nepotism. Abuse of connections was rampant in government departments and attempts by successive governments to contain corruption were doomed to failure. The Lebanese civil servant was also a victim of abuse and a low salary. With salaries at subsistence levels, and a public that was accustomed to preferential treatment and which stubbornly rejected being treated equitably, there was a temptation to accept the wheeling and dealing by both nationals and foreigners. Between 1940 and 1990, government employees were the lowest paid workers in the country; the public looked down upon government jobs and pitied those who said they were civil servants.

In the 1980s, salaries did not even cover commuting to work, let alone other expenses; they barely covered payment for food and shelter. In order to supplement their incomes, government employees started charging the public for regular services, which they did not see as a bribe or a commission but simply as informally switching half the burden of paying their salaries from the cash-starved government to the general public.

Western travellers in the non-oil-producing Middle East are bemused by the words *bakhshish* (tip) and *rashwa* (bribe); travelogues written by Westerners normally include a story or two about their experiences with these two words.[3] However, in the Levant, particularly in Lebanon, *bakhshish* and *rashwa* have a specific meaning that is irrelevant to the extra fee charged by a civil servant. In Lebanon, *bakhshish* refers to tipping a waiter at a restaurant, and *rashwa* refers to a criminal offence. The extra fee that goes into the pocket of the civil servant for a regular service is part of a system that tries to make everybody happy. Those who tried their luck and paid the regular fee had their files sitting in the drawer for months.

Another major source of income for the low-paid civil servant was moonlighting. It is normal in Lebanon and in many other developing countries for civil servants to become taxi drivers, vegetable vendors, school teachers or to work in a clothing store. Also, during the war, some civil servants were able to remain on the payroll and travel to the Gulf states or to the Americas where they would work while continuing to maintain their salaries in Lebanon.

The Lebanese who travelled to Europe or North America came back with stories about people standing in line to receive service, and equal treatment of citizens at government departments. These Lebanese had most often been the first ones to use the corrupt system at home. A person could tell wonderful stories about law and order in Sweden, and in the same conversation show you the expensive gold lighters and special bottles of alcohol that he had managed to get through customs by paying a small "fee". It was all right to complain about corruption while participating in it at the same time. At Beirut airport, when travellers had excess baggage, they would insist on keeping the extra weight, offering money and presenting petition cards from military officers or known militia leaders. Sometimes influential people would accompany their friends through customs without a word asked. Almost always, when those travellers arrived at their destinations abroad, they would have stories to tell about "corrupt airport employees".

A conscientious employee who rejected a bribe or a "reward" would have his arm twisted when a bigger reward went to his superior or a card arrived from a politician with a petition to "hurry up with the request". However, the corrupted system became a burden for law-abiding citizens.

Perhaps I can illustrate the state of the bureaucracy with an actual situation from daily life, when in 1978 I encountered a lengthy ritual to obtain a passport. I learnt that the starting point was to obtain a "fresh" civil registry card, for which I had to visit the Ministry of the Interior. I got there at 8 am to find a crowd of people already waiting for a particular civil servant. The man arrived at 9 am and promptly closed his door without looking round. When the door was finally opened, people rushed in and surrounded the employee, who signed their forms sporadically and in all directions. Before him on the desk were signs of a late breakfast: crumbs of a *zaatar* pizza and spots of oil on the newspaper. Formally, government offices should close around 2 pm. However, one spots very few employees after 12 noon. If my visit to the Civil Registry was typical, then one would only be able to complete one document a day. But why take the trouble? I was told that the *mokhtar*[4] could get all the required documents for a small fee. This way everybody won: I could use my time for other things, the *mokhtar* made some money, and the civil servant also got something.

Eventually, I completed my application. The next step was to present it at the *Sûreté Générale* to obtain a passport. As 1978 was also a year of chaos, what would normally have taken three days ended up taking much longer. I submitted my application, paid the regular fees and was told to expect delivery the next week. After two weeks and several visits I was told the passport was not back yet from the main office in Achrafié. When I asked for my file back, I found to my dismay that all this time it was still in the drawer of the first officer who had received the application.

Later I learnt that a certain civil servant in our neighbourhood could get the passport in one day for a fee that was five times greater than the official rate. When I met this man and gave him the money he pocketed it casually as if by right and murmured: "Tomorrow at two – my home." The following day, in Levantine fashion, I went to his home where his wife made coffee and we engaged in small talk about the situation. Then, as if that was not the purpose of the visit, he handed me the mint passport. Of course, it goes without saying that this employee was from a good law-abiding and God-fearing family.

This was the situation in Lebanon before, during and after the war: "Need a driver's licence, an import or export licence, forged university degrees, official school transcripts? You pay the fee and prompt delivery is promised." "Need water supply, bread and electricity when everything is in short supply? For the right price you get what you want." This behaviour was not limited to government employees, nor to private individuals. General directors and ministers could also take opportunities when they came. In 1969, the government decided to buy Crotal missiles from France and the Cabinet earmarked the budget for this purpose. Some months later, several ministers and military officers pilfered the funds, leaving little to complete the actual purchase. Fortunately, an inquiry identified a number of people who were involved in the scandal and they received lengthy jail sentences.

In 1990, under the first post-war government that promised to be different, a squad of policemen from the Ministry of the Interior stormed the Central Bank and broke into the governor's office, beat him up and wounded his aide. Newspapers reported the reason was that the Minister of the Interior, Elias al-Khazen, was upset that Governor Edmond Naim would not approve the funds needed to pay for printing new passports. The papers reported Naim's argument that the cost was purposely inflated to allow for the usual commissions and shares, and that Naim knew of another submission that had cost half the amount. Eventually, the episode ended with an apology to Naim and a denial from al-Khazen.

When the first round of fighting ended in 1976 and Beirut airport re-opened, nobody new that 1975–6 was only the first round in a series of wars that continued until 1990. In April 1976, the parliament elected the Governor of the Central Bank, the Chehabist Elias Sarkis, as president of Lebanon, and later that year Sarkis appointed the President of the Banking Control Commission, Salim al-Hoss, as prime minister. Al-Hoss formed a Cabinet on 8 December 1976 comprising well-known Chehabists, including Fouad Butros as Foreign Minister, Boutros Dib as Minister of Education, Farid Roufael as Minister of Finance and Farouk Abillama as Director of General Security. The Chehabist Michel al-Khouri replaced Sarkis as the Governor of the Bank of Lebanon.

With the euphoria and the optimism that accompanied the declaration of peace, the government felt it could go ahead with reconstruction. A new Council for Reconstruction and Development was created in January 1977 to replace the old Ministry of Planning. In 1978, the Council presented detailed studies and project schedules along with estimates of their financial requirements. The Council's task was not a small one: the destruction of Lebanon's industrial areas, the commercial district of Beirut and the tourist jewels of the mountain region had crippled the economy and created massive unemployment. National income had dropped 12 per cent in the first six months of the war in 1975, and 33 per cent in 1976 and 1977. While economic growth resumed at a rate of 6 per cent per annum until 1981, economic activity between 1978 and 1981 remained at half that achieved in 1974.

In 1977, the preliminary agenda of the Council called for the spending of US$7.5 billion. The government was hopeful that at least 50 per cent would come from the private sector and 50 per cent from the Arab countries. Initially, Sarkis was very enthusiastic and he pushed for a meeting of Arab Ministers of Finance to approve an aid package to Lebanon. However, the Israeli invasion of Lebanon in March 1978, and the war between the Syrian army and the Phalanges militia in east Beirut in the same year pushed the country back into the cycle of violence and postponed the government's reconstruction agenda.

Giving up on major projects, the government provided minor support to the damaged economic sectors. In tourism, businesses were allowed to postpone payment of taxes and loans, and some profits from the Casino du Liban were channelled to damaged hotels. Subsidies to tourism amounted to LL5 million annually between 1975 and 1979 (save for 1978 as the Casino was shut down). In 1977, the government-backed Bank of Industrial and Tourist Development assigned LL300 million to extend loans at low interest to help reconstruct tourist establishments.

However, government help was not sufficient to revive tourism as it was linked so closely to the security situation: Western tourists were no longer visiting. To cope with the situation, several establishments converted to other lines of business while many tourism employees departed for work in the Gulf and Saudi Arabia; many establishments closed permanently. After 1976, the shrinking tourist industry catered for a different type of guest. Whereas prior to the war most guests came for pleasure and to spend hard currency, after 1975, hotel guests were mainly foreign reporters covering the war, individuals escaping war in other parts of the country, militia leaders, Palestine Liberation Organization (PLO) officials and casual business visitors, such as arms dealers from Europe. In 1974, guests stayed 2.3 million nights, and in 1977, the total number of nights fell to around 400,000 – a loss of business of over 80 per cent.

The government's attempt to revive manufacturing also failed. In 1977, as an attempt to encourage investment in manufacturing, the government gave tax breaks for up to six years for investors who wished to start businesses in Beirut, and for up to ten years for investments outside Beirut. The decree specified that this tax break applied to firms with an initial investment of LL1 million and annual salaries of LL200,000. However, manufacturing remained dead for the next four years, and output dropped drastically as businesses were bombed, burnt-out and looted and the political situation in the country continued to deteriorate. Manufacturing had to wait until the late 1980s to experience new dynamism.

The al-Hoss government's limited steps in leading the country towards peace and recovery, coupled with existing statutory social programmes, played an important role in alleviating the suffering of low-income families during the war. The government's annual investments reached some 3 per cent to 5 per cent of GDP and its expenditures included generous subsidy programmes, social security and medical care funds, and free education from pre-school to university. In 15 years of war, people with limited means would have had no chance without these generous programmes. While the government spent generously, the sources of funds dried up and chronic deficits contributed to the decline of the national currency.

AMINE GEMAYEL AND GOVERNMENT COLLAPSE

After their third year in office, Sarkis and his government felt that they could not last even if they were able to control revenues. The destruction and the collapse was beyond their capacity. While the badly needed foreign aid never materialized, domestic sources of funds, such as customs duties and taxes, were either in decline or were being collected by the militias. Traditionally, customs and excise duties represented the largest single source of revenues to the government, accounting for 30 to 40 per cent of the total, while income taxes accounted for 15 per cent. Customs and excise taxes were the single most important source of revenue up to 1975, after which the militias took over the collection. Also after 1975, the government budget deficit started to accumulate, reaching several billion dollars by 1985 (Table 27 in the Statistical Appendix shows the rise in deficit from 1975 to 1983).

In the early 1970s, the government matched the shortfall in revenues by receiving small advances from the Central Bank. These advances ranged from a few million liras in 1970 to LL15 million in 1975. After the first leg of the war, to keep things running the government borrowed LL966 million in 1977, and LL851 million in 1978. With almost no revenue and little foreign aid, deficits were experienced every year after 1976. Government investments showed little or no profits, and taxes were not collected. To handle the situation, parliament granted the government borrowing authority and the power to issue securities. Borrowing took place largely through the issue of Treasury bills, which were offered to financial institutions and to the general public.

Illegal ports run by private militias mushroomed on the Lebanese coast and were used by almost everybody to import anything from cars to bottled beer, and export anything from paint to hashish and other drugs. Ports with modern facilities were built in many places – most notably at Ouzai, 2 kilometres south of Beirut, at Jiyé, 30 kilometres south of Beirut, at Aqua Marina, 30 kilometres north of Beirut and Chekka, 60 kilometres north of Beirut. According to conservative estimates, illegal ports and smuggling cost the government US$50 million per month in lost revenues. Government-run harbours were largely taken over by the militias who imposed their own duties and taxes on imports and exports (Table 25). As a ratio of imports, government customs revenues shrank to a small fraction of receipts. Between 1973 and 1982, the value of imports quadrupled, but government revenues were almost halved as most tariff revenues were collected by the various militias.[5] In the same period, exports were recovering, increasing to US$1.3 billion in 1981 from US$910 in 1980.

Finally, in 1979 during a summit of the heads of Arab states held in Tunis, citing the relative peace in Lebanon, a group of oil-rich countries committed themselves to granting Lebanon a sum of US$2 billion for reconstruction and development, paid in instalments over five years. However, the pledges by the donor countries were only partly respected. Between 1979 and December 1981, Lebanon received US$372 million, which was less than half of the US$800 million allotted for that period. Only the United Arab Emirates paid its quota in full; Saudi Arabia and Iraq paid only half their shares and Libya paid nothing. Saudi Arabia preferred to channel the other half of its quota (around US$60 million annually) through the businessman Rafic Hariri. The US$60 million became an annual Saudi tradition and, in 1991, Lebanon received US$60 million from the Saudi government to clear the debris and the streets of Beirut. Rafic Hariri established the Hariri Foundation to spend the money on various projects in Lebanon, including scholarships for university students.

After 1981, payments stopped altogether and the donor countries claimed that as long as the war continued in Lebanon no money could be allotted. Swept again by the internal conflict and by the lack of funds, the government switched its agenda to establishing "Peace Before Bread". By the time Sarkis ended his last year in office in 1982, the country was in a deeper abyss than it had been when he came to power in 1976. His term was crowned with another Israeli invasion in June 1982.

Between June 1982 and June 1985, the Israeli invasion and the three-year occupation of south Lebanon caused US$2 billion in economic damage. In 1983, the first year after the Israeli invasion, emergency humanitarian aid was badly needed and Lebanon received US$165 million. The Arab states were the main donors, followed by the United Nations, the International Red Cross and several non-governmental organizations (NGOs). The European Community paid US$50 million (of which Italy contributed US$19 million), the Banque Européenne de l'Investissement paid US$20 million and France extended a long-term credit to Lebanon for US$40 million. The United States of America also contributed. The USA had consistently offered Lebanon foreign aid over the past forty years. In the 1950s, following the Point IV programme,[6] Lebanon received amounts ranging from US$10 million to US$20 million from the US. The Marines landed in Beirut in 1958 to support Camille Chamoun and again in 1982 to participate in the Multinational Force that supervised the truce in Beirut following the Israeli withdrawal from the city.

Encouraged by the prospects of peace, in 1983, the Council for Reconstruction presented an update of its 1977 agenda of projects, with a total estimated cost of US$32 billion. The Lebanese government was optimistic that 75 per cent of the requirements for rebuilding the core of Beirut would come from foreign aid, and 25 per cent (US$8 billion) would be contributed by the Lebanese private sector, which had a major stake in the old commercial district. Optimism did not last long as the civil war resumed – this time between the Maronites and the Druze in the Aley and Chouf Mountains south-east of Beirut – and lasted for much of 1983 and 1984. In Tripoli, the second largest Lebanese city which had been spared for most of the war prior to 1983, a showdown occurred between rebel Palestinians and Yasser Arafat's organization, the PLO. A third battle began on 6 February 1984, when a Shiite–Druze alliance took over the western suburbs of Beirut. Following this battle, the Lebanese army, which had recently received American weapons and training, split along sectarian lines.

These events worked against the government's hopes for a quick economic recovery and the reconstruction of Beirut. Foreign donors and creditors refrained from providing more than emergency and humanitarian aid. The promised private investments did not materialize: patriotism aside, Lebanese entrepreneurs preferred the safety of foreign countries to the hell of war. Between September 1982 and June 1984 no major investments were recorded in Lebanon.

Between 1981 and 1990, battles around the country were erupting almost every year. In 1981, there was the battle for the town of Zahlé and the strategic Mount Sannine that escalated into a regional conflict between Syria and Israel. In 1982, the Israelis invaded the country. In 1983–5, a civil war started between the Maronites and the Druze in the Chouf. In 1983, a Palestinian civil war took place in Tripoli. In February 1984, the *Amal* militia and the Druze attacked west Beirut. In 1985, the battle for the Palestinian refugee camps started between *Amal* and the PLO. In 1983, several Lebanese militias invaded Tripoli to dislodge a radical Muslim militia. In 1986–7, the *Amal* and Druze militias battled for control over west Beirut. In 1986–90, an internal Maronite civil war flared up for the control of the Christian heartland. In 1989, a six-month "liberation war" was led by General Aoun. In 1986–90, an internal Shia civil war took place for the control of the Shia areas in Beirut and the south. Between 1991 and 2002, the Lebanese Army fought brief battles with Palestinian militants in the Ain Helwé refugee camp near Saida.

Faced with so many disasters, the Council for Reconstruction and Development's main efforts in the period 1983–90 went into maintenance of public utilities and roads, and emergency services to support the government work.

When Amine Gemayel became President of Lebanon in September 1982, the regional and international climate convinced him that he could rely on unlimited support from the USA and European countries. He toured the USA and Europe, and invited the British to send an army to Lebanon. He talked also about a Western aid package to Lebanon to the order of US$1.0 billion. His confidence in Western support even led him to alienate Syria and the Muslims of Lebanon. From the White House, with President Ronald Reagan standing next to him, he had very unkind words to say of President Hafez Assad and Syria.

Back in Beirut, the Lebanese army and the Phalanges militia behaved as victors, and treated Muslims and Palestinians very badly. Instead of taking a historic opportunity to build bridges with the Muslims by showing the best face of Maronite tolerance, the Gemayel government made things worse. After the Israeli invasion, which left 25,000 dead and cost US$2 billion in economic damage, the public expected the government would respond to such a national disaster by attending to the needs of the civilian population. The authorities chose instead to harass the populations of west Beirut and Saida who had sided with the Palestinians and the leftists before the Israeli invasion, with government troops victimizing male adults. They imposed excessive and strict searches and checkpoints, and started demolishing the slums of Ouzai where many of the displaced victims of the war resided.

From the start, the Muslims viewed the Gemayel government as belonging to the Phalanges militia and as their enemy. Reports mentioned 2,000 disappearances of people arrested by the army or kidnapped by the Phalanges. These incidents foretold bloodier episodes of the civil war which were on the way. Western and Arab observers remarked that Lebanon was not on the path of recovery and reconstruction, but was rather a country that was busily settling old scores.

AMINE GEMAYEL AND GOVERNMENT COLLAPSE

In April 1983, of the US$1 billion Gemayel sought, the USA promised US$251 million, of which US$100 million was destined to pay for the training of, and equipment for, the Lebanese army. The Gemayel government was keen to realize Bachir Gemayel's dream of building "an army of 100,000 men". Massive amounts of money that were badly needed for reconstruction and social services were spent on procurement of weapons. The cost of this armament was US$880 million,[7] and the first shipments were used to bomb the southern suburbs, stronghold of the Shia *Amal* militia that was challenging Gemayel and which began an uprising against his rule in February 1983. Much of the massive arsenal was later stolen and used by the various Lebanese militias to kill each other, or employed in Aoun's war against his foes.

Gemayel's dream of peace and a strong government quickly collapsed. As for Western support, only part of the US$251 million promised by the USA was paid; the rest was diverted to the US Marines for activities elsewhere in the world. The US Administration's priorities shifted elsewhere and in 1984 it informed Lebanon that the remaining US$40 million would not be paid.[8] Government debt kept growing: in 1983, the government received US$600 million in revenues and incurred a deficit of US$1.6 billion (LL3.543 billion) to match the spending of US$2.2 billion. This brought the domestic debt to US$3.7 billion in 1982[9] (LL16 billion) and to US$11.7 billion in 1983 (LL53.1 billion), exceeding the GNP in that year. Eventually, the government had to pay principal plus interest that amounted to a greater portion of expenditure.[10] Servicing the growing debt amounted to 17 per cent of the budget.

The Gemayel regime was so crippled that no government budgets were announced or presented between 1985 and 1990 because of the inability of the cabinet to reconvene. The Ministry of Finance introduced temporary measures that permitted the payment of salaries and the allotment of public funds to the various departments. The Central Bank established spending purses as accounts for the various ministries. For example, an account was set up for the Ministry of the Economy to import cereals and petroleum products, and another for the Ministry of Education to spend on public schools and the Université Libanaise.

Although this approach was a practical way to keep the government running in the absence of a Cabinet and a budget, it gave a free hand to the ministers and senior officials who spent funds without accountability to parliament and without following any priorities or guidelines.[11] In the absence of a budget document, revenues and expenditures were not known. Expenditures were committed to projects with no feasibility studies or economic evaluation, or even a sense of whether they were necessary. Some ministers even built new office blocks to house their departments and equipped them with modern furniture at a cost of millions of dollars.

In 1986, some attempts were made to trim expenditure. Consequently, government purchases abroad were halved and total expenditure was lowered by 39.4 per cent. The government encountered great difficulty securing foreign exchange funds and this situation became hopeless in 1987, when talk about using the massive gold reserves began.

The gold reserve

In 1987, attention focused on the 9.22 million ounces of pure gold bullion that were stored in the basement of the Central Bank on Rue Massraf Lubnan. The Governor of the Bank, Edmond Naim, physically guarded the place. How? He literally slept on a couch in his office at night and worked at his desk in the day.[12]

The argument for using the gold reserves was that bullion did not earn interest, and the government could sell the gold and invest the proceeds in secure bank accounts in Europe which paid at least US$300 to US$400 million in interest annually. Advocates of this idea argued that the interest earnings alone could eliminate the budget deficit and in time set public finances straight. Moreover, the dollar earnings would reduce the pressure on the lira in the foreign exchange market, thus reviving confidence in the national currency and encouraging the public to use it as a deposit in bank accounts. On the economic front, a strong lira could convince investors to come back to Lebanon, open up shop and create jobs.

This argument was not a winner. Parliament and several individual politicians opposed the plan and in order to ensure that nobody touched the gold, parliament withdrew the authority to handle reserves from the government and passed legislation requiring parliamentary approval for gold transactions. A stronger piece of legislation re-enforced this ban in 1990. The Finance Committee's report argued that the gold was a sacred national fund that gave psychological confidence to the holders of the lira and several disadvantages would result from selling it. Not least, it was unlikely that Lebanon could sell such a large quantity without making a downward impact on the world market.

Experience has shown that a fraction of one million ounces could make a big difference in the London gold market (gold prices dropped US$26 an ounce in four days in February 1990 following the dumping of 350,000 ounces of gold in London by Middle East sellers). Aside from the impact on the world market, the sale would give the wrong signal to the Beirut financial market and to the public that the government had finally collapsed. The message would lead to the erosion of any remaining public confidence in the lira, along with any hope of curing the economic and financial ills of the country.

Faced with such resistance, the government modified its position and proposed the sale of 20 per cent of the gold reserves, but the Central Bank dismissed this idea as a quick fix to inject funds into the coffers of a government that did not meet and had no budget or proper accountability system, and where officials were spending without paying attention to the state of affairs in the country. The sale of 20 per cent of the gold would not solve the crisis in the country. The Governor of the Central Bank wanted the use of the proceeds from the gold sale to be spelled out: were they going to be used to intervene to support the lira or to finance expenditures that amounted to US$450 million in 1987? "Who would guarantee that a further 20 per cent will not be sold later?" Naim asked.

Another less drastic proposal was made by the government. The idea was to use 20 per cent of the gold reserves as collateral for the government to borrow in foreign exchange markets. However, the Central Bank maintained its earlier line that whatever the amount to be borrowed it would be used to support the lira, in which case the amount would be swallowed easily by the Beirut market (as in 1986) and in no time the collapse would resume in a worsening environment under a situation of compromising the gold reserves. The Governor requested that the government should first start putting the house in order, tighten the screws, prepare a budget and curtail expenditure, and then it may not need to use the gold reserves at all. He suggested that cutting expenditure should start with axing subsidies and seeking cooperation in collecting taxes.

A private sector initiative was added to the debate but its contribution was short-lived. This initiative came from a committee calling itself the Economic Emergency Committee and comprised representatives of trade associations in the private sector such as the Bankers' Association and the Manufacturers' Association. Notable business leaders such as Walid Naja, Mohamed Cheaito, Joseph Faddoul and Fouad Abisaleh were in the membership. The committee met in August and issued a memorandum to the government addressing the economic crisis. The memo had seven recommendations.

1. Illegal seaports run by the militias should be shut down and handed over to the government; legal ports under militia control should be handed over to the authorities.
2. Tax collection should be enforced and militia authorities should help. Telephone, electricity and water fees should be collected, otherwise recipients should risk the withdrawal of service.
3. Subsidies should be scaled back and austerity measures introduced on social services.
4. The 1980 Consumer Cooperatives law calling for the establishment of consumer coops to impose discipline on consumer prices should be implemented.
5. The 1980 Medicine and Prescription Act calling for the establishment of the Medicine Bureau should be implemented.
6. A law to protect the consumer against fraudulent goods that use hazardous materials and expired foods should be introduced.
7. Housing initiatives to house the displaced families and the poor should be introduced.

While the first three recommendations addressed the budget deficit, the remaining four ironically called for more government spending. Even the recommendations that called for deficit reduction measures were mere fantasy. An attempt by the authorities to close down the illegal seaports triggered a battle in 1989 that cost 1,400 lives and caused massive damage to the country, while a subsequent attempt to seize control of the fourth and fifth basins of the Beirut harbour triggered another bloody battle that cost 1,000 lives and almost US$1.5 billion in damages to the economic infrastructure. In 1989–90, despite having 19,000 troops and heavy artillery the Lebanese army was unable to take over that portion of the Beirut harbour controlled by the Lebanese Forces militia, which only mustered 6,000 soldiers.

Public finance

With these prospects, the only route left for the government was to borrow more since cuts in spending or an increase in taxes were not possible. To sell its debt, the government had to create a market for its issues and the Central Bank obliged commercial banks to invest in Treasury bills. The banks were dissatisfied with this arrangement and they blocked the growth of the T-bill market by providing little or no facilities for active trading. The financial institutions felt their freedom was compromised and threatened by the spread of T-bills as an attractive investment to the public at the expense of bank deposits. With a lack of market commitment to buy and market the bills, the government sold a large portion of the issues to the Central Bank, which resulted in an inflationary monetary policy and the monetization of government debt. The more the lira flooded the market, the more the public was reluctant to hold it. The stock of money increased thirteen times in the period 1968–82 (from LL3,430 million to LL48.5 billion). This became worse in the 1980s when even a new supply in billions of liras was not considered a worry. The inflationary impact of this growth was reflected in domestic prices that doubled between 1974 and 1981.

On the foreign front, between 1975 and 1982, Lebanon continued to enjoy a strong currency, a balanced external sector and high gold and foreign currency reserves at the Central Bank. These foreign currency reserves increased from LL8.3 million in 1976 to LL27.7 million in March 1982. In that period, the health of the national currency remained intact, which kept the trade deficit tiny and the foreign currency debt of little concern. In 1983, the lira was recovering against the dollar in Beirut and a promise of economic recovery was again on the horizon. By May 1983, the government's foreign currency debt was as low as US$200 million, against foreign currency reserves of US$3 billion and gold reserves valued at US$3.6 billion.

To expand the T-bill market, the Central Bank followed the American Federal Reserve model and established wickets for the sale of T-bills to individuals in regional branches around the country – namely in Jounié, Tripoli, Zahlé, Saida, Baalbeck and Tyre. However, the growth of the T-bill market was of little concern as the interest cost of the debt to the government became inhibiting. Initially, as a measure to check inflation and the cost of borrowing, the Ministry of Finance imposed a ceiling on the yield on the three-month government T-bills at 19 per cent. But in 1986 the rates had to be increased to attract investors and the yield on the three-month bills shot up to 35 per cent. Even that rate was not good enough. With inflation in 1986–7 running at several hundred percentage points annually, there was no rate attractive enough to convince investors to buy lira-denominated securities or to keep lira deposits. Everybody preferred holding foreign currencies or investing in foreign currency paper that was not exposed to wild fluctuations and inflation pressures. By 1987, almost 70 per cent of commercial banks' reserves were linked to some kind of requirement or another.

A team from the International Monetary Fund (IMF) met regularly with the Lebanese monetary authorities. At a meeting in Paris in June 1987, the IMF approved the banks' credit policy to control credit expansion and check the growth of money. The IMF suggested further measures to contain money growth and check the collapse of the national currency. To achieve these goals, the growth of money supply had to be controlled. This was possible by restricting liquidity in the system and having financial institutions increase their capital base in proportion to the increase in the volume of their business. The IMF discouraged frequent intervention in the foreign exchange market on behalf of the lira as previous interventions had not stopped the fluctuation or discouraged speculation. Limited interventions with small amounts were advised until the banks built up their foreign currency reserves.

On the fiscal side, the delegation called for restraint on government spending especially on defence; advances and loans from the Central Bank to the government were strongly discouraged since they added to inflation and were not backed by real growth; and fuels and food subsidies were to be axed, as most subsidized items were smuggled outside the country. By 1987, the bank was using foreign currency reserves for monetary policy and to finance imports by the Ministry of the Economy. The Central Bank was faced with a double-edged sword. Reserves were used to supplement government expenditure which consisted of direct advances and the purchase by the Central Bank of a large volume of Treasury bills through the primary issue. This helped to monetize the debt.

Government domestic debt was composed mainly of T-bills and was largely owed to domestic financial institutions. It grew marginally from LL14.3 billion in 1985 to LL15.6 billion in 1986. Private individuals held 17 per cent of the total in the same period. Between 1986 and 1989, the debt grew at a moderate pace thanks to Central Bank reserves.

Net annual borrowing from financial institutions dropped to LL5 billion in 1986 against LL16.5 billion in 1985. However, after 1986, the lira collapsed and government finances deteriorated. Between 1987 and 1990, the Government was effectively bankrupt, with no budget, no Cabinet and no revenues. After 1988, the country entered another dark episode of civil strife and public debt reached LL1,000 billion (US$1.5 billion) in 1989 and almost LL2,500 billion (US$3.5 billion) in 1990. Between 1983 and 1989, the deficit grew from 65 per cent as a ratio of expenditures in 1983 to 82 per cent in 1984 and to 90 per cent in 1989.[13]

NOTES

1 Thomas Hobbes, *Leviathan*, London, Penguin, 1985, p. 186. Hobbes (1588–1679), an English philosopher, wrote an apology for the state to use coercive powers over its citizens to avoid civil war. This quote from Hobbes's book is relevant to the Lebanese context: ". . . to a time of war, where every man is enemy to every man; the same is consequent to time, wherein men live without other security, than what their own strength, and their own invention shall furnish them withal. In such condition, there is no place for industry; because the fruit thereof is uncertain; . . . no account of time; no arts; no letters; no society; and which is worst of all, continual fear, and danger of violent death; and the life of man, solitary, poor, nasty, brutish, and short."
2 Hazem Saghiyé, *Maronites from Lebanon* (in Arabic, *Mawarina min Lubnan*), Beirut, al-Markaz al-Arabi lil Malumat, 1988, p. 174.
3 See, for example, Thomas Lippman, *Egypt After Nasser*, New York, Paragon House Publishers, 1989.
4 A respected member of the community who is not a government employee but who is accredited by the government to sign and notarize applications for government documents. Usually the *mokhtar* runs a barber or a grocery shop.
5 *Arab Economic Report*, Arab League Information, 1986.
6 President Eisenhower's programme to assist pro-US governments in the Middle East against a potential Soviet threat.
7 Ministry of Finance, Republic of Lebanon, *Government Expenditures 1982–1985*, Beirut, p. 31.
8 The funding was redirected to Grenada, which had been invaded by the Marines in the previous year.
9 *Assafir*, Saturday 12 November 1984.
10 A government payment on mature debt has two components: the principal amount originally borrowed and the interest accumulated and payable on that amount.
11 Parliament voted on the budget after the Parliamentary Finance and Budgeting Committee scrutinized and approved each department's revenues and expenditures

as well as the general sources and uses of funds. The preparation of the budget document is usually the province of the Minister of Finance. The budget document would include projections of revenues and expenditures for the coming year, and requirements of each government department according to size and need. The fiscal year runs from January to December, and towards the end of October the government presents a budget to parliament for review and approval. Parliament reviews the budget within six weeks and the final document is passed by year-end.

Parliament has the power to amend single items, such as asking the government to re-allocate funds among the various programmes and regions, and individual deputies could plead for their ridings to ask for transfer of funds for health and education. However, the committee cannot alter the global amounts of revenues and expenditures, or the ways of raising money through taxation or borrowing. After 1985, a law was passed requiring the government to present the budget as a full document to be voted instead of the detailed and gradual approval.

12 Naim's experience was described in *The Banker*, July, 1989.
13 Makdisi, *Beirut Fragments*.

13

Roger Tamraz and Financial Collapse

The financial crisis of the 1980s was another deadly disaster to hit Lebanon. Until 1986, Lebanon had been plagued with endless wars, hyperinflation, foreign invasions, a massive exodus of people and the collapse of the national currency. However, this list was topped in 1986–9 with a major financial crisis. This was the second financial crisis in Lebanon's history and was similar to the first one of 1966. It had its origins in 1977, when the ten-year ban on the national establishment of banks was lifted. This ban had been introduced in 1967 following the 1966 financial crisis. Banks, large and small, increased in number between 1977 and 1982, but the growth was chaotic, and failures, mergers and acquisitions took place in larger numbers during the 1980s. In this period, actions by the Central Bank and the Banking Control Commission were not effective, and the Bank of Lebanon had to take over several banks and corporations in the country.

The financial sector suffered a major setback in 1975–6 and lost many of the gains of 1967–74. On the eve of the civil war in 1975, Westerners owned 43 per cent of the banks and controlled 52 per cent of deposits in the system. Long before 1975, banks were receiving reports on the increasingly dangerous situation in Lebanon following military confrontations between the Lebanese army and the PLO between 1969 and 1974, and the on-and-off skirmishes along the Lebanese–Israeli borders. In 1974 a group of masked gunmen attacked the offices of the Bank of America on Rue al-Massaref in downtown Beirut and held the mixed Lebanese and American staff hostage, requesting a ransom of US$10 million and a flight to Algeria. In those more stable times the Lebanese police acted quickly, raiding the bank and arresting the gunmen. Western banks took the hint and, with the first sign of trouble in Beirut in 1975, they slowly liquidated their activities and maintained a low profile.

After the first round of fighting in 1975–6, 25 foreign banks left Beirut and moved to Bahrain, Athens and Cairo, while at least 11 Lebanese banks moved to Paris. Of the 250 American companies operating in

Beirut in 1975 only ten remained by 1978. Some 26 branches of various banks were looted and burnt down, while 44 banks out of eighty in Lebanon declared that their branches had suffered damage from the fighting or had been looted by the combatants. The banks were especially hard hit in the commercial district and the hotels area in the chic Zeitouni district of Beirut. On 20 November 1976, the Lebanese Bankers Association (LBA) estimated losses in the banking sector between December 1975 and May 1976 at US$1 billion. The British Bank of the Middle East and Banco di Roma were the major losers. The media reported a sensational story about the looting of the British Bank's branch by the Phalanges. The militiamen had all the time they needed to open the safe, spending several days trying with different types of explosives and bombs until they cranked it open and retrieved millions of dollars in cash and gold. The money was subsequently used to purchase weapons on the open market in Europe.

Despite the setbacks, the banking sector was almost the only economic sector to survive the first round of the civil war and eventually all the subsequent rounds. Three days after the Israelis left Beirut in September 1982, the banks were again in full operation.

The years 1977–80 were a boom period for banks. Following the lifting of the ban on national establishments in 1977, national banks and their branches grew in number to 450 in 1980 against 250 in 1975. Employment in this sector increased at a rate of 4.3 per cent per year while wages rose 18 per cent annually. Along with lifting the ban, the government introduced a law that permitted offshore banking. As a result, branches of Lebanese banks abroad increased from five to thirty. In contrast, foreign banks were disappearing from the Beirut financial scene (see Table 30 in the Appendix, which shows the deterioration in the rank of foreign banks from 1971 to 1980). According to Table 30, the British Bank of the Middle East moved from rank 2 to rank 16, while Banco di Roma moved from rank 5 to 21. American banks moved from the top ten to the bottom of the list. They either maintained a small presence or moved their Middle East operations to Athens or Bahrain.

Warlord banking
The strong ties between financiers and warlords were a plus for the sector, providing immunity from the war and a constant stream of deposits.

Each bank was protected by a militia belonging to a de facto warlord in each canton.

In 1975–80, Lebanon was floating in cash according to a report in *Le Monde Diplomatique*:[1] almost US$120 million to US$150 million in remittances were sent by Lebanese workers in the Gulf to their families in Lebanon. These remittances peaked in 1981 at US$2 billion. The second source of deposits was the lucrative hashish business. The annual production of Lebanese hashish and other illegal drugs averaged 30,000 tons in 1975–81. At a price of US$65 to US$150 per kilogramme, drug revenues peaked at US$1.5 billion to US$2 billion annually. The third source of deposits was transfers from foreign governments to finance the war efforts of the various militias. Foreign governments poured millions of dollars into Beirut; newspapers casually reported on militia leaders who received something in the order of US$15 million to US$50 million every month. The Iranian Embassy alone dispensed US$100 million annually to its Lebanese allies and similar sums were spent by Israel on the South Lebanon Army (SLA) militia.

Iraq and Libya were equally big spenders and the Lebanese were very imaginative in their demands for more funds. The Libyan deputy prime minister, Abdel Salam Jalloud, visited Lebanon frequently to meet members of Kamal Joumblatt's leftist coalition and the Nasserite militias. In one visit in 1976, he was informed that a major attack was being planned against the Phalanges' stronghold at the Sodico Crossing in the heart of Beirut and that additional funds were needed for the task. Born in Libya and educated about the Battle of Alamein and the Second World War, Jalloud became curious and wanted to see for himself the magnitude of the Sodico front. When he finally got there, he saw several tanks and pieces of artillery, plus a few dozen militiamen. It was no Alamein.

Perhaps the largest depositors in Beirut's banks were the Palestinians. With headquarters in Beirut, the PLO had billions of dollars deposited in the city's banks. With the flow of cash from remittances, militia funds and drug sales, the banks were glad to offer their services and enjoyed the resulting prosperity. Bank deposits grew from US$3 billion in 1974, the last year of peace, to US$5 billion in 1980. French banks with Lebanese partnerships also grew in number. In 1981, out of the top ten banks, six were national in terms of deposits, against one national in the top ten banks in 1971.

Beginning of the crisis

In 1982 there were signs of the coming financial crisis. After 1981, the inflow of remittances and foreign aid fell sharply; the global oil glut that resulted in lower oil prices caused a recession in the oil states. Remittances from Lebanese workers in Saudi Arabia and the Gulf declined drastically and many returned home or left permanently for destinations in the Americas, Australia and West Africa. Things could only get worse. Faced with the continuous violence and lawlessness in Beirut, Arab countries postponed payments of approved aid packages to Lebanon until peace prevailed and the various factions reached an accord.

Lira deposits were badly hurt by inflation, which ran at 19 per cent annually between 1970 and 1981. This weakened the real exchange value of the lira against the dollar. Initially, the growth in deposits shrank from 18 per cent annually in 1974–81 to 16 per cent in 1982. However, after 1982, the share of foreign currency deposits began to grow as the share of lira deposits fell.

Perhaps the largest single factor that damaged the banking system was the departure of the PLO in 1982. After 1977, the largest bank in Beirut was again controlled by Palestinian capital. The Palestinian-owned and Jordanian registered Arab Bank Ltd had large deposits from the PLO and by 1981 had become the largest bank in Lebanon. Following the Israeli invasion in 1982, the PLO along with its economic, political and social infrastructure left Beirut and with it went the huge deposits held in Beirut's banks. The PLO's liquid assets in Beirut were estimated conservatively between US$1.5 billion to US$3.0 billion, with sizeable portions on deposit with the Arab Bank Ltd, while the PLO's expenditures in Lebanon amounted to 15 per cent of all economic activity in the country prior to the Israeli invasion. Consequently, the banking sector and the economy suffered a major setback.[2]

The large number of banks was another factor that led to the crisis. Encouraged by the lifting of the ban and benefiting from the lax atmosphere in the country, the financiers resumed clandestine deals, working under the Levantine ethic that getting that one extra dollar could be achieved by any possible means. Short-term credit deteriorated as several banks were involved in long-term investments, as well as speculation in foreign currencies and real estate. The Secrecy Law did not prevent some scandals from reaching the press. One such story was of a big Lebanese financier who obtained a bank loan of LL200 million (US$65 million) to speculate in the precious metals market.

The birth of dozens of small banks after 1977, coupled with a largely unregulated and disorderly banking sector, left most of the smaller banks exposed to shake-ups, takeover bids and bankruptcies, and the Banking Control Commission detected illegal activities everywhere. In 1982 two foreign financial institutions, Guy Butler and Tolt & Reilly, were shut down and there was a growing sense that the financial market was entering a difficult period. To prevent a repeat of the 1966 crisis, the government offered to negotiate with the Lebanese Bankers Association (LBA) to reach an agreement regarding the banks' credit policy and business practices. Armed with the Secrecy Law, the banks refused to deal openly with the Commission, and preferred a low-key contact with the Bank of Lebanon. However, in 1977, the Central Bank was not the baby of 1966, and following the investigation, it introduced a series of measures. The quick actions by the Bank and the board succeeded in putting some order in the market. But not for long, as speculation in the foreign exchange market continued unchecked, strengthened by the protection conferred on the bankers by the warlords.

Fears of a repeat of 1966 prompted the Banking Control Commission to act. The Commission was under the chairmanship of the banker Fouad Siniora. Siniora became the chairman of the Commission in November 1976 following the appointment of Salim al-Hoss to the post of prime minister. Siniora ordered an investigation into the books and records of several banks to make sure that they were abiding by the Law of Money and Credit and the established laws of business practices.

The bankers fought the Central Bank's measures and pushed for Siniora's resignation. Siniora's report created an uneasy atmosphere between the LBA and the government, and for that he became a target of criticism. The chance to punish Siniora came in 1982 when his contract expired and the government, under pressure, refused to renew it. This action antagonized the Central Bank and its governor, Michel al-Khouri, who threatened to resign on 27 August 1982 unless Siniora was re-instated. Al-Khouri complained that Siniora was being punished for doing his job to fend off a financial catastrophe. Siniora, a Sunni who hails from Saida, the hometown of Rafic Hariri, became finance minister in Hariri's cabinet in 1992 and again in 2000.

The veteran Chehabist Michel al-Khouri, son of former President Bechara al-Khouri and a professional banker, was appointed by his friend President Elias Sarkis as governor of the Bank of Lebanon in 1977. Following the end of the term of Sarkis and the election of Amine Gemayel as president, al-Khouri's disagreements with the government went beyond formalities and he resigned his post in 1983, citing retirement as a reason, although he stayed on until the end of 1984. Observers noted his disagreement with President Gemayel whose government was depleting the Treasury with purchases of American weapons for amounts reaching US$888 million. These weapons were eventually used in future civil wars.

The Finance Company
Early in 1982, the Lebanese Bankers Association (LBA) requested the Central Bank to help create a new institution to work as an intermediary between financial institutions and the Central Bank. On 30 December 1982, the Bank granted a new financial institution, the Finance Company of Lebanon (Société Financière du Liban (SOFL)), legal status, with capital of LL20 million (increased to LL40 million on 2 February 1987), as a private enterprise owned jointly by the Central Bank (50 per cent of shares) and a consortium of 45 foreign and national financial institutions. The Company was operational in 1983 with a board of directors representing the major banks. The Central Bank held the authority to approve the appointment of the Company's board of directors as well as the general director.

The Company was mandated to implement the monetary measures initiated by the Central Bank and to develop a secondary market for government securities so that government borrowing could be made easier without an adverse effect on the markets. Most of the company's functions were subject to approval by the Central Bank and the Banking Review Committee. The Company helped in the conduct of Open Market Operations on behalf of the Central Bank, and its work involved frequent intervention in the market to inject or withdraw funds and regulate banking activities. It helped in the exploration of investment opportunities in Lebanon and abroad, which gave direction to the banks to decide on worthy credit. It provided consulting services and had the function of a trust over all types of assets. The Finance Company traded in commercial paper and certificates of deposit to stimulate and develop the money market. In the foreign exchange market, the Company's function was to rationalize exchange rates and combat speculation, and to check the sudden outbursts of the dollar in Beirut. In summary, the Company was a unique finance establishment that covered the whole spectrum of financial activities.

From 1983 to 1987 the Company operated with no serious difficulty. However, the banks felt the impact of regulation and intervention, and grew impatient with the Company. On 15 January 1986, they simultaneously requested the Company to settle its LL4 billion debt with them. This request was undertaken in the knowledge that the Company could not possibly come up with the money since its liquid assets were locked in government securities. With the danger of default and bankruptcy, the Central Bank intervened and provided the required funds by purchasing securities from the Company to the amount of LL4.2 billion. However, this intervention meant a huge injection of money in the market and increased the banks' ability to extend credit. The added liquidity lowered the value of the lira against the dollar, which was trading at LL19 liras on 14 January, jumping to LL24.5 on 15 January. With the decline of net government borrowing to LL5 billion in 1986 from LL16.5 billion in 1985, the Finance Company deteriorated further, and its holdings of government paper dropped from LL4.7 billion to LL600 million in 1986.

After this episode, the Company recovered and launched a plan to create a Lebanese clearing house for interbank transactions in foreign currencies. Its rationale was that 85 per cent of banking activity was conducted in foreign currencies and most cheques were written in US dollars. These cheques had to be cleared in New York, a process that usually took 15 days and affected market efficiency. A company study estimated that it was costing US$10 to US$15 to process each cheque written in US dollars. The cost reflected the time it took to process the cheques, the commissions and charges, and the lost interest earnings. It was argued that a clearing house would eliminate these costs and would be a step towards greater market efficiency.

However, new developments made it impossible for the Company to implement this plan. In the summer of 1987, it was criticized and accused of abusing its function as an intermediary in the foreign exchange market, for being responsible for the collapse of the national currency and for making it easier for big speculators to conduct their business. There were demands that the government shut down the Company and investigate the accusations. The Company denied the accusations and argued that its intervention in the market on behalf of the lira was not a criminal offence but an essential task to protect the national currency and implement monetary policy. A spokesman for the Company said that without the Finance Company, the private sector would not adhere to the official exchange rate posted by the Central Bank at noon, and speculation against the national currency would increase. Its shutdown would only bring chaos and disorder to the markets.

However, the accusations were so strong that the court ordered the Company to shut down and undergo an official inquiry. Foreign exchange market reaction to the shutdown was strong and the dollar immediately jumped to LL300 from LL150. Despite this, the banks expressed relief that the ombudsmanship role of the Company had come to an end, while the LBA used the occasion as ammunition in its efforts to discredit the Central Bank and reduce its influence in the market. The irony was that the Company was established to answer to the needs of the banks for an intermediary with the Central Bank. However, these banks were first to abuse its absence. When the investigation was over, the Finance Company resumed its business but its image was tarnished and abilities subdued. The public believed the Company was used abusively to speculate against the lira.

Roger Tamraz
We saw in the aftermath of the financial crisis of 1966 the role played by Roger Tamraz, who represented the American firm, Kidder, Peabody and Co., who recommended the break-up of Intrabank and the distribution of its assets. The Intrabank episode improved Tamraz's credibility with the Gulf states. Tamraz left Lebanon in June 1975 when the civil war was in progress and didn't return until 1983 after his friend and former assistant, Amine Gemayel, became President of Lebanon. In the 1980s, Tamraz was again prominent in Lebanon and the Middle East, capitalizing on his connection with the Saudis and President Gemayel.

Tamraz's background showed that his rapid rise and beginnings were very similar to those of Youssef Beidas.[3] Like Beidas he was born and raised outside Lebanon, had an obscure family background, plus a strange-sounding name for Arabic speakers.[4] Born in March 1940 in Cairo to a Lebanese father and a Syrian mother, Tamraz went to

Cambridge University in the UK in 1960 to study economics and then to Harvard University in the USA where he graduated with an MBA. On graduating he joined the consulting firm Kidder, Peabody and Co. of New York, and at the age of 26, the firm sent him to review Intrabank. Tamraz had one advantage over Youssef Beidas: while Beidas was Palestinian and Christian Orthodox, both non-starters with the Maronites of Lebanon, Tamraz was Maronite and had a claim to Lebanese ancestry. For that matter it could be argued that even a father of Lebanese nationalism such as Pierre Gemayel had been born in Ismailiyya in Egypt.

Tamraz rose fast in big business. His work at Intrabank gained him a reputation in Lebanon and the Middle East as someone who could save institutions in difficulties or on the threshold of collapse.[5] Over the years, he was called upon to help float or establish several banks and institutions in Kuwait, Saudi Arabia, France and Iran where he worked with the natural gas firm, American Transcontinental. Like Beidas, Tamraz expanded his operations throughout the Middle East and abroad. In the early 1970s, he was the middleman for Egypt in financing the purchase of six Boeing 707s for US$60 million. In 1973, he launched new activities in the United States. Between 1975 and 1983, Tamraz devoted most of his time to running his international network along with his Saudi partners.

With support from the Saudi financiers Kamal Adham and Gaith Faraoun (who were prominent in the affair of the collapse of the Bank of Credit and Commerce in the USA), as well as from Ghassan Shaker, Salem Ben Laden and Prince Moussaed, Tamraz bought 60 per cent of the shares of the Bank of the Commonwealth in Detroit, and was involved in several other investments operating out of Detroit. He also bought Hotel Prince de Gaulle, the second oldest hotel in Paris after the Georges V. To manage his operations, he established the First Arabian Corporation along with Prince Moussaed and Salem Ben Laden. In March 1981, he bought 17 per cent of the US Kaiser Steel company for US$58 million. He also bought majority shares in Sunshine Mining Stocks,[6] and made offers to buy the Northern State Bank Corporation plus interests in Commonwealth Oil Refining and Lockheed Industries. With Saudi money, Tamraz proposed transferring US$100 million to Lockheed, which had financial difficulties at the time. However, the US government blocked the move, which would have given Arab interests a stake in the second largest defence manufacturer in the US.[7] In 1978,

Tamraz was involved in an offer to buy an oil refinery at Come-By-Chance in Canada.[8] The *New York Times* reported that "Tamraz owned, among other things, 76.7 per cent of the Commonwealth Bank of Detroit, with Saudi partners such as Prince Moussaed and Gaith Faraoun".[9]

On his return to Beirut in 1983, with Amine Gemayel's support Tamraz became involved with the Intrabank Group. Back in 1967, the assets of Beidas's defunct empire had been redistributed amongst claim holders, and were split between Intrabank Investments and Banque al-Machrek (see Chapter 7). In 1983, 45 per cent of the shares in the Intrabank Group were owned by the government and a new board of 12 directors was appointed, including Lebanese and Arab financiers from the Gulf states. Kuwait and Qatar, both of which had sizeable interests, occupied three seats on the board of directors. On 11 August 1983, Gemayel appointed Tamraz to Intrabank's board of directors along with the Lebanese financiers Kamal and Fouad Bohsali, Khaldoun Soubra, Robert Sursock, Jamil Mroueh, Ahmad al-Hage, Jamil Eskandar, Gaby Jalakh, the Kuwaitis Khaled Abousaoud and Mohamed al-Khorafi, and the Qatari Abdelkader al-Kadi.

It was not long before the line that separated what was owned by Tamraz and what was a joint interest in Intrabank became blurred. By 1988, Tamraz had built himself a large empire in Lebanon where he owned several companies, the largest of which was the Milcher Group. At that time he had important, if not majority shares, in the following companies: Middle East Airlines (MEA), the Beirut Harbour Corporation, Banque al-Machrek, the Real Estate Company of Lebanon, the Franco-Lebanese Real Estate Company, Baalbeck Studios, the Whole Mountain Company, the Trans-Orient Company, Intrabank Insurance, the Bank of Kuwait and the Arab World and St Louis Real Estate. He was also a major owner in the First Phoenician Bank, the Capital Trust and Crédit Libanais. In an interview with a weekly Beirut newspaper he said that he had 5,000 employees on the payroll in Lebanon alone.[10] In another interview he said that he was second only to the Central Bank, which held a majority of shares in Intrabank, and that he owned 42 per cent of al-Machrek through Milcher.[11] His overseas contacts were no less important. A Lebanese weekly reported that Tamraz was embarking on a major project that involved tourism and financial services in collaboration with Warren Avis, owner of an American car-rental company.[12]

Tamraz established another holding company in Beirut to control the air travel business. This company, called Jet Holdings, bought off Trans-Mediterranean Airlines (TMA), the only cargo carrier in Lebanon, and paid its US$40 million debt. Later Tamraz rejected an offer to sell TMA for US$70 million. In an effort to appease the Maronite warlords, he helped them build an illegal airport at Halat, north of Beirut. This airport became a popular idea with the Maronites, and a sign of independence and strength for the Christian enclave. The government opposed Halat and Middle East Airlines (MEA) carriers only used Beirut airport. However, the Christian militia waged a campaign to allow Halat to function and its TV station broadcast an announcement every few minutes that said: "Halat Hatman" (Halat Now). Tamraz contributed US$3 million to the airport and allowed loans from al-Machrek to complete the project that was designed to accommodate the Boeing 747 planes. He also gave shares in his companies as gifts to many politicians and friends.

Tamraz's activities brought him bad publicity as he developed the reputation of having a hand in everything. Eventually he came head to head with the directors of Intrabank who disliked his approach and disapproved of the involvement of his friends and political backers in the affairs of Intrabank. These backers and friends included many Lebanese warlords and financiers – indeed, President Gemayel was one of his most important backers – who, along with the media in east Beirut, were pushing for greater control of Intrabank by a close circle of Tamraz and a few others. The east Beirut media protested that Intrabank was again being influenced by non-Lebanese interests, pointing out that the Lebanese private sector controlled only 28 per cent of the voting shares, while 25 per cent belonged to Kuwait, 5 per cent to Qatar and 42 per cent to the Central Bank. In an attempt to draw closer to the Maronite warlords, Tamraz joined the chorus of protest, complaining that "the Gulf Arabs have controlled Intrabank for the past seventeen years and have a veto on everything. We cannot allow our economy to be run from the Gulf."[13]

Tamraz's ambitions widened in 1988: he wanted to be President of Lebanon. Relying on his connections and involvement in Lebanese finance, he announced his candidacy and, true to his style, he said that if he was elected he would introduce a Marshall Plan for Lebanon and "would bring at least US$3 billion from abroad for this purpose".[14] His sole qualifications by Lebanese standards were his Maronitism, followed by his wealth. However, in Lebanon, a candidate needed much more to be a president. Among the basic ingredients for a successful campaign were winning friends among the Sunni leadership, extending a hand to Syria, appeasing the warlords and the religious leadership in the country, and seeking the counsel of the Big Five countries in the world through their embassies in Beirut.[15]

Tamraz enjoyed none of these advantages, which had conversely existed in the young and radical Bachir Gemayel in 1982. Worse, there was the trouble of his non-Lebanese accent. Even the Palestinian Beidas eventually altered his accent so it became more Lebanese, but Tamraz had an Egyptian accent that was marred with heavy use of English expressions, a tribute to his years in the USA. In an interview with a Beirut daily, speaking about the need for reforms in the country, Tamraz wanted to say that he needed a *thawra* (revolution) from above. Instead, he used the word *tharwa* (fortune or booty). The journalist had to correct him for what he considered a Freudian slip from the money-orientated Tamraz.[16]

Amine Gemayel told Tamraz "You do not understand Lebanese ways". This was true, for again and again, Tamraz repeated Beidas's mistakes in disregarding and underestimating the warlords' power and the sectarian balance of the country, while emphasizing the principles of money and business. One example was Tamraz's attempt to dismiss Salim Salam as chairman of MEA and install one of his own men so that he could further establish his hegemony over the civil aviation industry. Salim was the brother of Saeb Salam and Tamraz should have known better than to tamper with such people. Although modern and business-like, MEA was not a corporation in an American context. Tamraz's logic was enshrined in business and finance, and this was too simplistic for the Lebanese context.

In his presidential campaign, Tamraz had several advisers to counsel him on a strategy to become elected. Whether on his own initiative or in response to requests, in an effort to win US support and Syria's blessing to his candidacy, he went to Damascus to see the Syrian vice-president Abdel Halim Khaddam – against the advice of Amine Gemayel. He told Khaddam with tongue in cheek that Syria should break its alliance with Iran and help win the release of the Western hostages in Lebanon. In return, he offered his financial services and international connections to help the Syrian economy. He told Khaddam: "You help us in security, we help you in the economy."[17] This episode was a joke for both the Syrians and the Lebanese, especially Tamraz's attempt to behave as a veteran Lebanese warlord and trying to ingratiate himself with Khaddam by using his nickname (*Abou* Jamal), a style common among the politicians of the Levant.

Despite his wealth and his Saudi and Lebanese connections, Tamraz failed to recognize his insignificance in Levantine affairs. One simply could not speak with such arrogance and openness; he should have spent more time learning the labyrinthine ways of the region and how to place himself "on the inside". Like Beidas, Tamraz's political activities and connections were to be his doom. The trouble started at Intrabank. In October 1983, two months after the appointment of the new board, the Kuwaitis and the Qataris boycotted the meetings, citing the security situation in Beirut for their failure to attend. A few months later, in May 1984, following disagreements over Tamraz's investment policies, Fouad Bohsali, Robert Sursock and Khaldoun Soubra submitted their resignations. Jamil Mroueh,[18] who also had strong Saudi connections, quit for different reasons and moved to London to publish the daily newspaper *al-Hayat* with Saudi financing. Mroueh later returned to Lebanon where he relaunched the English language newspaper *The Daily Star*.

With a smaller team, it was not possible for the board of Intrabank to vote on decisions. To resolve the impasse, the general assembly of shareholders met and lowered the number of directors to ten so that quorum could be achieved by six directors. Effectively, the board was controlled by Tamraz and five others.

Ever since 1983, the country had been divided between the Maronite warlords and their allies, and the opposition led by Walid Joumblatt, Sulieman Frangié and Nabih Berri. When Michel al-Khouri left the Central Bank as governor, the opposition pushed for a like-minded candidate. Hence, the lawyer Edmond Naim became governor in 1984. The Central Bank, which was legally the major shareholder in Intrabank, was represented in the Board of Directors and was well-informed about Tamraz's activities, while Walid Joumblatt and Nabih Berri were fuming over his connections with Amine Gemayel. Tamraz, along with Gemayel, had strong leverage over Intrabank and monopolized the proceedings and meetings that kept the Central Bank in the dark.

Early in 1987, when the board of Intrabank submitted the 1986 financial statement, the Central Bank moved and the Governor, Edmond Naim, ordered an investigation into Intrabank's books and balance sheets. The Bank was irritated by Tamraz's failure to call for a general shareholder meeting for 1985 and 1986, and by the unsatisfactory financial statements for the years 1984, 1985 and 1986. The Central Bank disapproved of the 1984 election of a new six-member board headed by Tamraz following the resignation of six members, and requested that the results of the election of the new smaller board be revoked.

By the time the Central Bank reacted to the events at Intrabank and to Tamraz's activities, several banks and institutions that were owned by or connected to Tamraz started to show signs of financial difficulties. Soon, several institutions declared bankruptcy and many others were hit by rumours. The Banking Control Commission reported that the following banks were in trouble: al-Machrek, Crédit Populaire, Crédit Libanais, the Milcher Group and the Lebanese–Arab Bank. To calm down the public, Naim rejected reports that the crisis was similar in proportion to that of 1966, explaining that the lax atmosphere allowed many individuals, such as Tamraz, to commit deplorable activities. It was a publicized fact that Tamraz was backed by President Amine Gemayel and top-level government officials, and this backing demonstrated itself forcefully in the way that the problems of al-Machrek and Crédit Libanais as well as other institutions were handled.

The Banking Control Commission reported that there were investments by al-Machrek worth US$60 million on deposit with al-Machrek Bahamas and that these investments were at risk since the Bahamas branch was effectively owned by a Panama-based holding company. An additional US$50 million was invested abroad by al-Machrek without any apparent guarantees. In its decision in July 1987, the Commission ordered Tamraz to return US$100 million invested abroad by al-Machrek according to a schedule so that the money could be reinvested under its supervision. But this was not carried out as Tamraz, with friends in high places, rebuked the request and the Commission was unable to enforce its decision. In his defence, Tamraz played down the situation at al-Machrek by declaring that there had been some disagreements over the bank's assets and their value, but that the issue was now considered settled. He boasted that he had saved Intrabank from bankruptcy when he arrived in 1983 and that "MEA was going under, Casino du Liban was incurring intolerable losses, the Bank of Kuwait was a small bank and al-Machrek was almost non-existent. Today, the Bank of Kuwait is in good shape, al-Machrek is one of the largest banks in Beirut, while MEA and the Casino are again doing good business."[19]

Eventually, the Central Bank forced Tamraz to resign as chairman of Intrabank.[20] He was replaced by Jamil Eskandar, while Majid Joumblatt joined the board of directors to represent the Bank. More trouble was on the way for Tamraz's Milcher Group. Al-Machrek was declared bankrupt in December 1988 and Crédit Libanais, the largest Lebanese bank, was in financial difficulty. In the same year, the First Phoenician Bank, owned by Tamraz, also failed and the Central Bank intervened to assume responsibility for its liabilities. The Bank paid all the Phoenician debts including foreign currency debt owed to foreign banks. In November 1989, the Central Bank bought shares in Crédit Libanais and al-Machrek for a sum of US$9.5 million, and assumed their debts and liabilities. This move gave the Bank of Lebanon, a state-owned corporation, 78 per cent of shares in Crédit Libanais, and its share of the Intrabank Group increased to 50 per cent.

The demise of Tamraz came at the end of Amine Gemayel's term of office in 1988. In the period 1983–8, Gemayel's opponents and critics were constantly calling for an investigation into the clandestine connections between Gemayel and Tamraz, and for the arrest of the latter. However, things changed when Gemayel's term as president ended. On the night before he left office, Gemayel appointed Michel Aoun as a caretaker prime minister. Aoun had his own ambitions and in an effort to consolidate his authority, he wanted to take over the control of Intrabank. For that purpose, he commissioned an investigation. Tamraz failed to comply with Aoun's wishes and a warrant was issued for his arrest. Tamraz managed to escape to west Beirut where he was protected by the old enemies. He was briefly a guest of Walid Joumblatt, where militiamen of the Socialist Progressive Party protected him. In 1988, he made contacts with militia leaders close to Damascus, hoping to get closer to Syria. On his way to Damascus he was kidnapped for ransom and held in an apartment in the town of Zahlé in the Bekaa. The kidnapping proved to be the worst ordeal for the business tycoon, as he was physically tortured until he paid hard cash to his captors. This experience destroyed all hopes for Tamraz in Lebanon and convinced him to leave. He eventually settled in the USA, where he had major business ventures – including a project to build oil and gas pipelines in the Caucasus region of the former Soviet Union.

In 1991, the giant Bank of Credit and Commerce collapsed throughout the world and reports mentioned several of Tamraz's partners, such as Kamal Adham and Gaith Faraoun, as important shareholders.

Gemayel also left Lebanon, going first to the United States then to France where he settled for ten years. In 2001, he returned to Beckfaya, the Gemayels' hometown in Mount Lebanon. However, the clandestine activities that had marred the years 1983–8 continued to surface in subsequent years, even as recently as 2002. One such activity was Tamraz's involvement in a scheme to sell 6,000 Lebanese passports to West Germany in return for several million dollars in 1986, and the mishandling of public funds in the purchase of French-made Puma helicopters for the Lebanese Army. Gemayel had reportedly given his blessing to the passports project which would have helped the Germans in their bid to deport several thousand Lebanese and Palestinians who had overstayed their welcome in West Germany as refugee claimants. The Germans had influence over Gemayel and Josef Strauss, the Governor of Bavaria, was his personal friend. In June 1991, Gemayel reportedly had lunch with Shimon Peres, then leader of the Israeli opposition, and in July 1991 he was summoned by a Lebanese court as a witness to the passports sales affair that involved Jamil Nomeh, Director of General Security in Lebanon who had the authority to certify the passports. Gemayel wrote two letters to the Prosecutor General, but never attended court.

In September 2002, one year after Gemayel's return to Lebanon, the Prosecutor General reopened the case of the Puma helicopters which was linked to the period of Gemayel's presidency and had involved mishandling public funds. Sami Maroun, one of Gemayel's closest advisors, was involved in the deal, and admitted to his habit of charging a commission on business deals. The helicopters were supposed to be new and French-made, but what Lebanon received at a hefty cost were used Romanian helicopters, which ended up being destroyed anyway by the Lebanese Forces Christian militia in their war against Michel Aoun in 1989. Gemayel's supporters maintained that accusations against the former president were politically motivated.[21]

Exporting the financial crisis

Another aspect of the financial crisis was the activities of Lebanese banks abroad. These banks benefited from a loophole in the Lebanese Law of Money and Credit, which specified a breakdown of assets and liabilities by currency. To manage their assets to liabilities the banks treated reserve requirement as the only requirement. Increasingly, the banks' foreign currency liabilities (deposits) exceeded their lira capital base and reserve requirements several times over. The banks defended their operations using the line they had used in 1955 and 1966. They argued that in an open market like Beirut, there should be no distinction between foreign currency deposits and lira deposits since they could readily be exchanged. They also argued that there would be no actual reduction in their capital base simply because their liabilities were in foreign currency, which in fact accounted for most of the deposits. These liabilities were equivalent to their foreign currency assets safely deposited with banks abroad. Hence, the capital base was matched by the small lira deposits and everything was fine.

In 1977, following the al-Hoss government's decision to allow offshore banking, many Lebanese banks opened branches abroad. These branches were used as conduits to siphon funds from Beirut, and to allow bankers more freedom to engage in lucrative activities with Europe, West Africa and the Middle East. We have seen that in 1986 the banks had resisted the Central Bank's effort to increase their capital base. The financial collapse in the 1980s weakened the hand of the Bank of Lebanon, and this weakness became apparent in the 1990s. While the relationship between the Central Bank and the Lebanese Bankers Association (LBA) became cordial after 1992, the cordiality came at the expense of a reduction in the power of the Central Bank in the conduct of monetary policy. As government debt rose from $1 billion in 1989 to $30 billion in 2002, the Central Bank was unfortunately unable to persuade banks to lower interest rates or to extend credit to businesses and individuals; both steps would have benefited the Lebanese economy.

This line was a non-starter for the Central Bank. If the banks chose to operate everywhere and escape scrutiny, then there was no way for the Central Bank to conduct a proper monetary policy. The capital requirement measures called for a ratio of 15 per cent of capital to be held in foreign currency. However, under the Secrecy Law it was impossible for the Bank to verify this requirement. Activities of banks in the foreign exchange market were extended to their branches abroad and the Central Bank made several attempts to monitor these offshore activities, especially when these foreign branches settled their foreign currency liabilities with financing from Beirut, thus draining the Beirut market of hard currency and decreasing the value of the lira.

Monetary authorities in other countries were keeping an eye on the practices of the Lebanese banks on their territory. In 1989, three Lebanese banks operating in Paris collapsed – an event that put all Lebanese banks operating in Paris in a difficult and embarrassing situation. The name of Roger Tamraz was prominent in this episode as he was the chairman of the Banque de Placement et Paiement (BPP), a branch of al-Machrek. The BPP was one of the banks that collapsed. Tamraz used BPP's credit to borrow large sums of money to finance his projects. In 1988, the Banque de France investigated BPP and found that it had a deficit of FF250 million.

The Intrabank Group was facing financial difficulties and it could not support BPP. At this point the French government requested the Bank of Lebanon in its capacity as a major shareholder of Intrabank, which owned al-Machrek, to float BPP. The Bank of Lebanon argued that its function as a central bank prevented it from extending its insurance of deposits to offshore banks and that such insurance applied to banks in Lebanon only. The French lost no time. They declared BPP to be in receivership and put it up for sale.

The second bank, the United Banking Company (UBC), owned by the Lebanese businessman Joe Kairouz, was brought into the open after the French police arrested a Lebanese national, Salim al-Lawi, as he was leaving the UBC branch in Paris carrying FF3.5 million in a handbag. The French authorities had been investigating UBC since 1986, forcing its owners to increase the paid-up capital several fold. UBC was involved in extending credit to a group of Lebanese businessmen amounting to several hundred million francs. The Central Bank learnt that most banks in Paris had rejected loan applications from these individuals, and that UBC, contrary to French law, had extended a series of loans totalling FF250 million to the same individuals, while UBC's official books showed that the sums went to several individuals and institutions with different names.

The third bank was the Lebanese Arab Bank, which extended loans to individuals who lacked the necessary creditworthiness. Investigations showed that the loans were being made to the same group that had been involved with UBC. What made the case harder for the banks was the claim by the Banque de France that the three banks' records and books had been tampered with immediately prior to the investigation.

The Bank of Lebanon against the Lebanese Bankers Association (LBA)

The problems at Intrabank and the banks' failures were not the end of the story as the Central Bank had to confront more forces in the system. The relationship between the Central Bank and the other financial institutions had been deteriorating since 1985 and in 1986–7 the cooperation between the LBA and the Bank of Lebanon reached a historic low. Finally, by the end of 1987 consultations were minimal and disputes rose on many fronts: the LBA's chairman, Adel Kassar, called on Edmond Naim to resign, and many bankers accused him of patronizing the opposition. At a meeting of the LBA, one member showed a pamphlet written by Naim in 1955 when he had been a member of Kamal Joumblatt's Progressive Socialist Party and editor of the socialist magazine *al-Anba*. The pamphlet, intended as evidence of Naim's "conspiratorial mentality", was entitled *Towards a Socialist Lebanon*, and was used in the barrage against the steadfast governor.

In 1989, the acquisitions by the Central Bank of more banking operations in the private sector added to its muscle in affecting monetary policy and directing the financial market. These moves were strongly opposed by the LBA, which argued that with the control of much of the banking sector, the Central Bank, as initiator of monetary policy and overlord of the Banking Control Commission and the Directory of Deposit Insurance, would be in a direct conflict of interest. The Central Bank defended its move as a necessary step towards floating important banks, and that Lebanon needed larger banks instead of the hundreds of small establishments, which were liable to bankruptcy and insolvability and were mostly inefficient. The problem of scale was important: a 1986 study showed the operating costs of small banks were 300 per cent of those of the bigger banks. Table 29 shows this size advantage in terms of the number of employees, capital base and the number of branches.

The banks were also furious at the monetary policy which crippled their ability to expand credit, and at the fines charged against violating institutions. These fines reached, at times, one-third of their paid-up capital base. The banks were equally unhappy with the policy of the Central Bank to force them to purchase Treasury bills, which they considered a risky investment. In fact, the Bank was unable to force them to buy the entire issues, and it had to absorb the remaining bills, effectively increasing the money supply.

Starting in 1986, to curb the growth of credit and its inflationary implications, the Central Bank tightened credit further by increasing primary reserve requirements, the holdings of T-bills and the capital base ratio to liabilities. Other measures included limiting the capital base in foreign currencies to 15 per cent. These measures aimed at checking credit expansion and the use of reserves to increase foreign currency holdings at the expense of the national currency. The hypothesis that banks would choose to hold zero liras and push the country into the abyss was pondered by some observers, while limiting holdings to borrowing in the interbank market to meet withdrawal requests.

The tightening was not a major obstacle to the banks in expanding their foreign currency holdings. They simply borrowed from each other to build up lira reserves to use for transactions and to maintain the desired reserves. This move pushed the Beirut interbank rate to 100 per cent in 1986, while speculation in the foreign exchange market continued undeterred causing ever greater harm to the lira, and leading to a glut of liras that nobody wanted. Some banks did not distribute earnings amongst shareholders, and instead used the proceeds to increase their capital base and reserve holdings.

The measures met stiff resistance and a negative response from the banks, and the Bank of Lebanon had to review alternatives similar to those practised by the Bank of England and the Federal Reserve System, eventually imposing strict guidelines for capital base requirements. Violating financial institutions were penalized by having their reserve requirements increased by 3.64 times and a fine that was deducted from the banks' deposits at the Central Bank. The Bank backed off under pressure from the LBA and following further negotiations, the requirement was reduced to 1.2 times only. The Association tried to waive the fines, arguing that these deposits at the Central Bank were ultimately owed to depositors who might lose confidence in the banking system if the banks' reserves at the Central Bank were used to pay the fines. But the Central Bank did not agree with the demand, arguing that fines had nothing to do with the public's deposit, and that the public's deposits were insured by the Central Bank and any bank that defaulted would be saved, as the series of bankruptcies in 1987–8 showed. An example was the Bank's rescue of the Tamraz-owned First Phoenician Bank. The Central Bank used the Phoenician's case as a showpiece to calm the market. Although under the law the Central Bank had no control over foreign currency holdings and deposits or even their size, it still insured all deposits.

Soon after introducing the tight measures, the Banking Control Commission realized that implementation was difficult. Although the Commission was able to keep watch over the largest ten banks, which held 50 per cent of total deposits in the system, it was close to impossible to look into the books of the dozens of small banks, several of which refused to cooperate or even to consider implementing the measures. The 1963 Money and Credit Act did not empower the Central Bank to intervene against the abuse of foreign currency deposits and holdings of banks.

An adverse impact of the Central Bank's measures was that banks lost their ability to extend credit and many recalled commercial credit to affect their daily transactions, which led to the exposure of promising investments and the collapse of many businesses. Successive business failures and the decline in business prospects convinced many banks that commercial credit was no longer profitable and they threw their weight into foreign currency speculation. The measures also had a positive impact. They decelerated credit expansion, improved lira deposits, which increased by 4 per cent in a few months, and checked the speedy fall of the lira by the end of 1987. Although the IMF suggested more credit tightening, the Central Bank was in no position to initiate new measures as the market was feeling that the current measures were already excessive.

The Central Bank's dispute with the LBA was out in the open and this worried depositors in lira-denominated accounts. There was also a public concern about the policies of the Central Bank. The public feared that the Bank was monetizing the economy by issuing more currency at the end of each month, thus pushing the lira further down. A psychology developed that the lira would fall further after each salary, and especially ahead of major holidays. Depositors were afraid that their lira deposits could be frozen by decree to help the government's finances or lose their value as the lira dropped.

The public had its share of blame in expanding credit. Depositors used cheques receivable as a form of payment simply by endorsing and passing them as payment for a transaction. These cheques were not cashed and were used again upon receipt before the three-day grace period. Individuals who used their cheques receivable as a form of payment benefited from the rise in the dollar instead of waiting for the cheque to clear. The government was aware of this problem which was adding liquidity to the inflated system. Thus, in October 1987 it introduced Law 761 requiring that cheques should be cleared before the funds could be used. The public also bought foreign exchange funds and deposited them with commercial banks, pushing the ratio of foreign currency denominated deposits to total deposits from 28 per cent in 1984 to more than 86 per cent in July 1987. The banks' holdings in the national currency became so small that sometimes for small transactions, bank employees would have to carry a bundle of dollars and go on foot to another bank to buy Lebanese liras. The alarming growth of liquidity in the lira led salaried employees to exchange their almost worthless liras for dollars upon receipt of wages.

Notes

1. "De quoi vivent les libanais", *Le Monde Diplomatique*, 15 February 1983.
2. Kamal Hamdane, *The Lebanese Crisis*, p. 207. The PLO in Lebanon was equipped with the apparatus of a full state. It boasted an annual budget equal to that of the Lebanese government and 40,000 employees on its payroll. It had various agencies responsible for the military and security, as well as for social services and the media.
3. For more detail on the similarities between the two men, see the November 1973 issue of *Fortune*. The comparison was also made on *Daily News Tonight*, New York, 27 March 1981.
4. Hazim Saghiyé quoted Tamraz as saying that his family came from the Caucasus. Therefore, he could have been of Armenian, Georgian or Circasse background (Saghiyé, *Maronites from Lebanon*, p. 313).
5. *Newsweek*, 10 February 1975.
6. *Daily News Tonight*, 27 March 1981.
7. *Newsweek*, op. cit.
8. *New York Times*, 4 May 1978.
9. Ibid.
10. *Annahar*, 8 August 1988.
11. *Al-Massira*, 11 July 1988.

12 *Assayad*, 26 September 1986.
13 *Al Massira*, op. cit.
14 *Annahar*, op. cit.
15 The Big Five being the United States of America, the Soviet Union, France, Britain and China.
16 *Assafir* newspaper, published in Saghiyé, *Maronites from Lebanon*, 1988.
17 Saghiyé, op. cit.
18 Son of editor Kamel Mroueh.
19 *Al-Massira*, op. cit.
20 As for Tamraz's political ambition, no presidential elections were held in September 1988, as the Parliament failed to reach a quorum, and the war resumed in February 1989. One year later, the Chehabist René Mouawad was elected president, but was subsequently assassinated. Elias Hrawi was elected to replace him.
21 Report by Fares Khachan in *Assafir*, 29 September 2002, and Nicolas Nassif in *Annahar*, 2 October 2002.

14

Supremacy of the Warlords

Switzerland of the East

In 1974, government pamphlets in English, French, German and Spanish invited Western toursits to visit Lebanon. Citing its beauty, lovely beaches and hotels, hospitals and educational institutions, and a hospitable people, the pamphlets ended with the line "Lebanon: Switzerland of the East" (*Lubnan Swissra al-Chark*). After 1975, the pretty Lebanon in the pamphlets disappeared and the warlordships that preceded the creation of the modern state resurfaced with a vengeance, signalling a return to the ghettos of the past. In 1976, these mini-states were sarcastically referred to by the local media as "Swiss cantons". After 1976, Lebanon was no longer compared to Switzerland in terms of beauty, but by the warlord counties that gave a cruel example of the canton system.

Between 1980 and 1990, a de facto system of cantons was dominant in Lebanon, undistinguished from the cantons of the period 1100–1864. Only a handful of the traditional mountain warlords and city *zaims* were left in the 1980s as most of the cantons were ruled by a new generation which, in 1975–6, was successful in eroding most of the traditional figures. The Shia Assads, Hamadis and al-Khalils, and the Sunni al-Solhs, Karamis and Salams were replaced by less well-known individuals. Even in the Maronite cantons power fell to individuals of humble background. Only the Druze and the northern Maronites were able to maintain traditional leadership – namely the Joumblatts in central Lebanon and the Frangiés in Zghorta.

Following the short civil war of 1958, in which 4,000 people were killed, President Fouad Chehab accepted the recommendations of a French think-tank to help develop the peripheral provinces and adjust the country's unbalanced economic and social development. It was ironic that Chehab's dream of a decentralized economic development with emphasis on the outlying regions needed a major civil war to put it on track. Between 1975 and 1980, the conflict brought many Lebanese out of their towns and villages to be displaced as refugees in their own country because of their religious or political affiliation. This movement led to a mini population transfer in Lebanon and created borderlines that defined the various cantons.

After November 1976, the Lebanese civil war was characterized by fixed trenches. Long-range artillery exchanges replaced actual frontline battles as the sectarian divide was drawn and each militia controlled a separate canton. This status quo continued until 1990, when central authority returned. Each warlord turned inward to establish his hegemony in his domains and this was successful to a large extent. At times it was not. The competition between leaders often led to mini-civil wars in each canton. The Joumblatts had competition from the Erslans in the Aley and Chouf regions; the Shia *Amal* movement had the opposition of Hizbollah in the south, south Beirut and the Bekaa; the Phalanges often fought against competing Christian factions in the eastern suburbs of Beirut, and so on.

Ironically, the cantonization of Lebanon led to greater economic activity in areas outside Beirut. Although the cantons became separate entities dominated by warlords, the economic reality dictated a continuation of business activities between the various cantons in Lebanon to secure markets and sources of financing, and the use of the transportation infrastructure inside Lebanon and with other countries.[1] The de facto local autonomy of the cantons was weakened by their inability to transform their symbolic independence into becoming meaningful economic entities. West Beirut continued to be the main, sometimes the only market, for the products of east Beirut, while east Beirut remained the only leisure destination for residents of west Beirut.

When Lebanon was created in 1920, the warlords of Mount Lebanon had descended on Beirut and with Beirut's collapse in 1975–6, money and skills fled the city. After 1977, economic activity increased in the cantons and regional development bloomed. In order to be independent and economically self-reliant, the Maronite, the Shia and the Druze warlords sent delegates to the rich and large Lebanese emigré communities in West Africa, the Americas and the Gulf states to attract investment into the cantons.[2] Funds were created with individual participants placing as much as US$25 million each. Canton-holding companies were in vogue as each warlord encouraged organized established firms and wealthy individuals in his territory into consortiums.

Developers made a windfall from the rise in demand for housing caused by the internal refugee problem. More apartment blocks and houses were built in each canton compared to pre-war levels. An incident occurred in Saida in 1983 that reminded the Lebanese of their historical precedents. The police reported that a tractor digging to prepare the terrain for construction had struck a mass grave. At first it was thought that the grave was one of many found in Lebanon in the aftermath of the Israeli invasion in 1982. But when forensic doctors examined the bones, they announced that the remains dated back several hundred years. The explanation provided was that the grave had been for victims of one or other of the endless civil wars in Lebanon. A similar find occurred in 1986 in the southern town of Ansar. In that area, construction workers ploughing the terrain found a mass grave containing almost 500 human skeletons and artefacts. Experts reported the dead bodies as dating back to 1749 when a battle between the Shia warlords and the forces of Youssef Chehab had taken place in the area.

In the 1980s, the areas with mixed populations were systematically destroyed. The destruction followed a line 50 kilometres long, going east from Beirut to Sofar in the mountain region, and straddling the old divide between Druze and Maronites along the Beirut–Damascus highway. The mixed area ran from the Beirut harbour and followed the Beirut–Damascus Road, through Kahalé, Aley, Bhamdoun, Sofar and ending in the Bekaa Valley. Between 1975 and 1977, the Maronites forcefully evacuated 250,000 Lebanese Shia, Palestinians and Kurds from their territories north and east of Beirut. The Muslims and the Druze also cleared Maronite towns in the Chouf and on the coast south of Beirut, which amounted to some 300,000 displaced citizens.

Internal tourism flourished in each canton, as several modern hotels and entertainment complexes were built in the suburbs of Beirut – namely Summerland (south of Beirut) and the Aqua Marina (north of Beirut). These establishments relied on a Lebanese clientele and on some foreign guests who ventured into Lebanon. The tourist establishments needed armed guards to operate, and were equipped with hydro and water lines that would run for several weeks if the public utility was interrupted. The number of registered travel agencies increased from 179 in 1974 to 300 in 1981 to serve mainly Lebanese travellers. Lebanese establishments outside Lebanon grew in number – notably in the hotel and restaurant business. In Paris, the Champs-Elysées boasted several

Lebanese restaurants. Entire street blocks in London, Montreal and, the Gulf states enjoyed healthy Lebanese business activity.

Illegal ports run by private militias mushroomed on the coast importing anything from cars to bottled beer, and exporting anything from pitta breads to hashish and other drugs. Ports with modern facilities were built at Ouzai (two miles south of Beirut), Jiyé (twenty miles south of Beirut) and Aqua Marina (twenty miles north of Beirut). According to conservative estimates, imports through illegal ports and smuggling had cost the government US$50 million per month in lost customs and excise revenues. Government harbours were taken over by the militias who imposed their own duties and taxes on imports and exports (Table 25 in the Statistical Appendix shows the value of customs revenues and imports). Judging from the value of imports in the period 1976 to 1990, government customs revenues shrank to a small fraction of actual receipts. Although the value of imports quadrupled between 1973 and 1982, government revenues were almost halved in the same period while most of the tariffs were collected by the treasuries of the various militias.[3]

To expand their authority and make more money, the warlords imposed taxes and placed tollbooths on every major crossing in the country. The tollbooths became the customs authority in each canton. By the mid-1980s, the tax structure of the warlords was so elaborate that taxes were imposed on real estate transactions, movement of goods, imports, exports, social services and on almost anything that moved. A document to transfer property needed to be stamped and approved by the local militia for a fee. Special levies were imposed "to support the war efforts" of the warlords.

Between 1977 and 1990, the Druze canton south of the Beirut–Damascus highway was led by Walid Joumblatt after the death of his father Kamal Joumblatt. The Maronite canton north of the Beirut–Damascus highway was initially led by Camille Chamoun and his allies, but later by the Gemayel family and the Phalanges military commanders. The Shia warlords were in control in their traditional strongholds in southern Lebanon and the northern Bekaa; they were a majority in south Beirut and had an important presence in Beirut itself. In the Shia community, the traditional leadership of the Assads and Hamadis was replaced by dynamic militiamen and outspoken new leaders. The urban Sunni militias were strong in Tripoli and Saida, but were outnumbered by the Shia and the Druze in Beirut.

The fragmentation of Beirut

Between 1975 and 1990, Beirut was the central shooting stage in the civil war. However, it remained an open city and this helped the government to use it as a test ground to spread central authority over the country. The western suburbs included 80 per cent of the city's core. They had a clear advantage in the fact that unlike the quasi-homogeneity of east Beirut, west Beirut remained a mixed area where Druze, Sunnis, Shia and Christians lived. Maronite leaders who disagreed with the warlords in east Beirut found refuge in west Beirut, and Muslim leaders who disagreed with the Muslim warlords fled to east Beirut. The Central Bank, with its gold reserves, the seat of government and many other important establishments were located in west Beirut.

Prior to the war, east Beirut had mainly been a quiet residential area. After 1975, Christian business activity moved away from devastated downtown Beirut to the eastern suburbs of Achrafié, Dora and Sinn al-Fil. The government had also maintained some presence in the east, including the headquarters of the Foreign Ministry, Électricité du Liban and the General Security Headquarters. The eastern sector was the best-equipped and most developed in terms of infrastructure in Lebanon. The Christian militias were in control of Beirut's harbour, the largest in the country, Jounié's harbour, the major energy utility in Lebanon at Zouk, the water supply station for the entire city of Beirut, the telecommunication systems, and the fuel depots and distribution centres. The expansion of east Beirut was healthier and more far-reaching than that of the western sector, as development and business activity extended further north into the port city of Jounié. What was called the eastern suburbs was in fact a huge area that went beyond the municipal borders of Beirut.

Beirut had mushroomed in every direction since the war began in 1975, swallowing the once tranquil villages of Dbaye, Sinn al-Fil, Ein Rummané, Forn Chebak, Dora, Bourj Hammoud, Chiyah, Ghobeiri, Ouzai, Khaldé and Bir Hassan. These villages became the four main suburbs that surrounded the core: the Shia suburb (known as ad-Dahiya, or literally "suburb", including: Chiyah, Ghobeiri, Hay Essellom, Ariss, Bir Hassan, Ouzai, al-Mouallem and Haret Houraik); the Druze suburb (Khaldé, Chouefat and Aramoun); the Armenian suburb (Bourj Hammoud, An-Nahr and Arax); and the Christian suburb (from Kfarchima, Hadeth, St Thérèse, Ein Rummané, Sinn al-Fil to Dora and up to Jalel Dib, Dbaye, Mkalles, Jisr al-Basha, Saddel Bucheriyé and Rawda).

In 1976, the Phalanges Militia (renamed the Lebanese Forces in 1978) was in total control of the eastern suburbs and remained so until 1990. In contrast, west Beirut changed hands eight times in the same period. In 1976, it fell to the leftist-Palestinian alliance, and in 1977–80, it was under the predominantly Syrian Arab Deterrence Force. When President Sarkis lost credibility with the Muslims, west Beirut turned into a gangland between 1980 and 1982. In 1982, it was besieged by the Israelis for three months, then taken over by the Multinational Force between September 1982 and October 1983. For the next three months, west Beirut was under the Phalanges-led administration of President Amine Gemayel who lost control when a Shia–Druze alliance stormed the sector and wrestled it from government troops in February 1984. In February 1987, following heavy fighting among the various militias in west Beirut, the Syrian army moved in and took control.

Therefore, between 1975 and 1990, the population of west Beirut became resigned to its unknown destiny as the central government was reduced to having a symbolic presence, controlling the prime minister's office in Beirut and the presidential palace at Baabda. By 1989–90, even the palace at Baabda was outside government authority and the newly elected President Elias Hrawi had to be content with an office in west Beirut.

The fate of west Beirut between 1975 and 1990 should not create the impression that east Beirut fared better under the control of the Christian militia. Lawlessness and warfare were the common themes on both sides. In 1975–6, the Phalanges fought the Palestinians and the Muslims in the eastern suburbs; in 1977–80, the war of dominance inside the Christian camp took its toll as the Gemayels tried to impose their will on the Frangiés canton in North Lebanon on 13 June 1978 and eradicated Chamoun's militia on 7 July 1980. The war inside the Christian heartland became open in 1982, when various leaders fought over the leadership of the Christian militia after the death of Bachir Gemayel. The disunity of the Christian warlords and merchants never recovered and continued in the political arena into the more peaceful 1990s and was even symptomatic of the Christian leadership in 2002. A major war that brought the Christian canton to its knees was the disastrous confrontation between the Christian militia led by Samir Geagea and the troops of General Michel Aoun in 1989–90.

The events on each side of the divide in Lebanon meant that no matter how each canton was "cleansed" in terms of religious affiliation, internal violence and continuous warfare haunted all the areas.

If that was the situation in Beirut between 1976 and 1990, outside the city, slowly but surely, the warlords established local authority with the trimmings of a government machinery. The typical canton was headed by a traditional family with a feudal background and a seat of power in a palace or in a historic town. The Lebanese cantons around Beirut had a centre of commerce, a seaport, a television station, a radio station and possibly an airport.

The Druze canton
After the death of Kamal Joumblatt, leadership of the Druze went to his son Walid. After the failed attempt by the leftists and the Palestinians to control the Lebanese state, the Joumblatts turned inwards to strengthen the Druze domains in central Mount Lebanon, and in the *caza*s of the Chouf and Aley. Except for the minor influence of the Erslans, the Joumblatts went unchallenged in leading the Druze throughout the Levant. Druze from Lebanon, Syria and Israel recognized the Joumblatts' leadership. Except for isolated events, the Maronite–Druze feud in Mount Lebanon was dormant from 1861 until 1976. Even when Kamal Joumblatt declared war on the "establishment", the civil war that started in 1975 did not turn into a Maronite–Druze war until at least 1983. The first signs of such a conflict occurred in March 1977, when Kamal Joumblatt was assassinated and Druze militiamen assaulted several villages in the Chouf and killed a few hundred Maronites.

Although the murder of Kamal Joumblatt crippled the leftist alliance and the cause of social reform, it helped to awaken the dormant Druze identity. Between 1977 and 1983, the Joumblatts strengthened Druze solidarity and built up their power. Before his death, Kamal Joumblatt had been even more influential than his ancestor Bachir Joumblatt (a contemporary of Bachir Chehab in 1792–1825). Kamal Joumblatt kept the Maronite leadership edgy and panicky as his verbal attacks and criticisms placed traditional politicians on the defensive. He always organized and led the opposition, and between 1969 and 1975, his efforts culminated with amassing all the disinherited and aggrieved groups in the country. By 1974, he had the prime minister of Lebanon, Rachid al-Solh, answering to his every whim.

Even Yasser Arafat did not escape Kamal Joumblatt's aura. In 1976, Joumblatt persuaded Arafat to fight Syria at Sofar and penetrate the village of Monteverde to relieve the besieged Palestinian camp of Tell Zaatar. The shrewd and calculating President Hafez Assad of Syria also got his turn with Joumblatt. In an eight-hour meeting in Damascus in 1976, the sharp Lebanese leader refused Assad's initiative to stop the fighting in Beirut, and pledged that he would not allow the Syrian Baath to rule in Lebanon. Joumblatt's reputation went beyond the Arab world to the international arena and was probably one of a few Lebanese who came to be known around the world. His prestige and influence were limited by the narrow sectarian politics of Lebanon.

After the murder of Joumblatt, the leadership fell to his son, the less doctrinaire but machiavellian Walid. The 1982 Israeli invasion allowed the Phalanges to move into areas in the Chouf which had not been entered since 1861. This step electrified the Druze and led to a repeat of a nineteenth-century-style Maronite–Druze civil war between 1983 and 1985. As in 1861, the Druze were able to defeat the Maronites after terrible battles and massacres, even pushing to areas that they had lost in 1976 and approaching Baabda, the seat of the Maronite president, in a surprising repeat of the 1861 events. However, pro-Maronite government troops in Souk al-Gharb led by General Michel Aoun halted their advance.

After 1985, the Druze canton remained peaceful. Meanwhile, Walid Joumblatt built a harbour at Jiyé (thirty kilometres south of Beirut), and established a radio station, Voice of the Mountain (*Sawt al-Jabal*). Tax collection booths were also installed at the entrances of the Druze canton. In Beirut, Joumblatt allied himself briefly with the moderate Shia and the Kurds, and tried to strengthen the hands of Chamoun's Christian followers by encouraging them to return to the Chouf. Later he became Minister of the Displaced under premier Rafic Hariri's first cabinet (1993–8) and opened up to his wartime enemies. He was reconciled with the Maronites and welcomed Patriarch Nessrallah Sfeir in the cleric's historic visit to the Chouf in 2001.

The Shia cantons

The Shia were even more divided than the Maronites. Between 1307 and 1975, the Shia were a fringe group in Lebanon (see Chapter 1). On the eve of the war in 1975, they were the most deprived and the poorest of the Lebanese communities. When the country became independent in 1943, the Shia had no educated elite, nor did they have a business class to speak for them. Shia warlords – the Hamadis of the Bekaa and the Assads of the south – were content to be subservient to the warlords and *zaim*s of the other communities. For their loyalty, the Shia warlords were given position of Speaker of Parliament, a ceremonial title. This position changed hands between Sabri Hamadi and Ahmed Assad (and Kamel Assad after the death of Ahmed Assad) over thirty years.

The Hamadis and the Assads didn't much care for the cause of progress of Lebanon's Shia; there were instances where they opposed progress and frowned on social protest. An oft-mentioned story about Ahmed Assad is worth re-telling here.

In the 1940s, Ahmed Assad, then a deputy representing a southern constituency, discouraged education and wanted his people to remain ignorant peasants. When a man asked him for help to send his brilliant son to high school in Beirut, he arrogantly answered: "Why do you want me to do that? Is it not enough for you that I am sending my son Kamel to school?"[4] By that, he meant that he was doing a favour to all the Shia. The story is retold by university-educated and wealthy Shia with a sense of accomplishment and success even against odds like the Assads.

While the Maronites were constantly conscious of their status and "communal" identity long before 1975, and entered the war mainly to defend their position, the Shia "communal" feeling did not exist prior to 1980. It was always the case that the Shia voiced their grievances through the leftist secular parties, and between 1975 and 1980, their men fought in the ranks of Kamal Joumblatt's coalition. On the fringe of the Shia community there was a tiny organization called *Amal*, established in 1974 by Moussa Sadr, a member of the Muslim clergy. *Amal* did attract a large number of common Shia, but failed to appeal to the intellectual and educated who disliked the organization's sectarian background and suspected it to be pro-establishment and pro-Syrian. In 1976, when Kamal Joumblatt called for war against Syria's allies in Lebanon, the Shia members in the leftist coalition were among the fighters who crushed and ended *Amal*'s presence in the leftist controlled areas. And when *Amal* established its authority in the southern suburbs, it crushed the leftist Shia with more ferocity in 1979.

A Shia identity started to emerge after the death of Kamal Joumblatt in 1977 as many were disappointed with the failure of Joumblatt's attempt at social reform. This particular event was the direct factor that led many Shia individuals to fall back on communal roots for survival in the new warlord system. Meanwhile, *Amal* was growing, and with Syria's support and the (unconfirmed) death of its mentor Imam Moussa Sadr, the tiny organization made important inroads in Shi'i Lebanon.

The educated and ideologically orientated Shia felt orphaned after the death of Joumblatt and were neglected by the government in Beirut. In southern Lebanon, they found themselves exposed to almost daily Israeli attacks; in south Beirut, they lived under the PLO's yoke; everywhere in the country, they suffered the same deprivation and poverty. These were the symptoms of the Shia grievances that Sadr had talked about daily before disappearing in August 1978.

Between 1978 and 1980, *Amal* grew significantly, and in 1980 it exerted its influence on the Lebanese government when it forced two Shia Cabinet ministers to resign because the government failed to win its approval for their appointment. Between 1983 and 1985, *Amal*'s boss, Nabih Berri, who was a Lebanese emigré in West Africa and a holder of American citizenship, suggested a Maronite–Shia pact to replace the Maronite–Sunni pact. This call appealed to some Maronite intellectuals who knew that the Shia were lukewarm about the Palestinian cause and Arab unity, noting that *Amal*'s battles were never against Maronites, but almost always against communists (who happened to be mainly Shia) and Palestinians.

In 1982, many Shia welcomed the Israeli invaders as signalling an end to PLO domination and to the violence that had engulfed southern Lebanon for more than fifteen years. However, when the Israelis enlarged their goals to cover all of Lebanon and impose a "New Order" (in Israeli Defence Minister Ariel Sharon's words), the Shia turned against them. Although *Amal*'s men put up a good fight against the Israelis alongside PLO men and leftists at the Khaldé Triangle (south of Beirut) in 1982, this did not win the Shia much leverage or sympathy in Lebanon or in the largely Sunni Arab world. The Arab world, in particular the Saudis, was interested in maintaining the Sunni share of any future deal on

Lebanon. The Sunni *zaim* Saeb Salam single-handedly monopolized the PLO–US–Israeli negotiations to end the war, while Rafic Hariri, a Sunni from Saida, was the dispenser of Saudi funds to help Lebanon. There was no reason for the Saudis to behave differently considering the rivalries among the big states (Iran, Egypt, Iraq and so on) of the Middle East.

Even after 1982, already considered the largest community in Lebanon in terms of number, the Shia had still not yet developed enough of an identity or a power base to make a difference to the political map of the country. It took a lengthy Israeli occupation of southern Lebanon and a cruel Phalanges government in Beirut to create a Shia psyche and improve *Amal*'s fortunes. This transformation occurred between 1983 and 1987. Following the departure of the Marines in 1983 and the bombardment of Shia areas in south Beirut by the Lebanese army, *Amal* and the Druze militia (led by Walid Joumblatt) assaulted west Beirut on 6 February 1984, and removed President Gemayel's authority from the western suburbs. This effectively split the government army along sectarian lines.

Having secured its victory in Beirut and the loyalty of the predominantly Shia sixth brigade of the Lebanese army, *Amal* now controlled west and south Beirut, and was moving to consolidate its control over Shia areas in southern Lebanon.

While *Amal* represented the moderate Shia who wanted to participate in the Lebanese state, another group of Shia was of a different opinion. In southern Lebanon, radical Shia were growing in numbers. In the years 1983–5, the Israelis waged an "iron fist" war (in the words of the then Israeli Defence Minister Itzhak Rabin) against the Shia, a disastrous policy that further radicalized the Shia against the Israelis and pushed young men to embrace fundamentalist Islam. The growth of a fundamentalist Shia organization called Hizbollah was the antithesis of the moderate *Amal*. A war for the leadership of the Shia community between the two organizations was waged for the remainder of the 1980s.

This struggle led to a bloody Shia civil war which became open warfare after the Israeli withdrawal from parts of south Lebanon in 1985, as both Shia groups were trying to establish control over the south. While *Amal*'s roots were with Imam Moussa Sadr who wanted to reform the Lebanese state, the radical Hizbollah received inspiration from the

1979 Islamic revolution in Iran. These radicals strived in the occupied south and waged suicide bomb attacks against the Israelis.[5]

Although Hizbollah was the group most familiar to Western audiences, there were many other radical Islamic Shia groups in Lebanon, such as the Islamic *Amal* (*Amal al-Islamiya*) of Hussein Mousawi in Baalbeck, the Islamic Jihad Organization (*Munazamat al-Jihad al-Islami*) of Imad Mughniyé and the pro-Iranian Organization of the Wretched on Earth (*Munazamat al-mustazafoun fil-Ard*). The radical Shia were not interested in a larger piece of the pie in the Lebanese government. Rather, they wanted an Islamic Lebanon based on the Iranian model. This radicalism was moderated when the war ended in Lebanon, as new voices in the fundamentalist camp called for participation in the Lebanese elections of 1992 in which the Islamic groups fielded many candidates and won many seats.

The dichotomy of the Shia went beyond zealots and moderates. It was also accentuated by a geographic split. Major differences were observed between the more militant and rural Shia of the northern Bekaa Valley, and the more moderate and urbane Shia of southern Lebanon. The northern Shia received a boost in 1982 when Iranian Revolutionary Guards entered Lebanon and established headquarters at the historic city of Baalbeck, and soon an Islamic Republic was declared there. While the counties of Hermel and Baalbeck traditionally followed Imam Sadr, founder of *Amal*, the population was radicalized in the 1980s and eventually *Amal* was forced out of the area. Thus, between 1986 and 1990, *Amal*'s monopoly of the representation of Lebanon's Shia was seriously challenged. The radicals secured large areas for themselves and were fighting to control Beirut and the south as well.

With Syria supporting the moderates and Iran supporting the radicals, the Shia war raged for four years. In the process, destruction and murder were two common themes in the Shia areas. In the town of Nabatié, the stronghold of *Amal*, in Iqlim Tofah (Region of the Apples, east of Saida) and in south Beirut, bloody battles were fought non-stop. While the Maronites were also at each others' necks in their areas, the Shia war in Beirut and south Lebanon accounted for 2,000 deaths and 6,000 wounded. Beautiful Lebanese towns in Iqlim Tofah like Jbaa and Habbouch were the scenes of bloody battles that caused serious damage to life and property. Civilian Shia were dislocated and made to suffer by their own people. The battle in south Beirut in the autumn and winter of 1987–8 was equally ferocious, where bloody scenes of civilians falling to their deaths were shown on television.

I visited Lebanon in December 1987, when the internal Shia and Maronite wars were raging. In Beirut, on the evening news, I watched anchorman Arafat Hejazi reading the details of the Maronite and Shia civil wars in a halting and sobbing tone. When the bloodied corpse of a small infant was shown, tears covered Hejazi's face and the newscast was interrupted for a video of a song by Julia Boutros about the suffering of the Lebanese people, showing scenes of war and destruction from 1975 to 1987. When the civil war ended in 1990, Hizbollah remained the only armed group in Lebanon to continue to function as a government-sanctioned resistance force against the Israeli occupation of southern Lebanon. In contrast, *Amal* was more involved in political activity. By 2003, both organizations were equally influential in the Shia community in Lebanon and had several representatives in parliament.

The Border Strip canton
Another canton was established in southern Lebanon by a pro-Israeli Lebanese militia. The origins of this canton date back to March 1976, when government troops mutinied under Colonel Ahmad Khatib and occupied several army barracks all over Lebanon. In the south, Khatib's supporters took over several barracks and started a shooting match against their colleagues who banded in another renegade brigade led by Major Saad Haddad in the village of Qilayaa. This fighting divided the border strip between a predominantly Christian area under the control of Saad Haddad, and another area under the control of the Palestinians and the Lebanese left and Khatib's faction of the Lebanese army.

Surrounded by the PLO and the Khatib faction who controlled Hasbaya and Marjayoun, and encouraged by former President Camille Chamoun, Saad Haddad established contacts with the Israelis and received weapons and support. The opportunity came for Haddad to expand his tiny territory in 1978. In that year, Israel invaded Lebanon and occupied the south. However, under US pressure it withdrew, leaving the South Lebanon Army (SLA) militia in control. Meanwhile, the UN decided to supervise a buffer zone between Israel and Lebanon, and for that purpose it sent a contingent of 6,000 troops.

The following episode was described to the author by two Lebanese writers who witnessed the birth of the Border Strip canton in 1978. The canton would last until May 2000: "On 13 June 1978, the United Nations Information Centre in Beirut invited the media to cover the deployment of the UNIFIL (the UN peacekeeping force in southern Lebanon). The delegation headed south early in the morning and reached Tyre at 9 am.[6] The UN convoy was gathered at the Ghassan Rahal Lebanese Army barracks, and left for a string of villages west of the city. The UN trucks and troop carriers climbed the steep hills where UN soldiers were spreading out in abandoned Israeli positions. The stretch of territory north-west of Tyre included the villages of Abassiyé and Borj Rahal, and ended at Deir Kanoun an-Nahr. This village overlooked the Litani River from a massive hill. At its edge we saw abandoned Israeli fortifications and met a British officer, General Cooke, looking through binoculars.

"In mid-afternoon, the UN force moved along the coast where it reached Jisr al-Hamra, south of the mouth of the Litani. There we met General Erskine, Commander of UNIFIL. He looked troubled and told us that his force was not able to enter certain areas on the maps and documents in his possession. This meant that the UN was unable to achieve its goal of extending Lebanese authority to the international border. The stand-off continued for another 22 years until the Israelis left abruptly on 24 May 2000.

"By 5 pm we arrived at the UN headquarters at Nakoura, the last major Lebanese town before the Israeli borders. Behind the UN complex we saw several Israeli soldiers inside Lebanon and further south was the border crossing, closed since 1948. The small town of Nakoura was located east of the UN centre. We represented a daily newspaper and another Beirut weekly magazine and we were curious to find out about the conditions of the Lebanese inhabitants of this remote area. As we walked towards Nakoura, we noticed a Lebanese flag of the size used by the Lebanese army posted at a checkpoint manned by the South Lebanon Army militia.

"The militiamen at the checkpoint were friendly, and offered biscuits and water and enquired about Beirut. Like the other Lebanese militias, they were very frank and arrogant in airing their beliefs. They said the 'liberation' of Lebanon would start from their canton. We enquired about the support they receive from Israel, which was evident:

they were trained by Israel; their tents, clothes, weapons and supplies all came from the Israelis. They said their enemies were the Syrians and the Palestinians, but not other Lebanese and certainly not the Israelis who welcomed their children in their hospitals. They believed that their Israeli-dominated area was the only free area of Lebanon and, *Inshallah* (God willing) they would take over the rest of Lebanon. Towards the end of the conversation, we learnt from the names that the militiamen at this checkpoint were a mixture of Christian and Shia Lebanese.

"As we chatted with the militiamen, a military Land Rover arrived carrying a bulky soldier with dark sunglasses and a black army beret, typical of the Lebanese Army Marines (*Maghawir*). When the man descended and greeted everybody, the militiamen stood in salute; this was the renegade Lebanese Army Major Sami Chediac, second in command to Saad Haddad in the South Lebanon Army (SLA) militia.

"With a dark black beard under a broad smile, Chediac talked to us casually about the situation, all the time looking into the distance at the surrounding hills and the UN compound down the road. The enclave, he said, extended from Hasbaya in the east to Nakoura on the coast. This included the major towns of Khiam, Marjayoun and Bint Jbail. Chediac explained that he had just had lunch with his superior, renegade Lebanese Army Major Saad Haddad, at Qilayaa. He said Israeli army officers attended the lunch and renewed their pledge of support to the enclave. We told him what many people thought of him in Beirut. Chediac's reaction was philosophical; he had an air that reminded us of the other militia leaders in Lebanon. He talked quietly about his group and what they were up to. Like leaders of the left, the Phalanges and the PLO, he was self-justified but not defensive. Of course he wanted an independent Lebanon, and no, he was not a stooge for the Israelis, who should surely leave Lebanon as soon as the Syrians and the PLO went. He added that seeing how the civil war had turned out in Beirut and Mount Lebanon, he would accept any help to defend the border strip and liberate Lebanon.

"We did not ask Chediac about the bloody role of the militia in the Israeli invasion in March, only ten weeks before, when Haddad's men had massacred old people in Khiam. David Hirst of *The Guardian* had reported that Haddad's men pulled gold teeth from the mouths of the elders, while many other civilians cried for help from under the rubble of bombed houses.

"It was already dark when we left the border strip on the back of a UN truck along with several local and Western journalists, one Canadian soldier and two Norwegians. We jokingly asked the Canadian soldier if he carried any Canada-Dry (a Canadian fizzy drink) in his knapsack as we were thirsty."

After 1982, the SLA militia grew stronger, and when Haddad died, the renegade Lebanese Army Colonel Antoine Lahd took over. After the Israeli withdrawal in 1985, the SLA territory expanded, as predicted by Chediac, and covered the county of Jezzine and a number of villages east of Saida. In 1993, the Border Strip canton contained almost half of southern Lebanon, overlooked Iqlim Tofah and controlled the Khardali bridge to Nabatié on the Litani River and the Beaufort Castle south of Nabatié. Like the other cantons the strip had a radio station, Sawt al-Amal, and a television station, Middle East Television (financed and run by American Evangelist Pat Robertson).

Throughout the civil war, the Lebanese government paid the salaries of teachers and civil servants of the Strip, and even paid the SLA regulars up to 1990. The SLA frequently shelled Saida and its Palestinian camps if the government shirked on prompt delivery of services. The civil war ended in Lebanon in 1990, but the Border Strip canton continued to exist for another ten years. On the morning of 24 May 2000, the militiamen and their families woke up to discover that the Israelis had withdrawn during the night and left them to face an uncertain destiny. An exodus ensued as over 7,000 individuals – militiamen and families – abandoned their homes and chose to seek refuge in Israel. Another 2,000 persons surrendered to the Lebanese authorities.

The Sunni cantons

Although all the Lebanese communities gave some form of support to the Palestinians while turning against them at times, the Sunnis were consistent in their support. In 1973, when Israeli agents killed several PLO leaders in Beirut, Prime Minister Saeb Salam resigned "because the Maronite-controlled Lebanese army failed to respond to the attack".[7] A demonstration of 250,000 people marched in support of the Palestinian Resistance. Salam's stand went beyond the symbolic Arab nationalist gesture. The Palestinians are 85 per cent Sunni, and the PLO in Lebanon, as Salam put it, was "the army of the Muslims", since he viewed the

Lebanese army as the guardian of Maronite privileges. After 1976, the Sunnis maintained their strongholds in Tripoli and Saida, and remained faithful allies of the Palestinians until the PLO left Beirut in 1982.

Saida became a canton in a dangerous environment. Its living space was constrained by Joumblatt in the north, Shia and PLO militias in the south, the SLA militia in the east, and the Israeli-controlled Mediterranean coast in the west. The Saida canton ran from the Awali River in the north to the Zahrani River in the south and ended at Scenic Bridge near the town of Ghaziyé.

Saida was the sister of Tyre in classical times and the seat of power for the whole country under the Ottomans when Beirut was a forgotten village. In the independent Lebanon, its role was eclipsed by Beirut and remained ignored for decades. The fact that Saida gave Lebanon the al-Solh *zaim*s did not pay any dividends as the al-Solhs resided in Beirut where they were engaged in politics and became prime ministers. Even in May 1992, an al-Solh (Takieddine) was appointed Prime Minister.

Saida's grievance with the Beirut regime crystallized in 1975. In 1974, Camille Chamoun established a fishing enterprise called Protein, aimed at large-scale exploitations of marine resources off the Lebanese coast. The fishermen of Saida feared for their livelihood if Chamoun had his way. In February 1975, Maarouf Saad, Saida's pan-Arab Nasserite mayor and parliamentarian, called for a general strike and a demonstration against Protein. During the protest, in which several thousands marched, Saad was shot and killed, reportedly by a government soldier.[8] This brought the Saads widespread sympathy and won the tiny Nasserite movement much credit with the public. Many analysts attribute the start of the civil war to this incident. For weeks after the murder of Saad, Saida was shut down. Protein's offices in Beirut were bombed (including one on Rue Abdul Aziz), and clashes with the army were reported. This situation continued for the next two months until the Lebanese conflict reached a point of no return and the skirmishes became open warfare on 13 April.

Saad's son Moustafa inherited the leadership of Saida and its Nasserite militia, the People's Nasserite Organization. Over the years, this militia took control of the city and established a police force and a tax collection system. It also controlled the ancient harbour and developed good but subdued friendships with the Palestinian camps south of the city. After 1985, Saida became a target of frequent shelling from the SLA who took over Jezzine and Kfar-Falous east of the city. The shelling of Saida became worse in 1986, when *Amal*'s war against the PLO flared south of Saida around the Palestinian camps of Ain Helwé and Miéou-Mié, and caused tragic losses of human life in the Christian town of Maghdouché.

Tripoli, the second largest Lebanese city after Beirut, was also a bastion of Arabism and Sunni Islam. Located wholly within the Syrian sphere of influence, Tripoli's move towards cantonization proved stillborn. After minor skirmishes with Maronite Zghorta in 1976, Rachid Karami, the Sunni *zaim* of Tripoli, and Sulieman Frangié, the warlord of Zghorta, brought peace to the north. Yet, the friendly and pro-Syrian Karami lost the monopoly of leadership in Tripoli. As in Beirut in the 1960s and the early 1970s, the leftists made important gains in Tripoli. In 1972, Abdel Majid Rafei, a leftist candidate, won a parliamentary seat against Karami's candidate. Aside from the left, Tripoli also witnessed the growth of some fringe Islamic groups, such as *Jundullah* (Soldiers of God), who were famous for commuting to the front lines against the Maronites on bicycles. When the Syrians moved into Lebanon in 1976, the leftists lost much of their influence and the status quo was maintained until 1980.

As had happened in other areas, the defeat of the left pushed many people to go back to their communal roots while maintaining the opposition of traditional *zaim*s and warlords. After 1980, many disillusioned young people were inspired by the Iranian revolution, and former members of the left, of the Islamic Jundullah and the outlawed Muslim Brothers joined together to reclaim Tripoli. In 1980, Tripoli's Muslim radicals reportedly provided assistance to the Muslim Brothers' uprising in the Syrian town of Hama. Over the following two years a well-organized paramilitary organization calling itself *Tawheed Islami* (Islamic Unification) appeared on the scene and manned the streets of Tripoli.

A major boost to Tawheed came from Yasser Arafat in 1983. Arafat, who had left Beirut in 1982, was able to sneak back to Lebanon and establish himself in the Palestinian camps of Beddaoui and Bared, east of Tripoli. The Syrians were angered by this move and were determined to dislodge Arafat from Tripoli. Thus, a bloody war followed, bidding the radical Muslim Tawheed militiamen of Tripoli and the PLO against the Syrian army and its Lebanese allies. In the process, observers witnessed a repeat of the siege of Beirut, with Arafat smiling to Western television crews and stating that "this great Islamic city will never surrender". Several hundred civilians were killed in this war, and hundreds of attractive modern buildings and other property were seriously damaged.

The Syrians and their allies won the battle and Tawheed sought a pact with the Syrians. However, the conflict resumed when the pro-Syrian Alawite community in east Tripoli, led by Ali Eid and his Arab Democratic Party began to show signs of power and hegemony. This posed a threat to *Tawheed*'s areas of influence, and thus another war flared between the Sunnis and the Alawis. The Syrians intervened once more, but this time they restored Rachid Karami's influence, who became Prime Minister of Lebanon again. However, Karami was assassinated by the Lebanese Forces Christian militia in May 1987 when a bomb exploded in his helicopter in northern Lebanon. His apolitical brother, Omar Karami, was appointed Prime Minister in 1990.

The Palestinian cantons
Since 1948, the Palestinians have been attacked by almost every country in the Levant, and remain homeless and victimized. They had several miserable and disastrous experiences, as the text below indicates.

- **In Palestine**. Over 1.3 million Palestinians lost their homes and became refugees in the 1948 and 1967 Arab–Israeli wars, which the Israelis won.
- **In Jordan**. The Palestinians were crushed in the Jordanian civil war of 1969–71.
- **In Lebanon**. Their camps were systematically destroyed and razed to the ground. Almost a dozen Palestinian camps existed in Lebanon in 1975 and were located near the major cities. The largest were Ain Helwé and Miéou-Mié near Saida. The camps were under the direct control of the PLO and didn't answer to the Lebanese authorities. The destruction of the PLO and the camps started in 1976.
    - **The Lebanese authorities**. The determination of the Lebanese government to establish its authority in the camps led to open conflict with the PLO starting in 1969. Battles and skirmishes marred every year between 1969 to 1991. Lebanon had to sign the Cairo Accord with the PLO effectively surrendering sovereignty over certain areas in southern Lebanon (al-Arkoub) so that

Palestinian guerrillas could wage their campaign against Israel. Several battles were waged between the Lebanese army and the PLO in the 1990s, and the most recent occurred in August 2002 in the Ain Helwé refugee camp near Saida.
- **The Phalanges**. After 1969, the PLO was seen by almost all Lebanese as a state within a state. The Phalanges, who fought the Palestinians since 1969, demolished many camps in 1976 including Tell Zaatar, Dbaye, Jisr al-Basha and Haret al-Ghawarné, and pushed their inhabitants to the Muslim side.
- **The Syrians**. The Syrian government was interested in reducing the PLO power in Lebanon, and Syrian troops participated in the war against the PLO in Beirut and the mountain region in 1976 and in Tripoli in 1983. The Syrians also assisted the *Amal* militia in the 1985 siege of the Palestinian camps.
- **The Israelis**. Between 1968 and 1993, the Israelis waged massive air and land assaults against the Palestinian camps and military bases throughout Lebanon, including assassinations of their leaders. The Israeli campaign culminated in two full-scale invasions in 1978 and 1982. The 1982 invasion was the largest Israeli operation in Lebanon, and resulted in destruction of the PLO structure in Lebanon and the death of 9,000 Palestinians.
- **The Shia**. The *Amal* militia also participated in the war against the Palestinians. After several skirmishes between 1979 and 1984, in 1985, *Amal* militiamen surrounded the camps of Sabra and Chatila, Bourj Brajné in Beirut, Ain Helwé and Miéou-Mié near Saida, and Bass and Rachidiyé near Tyre. The bloody War of the Camps ensued and caused much damage to human life and property.

- **In Kuwait**. The defeat of Iraq in Kuwait in February 1991 left its large Palestinian population open to retribution and revenge from the Kuwaitis. The large and prosperous community of Palestinians in Kuwait, almost 400,000, was reduced to less than 50,000 in 1992 and lost its wealth and influence. Individual Kuwaiti vigilante groups sealed entire Palestinian neighbourhoods in Kuwait City, and arrested and murdered many Palestinians. The PLO lost vital financial aid from the rich Arab states of the Gulf for Arafat's stand with Iraq in the Kuwait crisis.

Following the Palestinian–Israeli rapprochement in September 1993 and the creation of autonomous areas for the Palestinians in the West Bank and Gaza, there were renewed hopes in Lebanon that the Palestinian problem could eventually be resolved. The Lebanese government stand on the issue is enshrined in the 1989 Constitution, and calls for the restitution and resettlement of the Palestinian refugees in their former towns in Palestine. As of December 2002, there remained in Lebanon around 385,000 Palestinian refugees (United Nations Relief Works Agency (UNRWA) estimates).

NOTES

1 Hamdane, *The Lebanese Crisis*, p. 182.
2 It is established that the number of Lebanese expatriates and persons of Lebanese ancestry is larger than that in Lebanon. Conservative estimates put the number of the Lebanese diaspora at five to six million people, while the Lebanese World Cultural Organization comes up with the inflated number of thirteen million. Conservative estimates claim that almost four to five million people who trace their origin to Lebanon reside in the Americas, where Brazil alone has a community of two million and the United States has 1.5 million. Australia and the Arab countries come second with 200,000 each, while Europe has fewer than 50,000 and West Africa 75,000. The Lebanese Cultural Organization claims that twelve million Lebanese or persons of Lebanese ancestry live in the Americas, 500,000 in Australia and New Zealand, and another 500,000 in the rest of the world. The Lebanese diaspora is affluent and very successful and many of its members have become presidents and ministers and important business leaders in their adopted countries. (The Lebanese World Cultural Society, *The Lebanese Diaspora (Al-intishar al Lubnani*, quoted in *Who's Who in Lebanon*, Beirut, Publitec, 1991).
3 *Arab Economic Report*, Arab League Information, 1986.
4 Mentioned in Fouad Ajami, *The Vanished Imam: Musa al-Sadr and the Shia of Lebanon*, London, I.B. Tauris, 1986.
5 Robin Wright, *The Sacred Rage: The Wrath of Militant Islam*, New York, Simon and Schuster, 1986.
6 This episode is based on personal interviews with journalists.
7 Kamal Salibi, *Crossroads to Civil War: Lebanon 1958–1976*, New York, Caravan, 1976, p. 66.
8 This episode is considered by many observers as *the* first spark in the Lebanese civil war. While Georges Corm dates the start of the civil war to 1969 when the Phalanges fought the Palestinians, American Jonathan Randal makes the starting date a thousand years ago, in the eleventh century, when Druze, Maronites and Shia existed in Mount Lebanon and were the allies or the victims of this or that regional power (in Jonathan Randall, *La Guerre de mille ans*, Paris, Grasset, 1984).

15

Bachir Gemayel: Last of the Warlords

The Maronites have long experience of running the affairs of state in Lebanon. They ruled Mount Lebanon between 1770 and 1843, and Greater Lebanon between 1935 and 1988 (see Chapters 1 and 3), and continued to enjoy good representation after 1988. Not only did they control the government, but also they exerted significant economic influence in the country. Shortly after independence, they decided that since Lebanon's advantage was in services, it needed peace and security. The 1958 crisis proved the fragility of the warlord-based Lebanon in an explosive Middle East. Both the shabby internal social fabric and the difficult geographic location were detrimental to the growth of a services-dominated economy.

For a time, the Lebanese were able to convert each Middle East crisis into a net gain for Lebanon, and Lebanese economists casually wrote "Following the Palestine war, Arabian oil moved to Saida instead of the planned Haifa pipeline", or "The closure of the Suez Canal brought more business to Beirut", or "The socialist Arab regimes forced many wealthy Arabs to settle in Beirut" and so on. However, in the late 1960s, the problems eventually came back to haunt Lebanon. The Maronite warlords were aware of the social changes and the threats they posed to their privileged position. Several meetings were organized to address the situation, and Chamoun hosted a meeting in his palace at Saadiyat south of Beirut in 1966, which was followed by a military display of his private armed militia.

The social explosion in Lebanon started in 1968. The movement, which was initiated by the leftist parties led by a mixture of Muslim and Christian intellectuals, threatened the Maronite position in Lebanon. On the economic level, between 1968 and 1973, the no-war no-peace situation in the Middle East and the rise of the Palestinian guerrilla movement threatened Lebanon's role as a middleman in the area. It was the Druze leader Kamal Joumblatt who single-handedly brought the political opposition against the Maronites into a large umbrella under his leadership (see Chapter 9).

Pierre Gemayel

In the late 1960s, two warlords dominated the Maronite scene: Camille Chamoun and Pierre Gemayel. Chamoun's militia had its base in the Chouf, especially in Saadiyat (where Chamoun's palace was located), Damour and Deir al-Kamar. The less important but ambitious Gemayel had his base in the Upper Metn Region, centred in his hometown of Beckfaya.

Pierre Gemayel was born in Egypt in 1908 to a Maronite Lebanese family. In 1936, he established an organization in Beirut under the name the Social Democratic Party, alias the Phalanges. Many observers remarked that Gemayel founded the Phalanges following a visit he made to Nazi Germany where he was impressed with Nazi organization. This visit seduced many writers to make the deduction that the Phalanges had Nazi roots. The reality was that, except for fondness for organization, Gemayel never espoused Nazism, let alone any ideological doctrine. His Phalanges troopers who fought in the civil war in 1975–6 were the communal army of the Maronites, and for that matter every other community in Lebanon maintained a similar army. There was nothing profound about the average Phalanges member in 1975 any more than there was about the average Maronite mountaineer of 1860. This is not to accord the Phalanges little ideological credit, but to place them along with other groups in Lebanon, such as the Druze or the Shia, who had no ideology except the preservation of their own community. However, among the sectarian political organizations, the Phalanges could claim a form of Lebanese nationalism as an ideology.

Before 1958, the Phalanges were a minor force in Lebanese affairs. After supporting Chamoun in 1958, Phalanges cadets kept their guns, and in the late 1960s started arming themselves and making their presence felt. The social status of the Phalanges members was a minus for the movement in times of peace. The average Phalanges had no roots in the traditional feudal families and mostly descended from poor Maronite families. Even the Gemayels themselves could not compete with the big historical warlords of Lebanon.

The Phalanges was the number one military organization in Lebanon in terms of size, weaponry, popular support, intellectual cadre, participation and influence in the government, wealth, prestige and respectability. It was ruled by a politburo of largely educated Maronites who doubled as ministers in the government, or deputies in parliament.

The charisma of Pierre Gemayel dominated the politburo until his death in 1984. Between 1985 and 1990 the party was overrun by young militants as the elders were pushed aside.

As peace returned to Lebanon in 1990, the old guards of the Phalanges moved to isolate the military commanders and took back the membership cards from all the commoners who had fought the dirty wars on behalf of the Christians between 1975 and 1990. However, popular and grass-roots representation also added credit to the party. In the 1960s, the reformist President Chehab saw the Phalanges as a potential force for defying the warlords. He sponsored them in Parliamentary elections as a progressive Maronite movement, and sought their support against the more traditional Maronite warlords such as the Chamouns and the Frangiés.

In 1975, the Maronites were confident of a victory against the Lebanese leftists and the Palestinians. Contrary to the established wisdom at the time, the Phalanges were not interested in partitioning Lebanon; they truly believed that a swift victory against the marginal left would keep them on top of Lebanese politics. Thanks to their presence throughout the country and appeal to the traditional Muslim and Christian leadership, the Maronites scored some gains in the first year of the civil war. Even in west Beirut, large areas remained under Phalanges military control. Chamoun fared equally well in the first year of war. His men controlled the coastal highway between Nahmé and Jiyé south of Beirut, and in southern Lebanon, Chamoun's supporters controlled strategic areas such as Aichiyé and Marjayoun.

The confidence of the Maronites began to erode in January 1976. In that month it became clear that they could no longer use the state apparatus, including the army, to their advantage, and they discovered that their private militias, although capable of beating the small leftist Lebanese militias, were no match for the Palestinians, who joined the armed conflict on Kamal Joumblatt's side in 1976.

Bad luck met Chamoun's militia first. In January 1976, the coastal towns south of Beirut were stormed by the Palestinian-leftist forces. Chamoun's men, as well as a large number of Maronite civilians, especially in Damour, Nahmé and Saadiyat, fled to east Beirut. Later on, Aichiyé in south Lebanon met a similar destiny. In February and March 1976, the leftist–Palestinian alliance wiped out the Phalanges from west Beirut in successive campaigns. Encouraged by these results, the joint PLO-leftist forces attacked Phalanges lines on all fronts, and by spring 1976, the alliance was in control of 82 per cent of Lebanese territory. At that time, it seemed only a matter of weeks before Maronite power would be totally eradicated as the Palestinian–leftist coalition, led by Kamal Joumblatt, resumed its campaign by encircling the Maronite-held areas east and north of Beirut and in the mountain region. Bombs were falling on Jounié with increasing intensity, and Kamal Joumblatt was waiting at his house for the Maronite leaders to arrive and sign a pact with him agreeing to the reforms he espoused.[1]

By May 1976, the Maronites were cornered in Mount Lebanon with a coastal strip extending from Beirut's harbour to the Barbara Crossing at the edge of the Batroun county. This situation brought regional and international attention, as the threat of a PLO-backed leftist government headed by Joumblatt was becoming a reality. Neighbouring Israel and Syria were the two major players in latter events as the Israelis provided arms to the Phalanges, and the Syrians moved in against the PLO and the Lebanese left.

These interventions brought an end to Joumblatt and his coalition, but the Maronite position in the country was never again restored to pre-1975 eminence. This outcome was probably the major factor in convincing some Maronites in 1977–9 that it was time to create a Maronite canton along the lines of the 1840–60 events when Maronite power had been eliminated from the Chouf. While a de facto Maronite canton became a reality, after 1979, the idea of a separate Maronite entity was never pursued openly and never dominated mainstream Maronite thinking in Lebanon.

Bachir Gemayel

With the defeat of Chamoun in the Chouf and his flight to east Beirut, the Gemayels' ambitions came to the fore. While the Gemayels led the best organized militia in Lebanon, they lacked traditional warlord influence. On the other hand, the politburo of the party capitalized on the general belief that the Phalanges represented the common Maronite individual who had been exploited for centuries and belittled by the warlords. The Gemayels' plan was to lead the Maronite canton and negotiate from their strong position with the rest of Lebanon. Bachir, son of Pierre Gemayel, represented this ambition. He wanted to cleanse the canton and go on the offensive to reunite the whole of Lebanon under

Maronite leadership. Thus in 1976, a joint Maronite force defeated the Palestinians in Tell Zaatar and cleared the Muslim Lebanese from east Beirut. To counter the PLO–leftist alliance, the Gemayels and Chamoun were ready to ally themselves and receive help "even from the devil".[2]

The war against the Palestinian camps and the Muslim population of east Beirut was a milestone for Bachir.[3] Until 1976, the Phalanges militia had not been under the Gemayels' direct control, but under the leadership of other party officials, such as the commander William Hawi, an ex-army officer from the Greek Orthodox town of Bteghrine in the Upper Metn. In the battle for Tell Zaatar, Hawi was mysteriously assassinated, reportedly by someone from his own side. This assassination opened the way for Bachir to become the commander himself. Thus began Bachir's drive to destroy the Maronite traditional warlords and establish himself as a supreme leader of Maronite Lebanon and eventually, in 1982, as President of Lebanon. Inside the canton, Bachir turned to state-building. On 15 April 1976, he declared a civil administration in the Phalanges-controlled areas complete with a police force (Section Kataib de la Sécurité), courts and a postal service. In the summer he took over the fourth and fifth docks of Beirut's harbour, thus transferring to the militia's treasury almost LL2 billion of government revenues in customs duties alone. Casino du Liban, which netted the government almost LL200 million annually, also fell under his control.

At the regional level, Bachir was equally dynamic. For a full year following the arrival of the Syrian Army in east Beirut, the Phalanges lay low. However, when Syria broke off with Egypt (following Anwar Sadat's trip to Israel in November 1977), Bachir held a news conference in which he announced the divorce with Syria. In February 1978, attacks by Phalanges militiamen against Syrian positions at Fiyadiyé and Forn Chebak in the eastern suburbs of Beirut were followed by frequent attacks on the Rizk Tower in east Beirut, an important makeshift military base for Syrian troops. Fire broke out in the autumn of 1978, and open warfare started between Syria and the Phalanges ending with the Syrian army evacuating the Phalanges-administered areas. Bachir became an idol in the Maronite community, outdoing Chamoun in popularity and vying for absolute leadership in the community. By 1979, there was no more Muslim, Palestinian or Syrian presence to challenge Bachir in the Maronite canton. In the period 1979–81 he started eliminating Maronite opposition to his leadership. He began with the Frangié warlords of Zghorta.

The Frangiés

The Frangié warlords of Zghorta are traditional opponents to Chamoun and his Phalanges allies, in line with the historical animosity between the northern Maronites and the Maronites of central Lebanon. The Frangiés were challenged by other families on their own turf, such as the Douehis and Karams and the northern Maronite allies of Chamoun, and these in-house quarrels led to violent episodes between these families. In 1957, following a bloody encounter in the village of Mézyara, in which dozens of Douehi supporters were massacred by the Frangiés, Sulieman Frangié and his ally René Mouawad (both became presidents of Lebanon later) fled to Syria, where reportedly they were guests of the Assads (the family of Syrian President Hafez Assad).

In the 1958 civil war, the Frangiés stood against the Chamoun camp. After 1958, the Frangiés went through a historic transformation and allied themselves with the central Maronites, but returned to their traditional political stands in 1976. Between 1958 and 1964, President Chehab's anti-feudal stand as well as the new generation of Maronite leaders who supported his line of ruling Lebanon and eliminating the traditional warlords, brought a temporary rapprochement between the Frangiés and the Chamouns. This rapprochement was best exemplified by the 1970 presidential elections. In those elections, Camille Chamoun, Pierre Gemayel and Raymond Éddé (son of Emile Éddé), figured that with a docile parliament, the presidency would go to the Chehabist candidate Elias Sarkis. Chamoun did not fool himself about the strength of his alliance, for although the Muslim leadership and Kamal Joumblatt were equally fed up with the Chehabist style, they would never vote for an extreme Maronite hand-picked by Chamoun. Consequently, to attract the Muslims, the Maronite plan was that any Maronite should win but Sarkis. Therefore, Chamoun's foe Sulieman Frangié, who had many Muslim friends, was chosen to beat Sarkis. Pierre Gemayel and Raymond Éddé, both hopeful candidates, stood aside.

Frangié served his mandate amid awkward relations with Chamoun and the Gemayels, and as soon as his mandate was over in 1976, he turned against the Maronite alliance and returned to his home base in Zghorta. In Zghorta he embraced his (now deceased) brother Hamid's open friendship with Syria and the traditional Muslim leadership of Tripoli.

Out of public office in Beirut, Sulieman wished to re-establish himself as the warlord of Zghorta and northern Lebanon in 1976, but he had to surmount local challenges to his wish. During his absence as President in Beirut many things had changed in Zghorta. In 1976, the Phalanges were the strongest organization there, with an occasional display of military power. To his dismay, Frangié discovered that his wish of a separate hegemony in the north away from the civil war in Beirut was challenged by Bachir Gemayel.

Typical of the younger Phalanges who thought of themselves as modern and progressive, Bachir and his lieutenants attacked Frangié as "feudalist and old class". However, the Frangiés did not take Bachir's military prowess in Zghorta seriously and moved to check the Phalangist growth in Zghorta. In the events that followed, Frangié's militia killed Jude al-Bayeh, the Phalanges local chief, and this was the pretext for Bachir to flex his muscles in the north. Seeking revenge, a Phalanges platoon was expedited to the north. It was led by Samir Geagea, a Phalanges officer from the neighbouring town of Becharri, traditionally an old foe of Zghorta.

The platoon raided Ehden on 13 June 1978, and killed Frangié's son Tony and his family. Tony was the leader of the Frangié's Giants Brigade (*Liwaa al-Marada*) and Sulieman's heir apparent as leader of the north. Ehden was the hometown of Youssef Karam, who led the campaign against the popular Maronite uprising against the al-Khazen warlords in 1860. Phalanges propagandists pointed out with irony that their militiamen who came from the common people were revenged in 1978 for Karam's crushing of Chahine's uprising in 1858. The bronze statue of Youssef Karam in the main square of Ehden looked on as the Phalanges marched in.

The raid on Ehden produced the opposite to the intended effect. Reacting to the cold-blooded murder of his son and his family, Sulieman pledged that he would "never have a peace of mind until Bachir is done with". The Frangiés won much sympathy, especially after graphic pictures of the bloody massacre of Tony and his family were shown in Lebanese papers and on television.

After this incident, the Frangiés sealed their control over the entire northern Maronite region, banning all Phalangist presence. The Frangiés established effective economic control over the counties of Zghorta, Becharri and parts of Batroun and Koura, with a seaport near Chekka, a radio station, a television station and a seat of leadership in the town of Zghorta. They garnered "taxes" from the two largest cement factories in Lebanon located on the coast. The Giants Brigade defended the canton and in the early 1980s, the Frangiés expanded their control into the non-Maronite Orthodox Christian County of Koura, which was controlled by a traditional leadership and the secular Syrian Nationalist Party. The Koura region did not wish to be under the Zghorta yoke and offered stiff resistance in a battle against the Frangié militia in 1985, during which many Koura villages were attacked and pillaged, and many people killed.

In 1992, Sulieman Jr., the former president's grandson and son of the assassinated Tony Frangié, was elected to parliament and became a cabinet minister. He followed his family tradition of maintaining strong ties with the Lebanese Muslim leadership and with Syria, and distanced himself from the traditional Maronite leadership in Beirut and central Lebanon, refusing to be "a foot soldier to some lunatic (*majanin*) Christian leaders, as [had] been the case in the past".[4] From 2000, there was talk about Sulieman Jr. one day becoming president of Lebanon; even President Hafez Assad before he died in 2000 presented him with an expensive Arab mantle, which the media took to represent a Syrian blessing on the young Frangié.

The Chamouns
Between 1952 and 1975, Camille Chamoun was the most powerful Maronite warlord, eclipsing the Maronite presidents who succeeded him and the Maronite Patriarch himself. Maronite households placed his picture next to the Virgin Mary and the Last Supper, and the common people spoke of him with veneration. This was felt even during the mandate of the populist Fouad Chehab (1958–64). In religious celebrations, television crews employed by the government were pointedly ordered to focus the cameras on President Fouad Chehab receiving communion from the Maronite Patriarch so that people could see this on television and to counter the argument that Chehab had abandoned his Maronitism. But the common people loved Chamoun anyway.

Following the failure in the north, Bachir's northern borders were limited to within a line starting from the Barbara Crossing on the coast along the River Ibrahim up to the high slopes of the mountain range. Chamoun's followers who had fled the Chouf were the next target on Bachir's agenda. Following their defeat in the Chouf and Saadiyat in

1976, Chamoun's Tiger militiamen[5] became refugees in east Beirut where their independent military organization was under suspicion by the dominant Phalanges. Although Chamoun's men fought hard in Tell Zaatar under Phalange command and Chamoun's son and militia leader, Danny, was present to claim victory in August 1976, this did not get the Chamouns much credit with Bachir. On 7 July 1980, with Frangié out of the way and Chamoun an old man, Bachir's men uprooted the Tigers militia at Safra and Aqua Marina north of Beirut, killing 700 of them and throwing several bodies over the cliffs. Many of Chamoun's fighters fled to west Beirut and sought protection with the Muslims.

With his influence complete, Bachir declared a new unified militia, the *Forces Libanaises*. As the situation stabilized, the Gemayels' domains became the best equipped canton in Lebanon. Access roads to the canton became customs crossings, where duties were paid on goods and travellers paid crossing fees. An airport was built over a stretch of coastal highway at the town of Halat, financed by Roger Tamraz. The militia's television station, LBC (the Lebanese Broadcasting Corporation) became the most powerful television station in Lebanon and the neighbouring countries, and the radio station, the Voice of Lebanon (*Sawt Lubnan*), was popular. The Christian heartland was quickly transformed into a booming economy. Bachir decided it was time to enlarge the enclave.

In the winter of 1980–1, with the mountain region under his control, Bachir continued his ambitious project of claiming more Lebanese territory. He began his quiet plan to take over the Greek Catholic town of Zahlé in the Syrian-controlled Bekaa Valley. The plan involved building a major road from Mount Sannine to Zahlé. Syria viewed Bachir's move as compromising its strategic defences against Israel in the Bekaa, as his control of Zahlé would encircle Syrian positions against the Israelis. In response, Syrian troops blockaded Bachir's men in Zahlé and attacked them on Mount Sannine. The incident took a dangerous turn when Israeli planes shot down two Syrian helicopters and the Syrians responded by deploying SAM missiles in the Bekaa. When the Israelis threatened to bomb the SAMs, and before the situation deteriorated any further, the Americans sent in the White House Special Envoy Philip Habib, who defused the situation.

Bachir's ambitions were now out in the open and he could no longer look back. Now he was aiming for the presidency of Lebanon and spent months preparing for the presidential elections that were due to take place in August 1982. As the unchallenged leader of the Maronite community he stood a good chance. With Israeli tanks surrounding Beirut and occupying almost 50 per cent of Lebanese territory, Bachir was elected president at the Fiyadiyé Lebanese Army barracks overlooking Beirut.

What the Gemayels lacked in historical leadership they compensated for in brute force and foreign support. With Bachir as president, the Maronites felt that they were not only masters in their own home, but again in control of the whole country. For a moment they felt that things were going to be better than before 1975 "minus the Palestinians of course, and all the scum of the Lebanese left".[6] However, the assassination of Bachir in a tragic bombing in September 1982 abruptly ended these dreams, crippling the Phalanges with a blow similar to the one that had hit the leftists after the assassination of Kamal Joumblatt in 1977.

The new Maronite warlords

In September 1982, Amine Gemayel replaced Bachir as president of Lebanon. Amine was less desirous than his brother to be involved in the affairs of the Maronite enclave as he was now president of all of Lebanon. To establish his credibility with the Muslims and the Arab world, he relied on the Lebanese army and distanced himself from the Maronite militia. Meanwhile inside the canton, leadership of the Christian Lebanese Forces became less significant as it went to less charismatic and less influential figures such as Fadi Frem, brother in-law of the Gemayels, who lost the Battle of Bhamdoun in 1983, and Fouad Abinadder (son of Arzé Gemayel, sister of Bachir) who kept a low profile.

The young cadres of the Phalanges and the Lebanese Forces were unhappy about this situation. East Beirut was crowded with Maronite refugees from the Chouf and from Frangié's canton, and the sons of these refugees, who represented the rank and file of the Lebanese Forces, did not like Amine Gemayel's attempt to assume leadership of the Christian cantons as he was not close to the rank and file of the fighters like his brother Bachir. His role as president of Lebanon required rapprochement with the Muslims, and diehard Phalanges dubbed him *Mohamed al-Amine*. Accordingly, in March 1985, the trio of Elie Hobeika (a Maronite refugee from the Metn), Samir Geagea (a Maronite refugee from the Frangié domains) and Karim Pakradouni (an Armenian) joined forces and led a coup within the Lebanese Forces, further alienating Amine and his men. Hobeika, who is believed to be responsible for the Sabra and Chatila massacres, became the leader and started a dialogue with Syria. This open line with Syria led to writing down an agreement with the Druze and the Muslims in the latter part of 1985. But when Hobeika signed the agreement in Damascus that was intended to end the Lebanese conflict, he was deposed by Samir Geagea in January 1986.

Geagea belonged to one of the four minor warlord Maronite families in Becharri, and this background was reflected in his choice of aides and lieutenants in the Lebanese Forces who were young Maronites from the north – principally his cousins from the Rahmé family. Although his biography is not bloody like Bachir's, Geagea's military history was no less impressive. He led the raid against the Frangiés in Ehden in 1978, and fought the doomed war with the Druze in the Chouf in 1985 where, with a few militiamen, he defended the predominantly Maronite town of Deir al-Kamar against a Druze siege.

By the time he became leader in 1986, Geagea was not a fan of Amine Gemayel, and he effectively reduced the latter's authority to the traditional Gemayel domains of Upper Metn and the town of Beckfaya. Although he introduced many social services to the population of the Maronite canton, Geagea was not able to maintain peace in his domain. The internal Maronite feud continued with two attempted coups led by Hobeika against Geagea in 1987 and 1988, and with the rise of Michel Aoun, commander of the Lebanese army in 1988. Conflict between the Lebanese army and Geagea developed fast when the Lebanese army opened fire on a platoon of Geagea's men at the Monteverde Crossing in September 1987. Five militiamen belonging to the Rahmé clan were killed in that incident. In response, their brothers and family members in the Forces sought revenge and killed a high-ranking officer of the Lebanese army, Brigadier Khalil Kenaan.

By February 1989, the skirmishes between Aoun and Geagea turned into open warfare that lasted until October 1990. When Gemayel's mandate ended in September 1988, the Parliament failed to elect a new president and a Maronite council met at Baabda to face the possible situation of all executive powers falling to the hands of the Muslim prime minister, Salim al-Hoss, in line with the constitution. Following Danny Chamoun's suggestion, the council agreed to appoint Aoun, commander of the army, as a caretaker prime minister.

Aoun was a military man of humble origin who lived among the Muslims and was well established in the army corps. His family originated in the predominantly Shia suburb of Haret Houraik in south Beirut. He was confident that with well-trained and equipped troops he could unite the country behind him. Accordingly, he started a Liberation War against all the cantons in February 1989, which brought him face to face with the powerful Lebanese warlords and the Syrian army.

Aoun's solid stands and quick actions won him the admiration of the Maronites and a portion of other Lebanese. Ordinary Maronites decided that they had finally found in Aoun their lost saint after the deaths of Bachir in 1982 and Camille Chamoun on 7 August 1987. Aoun's popularity with the Maronites was enormous. Murals covered walls in the streets showing him as St George piercing the dragon with his harpoon. While these sentiments were all well and good, it was Aoun's adventurism and heroics that brought about the destruction of Maronite power in Lebanon. His six-month military campaign was the worst period of Lebanese violence. It ended without any gains to the Maronite community or to himself, and added much misery to the whole country.

After his failure to take on the Syrian-backed Walid Joumblatt, Aoun turned inward against Geagea and the war between the two split the already small Maronite enclave into two. Thus in the period 1989–90, there were at least four Maronite warlords dominating separate areas: Elie Hobeika in Zahlé; Sulieman Frangié Jr. in Zghorta, Becharri and the coast of Batroun; and Samir Geagea in parts of Beirut and its harbour and the county of Kesrouane north of Dog River. The remaining areas – namely those loyal to Amine Gemayel in the Metn, and parts of Beirut, including the state-owned television and radio stations – were under Aoun's control.

Ironically, the Maronites fought for fifteen years against the PLO, the Lebanese left and the Lebanese Muslims and held their own, but it was the Aoun–Geagea war that destroyed the will and military power of the Maronite enclave, and brought the Maronite leaders to their knees. This war opened the way for a political solution and the signing of the Taif Accord that officially ended the Lebanese civil war.

As for the trio who led the Christian militia in the 1980s, namely Samir Geagea, Elie Hobeika and Karim Pakradouni, peace had a different destiny for them. The sophisticated but less popular Pakradouni became the leader of the Phalanges Party in 2002. He built bridges across the whole political spectrum in Lebanon, but was challenged by the Gemayel clan (former President Amine Gemayel, his son Pierre Gemayel Jr. and nephew Nadim Bachir Gemayel), who enjoyed a strong following among the Phalanges. Hobeika, who changed sides in 1986 and became pro-Syrian, won a parliamentary seat in 1992 and was appointed cabinet minister. He lost both positions in the parliamentary election in 2000, and was mysteriously assassinated on 24 January 2002. Geagea continued to oppose the government in the period 1991–3 and reportedly refused a cabinet post. In 1994, he was arrested on a list of charges, including the assassination of Prime Minister Rachid Karami and the warlord Danny Chamoun, and the bombing of a church that killed many Christians. Although his organization (the *Forces Libanaises*) was banned, and he was still in jail in 2002, Geagea was very popular amongst the Maronite community. His supporters claimed that he was the only warlord to be brought to trial, and the courts exonerated him of the church bombing.

NOTES

1 Kamal Joumblatt, *Pour le Liban*, Paris, Stock, 1978.
2 Chamoun took up this phrase in echo of the words of Winston Churchill, spoken as England faced invasion from the Nazi armies in France.
3 In 1969, the PLO was proving its presence in Lebanon; the Phalanges militia and the Lebanese Army engaged the Palestinians in several battles between 1969 and 1973.
4 "Frangié: We refuse the rule that the Christians of the peripheral provinces should be foot soldiers for some lunatic Christians of Mount Lebanon", article in *Assafir*, August 18 2002.
5 Chamoun's militia was named after his father Nemr, which means Tiger.
6 This was the sentiment voiced by many jubilant Phalanges who celebrated the election of Bachir Gemayel as president and the victory against the Lebanese left and the Palestinians, two unexpected outcomes of the Israeli invasion.

16

Triumph of the Warlords and Merchants

The 1975–90 Lebanese experience is a case study in social psychology. The habits and values that shaped the day-to-day lives of people during the civil war have already disappeared as a new generation has emerged. The new generation has never experienced life in war and the old generation just wants to forget. As with the war years in Nazi Germany, it is possible for a society to be locked into behavioural patterns for a specific period of time, and for those patterns to dissolve completely with the beginning of a new era.

Cultural collapse
There were attempts in Lebanon to preserve the memory of the war whether in writing or through film-making. Two films came out in 1998, one entitled *West Beirut* by Ziad Doueiri, and the other *Civilisés* by Randa Chahal. Both of these made it to the international market and had wide success. Watching those movies, you could never escape the pain of déjà vu if you had experienced the war or the sense of disbelief if you had been too young at the time.

In June 1976, I stayed at home as schools were closed due to the ongoing fighting between the various militias. On most nights people had to run to underground shelters because bombs fell sporadically on residential areas – sometimes militiamen turned their heavy guns on civilian households in blind revenge. In the shelter, I developed a habit of listening to a transistor radio. My favourite programme was a popular radio show entitled *Baadna Taybeen! Ool Allah!* (*Praise God! We are still alive!*), which played on Beirut's Radio Liban. This show was produced and presented by the comedian Ziad Rahbani who, episode after episode, provided me with leg-slapping laughs in the grim shelter.[1] Every episode took the worst scenario of daily life in Lebanon and displayed it with sarcastic and tragi-comic humour that helped people to forget the bombs falling outside.

In one episode, a man was reading a newspaper when his wife started complaining about the shortage of cooking fuel, bread, vegetables and almost everything else. The man enquired calmly whether she had finished talking, then exploded in anger accusing her of being unpatriotic, whining about unimportant things while the battle continued in the Nicaraguan jungles against Somoza. This episode satirized the reality that ordinary folks were more interested in food and survival than in the causes of the various militias fighting in Lebanon, or in the foreign causes embraced by the Lebanese left out of "international solidarity with oppressed peoples".[2] That same year Ziad Rahbani also joked that guardians of Lebanese heritage were hiding in a secret lab somewhere in Beirut experimenting on blood samples to identify pure Phoenician blood.

During the war, Beirut became a surreal place. Life there resembled the twilight existence in Berlin during the Second World War, where people held wedding parties as the allies besieged and bombed the city. One summer evening in 1988, in the old Plage Saint Simon in Beirut (a once popular resort that was occupied by poor displaced Lebanese Muslims forced out of their homes in the eastern suburbs by the Phalanges in 1976), a fight between two local militias had ambulance sirens wailing all night as the wounded were taken to the hospitals and the dead to the morgue. Meanwhile, adjacent to the battle scene was the Summerland Hotel where clients simply sipped martinis and danced the night away. During the nightmarish Israeli bombardment of west Beirut in the summer of 1982, many Lebanese on beaches north of Beirut sat stoically in swimming trunks in the sun watching west Beirut as if it was "another planet" burning like hell a few miles away.

The Lebanese became numb; nothing hurt any more. Bullets scarred not only the buildings but also souls. In 1990, one could look around and see destroyed cities and villages; financial collapse and hyperinflation; poverty and social decay; displaced population on a massive scale; and dangerously high levels of emigration to other countries. Beirut's daily life was full of cruel surrealist dispositions.

Even the media became a source of surreal images. During my visits to Beirut, I read two daily newspapers, *Annahar* and *Assafir*. Almost every day, the front pages were covered with photographs of burning homes, exploded shells, carcasses of cars, dead bodies and invading armies. Below these on the bottom of the front page were advertisements featuring dance parties at expensive nightclubs, pictures of belly dancers and

Lebanese pop singers, such as Ragheb Alami or the Lebanese Madonna, and offering full-course meals.

Social events were devoid of meaning. Cultural life was reduced to song, lots of food and drink, and a good laugh. Anything else was taboo. Every time I visited the country, I was misled by the festive air that recalled the Carnival del Rio. Only those who stayed for lengthy periods could see how war was decaying society. Beirut's seafront and Mount Lebanon nightclubs presented popular performers who "revived" (that is, animated) the night with cheerful songs and lengthy recitals in the Arabic tradition, *tarab*. Restaurants featured endless supplies of a fifty-dish *mezzé* and *arak*. Most music shows were preceded by monologue stand-up comics. Somehow, this atmosphere convinced many short-term visitors and expatriate Lebanese that everything was all right.

Occasionally I travelled to areas outside the central region of Beirut and its immediate suburbs. Despite the war, many natural parks existed in the peripheral regions, including the River Awali to the south (popularly known as Multaka an-Nahrain), the coast of Chekka to the north, Jisr al-Kadi in the Chouf, and al-Bardawni River in the Bekaa. Typical picnics featured barbecued chicken and shish kebab (known in Lebanon as *lahem mechwi*) along with chilled water melons. Most picnickers brought along a tabla (traditional drum) to heighten the tempo. These picnics were almost ceremonial. The younger generation, however, behaved differently. I saw young energetic people dancing all night on the sidewalk on the Beirut seafront, not disco dancing, but rather the national *dabké* dance, and not to the usual pop music but to Arabic music played on tabla and *mizmar* (flute), with no food in sight.

The Beirut theatres were a different story. To be successful, Lebanese comedies had to elicit more laughs than the normal television sitcoms in North America. The Lebanese comedies, although produced under dire circumstances of war and chaos, were able to fire one joke after another, bringing roaring laughs from the receptive audiences. Another twist to Lebanese comedies is the use of traditional elements whereby the funny dialogue is interspersed with *dabké* dances, which are much admired by Lebanese party-goers. I doubted whether serious plays written by Shakespeare or the Egyptian Ahmad Shawki would command such crowds or be so much appreciated in Lebanon in that period.[3]

In the war years, the pop culture mentality was powerful in Lebanon to the extent that it easily spread abroad and dominated the nightlife of the Lebanese communities in the Americas, Africa and Australia. The expatriate Lebanese found themselves imitating the mother country's lifestyle, which they found more vibrant and fashionable than their comparatively stable and monotonous lifestyles. It seemed that the war-torn country had won on pop culture, albeit a pop culture that fizzled like beer and had no lasting impact.

Sadly, between 1980 and 1990, cultural life in Lebanon degenerated to such an extent that the presentation of an art show, a serious play, a world-class movie or a quality piece of music was no longer esteemed by the public. The arts were nowhere near what they had been in the period 1950–74. Sylvester Stallone and Arnold Schwarznegger became the idols of Beirut's movie-goers. The historical wonders of Baalbeck's Heliopolis Roman City became a shooting range for militia training.

Poets and cultural figures were threatened and sometimes assassinated. In 1976, I attended a poetry reading by the young Lebanese poet Hanibaal Atiyeh. Atiyeh, hailing from a long intellectual tradition in his family, recited with such passion and depth that I wanted to write down every verse. After his recital I had a lengthy conversation with him about his poetry and ideas. He said that he was attempting to maintain the Romantic tradition that had dominated Lebanese literary writings since the 1920s. In Canada, several years later, I fell upon an old Lebanese magazine. Yes, there he was. The Romantic Atiyeh. The caption said that the poet had been shot and killed while strolling down a sidewalk in Beirut. There were other stories of artists and performers who were heckled, slapped in the face or raped by militiamen.

Even with the effective division of the country into ten different cantons between 1980 and 1990, Lebanon maintained a kind of cultural unity. While it was sometimes not possible for Lebanese to meet residents of other cantons, they did so when they travelled abroad. Only then, away from home, did they realize that they did not differ much from one another. The social and cultural norms that tied the country together were numerous.

In the context of business, study, travel and social activities, the shared language and the common denominator of Levantine acquisitiveness usually assumed the dominant role in the Lebanese personality, while family and village loyalties were subdued and more or less passive. In business, it made little difference whether the client or the seller was Muslim or Christian. Most Lebanese people exhibited a mixture of hospitality, shrewdness, a passion for clandestine deals and a love of ostentatious luxury. Lebanese business culture is basically the same whether it is in Lebanon, Paris or Montreal. In Lebanese restaurants in Paris and Montreal, I witnessed "Abu Ali" toasting "Maroun", and the young "Mohammed" dancing to the steps of "Antoinette", the Maronite belly dancer while everybody else joined hands in the traditional *dabké* dance.

On the popular level, much in common could be established among the Lebanese. However, there was a serious vertical split that crossed the lines of religious allegiance. This vertical split produced three social groups – each one comprising a cross-section of Muslims, Christians and Druze.

The first group, representing roughly 20 per cent (500,000 people) of the population, was made up of those Lebanese who left the country and went abroad to settle in the Americas, Africa and Oceania. This group nostalgically remained hooked on the news and were more anxious than those who remained behind to learn the name and background of each victim falling on the streets of Beirut.

The second group were the common people, better known in Lebanon as "the silent majority". This group numbered roughly two to three million people. It was members of this group that lubricated the civil war with the blood of their children. Members included those who could not afford to leave the country, and those who manned the militias and acted as paid fighters in each warlords' war machine, and those who stayed in the countryside and paid no attention to the events in Beirut. Despite the tiny size of Lebanon one could still find remote villages where life was placid and monotonous. In 1987, on a tour of the southern Bekaa Valley, in a remote village we met an elderly woman tending her vegetables. During our brief conversation, she enquired casually whether Bechara al-Khouri (President of Lebanon in 1942–52) was all right and whether Hitler had really lost the Second World War.

The third group were the *kubar* (the upper class). Members of this group included the 200 or so aristocratic warlord and *zaim* families, which, with their entourage, numbered 80,000 to 120,000 individuals. These individuals led the militias, controlled parliament, the government, the army and the top positions in business and politics, and owned most of the sizeable businesses in the country.

While the Lebanese culture that flourished in 1950–74 went down the drain in 1980–90, the *kubar* resumed their routine lifestyle with an air of "business as usual". In the depths of the war, these people still read *Paris Match* and *La Revue du Liban*, bought the latest fashions and books from Paris, cut out recipes from French magazines, complained in Franco-Arabe to their visitors about the falling bombs outside, held impressive Ramadan banquets, visited Cairo and Damascus for fun and so on. It was in the *kubar*'s best interest to stay in the country. Their social status made them immune to the immediate hazards of war. With a network of connections covering the entire country, they were protected by the unwritten agreement that "You do not kill a known member of an enemy clan otherwise a blood feud will follow".

Although not in immediate danger from the civil war, the *kubar* had the most to lose: government posts, properties, relations, businesses, massive wealth and authority. In this sense the civil war was the war of the *kubar*. They therefore had a vested interest in staying in the country and leading their militias against their enemies. Members of this group would travel to any destination around the world for business or pleasure but would always come back. Between 1980 and 1990, it was not uncommon to see a Gemayel, a Chamoun or a Joumblatt in Switzerland, Canada, France or the United States, for a variety of reasons. Their stay abroad was normally brief, with apologies given that they must return to Beirut immediately.

After 1990, the 200 or so *kubar* families showed no signs of learning from the civil war. Indeed in the next round, if there were to be one, the same front lines and probably the same militias would re-emerge. Probably there is something in common here with the other *kubar* classes in the Middle East. After the war in Kuwait in 1990–1, a Kuwaiti cabinet minister in an interview on the American *60 Minutes* television show explained that the new Kuwait would review past practices and introduce new reforms. Pressed by the curious American reporter to elaborate, the Minister illustrated one type of reform with tongue in cheek: "Before the Iraqi invasion, Kuwaiti families had at least four domestic servants. Now servants should be limited to two per household." Pondering the apocalyptic dimensions of the war over Kuwait and the number of people killed or wounded in "Desert Storm", and the economic loss to the whole Middle East, and measuring these costs against the extent of reforms, one wonders whether the new Lebanese political system would be any different at the beginning of the twenty-first century than it had been during and before the civil war.

The ruling families in Lebanon are very conscious about status and this trait is closely imitated by the deprived population of Lebanon. Much of Lebanese social life is measured by levels of wealth and material success with no sense of modesty and tolerance. Awareness of status affects choices in marriage, friendship and education. Status is indicated by, among other things, the school where one sends one's children, the family background of the person one marries and the friends with whom one chooses to socialize.

The fabled hospitality of the Lebanese takes a curious twist when visiting a *kubar* household. This hospitality is a mixture of strange and well-orchestrated rituals. Clothing and furniture, especially the living room (the *salon*) are very important in Lebanon. For some, they are more important than food. During a visit to Beirut, I attended a party at the house of a known professor and literary writer. The *salon* was the most important room in the house, containing expensive chairs, couches and chandeliers, and covered with rugs. It is normally the place where households receive and entertain guests. It should not be confused with the North American "living room", which in Lebanon is the equivalent of an "all-purpose" room. In Lebanon, a living room is the room used by family and immediate relatives.

At this party, women wore excessively expensive clothes and jewellery, and their hairstyles were complex and sharply beautiful, a result of hours at the hairdresser. Even when travelling, Lebanese women could be seen in airports and stations in their best outfits and with wonderful hairstyles. I even saw glamorous-looking Lebanese women in Canada applying for refugee status and standing in line next to poor Sri Lankans and Somalis. In Lebanon the way you dress says much about your status, which explains why everybody dresses in a sophisticated manner. One might say that this is the case everywhere, but it is more so in Lebanon. Before 1974, Western tourists frequenting Beirut were laughed at and made fun of by Lebanese pedestrians and shopkeepers for the cheap clothing they wore in comparison to Lebanese standards. Western females were special targets of remarks for their baggy dresses, flowing T-shirts and jeans. One British journalist, a customer at a pub on Hamra Street, mentioned that these American travellers were probably doctors and lawyers in their country, and the way they dressed was because they were on vacation and therefore not concerned with dress codes.

Upon arrival at the party, visitors were seated on royal French chairs, but there was no sign yet of the professor or his wife. The former President Camille Chamoun had a ritual of his own: before his visitors were allowed in to see him, he would enter an anteroom next to his office. When the visitors were seated, he would walk in from the smaller room prompting the visitors to stand up and greet him rather than the other way around. Most Lebanese imitate this ritual and have their servants or children seat visitors who would then simmer in irritated silence. When the hosts walked in, visitors stood up in respect. This would be followed by rituals of hospitality: cigarettes and Turkish coffee; snobbish chatting, normally about the rainy weather in Paris during a visit there; a conversation mixed with name-dropping and a heavy use of French. Some Lebanese parents require their children to speak only in French with a complete ban on their mother tongue of Arabic, but would pay huge sums to acquire rare Arabic and Islamic artefacts to decorate their *salons*.

To contrast these rituals with those of North America, the populist culture and the small importance attached to class in the USA usually shocks Lebanese, Arab and European visitors. An American member of the 1947 Anglo-American Commission of Inquiry into Palestine described a visit by a British delegation to the US. During the visit, the British addressed others and responded to questions in a serious and solemn manner, so that when everyone walked through the corridors of the Department of Justice, conversation was hushed to mere whispering. Suddenly, a loud yell came out from an open door: "Where the hell are you, Texas Joe!" That was the Chief Justice of the United States of America looking for his friend, a judge from Texas. The British were appalled at the scene, never imagining that the Lord Justice of England would address a local judge in such a manner. At dinner, the British watched a US Marines band playing a Texas song for the pleasure of the US Chief Justice. When the band finished the Chief Justice leaned backward and sounded a very loud southern "*Yi-Pee-ee*!", which further shocked the British.

American populism found its way to influencing Lebanese manners early in the twentieth century. Many older people, especially graduates of the American University of Beirut (AUB) have a different outlook compared to the snobbish aristocracy. The behaviour of the early American teachers in Lebanon had an impact on the Lebanese graduates of the AUB. American professors who volunteered to serve in Lebanon such as

Cornelius Van Dyck, and Daniel and Howard Bliss, left a deep mark on the psyche of their Lebanese students.

The gentle puritan manners of these Americans changed the behaviour of many Lebanese families. Dr Van Dyck knew Arabic, and his simplicity and honesty and love of gardening impressed many people. In one episode in 1901, Van Dyck hired a young man to carry his shopping bags to his house. The shopping bags included a block of ice which was melting on the back of the young man who started cursing Van Dyck in Arabic by saying "Son of a dog, son of a bitch", and the like. When they arrived, Van Dyck invited the young man into his office, paid him and offered him a cold drink. As the young man drank the lemonade, Van Dyck showed him pictures of his family and the large portrait of his father hanging on the wall, then he turned to the young man and asked politely in perfect Arabic whether Van Dyck's father looked like a dog. The young man, taken aback by Van Dyck's knowledge of the meaning of his curses, apologized and left with admiration for a great man.

While most Americans would find the rituals of the Lebanese upper class awkward and uncomfortable, most Lebanese view them as the standard for everyone and imitate them very closely. The poor Lebanese are fatalistic. After years of war, they took sanctuary in refining the pursuit of leisure to counterbalance the fact that all too often life proved to be brutish and short. News about the war became irrelevant and ceasefire announcements were welcomed with cynicism. Death became a constant occurrence as the earlier reactions of disbelief and fear developed into a passive submission. The most repeated word in the war was *mashil-hal* (literally "all is well"). This idiom was used ironically when a bomb fell, a massacre took place, a car failed to start, water and electricity stopped flowing, garbage piled up, the airport was shut down, or for a dozen other possible disasters.

The sceptical Ziad Rahbani explored this attitude in his work.[4] His prophetic comedy, *What About Tomorrow? (Binnisbi laboukra shou)* tells the story of the economic miracle of Lebanon through the events of a bar-restaurant on Beirut's Hamra strip. It is a black comedy about the ups and downs of social climbing in Lebanon. Zacharia (played by Rahbani himself), the bartender and his wife Soraya, the waitress, are a couple whose lives rotate around the idea of becoming *kubar*. Their clients are a mix of Europeans, Americans and wealthy Arabs. The only Lebanese clients are those who want to do business with the foreigners, including a Lebanese poet who sells a package of poetry books and ladies' shoes to an emir from Abu Dhabi. Zacharia and his family, migrants from a poor mountain village, found the standards of Beirut and its *kubar* very demanding. This environment poisons them with luxuries and a modern lifestyle, and they become addicted: they buy a new car, rent a large apartment and send the children to a private school.

Their salaries are not enough to pay for the cherished status, but Soraya, unwilling to give up the new lifestyle, says: "What would people say about us if we leave the private school and sell the new car?" So they decide to "moonlight", and Soraya agrees to become a prostitute and offer her services discreetly to the clientele of the bar. Zacharia reasons that this would be fine as long as no Lebanese notice. As a precautionary measure, Soraya walks out ahead of the customer pretending to be sick so that Zacharia will tell her to go home. Things work as planned and the couple are able to maintain their lifestyle. However, a Spanish client grows fond of the seductive Soraya and one day, Soraya forgets to collect the money, so the Spanish man brings the envelope himself and hands it over to the ethically-minded Lebanese cook, Najib, to give to her. Najib reads the letter and meekly delivers it to Zacharia without a comment.

Zacharia becomes very irritated. His wife's moonlighting becomes public, and the manager Monsieur Antoine uses this to block any salary increase; he is pleased that the "moonlighting" has kept Zacharia mute about wage increases. Zacharia can no longer bear the dirty looks customers give his wife and the knowledge that any of them might be sleeping with his wife that night, nor the awkward atmosphere created by the Lebanese clients' and co-workers' knowledge of his wife's discreet occupation. Soraya finally says that she is ready to quit if an alternative source of money is provided.

In his attempt to find more money, Zacharia talks to Monsieur Antoine, but Antoine sheepishly enquires whether their two salaries plus the "overtime" are not enough. Zacharia answers that there will be no more overtime, and the salaries are insufficient to survive. The manager goes on complaining about the situation: "You have to recognize, my son, that Lebanon has no raw materials or oil. Private initiative is all we have got and the country cannot bear too many people. Maybe you should consider travelling abroad. I know an Arab sheikh who is building a modern hotel in Abu Dhabi with a rotating restaurant on the top floor. I could recommend you as a manager of that restaurant. This way you can make a fortune in the Gulf, and your wife could stay with us as a bartender and work overtime if she wishes." Zacharia asks coldly: "Do you know how many times that restaurant in Abu Dhabi rotates per hour?" Then he blasts Antoine asking how come the country supports people like him while the poor guy has to leave. Unable to get a raise, Zacharia accepts the miserable status quo, and his wife continues her activity.

One night, a drunk Belgian approaches Soraya, gives her flowers and insists that she should leave with him right away. Zacharia becomes angry and a shouting match starts between him and the Belgian. This develops into a fist-fight and Zacharia pulls a kitchen knife and stabs the man, who falls with blood on his shirt. Everybody in the bar is deeply shocked, as if this is the end of paradise, and darkness engulfs the place. In the following scene, Soraya is in black sunglasses with Antoine comforting her and reminding her that she has four children to look after, so there is no use in giving up because Zacharia is in jail. She agrees with Antoine and takes her husband's job. The curtains drop as activity and people of every nationality fill the restaurant again, similar to the opening scene.

Striving to be better is a legitimate endeavour in any culture, but in status-conscious Lebanon, it becomes an obsession. Things are tougher when status must come through a "clean" profession that requires no dirtying of hands or ploughing the soil. Such cultural inhibitions dictate politics and economics in modern Lebanon. The educated simply expect a "clean" profession with large offices and a comfortable environment. This explains why Lebanon was so dependent on the services sector, and why agriculture and manufacturing remained retarded. Youssef Beidas, founder of Intrabank (see Chapter 7) was an expert in Lebanese rituals. Next to his modern office at Intrabank headquarters in Beirut, Beidas maintained a very expensive Arabian-style *salon*, where Arabian coffee and expensive confectionery were served to exclusive clients. In that *salon*, Beidas had a table where gold bullion and investment certificates were neatly piled, a symbol that his clients' money was always at hand while the reality was that most of the deposits were invested in real estate.

Kamal Joumblatt subscribed to the view that the innate nature of a human being never changes. A Lebanese coming back to Lebanon after fifty years of absence would still demonstrate three basic characters: his village accent (whether in Arabic or in his adopted foreign language), a recurring sectarian mentality and village-style politics, and a love for Lebanese food (he might even show you the *jorn*[5] in which he had ground *kibbé* meat all these years). For a man who had spent fifty years abroad, and indeed for all the residents of Lebanon, warlords and *zaims*, old or new, were still the preferred figures of authority. These men could run a government, but they could never create a symbol of state authority (*raison d'état*) that transcended individuals, nor can they be replaced by the educated generation whom the public dismisses as "technocrats" – that is, those who were seen as "assistants" or "employees in the service of the *begs*".

Although the old warlord class was almost wiped out in the 1975–90 war, the warlord and *zaim* system would continue to be the dominant form of government until another conflict materialized.

NOTES

1 Son of the pop singer Fairuz, a multitalented genius in his own field. He is a musician, a performer, a comedian, a playwright, a songwriter and composer. He wrote in the style that matched the mood of the public. He wrote several long comedies – namely, *Auberge du Bonheur* (*Nazl a-Sourour*, 1974), *What about Tomorrow?* (1977), *A Long American Movie* (1979), *Failure* (1983) and *Marge d'Espoir* (*Lawla Fushatul Amali*, 1992). He also wrote and presented two radio shows: *Praise God! We Are Still Alive!* (1976) and *It is Good to be Smart* (1987).
2 During the 1975–6 period of the civil war, the Lebanese left and the Palestinians held several rallies around Lebanon, and the speakers often expressed solidarity with oppressed peoples around the world at the end of the speech. Ziad Rahbani picked on this theme to parody the public's cynicism towards the left and its idealism.
3 A joke circulated around that time about Shakespeare that the English playwright was in fact a Lebanese immigrant who went to England in the sixteenth century. People will even tell you that his correct name was Sheikh Esper, and that he was originally from Jbeil, a town north of Beirut.
4 See note 1 above.
5 A stone urn.

17

Rafic Hariri: Last of the Merchants

The war that started in 1975 reached its conclusion on 13 October 1990, thanks to the ebb and flow of regional and international conflicts. Relative peace in Lebanon was owed to external factors. Even in the summer of 1990, left to their own devices, there was no sign that the Lebanese warlords were coming to an agreement. Of all places, Saudi Arabia was the launching stage for two attempts at a peaceful conclusion to the war in Lebanon. After 1982, Saudi Arabia's chief spokesman in Beirut was the businessman Rafic Hariri, who rose to become the Prime Minister of Lebanon in 1992.

In 1976, a meeting between Anwar Sadat of Egypt and Hafez Assad of Syria ended the first round of civil war in Lebanon. The Riyadh Accord confirmed the Maronite–Sunni pact and recognized Syria's role in Lebanon. However, Egypt and Syria parted ways over Sadat's visit to Israel in 1977, and this ended the truce in Beirut. In a matter of months, violence engulfed Lebanon. In 1990, external factors again influenced events in Lebanon and brought the war to an end. When the Iran–Iraq War concluded in 1988, a triumphant Iraq wanted to resurrect its old influence in Lebanon and counter Syrian hegemony there. Thus, Iraq began supporting Aoun's bid to "Liberate Lebanon from Syrian occupation" in 1989. In 1990, the Kuwait crisis and Syria's stand against Iraq were the catalysts that renewed international blessing for Syria's role in Lebanon.

Early in 1990, in Taif, Saudi Arabia, Lebanese parliamentarians reached an agreement on reform. The Taif Accord allowed for equal representation of Muslims and Christians in Parliament, and introduced a new power-sharing formula that replaced the 1976 Riyadh Accord. The new formula created a *troika* leadership made up of a Maronite, a Shia and a Sunni. While the traditional offices continued – that is, a Maronite president, a Sunni premier and a Shia speaker of parliament – the new contract gave more powers to the speaker of parliament and fewer powers to the president. The implementation of the Accord was not possible until 1991, as two de facto governments co-existed in Beirut: one pro-Syrian, led by President Elias Hrawi; the other pro-Iraqi led by General Michel Aoun, who maintained his headquarters at the Presidential Palace. The Kuwait crisis permitted a swift expulsion of Iraq's supporters in Beirut. In October 1990, the USA, France and the Vatican gave the green light to dislodge Aoun and to open the way for a single government in Beirut. Further steps were taken to implement the Taif Accord, including "appointing" some 40 deputies to parliament, disarming the militias and restoring government property. A sign of the times came when Air France resumed flights to Beirut International Airport in June 1991, with several other airlines following suit. For the first time since 1974, government troops were again in control of the coast.

With the war over, the next three years were cruel as the Lebanese economy remained devastated and impoverished. The Kuwait crisis was disastrous for Lebanon. A United Nations report estimated Lebanon's losses as a result of the Kuwait crisis at US$2.9 billion, of which US$500 million were in lost remittances, US$500 million in deposits by Lebanese expatriates in Kuwaiti banks, US$250 million in additional costs of oil imports, and US$500 million in lost aid funds from the Gulf states. The war in Kuwait forced 50,000 Lebanese workers to return to Lebanon, creating another bottleneck for the struggling economy. In the summer of 1991, the minimum monthly wage in Lebanon dropped from US$63 to US$52.

The Taif Accord pledged close Syrian–Lebanese cooperation in all matters of economics and defence. With 40,000 soldiers in Lebanon since 1976 and a historical claim to parts of the country, Damascus secured a firm say in the future of Lebanon. On 3 May 1991, the Syrian government presented a document to the Lebanese government calling for special relations and virtual unity between the two countries with a joint leadership. The Syrian initiative was not new. Variations of the same proposal had been made to Lebanon since the break-up of the economic union in 1950. The Syrians presented the idea to President Gemayel in 1986, and he promptly rejected it. To circumvent him, Damascus got the Lebanese factions to sign a similar document in December 1986 known as the "Tri-Partite Agreement". This also failed after the Phalanges got rid of Elie Hobeika, who represented the Maronites in signing the document. On 22 May 1991, the Presidents of Syria and Lebanon signed a treaty that amounted to a virtual unity agreement, where all aspects of economic, political and cultural issues were to be harmonized within a few years.

Economic conditions remained at the top of the Lebanese priorities. On 6 May 1992, the people rose up in a social revolution that led to the collapse of the government. Despite the moves towards peace in 1990 and 1991, the spectre of the collapse and descent into poverty of Lebanon loomed larger now than during the war of the previous sixteen years. The country was still facing a multitude of problems. The Lebanese lira, one of the strongest currencies in the world in 1974, fell into a dark abyss in 1992, with the dollar trading at LL2,200 in May and at LL2,800 to LL3,000 in July and August. The destiny of 400,000 Palestinian refugees remained unresolved as their future was not to become clear until parties to the Middle East peace talks got round to discussing refugee matters. The Iranian factor in Lebanon was represented by the powerful Hizbollah militia and the influence exerted by Iran on Syria and on some Lebanese groups. This was strengthened in 1991 during a visit by Hashemi Rafsanjani, the President of Iran, to Damascus where he secured a promise that Hizbollah would not be disarmed in Lebanon. The situation in southern Lebanon was another problem, where the pro-Israeli SLA militia in the border strip were fighting an explosive war with pro-Syrian and pro-Iranian groups. There was also a failure of the warlords to reach consensus on social and political reform, thus paralyzing the peaceful recovery of Lebanon after 16 years of war.

The popular uprising of May 1992 brought hundreds of thousands of citizens representing the "silent majority" to the streets to protest against government inaction in tackling the catastrophes still pounding the country after two years of peace. Demonstrators attacked banks and commercial establishments, burnt tyres, cut off the main highways and called on Prime Minister Omar Karami to resign. The government of Omar Karami placed its wager on the prompt delivery of Arab and Western aid, which failed to materialize. However, in its budgets it behaved as if aid was coming, and doubled salaries, thus further inflating the economy and damaging the national currency.

Karami resigned and was promptly replaced by the economist Rachid al-Solh, the same person who had headed the government that witnessed the start of the civil war in 1975. Al-Solh administered parliamentary elections, which took place over the period August to October 1992, then duly resigned on 16 October to be replaced by businessman

Rafic Hariri on 22 October. Meanwhile, Nabih Berri, leader of the Shia *Amal* movement, was elected Head of Parliament on 20 October after winning a seat in a southern riding. The parliamentary elections, the first since 1972, resulted in a new parliament that comprised 64 Christian deputies and 64 Muslims, in observance of the new 50/50 formula of the Taif Accord.

With the entry of Hariri, Lebanon began a new era that would continue for the next dozen or so years. His presence on the scene dates back to 1982. In that year, following the departure of the Israelis and the arrival of the multinational force in Beirut, the Lebanese government was again optimistic about the chances of peace and reconstruction. The Lebanese banks were encouraged by the entry of Saudi-backed financiers into Lebanon, and by the plans for large-scale construction projects in Lebanon which needed banking services. Bankers were relieved when many banks were bought by the new financiers. Lebanon was witnessing the rise of a new breed of financiers educated abroad, preferably at American business schools and usually with MBAs, fluent in English, and armed with contacts with wealthy Saudi and other Arab personalities. These financiers bought off the assets of foreign banks, as well as their equipment and offices in Beirut. This previously unknown group gave the economy a new lease of life following the exit of Palestinian capital.

The party did not last long as the capital assets of the new financiers proved too large for the local players. Soon, larger financial institutions were taking over the smaller ones. The new owners stopped short of massive takeovers and consolidation, and maintained separate establishments under different names and boards of directors. Rafic Hariri and Roger Tamraz were two examples of the new merchants.[1]

Hariri, a Sunni from Saida, had established himself in Saudi Arabia and developed important contacts with the emirs and members of the Saudi royal family. He even obtained Saudi citizenship, a rarity for a foreigner. Following the Israeli invasion in 1982, the Saudi King Fahed appointed Hariri as dispenser of Saudi aid to Lebanon. In 1983, Hariri headed a consortium to rebuild the business core of Beirut through his construction company, Oger Liban, and later that year he bought the Banque de la Méditerranée from French bankers and established the Saudi-Lebanese Bank. Hariri set up separate boards of directors for these banks and maintained an independent organization for each bank. These banks grew and in 1989, Banque de la Méditerranée boasted more than

US$1 billion in assets. Hariri also established several business interests in Lebanon and abroad, mainly in France. In July 1990 and 1991, he was named as one of the world's top 20 billionaires by *Forbe's* magazine – his wealth estimated at US$2.5 billion.

In Saida, his hometown, Hariri built educational facilities at Kfar-Falous and an expressway that carried his name through the city. In Beirut, the lovely Boulevard Ramlet al-Baida became Boulevard Rafic Hariri, and several houses he owned on that boulevard became temporary residences of government figures including President Elias Hrawi in 1990. The media repeated his name often as a potential candidate for the office of prime minister. In 1983, he established the Hariri Foundation, which offered scholarships and grants to Lebanese students who wished to pursue higher education. The foundation sent thousands of students to the United States, Canada and Europe, and fully financed their studies and livelihood. The foundation became a familiar body to all university administrators in North America, with a major office in Washington, DC. Between 1982 and 1990, Hariri's fortunes and exploits were largely outside Lebanon. However, his big role in Lebanese politics started in 1991.

In the 1988 Lebanese presidential elections, Hariri had his own Maronite candidate, namely the former chief of Lebanese Military Intelligence, Johnny Abdou. He even invited the departing President Amine Gemayel's confidantes to France in April 1988 for a meeting to discuss the chances for Abdou's election. He reportedly offered Gemayel a sum of US$30 million to resign early and help elect Abdou with Hariri as prime minister. When quizzed by Gemayel's men what Hariri ought to do about the Syrians, Hariri reportedly answered that he was "willing to expend as much as US$500 million to get the Syrians on side".[2]

Hariri made a big contribution to the success of the Taif Accord and slowly built his name in Lebanese politics until he was chosen as prime minister in May 1992 with a mandate to rebuild the country and revive the collapsed economy. Over the next ten years, many reconstruction and development projects were completed, but the government was plunged into a $30 billion debt which was almost 160 per cent of the size of Lebanon's GDP.

In 1982, Hariri as a private businessman had a plan to reconstruct the business district of Beirut. In 1993, he was able to realise his ambitions as he now had the ability to succeed. For in 1993, in addition to his financial strength, he was also prime minister and could have a say in setting government priorities. The first step was setting up the Lebanese Real Estate Corporation (also known as Solidère: Société Libanaise pour le devéloppement et la reconstruction – The Lebanese Company for the Development and Reconstruction of Beirut's Central District) as a separate body from the Council for Reconstruction and Development, to own and develop the downtown area. The media pointed out that Hariri owned many shares in this corporation and that there was a conflict of interest with him as prime minister pushing a project that would further enrich him.

As Lebanon put the bad memories of a terrible war behind it, the Hariri team were facing a multitude of challenges: the rebuilding of Beirut's core area where much of the country's business activity would take place; the rehabilitation of the displaced into their own villages and homes (numbering in the region of 300,000 people); the plight of almost 385,000 Palestinian refugees in Lebanon in the light of the PLO–Israel Accord on 13 September 1993; the process of constitutional reform to put an end to sectarian politics in the educational system and the civil service; the prospects of peace with Israel and the liberation of southern Lebanon; and the development of the Lebanese economy to face the period of peace in the Middle East where its role as a middleman would be challenged by newcomers such as the Palestinians and the Israelis.

At the beginning of the third millennium, it seems that Lebanon is destined to be dominated by the warlord–merchant establishment that has shaped the landscape for the past 1,000 years. The same families whose names have filled the previous pages are still relevant in the twenty-first century in a way that remains unchanged from the year 1000. Whether Lebanon will move into a secular society led by the same clans is doubtful. The variety of groups and clans in Lebanon is a blessing and a curse at the same time. One cannot underestimate the value to the world of the Lebanese experience where 18 religious groups live in the same small piece of territory, or where ancient families continue to be visible. But if we are talking about nation-building, then Lebanon should abandon being an antique shop of social tradition and move to embrace modern governance.

Postscript

In the spring of 2003, yet another war started in the Middle East: the United States invaded Iraq with the ambitious aim of changing the regime in Baghdad. Meanwhile, a Palestinian uprising against the Israeli occupation of the West Bank and Gaza was already halfway through its third year. Naturally, being situated so near such troubled hotspots, these events influenced Lebanon, and my publisher asked if my optimism would be any different in light of these events. Since I did not want to end a book on Lebanon with a statement about Iraq and Israel/Palestine, a few remarks on what the events mean to Lebanon in the context of this book would be more appropriate.

In 2003, the Lebanese economy was adversely affected by the continued violence in the Middle East. Tourism remained at historic lows and was not able to recover to high levels last experienced in 1974; public debt spiralled out of control to almost $35 billion, almost 200% of the Gross Domestic Product; unemployment, emigration and poverty were exacting a heavy toll on the small country; and the internal situation was still dominated by alliances of warlords and merchants.

However, the events in Lebanon between 1975 and 1990, catastrophic as they were, dwarf in comparison to what has happened to Iraq since 1980. While the tally of the Lebanese war was 140,000 killed and $25 billion in damages, over 1.5 million died in Iraq with damages estimated at over $700 billion. Iraq has known many wars since 1980, and the US invasion in 2003 was just one of them. Over the past 23 years, Iraq has experienced a deadly war with Iran in the period 1980 to 1988, invaded Kuwait in 1990, was invaded by the US in 1991, had a civil war in 1991 and 1992, and was invaded again by the US in 2003. Consequently, Iraq has declined from being the most promising of the emerging independent Arab countries in the early 1970s, to a chaotic and poor place.

In 1990, Lebanon lost important remittances from Lebanese workers in Kuwait, and in 2003, it lost a sizeable market for Lebanese goods and services in Iraq. Both losses were augmented by the general security situation in the Middle East that is detrimental to economic activity. The violence in both Israel/Palestine and in Iraq has led to a drop in foreign and domestic investment and tourism and has hurt Lebanese chances for a prosperous future after its civil war.

Another observation on the events in 2003 is that this book can be used as a case study of the evolving Middle East. The situation of Lebanese warlords and merchants that I have described here can now be generalized to apply to many other countries in the Middle East. Coalitions of families are in control of business and politics not only in monarchic states, but also in supposedly republican ones. Hereditary political systems have been spreading in the region since 1970 when clannish arrangements led to warlord-merchant control in Iraq and Syria, which also materialized in Egypt in recent years and, to a lesser extent, in Yemen and Libya. Unelected presidents appoint their children to replace them, while most economic activities are run by a clique of related individuals. As the experience in Lebanon has revealed, I make the claim here that it is really difficult to change these arrangements. Lebanon has proven that not even foreign invasions can change family and tribal loyalties.

A third observation is the spread of powerful pan-Arab media that can compete on a world-scale. In the early 1980s, discussions took place between Third World countries and the advanced countries of the West about the blatant domination of the international flow of information by a few multinationals in the United States, the United Kingdom and France. The war over Kuwait in 1991 did not change that domination. But in 2003, the war in Iraq led to a revolution in international media. There was no more monopoly over news or information by CNN, Reuters, or Agence France Presse. Arab satellite TV channels, such as Al-Jazeera and Al-Arabiya, became household names all over the world and were seen as alternative sources of information. Lebanese expertise could help transform this revolution in the media into a winning situation for Lebanon. Already a new all-news TV station in Beirut, Alhayat-LBC, is making it on the airwaves. I remain optimistic that these media can inspire freedom of speech and may somehow contribute to more democracy and openness in the Middle East. And for that, I remain an optimist about the future of Lebanon and a believer in peace between the Arabs and Israel.

Notes

1 Tamraz was involved in many schemes and accused of illegal activities, which was not the case with Hariri despite statements to that effect by his political opponents. A 1997 book by Najah Wakim, a leftist deputy for Beirut, tellingly entitled *Black Hands*, provided detailed information about Hariri's business transactions. Although the book went into over twenty reprints due to popular demand, none of its contents warranted the establishment of a legal case against Hariri, as there was nothing against the law in Hariri's activities of amassing wealth, accumulating property, or appointing relatives in his ventures. This is not to say that the transactions mentioned in the book would have been totally legal in a European or North American context. But this should be blamed on the absence in Lebanon of separation between private business and public office and the need for business people who ran for public office to place their properties and stakes in blind trust. Najah Wakim, *Black Hands* (in Arabic, *Al-Ayadi al-Soud*), Beirut, Sharikat al-Matbouat, 1997.

2 Abdalla Bouhabib, *Yellow Light: Memoirs of Lebanon's Ambassador to the United States* (in Arabic, *Al dawe' al akhdar: muthakarrat safir Lubnan fi al milayat al mutahida*) Beirut, Sharikat al-Matbuat, 1992.

Statistical Appendix

TABLE 1
Distribution of economic sectors 1948 to 1965

Category	1948	1949	1950	1957	1964	1965
	(LL million)			(in per cent)		
Farm products	169	159	176	15.80	11.46	15.00
Utilities	21	23	33	na	2.50	na
Manufacturing	133	136	138	12.60	14.70	12.00
Construction	35	32	42	2.70	5.43	5.00
Transport and communication	34	35	38	5.30	6.80	7.00
Real estate	90	93	96	9.30	7.74	10.00
Finance	91	93	101	6.10	3.00	8.00
Other services	290	300	339	9.80	8.40	8.00
Commerce and social	280	309	339	31.20	32.30	26.00
Public sector	63	64	72	7.20	7.50	9.00
TOTAL	1,206	1,244	1,374	100.00	100.00	100.00

Source: Albert Badr and Assad Nasr, *National Accounts of Lebanon*, booklets 1–7, Beirut, Ministry of the Economy 1951, 1952, 1953, 1954; Kuwait Fund for Arab Economic Development, "Report on the Lebanese Economy and its Development Prospects", *Annual Report of the Kuwait Fund for Development Assistance*, Kuwait, June 1967.

TABLE 2
Distribution of national income 1966 to 1973 (LL million)

Category	1966	1967	1968	1969	1970	1971	1972	1973
Farm products	442	426	436	432	445	460	631	675
Utilities	88	93	99	104	113	118	129	140
Manufacturing	512	492	552	610	661	750	884	1,038
Construction	231	196	194	216	218	239	290	300
Transport and communication	310	329	380	383	401	438	478	513
Real estate	284	300	335	385	430	495	558	610
Finance	141	149	164	146	165	197	235	285
Other services	357	337	397	461	482	522	676	791
Commerce and social	1,183	1,160	1,359	1,435	1,527	1,723	2,007	2,241
Public sector	319	337	357	393	424	451	477	507
GDP at market prices	3,867	3,820	4,273	4,565	4,866	5,399	6,365	7,100
Indirect taxes less subsidies	-300	-267	-303	-342	-345	-412	-489	-562
GDP at factor cost	3,567	3,553	3,970	4,223	4,521	4,987	5,876	6,538
% of services	67.4		70.5		70.9		69.6	

Source: Ministry of Planning, Central Bureau of Statistics, *National Accounts of Lebanon*, Beirut, 1974.

TABLE 3
Structure of the Lebanese economy 1957 to 1974

	Shares of economic sectors (in per cent)				GDP (LL million)			
Year	Agriculture	Manufacturing	Services	Total	Agriculture	Manufacturing	Services	Total
1957	15.8	15.3	68.9	100	381	658	2,161	3,200
1964	11.6	20.1	68.1	100				
1965	15.0	17.0	68.0	100				
1966	11.4	21.5	67.1	100				
1967	11.2	20.4	68.4	100				
1968	10.2	19.8	70.0	100				
1969	9.5	20.4	70.1	100	432	929	3,204	4,565
1970	9.1	20.4	70.5	100				
1971	9.9	20.6	69.5	100				
1973	9.5	20.8	69.8	100				
1974	9.2	22.7	68.1	100	745	1,848	5,544	8,137

Source: Ministry of Planning, Central Bureau of Statistics, *National Accounts of Lebanon*, Beirut, 1974 and IRFED, *Les Besoins et possibilités du développement du Liban*, Beirut Ministry of Planning, 1962, Chapter 2, "Le revenu national", pp. 75–95.

TABLE 4
Active labour force by sector, 1967 and 1970

Category	1967		1970	
	Number of workers (1000s)	%	Number of workers (1000s)	%
Agriculture	300	44.0	102	17.3
Manufacturing	60	8.8	96	16.2
Construction	20	2.9	36	6.1
Finance	153	22.4	18	3.0
Transport and communication	30	4.4	38	6.4
Public service	17	2.5	25	4.2
Army and other	10	1.5	20	3.4
Real estate and other services	26	3.8	149	25.2
Utilities	4	0.6	15	2.5
Tourism	62	9.1	92	15.6
TOTAL	682	100.0	591	100.0

Source: For 1967: Kuwait Fund for Arab Economic Development, "Report on the Lebanese Economy and its Development Prospects", *Annual Report of the Kuwait Fund for Development Assistance*, Kuwait, June 1967. For 1970: Ministry of Planning, Central Bureau of Statistics, *Labour Report* (excluding Palestinians, Syrians and seasonal workers), Beirut, 1970.

STATISTICAL APPENDIX

TABLE 5
Capital base of manufacturing firms in 1950

Number of firms	Capital base (LL thousand)
25	1,000 and over
29	500–1,000
45	250–500
135	100–250
381	25–100
421	10–25
249	5–10

Source: Ministry of the Economy, *Quarterly Statistical Bulletin*, Beirut, October 1951. (By 1973, when the share of manufacturing in the national economy was rising, 140 establishments had more than 50 workers while 300 establishments had between 25 and 50 employees. At least 2,700 firms hired between 5 and 25 workers while 12,700 firms hired fewer than 5 employees.)

TABLE 6
Physical structure of manufacturing firms 1950 to 1971

Year	Number of firms	Number of workers (1,000s)	Capital (LL million)	Average size of firms — Workers	Average size of firms — Capital (LL thousand)
1950	1,285	22.0	144	17	112
1960	4,559	50.4	578	11	127
1961	5,901	59.5	641	10	109
1962	6,271	60.9	691	10	110
1963	6,647	63.1	806	9	121
1964	6,853	62.0	840	9	123
1965	6,138	60.5	869	10	142
1966	6,311	63.2	988	10	157
1967	6,459	61.7	999	10	155
1968	6,661	66.8	1,095	10	164
1969	6,970	71.0	1,122	10	161
1970	6,704	73.2	1,175	11	175
1971	8,114	82.8	1,321	10	163

Source: Ministry of the Economy, Manufacturing Sector Division, *Bulletin of the Manufacturing Sector Division*, Beirut, various years. Figures show registered establishments only.

[303]

TABLE 7
Structure of the manufacturing sector 1918 to 1964 (in per cent)

Year	Food, clothing, footwear	Raw materials	Metals: semi-processed and final products	Chemicals	Other products	Total
1918	75	7	4	1	13	100
1919–28	68	13	7	1	11	100
1929–39	50	17	16	2	15	100
1940–5	47	24	11	3	15	100
1946–50	45	28	9	4	14	100
1951–5	46	28	9	2	15	100
1954	54	21	8	2	15	100
1964	43	26	7	3	21	100

Source: A. Attallah and S. Khallat, *Lebanese Manufacturing and its Development*, Beirut, Ministry of the Economy, Manufacturing Division, 1969.

TABLE 8
Lebanese manufacturing by sector in 1950

Sub-sector	Number of firms	Workers (1000s)	Output (LL million)	Average number of workers per firm
Food	455	5.4	62	12
Beverages	123	1.3	12	11
Textile	60	5.0	40	85
Clothing	15	1.0	2	69
Wood	48	0.2	4	5
Furniture	95	1.2	10	13
Paper	9	0.1	1	9
Publishing	100	0.9	6	9
Leather	64	0.7	14	12
Rubber	6	0.4	2	75
Chemical products	64	1.1	16	17
Non-ferric products	156	2.8	22	18
Metals	30	0.6	11	21
Machinery	27	0.6	4	22
Electric appliances	4	0.2	2	54
Utilities (*)	–	–	39	–
Other	29	0.4	3	13
TOTAL (excluding*)	1,285	21.9	250	–

Source: Albert Badr and Assad Nasr, *National Accounts of Lebanon*, booklet 3, "Income in the manufacturing sector", Beirut, Ministry of the Economy, May 1953.

TABLE 9
Imports of manufactured goods 1957 to 1965

Year	Final LL million	(%)	Semi-final LL million	(%)	Raw materials LL million	(%)	Total imports LL million	(%)	Total output
1957	25	5	102	19	45	8	172	32	542
1958	28	6	80	17	30	6	138	32	461
1959	24	4	98	18	41	8	138	30	555
1960	26	4	125	19	41	6	192	29	669
1961	33	5	124	17	43	6	221	28	725
1962	24	3	135	17	64	8	205	29	779
1963	30	4	150	18	59	8	329	29	837
1964	54	4	228	19	81	8	363	29	921
1965	66	5	256	19	86	6	308	30	1,481

Source: A. Attallah and S. Khallat, *Lebanese Manufacturing and its Development*, Beirut, Ministry of the Economy, Manufacturing Division, 1969.

TABLE 10
Trade in agricultural products (1964) (LL million)

Product	Imports	Exports	Balance
Grains	77	1	-76
Fruits	14	47	+33
Processed	51	14	-37
Vegetables/flowers	22	16	-6
Forestry	6	0	-6
TOTAL*	172	79	-93

*Figures rounded to nearest decimal.
Source: Kuwait Fund for Arab Economic Development, *Annual Report of the Kuwait Fund for Development Assistance*, Kuwait, June 1967.

TABLE 11
Exports 1971 to 1982 (LL million)

Year	Agricultural products LL million	%	Manufactured goods LL million	%	Total exports
1971	263	33	485	61	789
1972	333	28	807	68	1,180
1973	370	17	1,060	48	2,193
1974	338	19	1,304	75	1,740
1975	214	15	1,133	80	1,425
1976	233	29	500	63	800
1977	309	13	1,892	80	2,365
1978	250	12	1,544	71	2,162
1979	332	11	2,158	71	3,024
1980	334	8	3,328	80	4,160
1981	319	6	4,355	80	5,444
1982	257	7	2,500	65	3,866

Source: Beirut Chamber of Commerce, *Annual Report*, Beirut, various years; *Lebanese and Arab Economies Monthly* (in Arabic, *Al-Iktissad al-Lubnani wal Arabi*), January 1982, p. 22.

TABLE 12
Lebanese imports 1957 to 1981 (LL million)

Year	Manufactured goods LL million	%	Other imports	Total imports
1957	172	32	370	542
1958	138	30	323	461
1959	138	25	417	555
1960	192	29	477	669
1961	221	30	504	725
1962	205	26	574	779
1963	329	39	508	837
1964	363	39	558	921
1965	308	21	1,173	1,481
1971				2,169
1972				2,605
1973				3,168
1974				4,200
1975				3,850
1976				1,800
1977				4,500
1978				5,100
1979				7,500
1980				10,000
1981				11,500

Source: A. Attallah and S. Khallat, *Lebanese Manufacturing and its Development*, Beirut, Ministry of the Economy, Manufacturing Division, 1969; *Lebanese and Arab Economies Monthly* (in Arabic, *Al-Iktissad al-Lubnani wal Arabi*), January 1982, p. 22.

TABLE 13
Lebanese trade by region, 1971 and 1972 (LL million)

	Imports 1971	Imports 1972	Exports 1971	Exports 1972
Arab Countries	216.3	305.5	515.3	679.3
Saudi Arabia	32.9	48.7	124.9	190.2
Kuwait	5.4	8.2	88.9	110.5
Syria	35.0	71.1	75.2	83.3
East Asia	175.9	229.3	13.9	26.6
Japan	102.9	119.2	1.3	4.7
North America	267.4	360.7	24.7	74.3
USA	250.0	321.5	23.1	71.6
South America	50.6	46.5	4.9	10.3
EC	809.5	916.2	54.1	96.3
France	265.9	281.8	14.4	52.8
West Germany	245.2	284.5	13.8	12.1
Italy	186.5	233.8	14.9	16.9
Eastern Europe	228.5	218.9	37.0	57.3
Other Europe	521.1	522.7	76.2	126.5
UK	197.1	232.5	0	0
Switzerland	229.7	183.6	0	0
Sub-Saharan Africa	26.3	45.5	25.2	24.8
Supplies to aeroplanes and ships	0	0	55.9	72.1
TOTAL	2,525.3	2,828.9	807.8	1,168.6

Source: Beirut Chamber of Commerce, *Annual Report*, Beirut, 1974.

TABLE 14
Remittances against trade deficit 1971 to 1981

Year	(US$ million)	(LL million)
1971	250	-1,385
1972	307	-1,511
1973	361	-1,875
1974	912	-2,460
1975	515	-2,425
1976	27	-1,000
1977	1,114	-2,135
1978	685	-2,938
1979	1,772	-4,476
1980	2,254	-5,840
1981	1,920	-6,006

Source: *Lebanese and Arab Economies Monthly* (in Arabic, *Al-Iktissad al-Lubnani wal Arabi*), January 1982, p. 22.

TABLE 15
Income distribution 1960

Category	Population (%)	Annual income (LL)	Annual income (US$)
Poor	9	1,199 or less	399 or less
Low income	40	1,200–2,499	400–829
Middle income	3	2,500–4,999	830–1,659
Upper middle	14	5,000–14,999	1,660–4,999
High income	4	15,000 or more	5,000 or more

Source: IRFED, *Les Besoins et possibilités du développement du Liban*, Beirut, Ministry of Planning, 1962.

TABLE 16
Income distribution 1966

Category	Families	Persons	% of population	Yearly income per family (LL)	Yearly salary per person (LL)
Poor	605	2,828	20	1,000–6,000	1,580
Low income	920	5,053	37	6,001–12,000	2,638
Middle income	457	2,560	19	12,001–18,000	3,638
Upper income	341	1,997	14	18,001–30,000	4,334
High income	224	1,402	10	30,001 and over	7,653 and over
TOTAL	2,547	13,840	100		

Source: Ministry of Planning, *Statistical Bulletin*, 1966.

TABLE 17
Minimum monthly salaries in Lebanon 1972 to 1983

Year	Minimum salary (LL)	Annual salary increase (%)
1972	205	–
1973	225	5
1974	275	10
1975	325	10
1979	550	69
1980	710	29
1981	815	15
1982	955	17
1983	1,100	12

Source: *Annahar al-Arabi*, 17 August 1986.

TABLE 18
Lebanese paramilitary organizations 1990

Militia	Affiliation	Number of armed members
South Lebanon Army	Christian and Shia Muslim	2,500
Forces Libanaises	Maronite	10,000
Al-Waad Party (Elie Hobeika)	Christian	700
Giants Brigade (Frangié)	Maronite	800
Progressive Socialist Party (Joumblatt)	Druze	6,000
Amal	Shia Muslim	4,000
Hizbollah	Shia Muslim	4,500
People's Nasserite Organization (Mustafa Saad)	Sunni Muslim	600
Arab Democratic Party (Ali Eid)	Alawite	500
Syrian Social Nationalist Party	Secular (mixed)	1,000
Communist Party of Lebanon	Secular (mixed)	700
Ba'ath Socialist Party	Secular (mostly Muslim)	500
TOTAL		31,800

Source: Nabil Beyhum, "The Lebanese War and the Sectarian System", in Kamal Hamdane, *The Lebanese Crisis* (in Arabic, *Al-Azma al-Lubnaniya*), Beirut, Dar al-Farabi with UNRISF, 1998, p. 179.

TABLE 19
Population of Lebanon 1944 to 1990 (in millions)

Year	Population	Year	Population
1944	1.06	1973	2.66
1950	1.62	1974	2.73
1955	1.85	1975	2.77
1958	2.00	1976	2.77
1959	2.01	1977	2.76
1960	2.03	1978	2.73
1961	2.05	1979	2.70
1962	2.07	1980	2.67
1963	2.10	1981	2.65
1964	2.13	1982	2.64
1965	2.15	1983	2.64
1966	2.21	1984	2.64
1967	2.27	1985	2.90
1968	2.34	1986	2.90
1969	2.40	1987	3.00
1970	2.47	1988	3.00
1971	2.53	1989	3.10
1972	2.60	1990	3.10

Source: International Monetary Fund, *International Financial Statistics Yearbook*, Washington DC, various years.

TABLE 20
Lebanon's merchandise trade balance 1955 to 1985 (US$ million)

Year	Exports	Imports	Year	Exports	Imports
1955	33	218	1972	377	924
1958	32	214	1973	837	1,541
1959	40	258	1974	1,487	2,355
1960	43	290	1975	1,121	2,048
1961	41	319	1976	496	612
1962	59	331	1977	691	1,539
1963	57	354	1978	755	1,922
1964	65	509	1979	773	2,700
1965	87	543	1980	868	3,650
1966	103	608	1981	836	3,499
1967	118	549	1982	727	3,391
1968	147	594	1983	691	3,661
1969	165	610	1984	582	2,948
1970	192	653	1985	482	2,203
1971	247	731			

Source: International Monetary Fund, *International Financial Statistics Yearbook*, Washington DC, various years.

TABLE 21
Closings of the US dollar in 1986 to 1987 (LL)

	1986	1987
January	24.50	91.00
February	19.50	89.30
March	22.55	108.75
April	25.90	118.25
May	38.80	122.25
June	42.50	142.38
July	45.75	181.50
August	40.75	269.00
September	45.00	289.50
October	51.60	511.00
November	68.00	520.00
December	87.00	455.00
1 May*	25.80	119.25
2	26.50	119.75
4	27.75	115.00
27	30.50	122.00
28	31.25	127.00
24–30	28.90	122.00
1 June	32.40	122.00

*Karami's assasination
Source: Banque du Liban, *Bulletin mensuel*, Beirut.

TABLE 22
Beirut's interest rates 1964 to 1984 (in per cent)

Year	Discount rate	T-bill rate	Year	Discount rate	T-bill rate
1964	3.00	–	1974	7.00	–
1965	3.00	–	1975	7.00	–
1966	3.00	–	1976	6.00	–
1967	3.00	–	1977	6.00	–
1968	3.00	–	1978	6.00	–
1969	3.00	–	1979	8.50	–
1970	3.00	–	1980	10.00	10.40
1963	–	–	1981	13.00	14.00
1971	3.00	–	1982	12.00	13.95
1972	3.00	–	1983	12.00	9.45
1973	5.00	–	1984	12.00	13.44

Source: International Monetary Fund, *International Financial Statistics Yearbook*, Washington DC, 1994.

TABLE 23
Financial position of banks 1959 to 1983 (LL million)

Assets

Year	Number of banks	Number of branches	Reserves	Foreign capital	Credit	Total
1959	29					
1963	70					
1964	76		100	1,460	1,945	3,505
1965	80		108	1,848	2,310	4,266
1966	99		188	1,684	2,236	4,108
1977	80	372				
1978	80	480				

Liabilities

Year	Demand deposits	Notice deposits	Demand deposits	Other deposits	Total
1964	890	1,271	1,023	322	3,506
1965	962	1,705	1,156	443	4,266
1966	894	1,891	820	503	4,108

Source: F. Qubain, *Crisis in Lebanon*, Washington DC, Middle East Institute, 1961, p. 5; Kuwait Fund for Arab Economic Development, *Annual Report of the Kuwait Fund for Development Assistance*, Kuwait, June 1967; *Lebanese and Arab Economics Monthly* (in Arabic, *Al-Iktissad al-Lubnani wal Arabi*), December 1982.

TABLE 24
Largest banks in 1966 (LL million)

Name of bank	Number of branches	Capital
Intrabank	60	766.0
Bank of Beirut and Riyadh	25	68.5
Lebanon and the Middle East	15	147.7
Banque Populaire	10	152.0
Union Libanais	10	26.6
Banque du Développement	8	34.6
Banque du Commerce	5	157.5
Banque Belgique-Libanaise	5	62.0
Banque du Liban et d'Outre-mer	5	60.2

Source: Kuwait Fund for Arab Economic Development, *Annual Report of the Kuwait Fund for Development Assistance*, Kuwait, June 1967.

TABLE 25
Tarif revenues and imports 1975 to 1983 (LL million)

Year	Tarifs	Imports
1973	363	3,168
1974	477	4,200
1975	335	3,850
1976	65	1,800
1977	480	4,500
1978	541	5,100
1979	682	7,500
1980	683	10,000
1981	476	11,500
1982	273	na

Source: *Lebanese and Arab Economies Monthly* (in Arabic, *Al-Iktissad al-Lubnani wal Arabi*), December 1982, p. 22; *Assafir* (Beirut daily), 18 March 1983.

STATISTICAL APPENDIX

TABLE 26
Lebanese government revenues and expenditures
1939 to 1954 (LL million)

	1939	1948	1949	1950	1951	1952	1953	1954
Revenues								
Direct taxes	1.20	11.73	12.93	12.89	14.46	17.27	15.20	16.65
Property taxes	0.00	1.28	1.09	1.09	1.01	0.63	0.65	0.70
Fees/Licenses	0.00	6.41	7.00	7.66	8.77	10.48	10.48	11.48
Customs/Excise	4.35	23.38	26.09	20.51	33.53	36.77	34.30	38.75
Indirect taxes	0.00	29.09	32.77	37.97	37.60	42.57	37.58	41.63
Other revenues	1.65	6.77	7.24	7.09	9.73	17.04	14.47	14.66
TOTAL	7.20	78.66	87.21	83.21	105.10	124.76	112.68	123.87
Expenditures								
Education	0.05	5.69	6.77	7.86	9.56	9.96	13.55	15.51
Health	0.28	3.73	4.82	4.82	4.56	4.66	5.81	6.27
Defence	0.81	13.31	17.32	14.56	17.08	17.42	19.06	20.92
Public works	1.14	17.70	17.56	20.33	17.95	14.77	15.82	19.06
Other	4.45	29.64	36.93	36.93	40.90	41.70	58.60	61.64
TOTAL	6.73	70.07	83.40	84.50	90.05	88.51	112.84	123.40
Deficit/Surplus	0.47	8.59	3.72	2.71	15.05	36.25	-0.16	0.47

Source: UN Bureau of Economic Affairs, *Annual Report* 1957.

TABLE 27
Government budget deficit 1975 to 1983 (LL million)

Year	Projected	Actual
1975	218	218
1976	299	299
1977	577	567
1978	857	526
1979	994	992
1980	811	1,792
1981	1,048	1,965
1982	2,755	3,132
1983	1,700	3,453

Source: *Lebanese and Arab Economies Monthly* (in Arabic, *Al-Iktissad al-Lubnani wal Arabi*), December 1982, p. 22; *Assafir*, 13 January 1984.

TABLE 28
Stock of money 1972 to 1982 (LL million)

Year	M1*	M2**	Total
1972	2,275	5,762	6,833
1973	2,619	6,754	8,290
1974	2,998	8,063	9,955
1975	3,836	8,917	11,003
1976	4,905	9,830	11,611
1977	5,062	12,164	14,759
1978	6,148	14,925	17,620
1979	6,684	16,575	22,187
1980	7,733	20,204	29,201
1981	9,005	26,123	40,910
1982	na	32,692	48,500

*Demand deposits and money in circulation
**M1 and Notice deposits
Source: Robert Casparian, *Bulletin Trimestriel de la Banque du Liban*, Beirut, no. 12, 1982.

TABLE 29
Cost ratios for Lebanese banks in 1986

Number of employees	Cost ratio	Capital base ($1,000)	Cost ratio	Number of branches	Cost ratio
100–200	2.7%	1,000–5,000	3.8%	1–2	2.6%
200–400	1.6%	5,000–10,000	1.6%	3–5	2.0%
400 or more	1.3%	15,000–25,000	1.2%	20 or more	1.3%

Source: *Al-Minbar*, Paris, no. 49. March 1990, pp. 50–3.

TABLE 30
Top banks in Lebanon (in terms of assets)

Position	In 1971	In 1980
1	Arab Bank Ltd	Arab Bank Ltd
2	British Bank of the Middle East	Banque Libano-Française
3	Banque de la Syrie et du Liban	Banque Liban et d'Outre-mer
4	Sabbagh Bank (Banque Française)	Banque Audi du Moyen Orient
5	Banco di Roma	Fransabank
6	Banque Nationale de Paris	Crédit Libanais
7	Banque Libanaise pour le Commerce	Banque Libanaise pour le Commerce
8	Citibank	Banque Nationale de Paris
9	Bank of America	Banque de la Méditerranée
10	Crédit Lyonnais (Trad Bank)	Bank Byblos
11	Banque Liban et d'Outre-mer	Banque de la Syrie et du Liban
12	Bank Egypte-Liban	Bank of Beirut and Riyadh
13	Société Bancaire Libano-Européenne	Bank of Beirut and the Arab Countries
14	Chase Manhattan	Banque al-Machrek
15	Bank of Beirut and Riyadh	Société Bancaire Libano-Européenne
16	Banque Arabe-Africaine	British Bank for the Middle East
17	Crédit Libanais	Crédit Lyonnais
18	Bank Audi	Bank Saradar
19	Nova Scotia	Crédit Populaire
20	Bank Byblos	MEBCO Bank
21	Bank of Beirut and the Arab Countries	Banco di Roma
22	Royal Bank of Canada	Bank of Lebanon and Brazil
23	Rif Bank	Banque Egypte-Liban
24	Banque du Travail et de l'Industrie Commerce	Banque du Travail et de l'Industrie Commerce

Source: Lebanese Bankers' Association, *Annual Consolidated Report*, Beirut, 1982.

TABLE 31
US dollar trading in the Beirut market 1949 to 1964 (LL million)

Year	Average	Minimum	Maximum
1949	3.26	3.21	3.31
1950	3.47	3.42	3.52
1951	3.73	3.68	3.78
1952	3.66	3.61	3.71
1953	3.42	3.37	3.47
1954	3.22	3.07	3.26
1955	3.24	3.23	3.26
1956	3.22	3.18	3.25
1957	3.18	3.12	3.21
1958	3.18	3.16	3.30
1959	3.16	3.14	3.18
1960	3.17	3.14	3.19
1961	3.08	3.01	3.15
1962	3.01	2.99	3.08
1963	3.11	3.05	3.17
1964	3.07	3.04	3.12

Source: Abdul Amir Badruddin, *The Bank of Lebanon: Central Banking in a Financial Centre and a Financial Entrepôt*, London, Pinter, 1984.

TABLE 32
The 1921 Census of Mount Lebanon and the Annexed Territories

	Total	Maronites	Other Christians
Mount Lebanon	414,800	242,300	86,000
Annexed areas	350,647	43,091	69,135
Directorates of the annexed areas			
Beirut	94,500	17,600	17,000
Saida	32,254	2,698	1,465
Tyre	41,214	2,432	3,300
Marjayoun	11,028	970	4,000
Hasbaya	9,359	511	2,410
Rachaya	12,808	406	4,500
Lower Bekaa	39,674	7,535	16,400
Baalbeck	31,771	3,018	5,600
Hermel	8,795	414	25
Akkar	34,732	5,847	10,300
Tripoli	34,512	1,687	4,500
Total residents	579,779	178,257	113,939
Lebanese overseas	185,668	107,134	41,196
Total Greater Lebanon	765,447	285,391	155,135
Percentage of population		38%	20%

Source: This information is based on the 1921 Census of the population of Greater Lebanon. This Census was commissioned for the next 11 years and 1932 saw the last ever Lebanon official Census. Since this date the Lebanese government has relied on surveys and estimates for current demographic counts.

Notes: Other Christians include Greek Orthodox, Greek Catholics and Protestants. The non-Christian population includes Druze, Shias and Sunnis. "Lebanese overseas" denotes those who emigrated to Egypt and the Americas and continued to claim citizenship by way of their Ottoman passports.

TABLE 33
The 1932 Census of Lebanon under French mandate

Religious community	Number	% of population
Maronites	228,398	29.0
Greek Catholic	45,000	5.7
Greek Orthodox	76,522	9.7
Armenians	31,156	4.0
Other (incl. Jews, Latin rite, Protestants, Copts)	22,308	2.8
Total Christians and Jews	403,384	51.3
Sunni Muslim	175,925	22.4
Shia Muslim	154,208	19.6
Druze	53,047	6.7
Total Muslims	383,180	48.7
Total population	786,564	100.0

Source: Said Murad, *The Bid for a United Lebanon* (in Arabic, *Al-Haraka al-Wahdawiya fi Luban*), Beirut, Markaz ad-Dirasat al-Arabiya, 1986, p. 210.

Select Bibliography

This bibliography provides a short list of further reading. For additional sources and titles please consult the endnotes in the individual chapters of this book.

Aboukhalil, Joseph. *The Story of the Maronites in the Lebanon War* (in Arabic, *Qissat al Mawarina fi Harb Lubnan*), Beirut, Sharikat al-Matbouat, 1990.

Abu-Rish, Said. *Beirut Spy: The Story of the St Georges Hotel*, London, Bloomsbury, 1990.

Ajami, Fouad. *The Vanished Imam: Musa al-Sadr and the Shia of Lebanon*, London, I.B. Tauris, 1986.

Alamuddine, Najib. *The Flying Sheik: Story of Middle East Airlines*, London, Quartet Books, 1987.

Ayache, Ghassan. *Crisis of Public Finance in Lebanon 1982–1992* (in Arabic, *Azmat al Maliyya al-Amma fi Lubnan 1982–1992*), Beirut, Dar Annahar, 1997.

Badruddin, Abdul Amir. *The Bank of Lebanon: Central Banking in a Financial Centre and a Financial Entrepôt*, London, Pinter, 1984.

Barakat, Halim. *Lebanon in Strife*, Austin, University of Texas Press, 1985.

Beirut Chamber of Commerce. *Annual Report*, Beirut, various years.

Betkovitch, Constantine. *Lebanon and the Lebanese: Memoirs of the Russian Consul in Beirut 1869–1882* (in Arabic, *Lubnan wa al Lubnaniyoun: muzakaraat al consul al roussi fi Bayrout, 1869–1882*), Beirut, Dar al Mada, 1987.

Binder, Leonard. *Politics in Lebanon*, New York, John Wiley, 1966.

Bouhabib, Abdalla. *Yellow Light: Memoirs of Lebanon's Ambassador to the United States* (in Arabic, *Al dawe' al akhdar: muthakarrat safir Lubnan fi al wilayat al mutahida*), Beirut, Sharikat al-Matbouat, 1992.

Chebaro, Issam. *A History of Beirut from Ancient Times to the Twentieth Century* (in Arabic, *Tarikh Bayrout min Aqdam al-Ossour ila al-Qarn al-Ishrin*), Beirut, Dar Misbah al-Fikr, 1987.

Chevallier, Dominique. *La Société du Mont Liban à l'époque de la révolution industrielle en Europe*, Paris, Geuthner, 1971. (Arabic edition, Dar al Hakika, 1993.)

Chiha, Michel. *Visage et présence du Liban*, Beirut, Presse Orientale, 1964.

—*Propos d'économie Libanaise*, Beirut, Trident, 1965.

Cobban, Helena. *The Making of Modern Lebanon*, London, Hutchinson, 1985.

Copeland, Miles. *The Games of Nations*, London, Weidenfeld and Nicholson, 1969.

Corm, Georges. *Politique économique et planification au Liban, 1954–1964*. Beirut, Imprimerie universelle, 1964.

—*Histoire du pluralisme religieux dans le Bassin méditerranéen*, Paris, Geuthner, 1998.

—*Liban: les guerres de l'Europe et de l'Orient, 1840–1992*, Paris, Gallimard Folio Actuel, 1992.

—*Le Proche-Orient éclaté 1956–2000*, Paris, Gallimard Folio Actuel, 1999.

Daher, Massoud. *A Social History of Lebanon 1914–1926* (in Arabic, *Tarikh Lubnan al Ijtima'l*), Beirut, Dar al-Matbouat al Charquiya, 1984.

—*Lebanon: Independence, Accord and Entente* (in Arabic, *Lubnan al Istiqlal, al sigha wal mithaq*), Beirut, Dar al-Matbouat al Charquiya, 1984.

Daou, Butros. *A History of the Maronites* (three volumes; in Arabic, *Tarikh al-Mawarina*), Beirut, Dar Annahar, 1970.

Dib, Kamal. *The Economic Cost of War in Lebanon* (in Arabic, *Thaman al-Dam wad-Damar*), Beirut, Geoprojects – Sharikat al-Matbouat, 2001.

—*Orient Gate: Lebanese Experiences* (in Arabic, *Ala Bawabat al-Chark*), Beirut, Dar al-Farabi, 2003.

Fawaz-Tarazi, Leila. *An Occasion for War: Civil Conflict in Lebanon and Damascus in 1860*, London, Oxford Centre for Lebanese Studies, I.B. Tauris, 1994.

Fisk, Robert. *Pity the Nation: The Abduction of Lebanon*, Oxford, Oxford University Press, 1991.

Friedman, Thomas L. *From Beirut to Jerusalem*, New York, Farrar Strauss Giroux, 1989.

Select Bibliography

Giannou, Chris. *Besieged*, Toronto, Porter Books, 1990.

Gilmour, David. *Lebanon, A Fractured Country*, London, Sphere Books Ltd, 1984.

Glass, Charles. *Tribes with Flags: A Dangerous Passage through the Chaos of the Middle East*, New York, Atlantic Monthly Press, 1990.

Gordon, David. *Lebanon: The Fragmented Nation*, London, Croom Helm, 1980.

—*The Republic of Lebanon: Nation in Jeopardy*, Boulder, Colorado, Westview Press, 1983.

Hamdane, Kamal. *The Lebanese Crisis* (in Arabic, *Al-Azma al-Lubnaniya*), Beirut, Dar al-Farabi with UNRISF, 1998.

Harik, Iliya. *Politics and Change in a Traditional Society: Lebanon 1711–1845*, Princeton, Princeton University Press, 1968.

Hélou, Charles. *Memoirs* (in Arabic, *Muthakaraat*), Beirut, Dar Annahar, 1995.

Hitti, Philip. *History of Syria including Lebanon and Palestine*, New York, Macmillan, 1951.

—*A History of Lebanon* (in Arabic, *Tarikh Lubnan*), Beirut, Dar al-Kitab al-Lubani, 1980.

Holt, P. M. *Egypt and the Fertile Crescent 1516–1922*, Ithaca, Cornell University Press, 1985.

Hudson, Michael. *The Precarious Republic: Political Modernisation in Lebanon*, New York, Random House, 1972.

Huxley, Julian. *From An Antique Land*, London, Max Parrish, 1954.

International Monetary Fund. *Lebanon Staff Report*, Washington DC, 1993.

IRFED. *Les Besoins et les possibilités du dévéloppement du Liban*, Beirut, Ministry of Planning, 1962.

Joumblatt, Kamal. *Pour le Liban*, Paris, Stock, 1978.

—*I Speak for Lebanon*, London, Zed Books, 1983.

Al-Khazen, Farid. *The Breakdown of the State in Lebanon 1967–1976*, London, I.B. Tauris, 2000.

Krimski, Agatangel. *Beirut and Mount Lebanon: Memoirs of a Russian Social Scientist 1896–1898* (in Arabic, *Muthakaraat alem roussi min Lubnan, 1896–1898*), Beirut, Dar al Mada, 1986.

Labaki, Boutros and Khalil Abourjeili. *Bilan des guerres du Liban 1975–1990*, Paris, L'Harmattan, 1993.

Lamb, David. *The Arabs*, New York, Random House, 1988.

Lammens, Henri. *La Syrie*, Volumes I and II. Beirut, Imprimerie Catholique, 1921.

Longrigg, Stephen. *Syria and Lebanon under French Mandate*, London, Oxford University Press, 1958.

Mackey, Sandra. *Lebanon: Death of a Nation*, New York, Anchor Books, 1991.

Mahfouz, Youssef. *A Short History of the Maronites* (in Arabic, *Mukhtassar fi Tarikh al Mawarina*), Kasslik, Kasslik Presses, 1984.

Makdisi, Jean. *Beirut Fragments*, New York, Persea Books, 1990.

Makdisi, Samir. *Financial Policy and Economic Growth: The Lebanese Experience*, New York, Columbia University Press, 1979.

Maki, Mohamed Ali. *History of Lebanon between 732 and 1516* (in Arabic, *Tarikh Lubnan bayna 732 wa 1516*), Beirut, Dar Annahar, 1977.

Meo, Leila. *Lebanon: The Improbable Republic*, Westpoint, Connecticut, Greenwood Press, 1972.

Morris, Jan. *The Venetian Empire*, London, Penguin, 1989.

Nasr, Salim and Claude Dutar. *Les Classes sociales au Liban*, Paris, Presse de la fondation nationale des sciences politiques, 1976.

Odeh, B. J. *Lebanon: Dynamics of Conflict*, London, Zed Books, 1984.

Oughourlian, Joseph. *Histoire de la monnaie libanaise*, Toulouse, Éditions Erés, 1983.

Pakradouni, Karim. *Curse of a Nation* (in Arabic, *Laanat Watan*), Beirut, Trans Orient Press, 1991.

Qubain, F. *Crisis in Lebanon*, Washington DC, Middle East Institute, 1961.

Rabinovich, Itimar. *The War for Lebanon*, Ithaca, Cornell University Press, 1985.

Randall, Jonathan. *La Guerre de mille ans*, Paris, Grasset, 1984.

Saghiyé, Hazem. *Maronites from Lebanon* (in Arabic, *Mawarina min Lubnan*), Beirut, Al-Markaz al-Arabi lil Malumat, 1988.

Said, Abdalla. *Development of Private Property in Mount Lebanon during the Mutassaref Regime* (in Arabic, *Tatawor al mulkiya al akariyya fi jabal Lubnan fi ahd al mutassarifiyya*), Beirut, Dar al Mada, 1987.

Said, Edward. *The Question of Palestine*, New York, Vintage Books, reissued 1992.

—*Peace and its Discontents: Essays on Palestine in the Middle East Peace Process*, New York, Vintage Books, 1996.

—*The Politics of Dispossession: The Struggle for Palestinian Self-determination, 1969–1994*, New York, Vintage Books, 1995.

Salamé, Youssef. *Memoirs* (in Arabic, *Hadathani Ya Sine, Qal*), Lind, Dar Neilsen, 1988.

Salibi, Kamal. *A Modern History of Lebanon* (in Arabic, *Tarikh Lubnan al Hadith*), London, Weidenfeld and Nicolson, 1965. (Arabic edition, Beirut, Dar Annahar, 1971 and 1991.)

—*Crossroads to Civil War: Lebanon 1958–1976*, New York, Caravan Books, 1976.

—*House of Many Mansions: The History of Lebanon Reconsidered*, Berkley, University of California Press, 1990.

Tibawi, Abdul Latif. *A Modern History of Syria including Lebanon and Palestine*, London, Macmillan, 1969.

UNESCO, International Peace Research Institute. *Peace and Development in Lebanon*, Paris, 1990.

Who's Who in Lebanon, Beirut, Publitec, 1991.

Wright, Robin. *The Sacred Rage: The Wrath of Militant Islam*, New York, Simon and Schuster, 1986.

Zamir, Meir. *The Formation of Modern Lebanon*, London, Croom Helm, 1985.

Index

A

Abbasids 18, 71
Abillama family 29, 40, 51
  Abillama, Farouk 107, 205
  Abillama, Ra'if 39
Aboufadel, Mounir 103–4, 109–10
Abousaoud, Khaled 228
Abu Dhabi 104, 288–9
Achrafié 70, 87, 204, 247
Acre 11, 21, 23–4, 36, 41–2, 46, 66, 70, 74, 103
Africa 12–13, 62, 90, 173, 183, 282–3, 305, 313
  North Africa 13–14, 22, 39, 63, 77, 85
  West Africa 62, 100, 134, 183, 198, 222, 235, 244, 252, 263
al-Ahdab family 54, 55
  al-Ahdab, Aziz 146, 164
  al-Ahdab, Kheireddine 55, 79
Ain Dara 25, 29, 51, 153
Ain Helwé 210, 260–2
Akkar 24–5, 53, 91, 136, 314
Alamuddine family 28–9, 141
  Alamuddine, Ali 28
  Alamuddine, Najib 103, 113–14, 118, 124–5, 141, 150
Alawi mountains 15, 19, 261
Aleppo 11, 19, 23–7, 31, 33, 69, 71
Alexandria 11, 30, 44, 67, 73
Aley 152–3, 209, 244–5, 249
Algeria 85, 173, 219
Ali, Caliph 13, 18, 22–3, 30
All-Syrian Congress 55
Amal militia 158, 162, 210, 211, 244, 251–5, 260, 262, 294
American University of Beirut 70, 74, 85, 136, 159, 163, 177, 180, 200, 286
Amman 11, 89
Anatolia 57–8
Anglo-American Commission of Inquiry into Palestine 286

Ansar 245
Aoun, Michel 31, 152, 158, 162, 178–9, 190, 210, 211, 233, 234, 248, 250, 275–6, 291, 292
Aqua Marina 155, 160, 207, 245, 246, 273
Arab Bank Ltd 103, 115, 138, 222, 313
Arab Democratic Party 261
Arab Deterrence Force 248
Arab League 217
Arabia 12–18, 23, 30, 36, 65, 84
Arafat, Yasser 209, 250, 260, 262
ARAMCO (Arab-American Oil Company) 183
Arida family 50, 73, 128, 200
  Arida, Alphonse 119
  Arida, Carlos 116–17, 119
  Arida, Maronite Patriarch 78
  Arida Brothers Company 188
arms dealing 160–1
Asia Minor 14, 44, 48, 58
Assad family 51, 87, 141, 243, 246, 251
  Assad, Ahmed 51, 87, 251
  Assad, Hafez 36, 210, 250, 270, 272, 291
  Assad, Kamel 51, 142, 143, 251
Assaf family 23, 24, 25, 29, 31, 67–8, 128
  Assaf, Mansour 67
  Assaf, Tawfic 128
Assaf Mosque 31, 67
Athens 44, 150, 219, 220
Awali, River 259, 281
Ayoub, Iskandar 117, 123
Ayubids 12, 19, 65

B

Baabda 48–50, 56, 58, 76, 77, 87, 118, 155, 179, 248, 250, 275
Baakline 23, 25, 30, 43, 314
Baalbeck 11, 21, 92, 135, 216, 254, 282
Baath Party 55, 250

[325]

Bab Idriss 62, 117
Baghdad 12, 13, 18, 56, 71, 88
Baghdad Pact 86, 87
Bahrain 219, 220
Banco di Roma 220, 313
Bank of America 104, 113, 122, 219, 313
Bank of Credit and Commerce 227, 234
Bank of England 238
Bank of Kuwait and the Arab World 228, 233
Bank of Lebanon 99, 101, 173–4, 180, 205, 219, 233, 235–9
Banque al-Machrek 122, 228, 229, 232–3, 236, 313
Banque de France 236–7
Banque de la Méditerranée 294, 313
Banque de la Syrie et du Liban (BSL) 96, 171, 313
Banque Libano-Française 100, 313
Bassoul 52
Basta 86–7
Batroun 19, 268, 271, 276
Becharri 49, 50–1, 271, 275, 276
Beckfaya 234, 266, 275
Beidas, Youssef 103–14, 115, 116–17, 118–19, 120, 123, 124–5, 226–7, 228, 230, 231, 289
Beirut
  Chamber of Commerce 130, 140, 185, 199
  destruction of 143–50
  fragmentation 247–9
  Harbour Corporation 107, 148, 228
  international airport 61, 148–50, 164, 292
  migration of Palestinian wealth 103–24
  stock market 130–2
Beiteddine 43, 50
Bekaa Valley 19, 20, 21, 24, 27, 29, 48, 49, 51, 53, 87, 91, 92, 93, 101, 134–6, 140, 152, 233, 244, 245, 246, 251, 254, 273, 281, 283, 314
Berri, Nabih 231, 252, 294
Beyhum 52, 54
Bhamdoun 152, 153, 245, 274
Bonaparte, Napoleon 42, 44, 57, 128
Boulos family 50
  Boulos, Badih 109

Boulos, Philip 109
al-Boustani family 50
al-Boustani, Butros 39
al-Boustani, Emile 83, 87–8
Britain 14, 66, 84–5, 106, 174, 290
British Bank of the Middle East 159, 220, 313
Buhtur family 23, 28
Bustros 52, 71
Butros, Fouad 205
Byblos 34, 57, 62, 79
Byzantium 12, 71

C
Cairo 13, 22, 31, 44, 46, 56, 57, 65, 219, 226, 284
  Cairo Accord 261
Canada 1, 282, 284, 285, 295
Carthage 36, 62–3
Casino du Liban 107, 194, 206, 232–3, 269
Caucasus 234, 240
Chahine, Tanyous 47–9, 271
Chamoun family 2, 51, 108, 141, 267, 269–70, 272–3, 284
  Chamoun, Camille 40, 56, 83–4, 86–8, 95, 98, 110, 158–61, 165, 201, 209, 246, 248, 250, 255, 259, 265, 266–70, 272–3, 276, 277, 285
  Chamoun, Danny 83, 161, 165, 273, 275, 277
  Chamoun, Dori 83
  Chamoun, Nemr 51, 83, 86, 277
Chase Manhattan Bank 104–6, 113, 122, 313
Chatila refugee camp 136, 262, 275
Chediac, Sami 257–8
Chehab family 23, 28–9, 35, 41, 47–8, 50, 58, 59, 80, 141
  Chehab, Adel 107
  Chehab, Bachir II 17, 42–3, 45–6, 249
  Chehab, Bachir III 46–7
  Chehab, Fouad 80, 84, 87–9, 95, 100, 108, 110–11, 137, 178, 201, 243, 267, 270, 272
  Chehab, Haidar 28
  Chehab, Maurice 107

Chehab, Melhem   40
Chehab, Youssef   21–2, 40–2, 245
Chekka   207, 271, 281
Chiha family   52, 71, 72, 76–7, 96
  Chiha, Michel   76–8, 81, 83, 100, 109
Chouf region   22–9, 40, 43, 48–51, 68, 75, 77, 80, 83, 87–8, 110, 153, 209–10, 244–5, 249–50, 268, 272, 274–5, 281
Citibank   122, 313
civil service   201–5
Cold War rivalry   86–9
Conseil de Discipline   201
Constantinople   11–13, 17, 25–30, 40, 44, 46
Corm, Charles   35, 78
Corm, Georges   164–5
Council for Reconstruction and Development   200, 205, 209–10, 296
Crédit Libanais   228, 232, 233, 313
Crédit Lyonnais   69, 96, 313
Crédit Populaire   232, 313
Crusader period   65–6
Cyprus   20, 26–7, 34, 66, 89, 135, 149, 187

D

Damascus   2, 11–20, 22–30, 36, 41, 43, 47, 52–6, 70–6, 92, 147, 152–4, 160, 230, 233, 245–6, 250, 275, 284, 292–3
Damour   154, 195, 266, 267
Daoud Pasha   50
Daouk family   54
  Daouk, Ahmed   80
Debbas, Charles   76–7
Deir al-Kamar   25, 30, 43, 48, 51, 83, 154, 266, 275
*dhimmi*s   45, 58
Dib, Boutros   205
Dikuané   151
Dog River   25, 37, 276
Dora   190, 247
Douehi family   50, 87, 270
Doumit family   128
Druze   11, 15, 22–5, 28–9, 40–54, 58–9, 68–9, 75, 83, 87, 89, 141–3, 152–4, 158, 162, 209–10, 243–50, 253, 263, 265–6, 275
Druze canton   249–50
Druze civil war, 1711   28–30
Druze, origins of   22–3

E

economy
  1920–50   91–5
  1966–74   127–40
  banking sector   95–101, 219–21
  benefits of Middle East conflicts   265
  budget deficits   215–17
  collapse of national currency   170–9
  drugs trade   132–5
  financial crisis   113–21, 222–40, 293
  fuel subsidies   188–90
  gold reserve   212–15
  Hoss government   205–7
  housing   195–9
  hyperinflation   182–7
  monetary union with Syria   97–8
  municipalities   193–5
  personal income   135–7
  power utilities   187–8
  social security   190–3
  Syrian intervention in   138–40
Éddé family   108
  Éddé, Emile   73, 75–80, 81, 110, 270
  Éddé, Pierre   118
  Éddé, Raymond   270
Egypt   11–14, 18–24, 39, 42–5, 50, 55, 57, 67, 85–6, 89, 108, 116, 133, 135, 217, 227, 253, 266, 269, 291
  intervention in Lebanon in 1958   86–9
  occupation of the Levant in 1773   41
  occupation of the Levant in 1831   43–6
Ehden   49, 50, 271
Eid, Ali   261
Ein Rummané   144, 247
Eisenhower, Dwight   115, 217
Électricité du Liban   73, 188, 194, 247
Erslan family   29, 51, 141, 244, 249
  Erslan, Majid   80, 87, 141
Eskandar, Jamil   228, 233
Eskenderun   11, 89
Essaili   73, 128
European Community   208

F

Fahed, King of Saudi Arabia   294
Fairuz   31, 290
Faisal, Emir   52, 76
Faisal, King of Saudi Arabia   116
Fakhreddine II, Emir   23, 24–8
families   72–3, 77–8, 80–1, 83–4, 127–8, 141
Faraoun family   52, 71, 77, 96
    Faraoun, Gaith   227–8, 234
    Faraoun, Henri   145, 148
Fatah   161
Fatimids   20, 22, 43, 65
Federal Reserve System   216, 238
Finance Company of Lebanon   224–6
First Phoenician Bank   228, 233, 239
Fiyadiyé   269, 274
Forn Chebak   247, 269
France   3, 13, 14, 28, 35, 38–40, 44, 49, 53, 56, 63, 68, 72–9, 81, 85, 90, 106–7, 171, 173–4, 204, 209, 227, 234, 241, 277, 284, 292, 295
Frangié family   2, 87, 108, 243, 267, 269, 270–2
    Frangié, Hamid   86, 270
    Frangié, Kabalan   50
    Frangié, Sulieman   4, 51, 80, 141–2, 150, 231, 260, 270–4
    Frangié Jr., Sulieman   272, 276
    Frangié, Tony   271
French Mandate   15, 75–6

G

Galilee   23, 30
Gaza   11, 263
Geagea family   50
    Geagea, Samir   9, 51, 162, 178, 248, 271, 274–7
Gemayel family   2, 108, 234, 246, 248, 266, 268–9, 273–7, 284
    Gemayel, Amine   81, 108, 152, 201, 210–11, 224, 226, 228, 229, 230, 231, 232, 233–4, 248, 253, 274–7, 292, 295
    Gemayel, Antoun   39
    Gemayel, Arzé   274
    Gemayel, Bachir   4, 5, 8, 39, 57, 143, 164, 165, 211, 230, 248, 265, 268–9, 271, 272–4, 275, 276, 277

Gemayel, Nadim Bachir   277
Gemayel, Pierre   8, 87, 227, 266–8, 270
Gemayel Jr., Pierre   277
Germany   79, 106, 179, 181, 234, 266, 279
Ghandour   73, 128
Ghassan tribe   14
Ghazir   24, 67
Giants Brigade   271–2
Gibran, Khalil   39, 50
Greater Lebanon, State of   52–3
Greece   12–14, 34, 37, 44, 58
    Greek Catholics   49, 71, 273
    Greek Orthodox   52, 54, 76–9, 89, 143, 269

H

Habib, Philip   273
Haddad, Mounir   109
Haddad, Saad   255, 257–8
al-Hakem, Fatimid Caliph   22–3
Haifa   46, 265
Halat   229, 273
Hama   11, 260
Hamadi family   21, 51, 141, 243, 246, 251
    Hamadi, Saad   51
    Hamadi, Sabri   87, 143, 251
    Hamadi, Said   51
Haret Houraik   247, 276
Hariri Foundation   208, 295
Hariri, Rafic   64, 179, 195, 208, 223, 250, 253, 291, 294–7
    first government: 1992   294–7
    rise of   294
Hasbaya   255, 257
Hawi, Georges   143
Hejaz   30, 44
Hélou family   52
    Hélou, Charles   78, 109, 110–13, 114, 115, 124–5, 141
Hermel   21, 135, 254
Hitti, Philip   30, 74
Hizbollah   161, 162, 244, 253–4, 255, 293
Hobeich family   23, 29
    Hobeich, Maronite Patriarch   47, 75

[328]

Index

Hobeika, Elie 274–5, 276–7, 292
Hong Kong 110, 129
al-Hoss, Fawzi 87
al-Hoss, Salim 100, 120, 122, 178, 200, 205–6, 223, 235, 275
Hoyek, Maronite Patriarch Elias 52
Hrawi, Elias 81, 179, 241, 248, 292, 295
Hussein, King of Jordan 88

I
Ibn Munqidh, Osama 20
Ibrahim, Mohsen 143
India 13, 90
Institut International de Recherche et de Formation Éducation du Développement (IRFED) 137, 201
International Red Cross 208
International Monetary Fund (IMF) 175, 176, 216, 239
Intrabank 95, 101–24, 138, 144, 226–37, 289
  Intrabank Group 228, 233, 236
  Intrabank Insurance 228
  Intrabank Investment Company 122, 228
Iqlim Tofah 254, 258
Iran 21, 86, 227, 230, 253–4, 293
Iran–Iraq War 291
Iranian Revolutionary Guard 254
Iraq 12, 18, 23, 27, 88–89, 101, 106, 116, 139, 161, 189, 208, 221, 253, 262, 291
Irmia, Maronite Patriarch 38
Islam 12, 35, 45, 58, 74
  schisms 18–19
Islamic Benevolent Society 56
Islamic Jihad Organization 254
Israel 5, 7, 23, 73, 85–6, 90, 135, 138–40, 160, 221, 249, 255, 257–8, 261–2, 268–9, 291, 296
Italy 26, 68, 79, 101, 106, 174, 179, 209

J
Jabal al-Arab 16
Jabal Druze 23, 47, 53
Jabbour 128
Jabre 73, 128
Jallad 128

al-Jazzar, Ahmad Pasha 21, 41–2
Jbeil 19, 33, 34, 75, 290
Jebel Amil 19, 20, 21, 24, 41, 53, 55
Jerusalem 11, 22, 30, 41, 103, 110
Jezzine 21, 50, 258, 260
al-Jisr family 54, 55
  al-Jisr, Mohamed 55, 77–8
Jisr al-Basha 93, 136, 151, 247, 262
Jiyé 188, 207, 246, 250, 267
Jordan 23, 25, 31, 84, 88–9, 101, 106, 139, 261
  River Jordan 22, 25
Joumblatt family 27–9, 51, 87, 141, 243–4, 249, 284
  Joumblatt, Ali 27
  Joumblatt, Bachir 43, 249
  Joumblatt, Hussain 27
  Joumblatt, Kamal 31, 51, 57, 83, 86–7, 137, 140, 142–3, 161, 164–5, 201, 221, 237, 246, 249–52, 265, 267–8, 274, 277, 289
  Joumblatt, Majid 233
  Joumblatt, Walid 1–2, 108, 231, 233, 246, 249–50, 253, 276
Jounié 24, 46, 51, 143, 154, 159, 216, 247
Jundullah (Soldiers of God) 260

K
Kahalé 153, 245
Kairouz family 50
  Kairouz, Joe 236
Kansou, Assem 143
Kantari 145–6
Karam family 270
  Karam, Assad 50
  Karam, Youssef 49–50, 75, 271
Karami family 54–5, 141, 243
  Karami, Abdel Hamid 55
  Karami, Omar 56, 261, 293
  Karami, Rachid 86–8, 143, 260–1, 277
Kassir, Victor 182
al-Kebir, Ali 12, 22, 43
al-Kebir, Mohamed Ali 43–4
Kesrouane 19–20, 23–5, 29, 48–51, 75, 276
Kettané 73, 128
Kfarchima 93, 247

Kfar-Falous 260, 295
Khaddam, Abdel Halim 230–1
Khaldé 73, 88, 148, 150, 154, 247, 252
al-Khalil family 51, 243
  al-Khalil, Kazem 87, 143
Khatib, Ahmad 255
al-Khazen family 29, 47–50, 68, 271
  al-Khazen, Elias 204
  al-Khazen, Naufal 68
al-Khouri family 50, 72, 77–80, 95, 108, 119, 128
  al-Khouri, Bechara 55, 56, 75–6, 77–81, 83–4, 95, 100, 109, 110, 202, 224, 283
  al-Khouri, Butros 119, 128
  al-Khouri, Fouad 128
  al-Khouri, Michel 100, 205, 223–4, 231
  al-Khouri, Mounir 109
  al-Khouri Saleh 75
  al-Khouri, Salim 83
Kidder, Peabody and Co. 121, 122, 226
King-Crane Commission 85
Koura 54, 65, 271–2
Kuleilat, Ibrahim 143, 164
Kuwait 57, 89, 104, 122, 132, 139, 153, 179, 190, 228–9, 262, 284, 227, 291–2
  Kuwait crisis, impact on Lebanon 292

L

Lahoud family 52
  Lahoud, Emile 81
Lammens, Henri 15, 30
Latakia 11, 36, 70–1
League of Nations 76, 85
Lebanese Arab Bank 232, 236
Lebanese Bankers Association (LBA) 130, 220, 223, 224, 226, 235, 237, 238–9
Lebanese Broadcasting Corporation (LBC) 273
Lebanese Real Estate Corporation 296
Lebanese Finance Company (SOFL) 132
Lebanese Forces 4, 162, 214, 234, 248, 261, 273–7
Lebanon
  ancient origins 14–15
  US involvement in 84–6, 209–11

Levant
  European domination of 66–72
  Italian intervention in 25–6
Libya 74, 161, 208, 221
Litani River 92, 155, 256, 258
London 5, 31, 57, 74, 80 1, 84, 90, 101, 117, 155, 160, 164–5, 213, 217, 231, 246, 263
Ludwig, Daniel 116, 119, 123

M

Maan family 23, 25, 28, 29, 35, 43, 68
  Maan, Ahmed 29
  Maan, Fakhreddine II 23, 25–8, 29, 30, 31, 41, 42, 43, 45, 47, 68
  Maan, Hussein 28
  Maan, Kurkumaz 24, 45
Maghdouché 260
Maissaloun 53
Malta 17, 36, 46, 63, 66
Mansour, Albert 143
Marjayoun 257, 267
Maronite Church 49, 58, 72
  origins of 33–4
Maronites ix, 19–23, 34–59, 68–9, 71–80, 83, 87, 89, 108, 141–3, 152–4, 159, 162, 164–5, 178, 209–10, 227, 229, 231, 241, 243–52, 255, 258–60, 263, 265–76, 292
  civil wars 1978–90 270–7
  links to Europe 38–40
Maroun, Sami 234
Maroun, Youhanna 33
Marseilles 63, 107, 171
Marshall Plan 7, 229
Matni, Nassib 87
Mazraat Chouf 27
Mecca 12–13, 18, 74
Medicis 25
  di Medici, Prince Cosimo 26
Medina 19
Memlukes 19, 21, 43, 45, 65–8
Metn 50, 77, 87, 110, 152, 266, 269, 275–6
Middle East Airlines (MEA) 113–14, 116–17, 118, 119, 124, 141, 148, 150, 183, 200, 228–9, 230, 232–3
Middle East Television 258

INDEX

Miéou-Mié   260, 261, 262
Milcher Group   228, 232–3
Mokhtara   2, 27
Monteverde Crossing   250, 275
Montreal   155, 246, 283
Mouawad family   87
  Mouawad, Mikhail   50
  Mouawad, René   51, 179, 241, 270
Mouaya, Umayad Caliph   18
Mount Lebanon   3, 15–18, 19–20, 22, 23, 24–5, 26, 27–8, 33, 38, 40, 41, 42, 43, 46, 48–54, 57, 68, 69, 71–2, 75–6, 83, 91, 129, 136, 151, 158, 198, 234, 244, 249, 257, 263, 265, 268, 277, 314
  early settlement   16–17
  Memluke invasion   20
  popular uprising   47–8
Mount Sannine   209, 273
al-Mourabitoun (Independent Nasserite Movement)   164
Muhammad, the Prophet   13, 18–19, 30
Murr Tower   145, 147
Muslim Brothers   260
Mutassarefiya   49–51, 75

N

Nabaa   136, 151, 154
Nabatié   93, 254, 258
Naccache family   52
  Naccache, Alfred   80
  Naccache, Georges   102
Nahmé   93, 267
Naim, Edmond   204, 212, 213, 218, 231–2, 237
Naja, Rafic   101, 102, 118
Nakad   73
Nakoura   74, 256–7
Napoleon III   48
Nassar, Nassif   21, 41
Nasser, Gamal Abdel   12, 55, 57, 73, 85, 87–8, 98, 108, 116, 143, 164, 217
nationalism   34–7, 78–81
Nawfal   73
Nixon, Richard   173

O

Oger Liban   64, 195, 294
Oghourlian, Joseph   114, 118, 125

al-Omar, Daher   21–2, 41, 42
Organization of the Wretched on Earth   254
Orontes Valley   19, 33–4, 92
Orthodox Christians   40–1, 53–4, 59, 65, 68–71, 143, 227, 272
Ottoman Bank   69, 96
Ottoman Empire
  1760 Arab uprising   21
  Druze uprising   24–5
Ouzai   154, 207, 210, 246, 247

P

Pakradouni, Karim   57, 274, 276
Palestine   21, 30, 36, 40–2, 46, 67, 73, 84–5, 89, 103, 109, 138, 261, 263
Palestine Liberation Organization (PLO)   115–16, 138, 139–40, 150, 153, 158–61, 206, 209–10, 221, 222, 240, 252–3, 255, 257–62, 267–9, 276–7, 296
Palestinian refugees   138, 261–3
Paris   5, 30, 61, 68, 76, 84, 105, 107, 113, 118, 127, 136, 140, 155, 160, 171, 175, 179, 191, 216, 219, 227, 236, 245, 263, 277, 283, 286
Parker, Paul   113, 118–19, 120, 121, 123
People's Nasserite Organization   259
Peres, Shimon   234
Persia   12–13, 19, 21, 65
Phalanges Party   8, 31, 143–7, 150–65, 195, 205, 211, 220–1, 244, 246, 248, 250, 253, 257, 262, 266–74, 277, 280, 292
Phoenicia   30, 35–7, 62, 92–5
Place des Martyres   74, 144, 147
Progressive Socialist Party   237

Q

Qatar   104, 106, 122, 153, 228–9
Qilayaa   255, 257

R

Rabin, Itzhak   253
Rafei, Abdel Majid   143, 260
Rafsanjani, Hashemi   293
Rahbani, Ziad   279–80, 287, 290
Ras Beirut   70, 118
Riyadh Accord   291

[331]

Rockefeller, David   104, 113
Rockefeller, Nelson   104
Roman Catholic Church   38, 68, 71, 76
Rome   34, 37–9, 63–4, 71
Roufael, Farid   100–1, 205
Russia   14, 40–4, 66, 68–9
　Russian intervention in the Levant
　　40–1

S

Saad family   259
　Saad, Maarouf   259
　Saad, Moustafa   164, 259
al-Saad, Habib Pasha   9, 52, 75–8
Saadiyat   159, 265, 266, 267, 272–3
Sabra refugee camp   136, 262, 275
Sadat, Anwar   269, 291
Sadr, Moussa   142, 251–3
Safad   68
Saghir family   21
Said, Edward   67
Saida   11, 19, 21, 24–7, 41, 46, 53–5, 62, 66, 68, 70, 74, 80, 84, 92–3, 141, 195, 210, 216, 223, 245–6, 253–4, 258–62, 265, 294–5
Saifa   24–5
Saladin   72
Salam family   54, 141, 243
　Salam, Hani   125
　Salam, Saeb   86–7, 89, 115, 125, 141, 142, 143, 163, 230, 258
　Salam, Salim   55, 79, 230
Salamé, Elias   120
Salamé, Widad   103
Salamé, Youssef   101, 104–5, 114, 118, 123, 124, 125
Salha family   128
　Salha, Najib   101, 102, 113, 118, 121
Salibi, Kamal   30–1, 36, 57, 58, 59, 81, 263
Sanayeh   145, 155
Sarkis, Elias   100–1, 109–11, 118, 120–1, 141, 155, 163, 205, 207–8, 224, 248, 270
Saudi Arabia   116, 133, 139, 179, 206, 208, 222, 227, 291, 294
Saudi-Lebanese Bank   294
Sfeir, Maronite Patriarch Nessralla   153, 250

Shah of Iran   160, 163
Shia cantons   251–5
Shia Muslims   19–22, 41, 45–6, 51–4, 87, 89, 141, 143, 158, 162, 164, 210–11, 243–8, 251–7, 262–3, 266, 276
Siniora, Fouad   223
Sinn al-Fil   93, 247
Smyrna   11, 30, 158
Social Democratic Party (*see also* Phalanges Party)   266
Social Security Fund   191–3
Socialist Progressive Party   233
Société Foncière du Liban (SOFL)
　see Lebanese Finance Company
Sodico Crossing   147, 221
Sofar   152–3, 245
al-Solh family   54, 55, 141, 142, 243, 259
　al-Solh, Rachid   250, 293
　al-Solh, Riad   55, 80, 84, 89–90
　al-Solh, Rida   55
　al-Solh, Sami   80, 87
　al-Solh, Takieddine   259
Souk al-Gharb   152, 250
South Lebanon Army (SLA)   221, 255–9
South Lebanon, canton of   255–8
Spears, General Sir Edward   78, 80
Stalin, Josef   86
State Bank of India   173
Sudan   45
Sunni cantons   258–61
Sunni Muslims   23–4, 45, 54–9, 67, 69–71, 77, 79–81, 87–9, 141, 143, 230, 243, 246–7, 252, 258–61
Sursock family   52, 71, 96, 228, 231
Switzerland   7, 106–7, 120, 123, 165, 191, 243, 284
Syria   11–19, 23, 27, 30, 33, 36, 46, 51, 54–5, 57, 59, 67, 71–2, 79, 85–6, 89, 92, 96–7, 101, 106, 131, 135, 138–40, 150, 165, 170–1, 179, 182–3, 187, 209–10, 230, 233, 249–51, 254, 268–70, 272–3, 275, 291–3
Syrian Nationalist Party   79, 89, 272
Syrian Protestant College   70, 85

T

Tabet family   52
　Tabet, Zalfa Nicolas   83

Taif Accord   4, 276, 291–5
Takla family   71
  Takla, Philip   110, 118, 120
Talhouk family   23
Tamraz, Roger   121–5, 219, 226–40, 273, 294, 297
Tanukh family   23
al-Tanzim al-Nasseri (Union of Working People's Forces Nasserite Organization)   164
Taraboulsi family   73
Tawheed Islami (Islamic Unification)   260, 261
Tell Zaatar   93, 136, 151, 154, 250, 262, 269, 273
Tiger militia   158–9, 273
Trans-Arabian Pipeline (Tapline)   84, 88, 190
Trans-Mediterranean Airlines (TMA)   150, 165, 229
Tripoli, Lebanon   11, 19, 24, 29, 33–4, 38, 53–5, 66, 70, 74, 77, 79, 91–3, 128, 141, 143, 154, 179, 189–90, 210, 216, 246, 259–62, 270
Tripoli, Libya   85, 90
Tueni family   52, 71
  Tueni, Ghassan   8
Tunisia   19, 22, 36, 63
Turkey   11, 23, 30–1, 44, 57, 76, 86, 89, 132, 135, 138
TWA   149
Tyre   11, 16, 19, 37, 46, 51, 53, 62–3, 66, 70, 74, 92–3, 160, 216, 259, 262

U
Umayads   18
UNIFIL   256
United Arab Emirates   208
United Arab Republic (UAR)   86
United Banking Company (UBC)   236–7
United Nations (UN)   73, 208, 255–8, 292
United Nations Relief Works Agency (UNRWA)   263
United States of America   37, 84–8, 90, 104, 106–7, 113, 116, 122–3, 132–3, 148, 149, 150, 160, 163, 165, 168, 172, 173, 174, 202, 209, 210–11, 227, 230, 233, 234, 241, 253, 263, 273, 281, 284, 286, 292, 295

V
Vatican   38, 40, 71, 292
Venice   2, 31, 66, 158, 165

W
Wadi al-Taim   23, 28, 47
Wakim, Najah   143, 164, 297
war, civil
  1841–3   46–7
  1860   48–9
  1958   85–9
  1975–90
    Battle for Mount Lebanon   151–4
    cost of destruction   154–7
    cultural collapse   279–90
    films and theatre   279–83
    financing the war   157–61
    ghettoization   243–77
    human cost   161–3
    leftist coalition   142–3
    Syrian–Egyptian rapprochement   291
    Syrian intervention   150–1
    Taif Agreement   291–2
  1983   210
  media coverage   6–7
World Bank   173, 195

Y
al-Yafi, house of   141
  al-Yafi, Abdalla   87, 109, 110, 114, 118

Z
Zahlé   49, 92, 101, 209, 216, 233, 273, 276
Zeitouni   62, 107, 145, 220
Zghorta   48, 50, 87, 243, 260, 269–72, 276

Also available

Labor and Human Capital in the Middle East
Studies of Markets and Household Behavior
2002 • 424pp • 235 x 155 mm • Paper £14.95 • ISBN 0 86372 295 4

Iraq's Economic Predicament
2002 • 388pp • 235 x 155 mm • Cased £35.00 • ISBN 0 86372 276 8

State and Agriculture in Iraq
Modern Development, Stagnation and the Impact of Oil
2002 • 400pp • 235 x 155 mm • Cased £35.00 • ISBN 0 86372 279 2

Lebanon's Renaissance
The Political Economy of Reconstruction
2001 • 276pp • 235 x 155 mm • Cased £35.00 • ISBN 0 86372 252 0

Nationals and Expatriates
Population and Labour Dilemmas of the Gulf Cooperation Council States
2001 • 300pp • 235 x 155 mm • Cased £35.00 • ISBN 0 86372 275 X

Water in the Arabian Peninsula
Problems and Policies
2001 • 412pp • 235 x 155 mm • Cased £35.00 • ISBN 0 86372 246 6

Available from your local bookshop; alternatively, contact our Sales Department on +44 (0)118 959 7847 or email on **orders@garnet-ithaca.co.uk** to order copies of these books.